Domain-Specific Languages in Practice

Antonio Bucchiarone • Antonio Cicchetti •
Federico Ciccozzi • Alfonso Pierantonio
Editors

Domain-Specific Languages in Practice

with JetBrains MPS

Editors
Antonio Bucchiarone (iD)
Fondazione Bruno Kessler (FBK) - MoDiS
Trento, Italy

Antonio Cicchetti (iD)
School of Innovation, Design and
Engineering (IDT)
Mälardalen University
Västerås, Sweden

Federico Ciccozzi (iD)
School of Innovation, Design and
Engineering (IDT)
Mälardalen University
Västerås, Sweden

Alfonso Pierantonio (iD)
University of L'Aquila
L'Aquila, Italy

ISBN 978-3-030-73760-3   ISBN 978-3-030-73758-0   (eBook)
https://doi.org/10.1007/978-3-030-73758-0

This Springer imprint is published by the registered company Springer Nature Switzerland AG.
The registered company address is: Gewerbestrasse 11, 6330 Cham, Switzerland

Preface

The fundamental vision proposed by **Model-Driven Engineering (MDE)** is coping with the complexity of reality by means of abstraction: The relevant aspects for a certain application domain are described with models, which by definition are simplified representations of a system in the real world [1]. In particular, models are abstractions of real problems and are defined using a set of well-defined concepts and their relationships, typically formalized in a modeling language definition. **Domain-Specific Languages (DSLs)** have been introduced with the aim of meeting the needs of particular application domains, industry, or business challenges, which would be less efficiently addressed by using mainstream general-purpose languages. In fact, DSLs are languages specifically defined to express problems and/or solutions by using terms appropriate for the specific application domain and hence familiar to domain experts [2].

Language workbenches are tools with which DSLs can be designed, implemented, tested, and in some cases used. In this respect, they play a critical role for DSL development. A workbench should allow for a relatively easy language specification while still providing language engineers with powerful editing and automation features. Domain-specific concepts and their relationships should be specified together with corresponding semantics and notations, while the workbench is expected to offer generative mechanisms or interpreters deriving the necessary programming environment, notably editors, palettes, auto-completion and validation features, persistence and versioning, and so forth [3]. Needless to say, additional capabilities for supporting language extension, refinement, and maintenance are of paramount relevance for the success of industry-strength DSLs too.

MPS, short for **Meta Programming System,** is an open source language workbench developed by JetBrains over the last 15 years. It is used to implement languages for real-world use. Its distinguishing feature is projectional editing, which supports almost unlimited language extension and composition possibilities [4] as well as a flexible mix of a wide range of textual, tabular, mathematical, and graphical notations [5].

This book is designed as an accessible means to introduce the readers to and/or deepen their existing knowledge of **MPS**.

The book begins with an overview of the domain of language workbenches, which provides perspectives and motivations underpinning the creation of MPS. Moreover, technical details of the language underneath MPS together with the definition of the tool's main features are discussed in chapter "JetBrains MPS: Why Modern Language Workbenches Matter". Following this Introduction, the volume is organized into three parts, each dedicated to a specific aspect of the topic.

MPS in Industrial Applications

Chapters "Use MPS to Unleash the Creativity of Domain Experts: Language Engineering Is a Key Enabler for Bringing Innovation in Industry", "JetBrains MPS as Core DSL Technology for Developing Professional Digital Printers", "A Domain-Specific Language for Payroll Calculations: An Experience Report from DATEV", "FASTEN: An Extensible Platform to Experiment with Rigorous Modeling of Safety-Critical Systems" and "Migrating Insurance Calculation Rule Descriptions from Word to MPS" present the use of MPS in industrial applications. They cover the challenges and inadequacies of general-purpose languages used in companies, as opposed to the reasons why DSLs are essential, together with their benefits and efficiency; moreover, they summarize lessons learnt by using MPS.

Chapter "Use MPS to Unleash the Creativity of Domain Experts: Language Engineering Is a Key Enabler for Bringing Innovation in Industry" introduces the experiences gained by utilizing MPS in smart factory, finance, and medical domains. The chapter describes how appropriate DSLs could be defined by means of MPS together with their effectiveness in allowing experts to explore and enhance their domain-specific knowledge. Moreover, the chapter places MPS in a broader perspective of core DSL engineering by discussing language adoption and the most frequently used features. Chapter "JetBrains MPS as Core DSL Technology for Developing Professional Digital Printers" reports on how the adoption of MPS can lead to efficient and continuous innovation with sustainable quality. The innovation is brought by means of new DSLs supporting feature management and tool chaining for an industrial production application. Once a new DSL is introduced in the industrial ecosystem, its functionality and suitability are tested and evaluated. Chapter "A Domain-Specific Language for Payroll Calculations: An Experience Report from DATEV" reviews the development process of a DSL for payroll calculations by means of MPS. Interestingly, the introduction of the DSL is based on the demonstrated higher efficiency of using a DSL to deal with domain complexity drivers in comparison to a general-purpose language. The implemented DSL has reached an advanced maturity level and includes relevant features such as versioning, re-use, and testing. Chapter "FASTEN: An Extensible Platform to Experiment with Rigorous Modeling of Safety-Critical Systems" introduces an open source research environment for model-based specification and design of safety-critical applications and describes its characteristics as a collection of DSLs. The chapter surveys the DSLs, and their development and utilization, and then proposes a discussion of the lessons learnt by implementing them focusing on the features of MPS that enabled that. Another industrial application is reported in chapter "Migrating Insurance Calculation Rule Descriptions from Word to MPS", where existing C code plus natural language specifications in Word were reverse-engineered toward a DSL under adoption in the assurance domain. Indeed, the underlying goal is to perform a structural cleanup and splitting into small independent units of the existing routines. The incremental adoption process of the DSL is discussed together with a demonstration of its effective results, especially with respect to versioning and memory handling.

MPS in Research Projects

MPS implementations in research projects are discussed in chapters "Projecting Textual Languages", "Engineering Gameful Applications with MPS", and "Learning Data Analysis with MetaR": these projects cover the benefits of text-based languages, the design and development of gamification applications, and research fields with generally low expertise in language engineering. One of the strengths of MPS, the provision of a mixture of different notations, is discussed in chapter "Projecting Textual Languages". In particular, the chapter presents an approach to automatically map grammar-based language definitions toward corresponding DSLs specified by MPS. Another research effort based on MPS features is presented in chapter "Engineering Gameful Applications with MPS", which illustrates the creation of a gamification design framework as a collection of DSLs. Each DSL addresses specific concerns of a gamification application design and deployment, while the MPS language workbench provides consistency by construction through language extension mechanisms. Chapter "Learning Data Analysis with MetaR" introduces a case study related to a tool designed to facilitate the use of DSLs by researchers with nontechnical background. In other words, a DSL created by means of MPS acts as a meta-tool to enhance the user-friendliness of the base tool. Yet, thanks to the features embedded in MPS, the tool includes language composition for expert users, such that the meta-tool can be further extended and tailored to specific needs.

Teaching and Learning with MPS

Chapters "Teaching MPS: Experiences from Industry and Academia" and "Teaching Language Engineering Using MPS" present experiences on teaching and learning with MPS. Chapter "Teaching MPS: Experiences from Industry and Academia" focuses on teaching both industrial professionals and academic students. In particular, the chapter discusses the organization of academic courses on MPS: first, the basics of text-based language workbenches are provided, and then the technical details of MPS are presented. In this way, students can capture the distinctive characteristics of MPS. Instead, chapter "Teaching Language Engineering Using MPS" introduces the principles involved in DSL design and development in conjunction with compiler theory, and then shows how MPS can be exploited for the practical implementation of those principles.

To summarize, this book covers several topics related to DSL engineering in general and how they can be handled by means of the JetBrains MPS. The number and diversity of the presented use-case demonstrate the strength and malleability of the DSLs defined using MPS. The selected contributions, which represent the current state of the art and practice in using JetBrains MPS to implement languages for real-world applications, are expected to be of great interest for the Model-Driven and Software Languages Engineering communities.

Perspectives

The insights brought by the book indicate that MDE's state of the art and practice display the growing success of language workbenches supporting various, sometimes blended [6], notations (Rascal [7], xText [8], and MPS, to mention a few). Seamless blended notations can bring several benefits, among them flexible separation of concerns, multiview modeling based on multiple notations, convenient text-based editing operations (inside and outside the modeling environment), and eventually faster modeling activities [9]. In this respect, specifying models as text may provide great advantages via the leverage of text manipulation tools, such as text-based diff/merge, while leaving open the possibility of rendering portions of models in a diagrammatic form (interestingly, the upcoming SysML v2 [10] takes this direction by providing a textual syntax).

One of the reasons for the success of text-based language workbenches is their pragmatic approach: the simple definition of a (E)BNF grammar, i.e., the abstract syntax, is usually enough to create the first prototype of a DSL, while concrete syntaxes can be incrementally refined. This is the case for MPS, which allows the quick creation of fully fledged text-based DSLs with limited effort, by defining a set of concepts, their properties, and relationships. Moreover, its projectional editing conveys a structured approach to the creation, visualization, and editing of models.

An open issue, common to most language workbenches, is the effort required for large customizations, including their maintenance in case of language evolution. In this respect, MPS provides the possibility to alleviate maintenance issues through a powerful language extension mechanism. Indeed, several chapters in the book refer to these mechanisms as one of the most relevant features of MPS. Moreover, the movement toward web- and cloud-based solutions has affected the way language workbenches are designed and evolved; this applies to MPS too, for which fully fledged web-based solutions (e.g., Modelix DSL[1]) are under development.

---

[1] https://modelix.github.io/

Acknowledgments

The editors would like to express their deepest gratitude to all the authors who have submitted their valuable contributions and have provided their highly qualified expertise in reviewing the chapters included in this book. Moreover, they would like to thank Robert Walter—Senior Software Developer at Unity Technologies—and Federico Tomassetti—Software Language Engineering expert and Co-founder at Strumenta—for their professional support in reviewing some of the chapters. The editors would also like to thank the Springer staff for their continuous support and dedication. In particular, the tireless support from Ralf Gerstner, Executive Editor for Computer Science at Springer, has been greatly appreciated.

Trento, Italy   Antonio Bucchiarone
Västerås, Sweden   Antonio Cicchetti
Västerås, Sweden   Federico Ciccozzi
L'Aquila, Italy   Alfonso Pierantonio

References

1. Schmidt, D.C.: Guest Editor's Introduction: Model-driven engineering. Computer, **39**(2), 25–31 (2006). https://doi.org/10.1109/MC.2006.58
2. van Deursen, A., Klint, P., Visser, J.: Domain-specific languages: an annotated bibliography. SIGPLAN Not. **35**(6), 26–36.
   https://doi.org/10.1145/352029.352035
3. Voelter, M., Benz, S., Dietrich, C., Engelmann, B., Helander, M., Kats, L.C.L., Visser, E., Wachsmuth, G.: DSL engineering – designing, implementing and using domain-specific languages, pp. 1–558. dslbook.org, ISBN 978-1-4812-1858-0 (2013)
4. Voelter, M.: Language and IDE modularization and composition with MPS. In: Generative and transformational techniques in software engineering IV, pp 383–430. Springer (2013)
5. Voelter, M., Lisson, S.: Supporting diverse notations in MPS' projectional editor. GEMOC@MoDELS 2014, pp. 7–16
6. Ciccozzi, F., Tichy, M., Vangheluwe, H., Weyns, D.: Blended modelling-what, why and how. In: 2019 ACM/IEEE 22nd International Conference on Model Driven Engineering Languages and Systems Companion (MODELS-C), pp. 425–430. IEEE (2019)
7. Klint, P., van der Storm, T., Vinju, J.J.: RASCAL: A domain specific language for source code analysis and manipulation. In: SCAM, pp. 168–177. IEEE (2009)
8. Eysholdt, M., Behrens, H.: Xtext: Implement your language faster than the quick and dirty way. In: SPLASH Companion, pp. 307–309. ACM (2010)

9. Addazi, L., Ciccozzi, F. (2021). Blended graphical and textual modelling for UML profiles: a proof-of-concept implementation and experiment. J. Syst. Softw. 110912

10. Object Management Group. https://www.omgsysml.org/

Contents

JetBrains MPS: Why Modern Language Workbenches Matter

Václav Pech

Abstract The goal of this chapter is to give a perspective on language work-benches, as well as to provide an overview of the MPS features. It starts with an introduction to language workbenches and motivations for DSL development. It then continues with an overview of how languages are created in MPS. Projectional editing is explained and its benefits for DSL design discussed. Other essential aspects of language definition, such as language testing and migration, are covered as well. Finally, useful pointers regarding the MPS ecosystem and the user community are provided.

1 Introduction to the Domain of Language Workbenches

MPS is an open-source language workbench by JetBrains that focuses on domain-specific languages. The name of the tool, MPS, is an acronym for Meta-programming System, which emphasizes the focus on meta-programming, i.e,. creating languages and comprehensive tooling for programming.

Domain-specific languages (DSL) is a fairly established idea of using custom-tailored languages to describe programs or parts of them, such as algorithms or configuration specifications, using notations specific to a particular domain. DSLs proponents claim that using a mixture of single-purpose DSLs in concert brings benefits such as higher abstraction level, fewer errors in code, smaller technology lock-in, and better communication between developers and business people compared to using a single general-purpose language (GPL). They also state that these benefits are likely to outweigh the additional costs of language development and maintenance for many projects.

V. Pech (✉)
JetBrains s.r.o. Kavčí Hory Office Park, Praha 4 – Nusle, Czech Republic
e-mail: vaclav.pech@jetbrains.com

© The Author(s), under exclusive license to Springer Nature Switzerland AG 2021
A. Bucchiarone et al. (eds.), *Domain-Specific Languages in Practice*,
https://doi.org/10.1007/978-3-030-73758-0_1

DSLs have been gradually gaining popularity both in academia and in industry over the past two decades. On one hand, it was various internal DSLs such as Cypher (a query language for the Neo4J graph database), Gradle (a build tool), Spock (a test framework), and many other utility-like DSLs that aimed at simplifying life for developers. On the other hand, there were external, in other words "standalone," DSLs, which do not depend on a host programming language. VHDL, MATLAB, YACC, and SQL can be considered typical examples. As Martin Fowler states in his famous article [1], external DSLs, unlike internal ones, offer much richer and more flexible notations, but typically lack advanced tooling and integrate only loosely with the rest of the codebase of a system that they are part of.

While the available IDEs can provide assistance to developers when manipulating code written in some internal DSLs, building tools for external DSLs that would be comparable in functionality with traditional IDEs requires non-trivial additional effort. Thus the greater potential of external DSLs is hindered by the lack of (or the cost of) proper tooling. This gave rise to language workbenches.

Language workbenches were created with two main goals in mind:

1. To simplify the language-definition process and help maintain the whole language lifecycle
2. To simplify or automate the process of creating tooling for the languages

A language workbench can be described as a factory for building languages and tooling for them. The tooling aspect of language workbenches must not be underestimated, especially if the DLSs are supposed to be integrated into a larger code base written in a GPL. In addition, proper tooling, especially an intuitive editor, may help non-programmers interact with the code in a DSL. This would lower the bar for domain experts to join the development team and participate in a software project as active code authors.

The tooling aspect typically includes:

- Syntax coloring in the editor
- Code completion that gives suggestions as to what code can be entered at the current cursor position
- Navigation in code (go to definition of a reference, find/highlight usages of a definition, find an element by its name)
- Error highlighting in code on the fly as well as on demand in a report
- Static code analysis that detects erroneous or suspicious pieces of code and reports them to the developer
- Refactoring (rename an element, move an element to a different location, safe delete, extract some code into a new definition, inline a definition, etc.)
- Integrated test runner to quickly test the correctness of the code
- A debugger that interactively runs a program step-by-step and allows the developer to inspect the state of the program at various moments of its execution
- Integrated support for version control systems (VCS) that offers intuitive diff views and conflict resolution
- Integrated code generator and/or a compiler that transforms the DSL code into its runnable form

- A way to split large code base into smaller parts and manage dependencies between these parts
- Offering a notion of a language version and defining a process to migrate code to a particular version of a language, ideally automatically

1.1 A Brief History of the MPS Project

MPS was created by JetBrains. JetBrains is a software company founded in 2000, which since its beginning has focused on building tools for developers. The product portfolio contains mostly IDEs for popular programming languages and platforms, including Java, Android, C/C++, .Net, Ruby, and Python. JetBrains also makes tools for team cooperation. The company has over 1200 employees and is headquartered in Prague, Czech Republic, with offices worldwide.

The MPS project was started in 2003 as an internal experiment to try innovative concepts, such as projectional editor and code generation, on the Java platform. It has gradually evolved into a regular tool that is ready for use in the industry. The open-source license permits users to use MPS in commercial as well as open-source and academic projects without fees or any liabilities for JetBrains. JetBrains offers consultancy, training, and commercial support to customers to fund further development of the tool.

MPS is a universal language workbench, and is capable of supporting a wide range of domains. Thus far, MPS has been tried in domains as varied as

- Health and medicine [2]
- Data science [3]
- Tax legislation [4]
- Formal systems specification [5]
- Automotive [6]
- Aerospace [6]
- Robotics [6]
- Embedded software [6]

MPS does not contain any restrictions or limitations that would prevent it from addressing more domains in the future.

1.2 The Business Value of Language Workbenches

There are three main benefits of using Language Engineering for building software:

- Productivity
- Quality
- Leveraging expertise

1.2.1 Productivity

The main gains in productivity come from removing repetition from code and from raising the abstraction level closer to the problem domain. Higher levels of abstraction support the programmer's focus and reduce the abstraction gap between the domain and the language. This also applies to the maintenance phase. Reading and understanding code can be greatly improved by raising the level of abstraction.

When comparing the traditional approach using GPLs with language engineering, the productivity increase comes at the price of higher initial costs—the languages must first be designed and implemented. Luckily, language workbenches often support language evolution—languages can be developed and used at the same time. Code gets automatically migrated to the most recent version of the languages. Language development can be done iteratively.

1.2.2 Quality

Code written using DSLs tends to contain fewer defects, mainly due to the following reasons:

- The code is shorter than when written using a GPL.
- The code is easier to analyze by tools and reviewed by humans.
- The language can forbid dangerous or suspicious code constructs, e.g., pointer manipulation or null values.
- Error messages that the IDE shows to the user can be domain-specific, e.g., "Symbol is not available on a phone keyboard."
- The generator generates code with consistent quality—new features (aka business rules, menus, etc.) have the same quality as the old ones, since the generator used to generate runnable code for them is the same.

1.2.3 Leveraging Expertise

Language engineering separates the concerns of the problem domain and the implementation domain.

Problem domain—is covered by the user models written in DSLs. Domain experts understand this domain and thus benefit from being able to read or write code that targets the problem domain. The domain experts' expertise is encoded in the user models. These are typically preserved in version control systems and evolve at the pace of evolution of the business.

Implementation domain—is covered by the generator and the generator runtime frameworks. Professional programmers understand this domain and use GPLs to implement the logic. The logic of efficient implementation is encoded in the generator and evolves at the pace of evolution of the implementation technology (e.g., Java, the database, the operating system).

- The separation of the two concerns enables business to evolve each domain at its own pace and react to challenges in either of them independently.
- Domain experts who join the team can understand the business rules covered by the models from reading the user models, since the problem domain is not cluttered with alien implementation logic.
- Switching the implementation technology should ideally only mean defining a new generator.
- The user models, which hold the essential business logic, remain valid and usable even when the implementation technology changes dramatically.

2 MPS Terminology and Notations

People sometimes get confused about how code is represented in computer programs. Compilers, interpreters and IDEs need to manipulate code that the user has provided. Code is typically stored in text files and the extension of the file indicates the language used by that file. Computer programs, in order to represent the code in memory, need to read the files and process them with a special tool, called parser. Parser uses the known grammar of the language to distinguish individual tokens in the text file and to assign meaning to them. As parser reads the file it gradually builds a data structure that is known as the Abstract Syntax Tree. The structure represents the code fully and unambiguously. Abstract Syntax Trees (AST for short) are used by the IDEs to provide assistance to the user, and are used by the compilers to perform transformations that gradually convert the tree into runnable binary code.

2.1 Abstract Syntax Tree

MPS differentiates itself from many other language workbenches by avoiding the text form. The programs are always represented by an AST—on disk, in memory, and during transformations and code generation. This means that no grammar definitions or parsers are needed to define a language in MPS.

2.2 Node

Nodes form an AST. Each node has a parent node, child nodes, properties, and references to other nodes. The nodes that don't have a parent are called root nodes. These are the top-most elements of ASTs. For example, in Java the root nodes are classes, interfaces, and enums.

2.3 Concept

Nodes can be very different from one another—an if statement certainly looks different than a variable declaration. It is the concept of a node that codifies how a node will behave and what purpose it has in code. Each node stores a reference to its concept. The concept defines the class of nodes and coins the structure of nodes in that class. It specifies which children, properties, and references an instance of a node can have. Concept declarations form an inheritance hierarchy. If one concept extends another, it inherits all children, properties, and references from its super-concept.

While nodes compose ASTs, concepts define the possible "categories" of nodes.

2.4 Models vs. Meta-models

The terms models and meta-models are known from model-driven software design. While "models" represent user code, "meta-models" represent the "abstractions" available for creating those "models." This is somewhat similar to the distinction between "instances" and "classes" in object-oriented programming, where "classes" provide the framework and developers create "instances" of these "classes" in order to create functional systems.

In MPS "meta-models" are represented as languages, which hold concepts, and "models" are represented as user code, which consists of nodes in ASTs.

2.5 Language

A language in MPS is a set of concepts with some additional information. The additional information includes details on editors, completion menus, intentions, typesystem, dataflow, etc. associated with the language. A language can extend another language and thus define additional qualities for concepts defined in the extended language.

2.6 Modules

Projects in MPS consist of modules. Modules are independent reusable collections of code. There are four types of modules in MPS:

- Solution—represents a piece of user code and is equivalent to how code is structured in traditional IDEs.
- Language—represents language definition.

- Generator—represents definition of code transformations into another language.
- DevKit—groups modules (Solutions and Languages) for easy reference; does not add any new code or functionality. A module can be part of multiple DevKits.

2.7 Models

Internally, modules are structured into models. Models are a language-agnostic equivalent of Java's packages, Ruby's modules, or JavaScript folders. Models hold root nodes, which are a rough equivalent to files in traditional languages. Root nodes "are" the code. Technically, they represent the roots of trees (aka Abstract Syntax Tree) and hold other nodes organized into a tree-like hierarchy.

Additionally, MPS has the capacity to organize code inside models hierarchically into what are called virtual packages.

2.8 Generator

The generator gives the code meaning. It transforms the model into a model that uses a different language, typically on a lower level of abstraction. Generation in MPS is done in phases—the output of one generator can become the input for another generator in a pipeline. An optional model-to-text conversion phase (*TextGen*) may follow to generate code in a textual format. This staged approach helps bridge potentially big semantics gaps between the original problem domain and the technical implementation domain. It also encourages reuse of generators.

3 BaseLanguage

MPS comes with a clone of the Java language, called BaseLanguage. Since Java is a traditional parser-based GPL, it cannot be used directly in MPS as is, but had to be re-implemented using the MPS language definition mechanisms. This re-implementation is called BaseLanguage. The word *base* highlights that it is:

1. The fundamental language used throughout MPS to write language definitions logic.
2. A typical target of code generation—high-level DSL code is generated into BaseLanguage, which in turn can be represented as Java source code and then compiled with a Java compiler.

Although originally BaseLanguage copied Java in version 6, numerous extensions have been created over time to provide additional capabilities and bring in many of the later Java features.

However convenient, BaseLanguage is not the only desired target language for code generation. The generator can transform models between any languages, provided they all have their MPS-based definitions available. To date, MPS implementations of these traditional GPLs languages exist and are readily available—Java, XML, Html, CSS, C, C#, JavaScript, Text, PDF, and LaTex.

In order to generate other languages than these, the intended languages must first be defined in terms of MPS.

4 Projectional Editor

Editing code in MPS differs fundamentally from other, more traditional, tools. MPS is based on the concept of projectional editor, which is an invention from the 1970s that has been so far adopted mostly by tools outside of the programming mainstream. In essence, a projectional editor lets the developer manipulate the in-memory representation of the code directly, instead of letting them type characters that need to be parsed by the tool.

From the user perspective this feels somewhat similar to editing math formulas in popular text processors. The editor takes care of the structure of the code and the developer fills in the blanks. Since the code is never represented in a plain text form, there is no need for parsing text in order to build the in-memory representation of code. The code is always in this form—on disk as well as in memory.

The challenge for projectional editors is to hide the fact that the user is manipulating the AST. Historically, the editors were not very successful in making text editing convenient enough for the programming community to adopt it widely. Its applicability has thus been limited to only a few domains.

MPS has made an attempt to improve projectional editing and make it universally applicable to a wide range of possible notations. The key element of the MPS projectional editor is the idea of node transformations. When the user presses a key on the keyboard, it is not understood as a character that needs to be inserted into a text document, but instead it is handled as an event by the part of the AST that holds the cursor at that moment. A key event is announced to the registered listeners on that particular node of the AST and they will handle the event, typically by transforming the AST to reflect the character represented by the event (Fig. 1).

4.1 Notations

The notation directly influences the success of a language. People frequently adopt or refuse a language depending on how familiar they feel when interacting with the code. The notation should be simple and concise and provide sensible defaults. If a preferred notation exists already in the domain, it is advisable to reuse or adapt it in the new language.

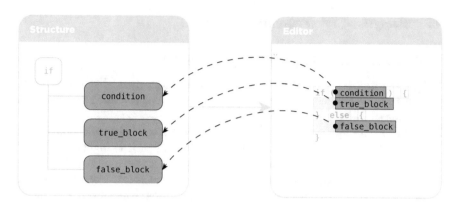

Fig. 1 Mapping of children of the concept for conditional statement to cells of the projectional editor

Finally, the support that the IDE provides (code completion, scoping, intentions, refactorings, navigation, error detection, etc.) adds to the usability of the notation itself. It is not only the static syntax of the language but also the possibility of efficient interaction with the code that users care about when it comes to language notations.

The long history of parser-based languages has made many engineers believe that textual notations are the generally preferred ones, while, in fact, they may not be optimal for numerous problem domains. Abstract Syntax Trees (AST) as a data structure are not limited to representing text. They can easily represent diagrams, tables, or anything that can be mapped to a structure of a hierarchy with references. It is the textual editor of the traditional IDEs that puts restrictions on the allowed notations. Tools such as MPS that build on the principles of projectional (sometimes called structured) editing can offer a wide range of notations.

Symbols—notations that combine text with non-textual symbols. Math, for example, has been using symbols for centuries, and there are good reasons to support these symbols in languages used in math-heavy computations.

Tables—the wide use of spreadsheets proves that tabular notations are handy for certain types of tasks, for example as spreadsheets or decision tables.

Forms—rich text editors are also frequently utilized for encoding rules of various sorts. Requirement documents, business rules specifications, and formalized contract agreements are examples of documents that can be treated as regular models with all the benefits of tooling, automation, and transformations.

Diagrams—numerous problems are best solved in graphics—electrical circuits, organizational charts, workflows, etc.

State machines—some domains, such as embedded software and robotics, use state machines to model systems that react to external events and change their internal state following a predefined set of rules. To express the transitions in individual states after the arrival of certain events a table or a diagram can be used with high success rates.

4.2 Benefits of Projectional Editing

There are three main benefits of using a projectional editor:

1. **Rich notations**—since AST can represent textual as well as tabular or graphical notations, the absence of a parser opens up the possibility of using non-parseable notations.
2. **Multiple notations**—since the persistence format of code in a projectional editor stores the AST, which is independent of the notation, it is highly possible to define multiple notations for a single language and let the user switch between them at will. The code can, for example, be presented as text when created, as a table when conducting a code review, and as a diagram when resolving a merge conflict.
3. **Language modularity**—the problem of multiple parsers is completely avoided by projectional languages. The nodes of an AST are disambiguated by the user when created and hence the tool is always certain about what concept is represented by a given node. Nodes belonging to different languages can be combined in a single code base, even in a single AST. Families of languages and their extensions can be designed in a way that permits reuse, cross-referencing, embedding, and extension of elements of one language by elements of another language. This helps to avoid the need to design bloated "all-world" language and instead encourages minimalistic purpose-oriented languages that can be combined at will.

4.3 Notations Trade-Offs

For beginners or infrequent users of a language, a chatty, highly descriptive syntax with enough visual guidance should be preferred—a learnable notation. For experienced and frequent users, an efficient, perhaps even cryptic, fast to type notation with numerous keyboard shortcuts will allow the users to achieve their tasks faster.

Orthogonally, notations can be optimized toward easy readability or writability. Ceremony in code helps in understanding context, but slows people down when they have to write the code. Compact syntaxes, on the other hand, may sometimes be challenging to read.

Since MPS enables language designers to provide multiple notations for a language, which the users can choose from when editing code, the trade-off between learnability and effectiveness, as well as between readability and writability, does not need to be made in MPS languages. Instead, languages can address these competing concerns with multiple notations, each optimized for a particular task or role. For example, when encoding a state machine, a textual notation could be used by experienced users to efficiently create definitions (weight toward effectivity and writability), while a diagram notation may be used for code reviews (readability).

4.4   Reflective Editor

Although the editor in MPS hides the real code (AST) under the hood and instead only permits the developers to interact with the code through one of several projections, there is a way for the developer to see and touch the AST directly. MPS offers Reflective editor, which is a default visualization available for all languages automatically. It simply projects the AST onto the screen as a tree and lets the user edit the values in a default way. This is especially handy in the early prototyping stages of language development when the editors are broken or non-existent. Having such a fallback editor option might be useful even at later phases of development if none of the provided editors supports the desired editing task.

5   The MPS Way of Defining Languages

The definition of a language in MPS is split into several aspects. Each aspect is represented as an independent model inside the language definition.

- *Structure*—Holds the abstract syntax (concepts) of the language.
- *Editor*—Contains editor definitions (notations) for the concepts of the language.
- *Constraints*—Puts additional constraints on what values properties can have, what targets references can point to, and what children a node can have beyond the cardinality restriction specified in the Structure aspect.
- *Typesystem*—Holds rules that the typesystem engine should use when calculating types for nodes. Additionally, it defines checking rules that represent static code analysis checks that should be performed against models that use the language.
- *Dataflow*—Defines the control and dataflow rules for individual concepts. Based on these control and dataflows, a detailed analysis can be performed and issues such as "unreachable code" and "potential null-pointer exception" can be discovered.
- *Intentions*—Collects handy intentions that will assist the user with quick hints on how to refactor or reorganize the code.
- *TextGen*—Useful only for languages that can have their models directly converted to textual files (aka base languages). Defines rules that help MPS flush the AST into a textual buffer to create textual source files.
- *Generator*—This aspect is actually a whole module not just a model. It contains rules and templates to convert models written in this language into another language.

```
concept IfStatement extends    AbstractCommand
                    implements <none>


instance can be root: false
alias: if
short description: <no short description>


properties:
<< ... >>


children:
condition    : LogicalExpression[1]
trueBranch   : CommandList[1]
falseBranch  : CommandList[1]
```

Fig. 2 The definition of a typical conditional statement in MPS

5.1 Structure

Language definition in MPS starts with the abstract syntax, which MPS calls "Structure." This is quite different from how traditional parser-based systems approach it, since these focus on the concrete syntax (aka notation) first. In MPS it is the conceptual view that is taken first—the language author defines the concepts, their properties, their references, and their mutual relationships of inheritance or aggregation (Fig. 2). The reflective editor helps a great deal with quick prototyping in this early stage of language design when editors do not exist yet or are only rudimentary.

5.2 Editor

Once the concepts are defined, their visual representation can be created. The language author is not restricted to only one visual representation of a concept; the language may offer multiple notations. One of them must be marked as "default," and the others are identified by textual identifiers (hints), allowing the final user to select these alternative notations by selecting the corresponding hint from the list.

An editor definition consists of one or more cells. A cell can contain a fixed text value, be bound to a property or a reference value of a node, or represent an editor of a child node. Cells can be styled with colors, padding, font styles, and sizes in a way similar to how CSS is used to style HTML elements. Modularization of the editor definition is allowed by using "Editor Components," the sub-concepts of which can override and thus customize their visual representation from what they have inherited.

The ability to customize the transformations of nodes is also very important, as it directly influences the dynamic behavior of the editor. The language author can customize the content of the completion menu in given contexts, allow fluent textual editing, and offer handy visual indicators to the user.

5.3 Constraints

When a property of a concept must only allow certain values (e.g., an integer value must be between 0 and 100; a text value must meet a regular expression), it must be specified in the constraints aspect. Similarly, it should be used when the scope of a reference (the set of available targets) must be limited. Additionally, the parent-child relationship as specified in the Structure aspect may be subject to further restrictions, which the Constraints aspect allows to be specified in the "can be child," "can be parent," and "can be ancestor" rules. The constraints represent rules that the editor prevents from being violated. Thus the user is not allowed to insert an invalid value into a property or an out-of-scope target into a reference. Such violations are reported by the color red in the editor.

5.4 Typesystem

The typesystem serves two purposes—type calculation and static code analysis. We will briefly look into both.

5.4.1 Type Calculation

The type inference engine in MPS will attempt to assign types to all nodes in the AST. If it fails to assign a type to a node or if some rules contradict each other in terms of what type a node should have, the typesystem will report a typesystem error to the user.

The language author uses inference rules in the typesystem aspect to define rules on how types should be calculated for nodes. For example, look at the following code:

```
var a = 10
increment(a)
def increment(integer p) {return p+1}
```

Line 1 declares a variable, line 2 passes a variable reference to a method call, and finally line 3 declares the method called increment. In a straightforward typesystem implementation for such a language there would be the following inference rules involved in computing the type of the variable "a":

1. The type of "10" is integer.
2. The type of a variable declaration equals the type of its initializer.
3. The type of a variable reference equals the type of the variable declaration that it references.
4. The type of the parameter of method "increment" is integer.

These rules are enough for the typesystem to annotate completely and unambiguously all nodes in the code snippet with types. Additionally, a check should be inserted into the ruleset that, once the types are calculated, will verify that we are passing an integer into the "increment" method: "The type of the argument when calling the increment method must equal to the type of the parameter in the declaration of the method."

In this way the typesystem can detect situations when a value of an invalid type is being passed into the method.

5.4.2 Static Code Analysis

The typesystem offers checking rules to define code structures that should be reported to the user. This is typically used to inform the user about suboptimal code structure, potential semantics errors, unused definitions, misplaced constructs, etc. There are three levels of severity to report:

- Error
- Warning
- Informational message

Unlike for constraints, the typesystem checking rules do not prevent problems from happening. Instead, they report already present problems to the user and allow the user to trigger an associated quick-fix, if available, that will correct a particular issue.

5.5 *Generator*

While languages allow their users to create code, which MPS stores in models, generators can transform these source models into target models. Generators perform model-to-model transformations on models. The target models use different languages than the source models (typically the abstraction level is reduced/lowered during a generation transformation) and serve one or more purposes:

- Models can be converted to text source files and then compiled with standard compilers (Java, C, etc.).

- Models can be converted to text documents and used as such (configuration, documentation—property files, XML, PDF, html, latex).
- Models can be directly interpreted.
- Models can be used for code analysis or formal verification by a third-party tool (CBMS, state-machine reachability analysis, etc.).
- Models can be used for simulation of the real system.

It is possible for there to be several generators for the same DSL, each generating different implementation code. These generators may all be used at the same time to target multiple platforms, or they may evolve over time, one replacing the other as the needs for the run-time platform evolve. Regardless, it is sensible to follow this rule: A generator must not influence the design of the language.

The lifetime of a generator is usually shorter than the lifetime of the language and the models created with it. It is the user models that hold the biggest value for the customer as the user-written models contain the business knowledge collected over time by domain experts. This value must be preserved even if the implementation platform of the system may change over time.

A generator consists of stable and variable parts. The stable parts is the code that is always generated unchanged, no matter how the user implements the logic in the DSL. Large portions of the stable parts are frequently extracted away from the generator and implemented as a library that bundles with the generated code at run-time. The variable parts, on the other hand, reflect the actual DSL code. The generator thus has to support parametrization of the generated code to reflect the values in the input model.

The generator in MPS takes a templating approach. Each generator contains a set of rules that specify what templates to apply to what nodes in what context. The generator also contains the templates that specify code snippets in the target language into which a node should be translated.

When, for example, generating code written in language A into code written in language B, the generator author must specify rules that for each concept in language A define a template written in language B, which should be used to replace nodes of this concept in code with snippets of code in language B. These templates are parameterized with values from nodes of the original model. The parameterization is done using a family of macros that annotate the nodes of language B in the templates or their properties, children, and references, and specify how to set values depending on values in the input model.

6   Integration with Other Systems

6.1   Language Plugins

MPS builds on the modular IntelliJ platform. Its functionality can be enhanced through plugins that the users install through the UI, either from the JetBrains plugin repository or directly from a plugin zip file. This is a convenient option for languages to be shared among developers—a language or a set of related languages is packaged as a plugin for the IntelliJ platform and then distributed to the users, either directly or via the JetBrains plugin repository. On the receiver end it is just a matter of choosing the plugin from a list in the MPS UI and the languages can be instantly used to write models.

6.2 Standalone IDEs

Being a language workbench, MPS is a fairly large and complex tool. While it is acceptable for language designers to manage its complexity, for the intended users of the languages themselves a much simpler tool is typically needed. All the language design tooling and UI elements can safely be dropped in a tool, the single purpose of which is to let the user create and edit models in some languages and possibly generate them into the desired implementation code. By leveraging the IntelliJ platform, MPS enables the language authors to package a language or a collection of languages together with the core IDE functionality into a single-purpose tool—a custom IDE. This Java-based IDE, which is a single-purpose modeling tool, is then distributed to the users. The tool holds very little MPS-related heritage.

This is the favorite distribution path for most languages and their associated tooling, when the target users are non-programming domain experts.

6.3 Build Language

MPS has its own build automation facilities that allow language authors to create modular descriptions of how their languages should be built, what dependencies they have, and into which locations the output should be packaged.

The MPS build language is an essential component of this whole process. Build Language is an extensible build automation DSL for defining builds in a declarative way. Generated into Ant, it leverages the Ant execution power while keeping the sources clean and free from clutter and irrelevant details. Organized as a stack of MPS languages with Ant at the bottom, it allows each part of the build procedure to be expressed at a different abstraction level.

The build scripts can be used to create language plugins and standalone custom language IDEs, and to run language tests. Since Ant was chosen as the implementation technology for the MPS build scripts, all of these tasks can be performed from the command line as well as automatically on the continuous integration server. This enables MPS to participate in the automated build processes and thus produce or consume artifacts that together form a complete software application.

6.4 Persistence

Since all code in MPS persists in its AST form, a hierarchical structure must be present in the file that represents an MPS model on disk. By default, XML is utilized by MPS, with a proprietary binary format being an alternative. Custom persistence formats, such as database, JSON, and custom-formatted text files, can be plugged into MPS by providing a model serializer and a de-serializer.

6.5 Version Control

MPS leverages the IntelliJ platform to integrate with the most popular VCSs such as Git and Subversion. Since the users do not expect to manipulate code in its raw persistence format (XML or another structured format), MPS provides its own UI for diff view as well as for conflict resolution. The projectional editor is displayed to the user to render the particular code version. If multiple projections are available in the language, the user can conveniently choose which projection to use in the view.

6.6 Third-Party Tooling

From the software architecture point of view MPS is a modular Java application. It enables developers to enhance it with additional tools and useful visual elements. Typical examples include:

- External code analysis tools that need to be triggered from MPS in order to check the MPS models
- Code verifiers that need the models to be transformed into a particular format, then perform the verification, and finally present the results to the user in an intuitive way
- External debuggers
- Additional model visualizations that provide the user with a different view on the models
- Intuitive visual reports or consolidated statistics calculated from the models and presented to the user in an arbitrary way

7 Language Versioning and Migrations

Languages, like any piece of software, need to evolve over time. When changes are introduced into a language, existing code may break. Migrations automate the process of fixing such broken code by upgrading it to the recent version of the language.

After a language has been published and users have started using it, the language authors have to be careful with further changes to the language definition. Some changes to a language break code; some don't. In particular, removing concepts or adding and removing properties, children, and references to concepts will introduce incompatibilities between the current and the next language versions. This impacts the users of the language if they switch to the next language version. Failures to match the language definition will be presented to the user as errors reported in their models.

Breaking changes should always be accompanied by migrations to avoid problems on the user side. Migrations may also be useful for user convenience to automatically leverage non-breaking changes in their models.

Non-breaking changes:

- Add a new concept.
- Add properties to a concept.
- Add children and references to a concept, provided they are optional.
- Rename concepts, properties, children, and references.
- Loosen constraints.

Breaking changes:

- Add mandatory children and references (cardinality 1, 1...n).
- Remove concepts, properties, children, and references.
- Tighten constraints.

MPS tracks versions of languages used in projects and provides automatic migrations to upgrade the usages of a language to the most recent version of the language. The language designers can create maintenance "migration" code to run automatically against the user code and thus change the user's code so that it complies with the changes made to the language definition. This is called language migration.

8 Testing Language Definitions

Modern software development relies on automated testing as a way to increase reliability. The same holds true for languages in MPS—many different aspects of the language definition can be tested automatically. Structure, editor, constraints, typesystem, scoping, intentions, migrations, and the generator can all be tested with automated scripts. Let's cover the individual options that developers have in order to test the language definitions.

8.1   Debugging

MPS comes with a Java debugger and offers integration points for other external debuggers. Since MPS languages are implemented in Java, the built-in Java debugger can be used to debug language definitions. Extensive support is also available for trace and log messages to be inserted in code and then explored in the log.

8.2   Editor Tests

Editor tests allow language designers to test the editor definition and its reaction to user actions. Each editor test consists of three parts:

1. A starting piece of code and a starting cursor position
2. An expected resulting piece of code and optionally a resulting cursor position
3. A sequence of user-initialized events, such as text typed, keys pressed, or actions triggered, plus assertions of the editor state

Editor tests are run against the desired MPS editor definition, while the user actions are simulated and the resulting code is compared with the expected result. Additionally, the test can make assertions against the state of the editor context at any moment during its execution. This can be handy, for example, to test the available options in a completion menu or the visibility and properties of a particular editor cell.

8.3   Node Tests

Node tests focus on testing the Structure, Constraints, Typesystem, and Dataflow aspects of language definition. The test contains a piece of code together with assertions about its correctness. These arrestors can either be inserted as annotations into the code itself or expressed in an imperative style in one or more test methods. The assertions typically check:

- The presence or absence of errors on nodes
- The presence or absence of warnings on nodes
- The type calculated by the typesystem for a node
- The scope of a reference
- Violations on constraints

8.4   Migration Tests

Migrations tests can be used to check that migration scripts produce expected results when run against a specified input. A migration test can test a single migration or multiple migrations applied together. The test defines:

- The migration or multiple migrations to apply
- The nodes to apply the migrations to
- The nodes that represent the expected outcome of the test

8.5   Generator Tests

Generators can be tested with generator tests. Their goal is to ensure that a generator, or set of generators, conducts its transformations as expected. As with most tests in MPS the user specifies:

- The pre-conditions in the form of input models
- The expected output of the generator in the form of output models
- The set of generators to apply to the input models

A failure to match the generator output with the expected output is presented to the user in the test report.

9   The MPS Community

The community around MPS has been growing steadily since the early days of MPS. At first it was formed mostly by innovators who were seeking efficient ways to create complex software systems. Many of these luminaries, such as Markus Voelter [7] and Fabian Campagne [8], helped spread the word among early adopters. Soon interesting experimental projects started popping up.

- mbeddr [9]—an extensible C implementation for embedded software development
- MetaR [10]—an R IDE for people with limited computer science background
- NYoSH [11]—a tool designed as a modern replacement for Unix/Linux command line shells
- iets3 [12]—base language for system modeling and specification including basics abstractions for components, expression, variability, etc.

This pioneering work led to first customers adopting MPS for their business. Many of these describe their projects later in this book.

9.1 Sources of Information

There are several places where MPS community members go for information and advice:

- Online forum [13]—this is a discussion forum where people can ask and answer questions related to the MPS technology as well as to language design in general.
- Blog [14]—the MPS team regularly informs the community about new releases, interesting features, and upcoming events through the blog.
- Slack [15]—the official slack channel, where the users can talk to the developers as well as the other members of the MPS community.
- MPS rocks [16]—an informational portal on everything about MPS run by Kolja Dummann.
- Publications page [17]—MPS, being open-source software, encourages researchers from academia to use it for their experiments with languages. The MPS team maintains a list of relevant papers that have been published by people from academia as well as from the industry.

9.2 MPS Extensions

The mbeddr team has gradually built a comprehensive collection of utilities and utility languages that were not specific to their primary domain of focus, which was embedded systems. They generously extracted these handy gadgets that solve many recurring problems in language engineering into an independent package and shared it with the community. The library is available as a download [18] separate from MPS itself. In addition, the individual tools have been deployed as plugins into the JetBrains plugin repository for easy installation.

9.3 Language Repository

The collection of publicly available MPS-based languages is growing. Some of them are readily available in the JetBrains plugin repository [19]. The language repository page [20] is an attempt to keep a list of all available languages in one place.

10 Conclusion and Future Developments

The development of MPS continues. To stay relevant, MPS has to adapt to new technologies and engineering processes. The underlying IntelliJ platform covers most of these changes, although integrating some of them with the projectional editor imposes challenges. The MPS team continues to search for ways to overcome the limitations of the individual aspects of language definition:

- The constraints aspect now offers an experimental approach to constraint definition that allows the designer to componentize the individual rules and to customize the error messages.
- A new typesystem aspect will be introduced to considerably improve the expressiveness of the typesystem rules.
- The definitions of menu transformations in the editor aspect should be simplified, at least for the typical scenarios.
- The support for cross-model generation and incrementality of the generator must be enhanced.

Separately, JetBrains continues to develop a web-based projection editor that could eventually become a cornerstone of new generation language workbenches.

References

1. Language workbenches: the killer-app for domain specific languages? https://www.martinfowler.com/articles/languageWorkbench.html
2. Case Study: How DSLs transformed Voluntis in the worldwide leader in Digital Therapeutics algorithms. https://strumenta.com/wp-content/uploads/2020/05/Voluntis-Case-Study.pdf
3. The MetaR project case study. https://resources.jetbrains.com/storage/products/mps/docs/MPS_MetaR_Case_Study.pdf
4. The Dutch Tax Office case study. https://resources.jetbrains.com/storage/products/mps/docs/MPS_DTO_Case_Study.pdf
5. FASTEN.Safe: A model-driven engineering tool to experiment with checkable assurance cases, by C. Carlan, D. Ratiu, 39th International Conference on Computer Safety, Reliability and Security (SAFECOMP), 2020. https://drive.google.com/file/d/18O7iY1MkkECj%2D%2DujO-Zx5hNX7DazGMkL/view?usp=sharing
6. The mbeddr project case study. https://resources.jetbrains.com/storage/products/mps/docs/MPS_mbeddr_Case_Study.pdf
7. Markus Voelter homepage. http://voelter.de/
8. Fabian Campagne's laboratory homepage. http://campagnelab.org/
9. The mbeddr project homepage. http://mbeddr.com/
10. The MetaR project homepage. http://campagnelab.org/software/metar/
11. The NYoSH project homepage. http://campagnelab.org/software/nyosh/
12. The iets3 project source code repository. https://github.com/IETS3/iets3.opensource
13. The MPS online discussion forum. https://mps-support.jetbrains.com/hc/en-us/community/topics/200363779-MPS
14. The official blog of the MPS project. https://blog.jetbrains.com/mps/
15. The official slack discussion for the MPS community. https://jetbrains-mps.slack.com
16. The "MPS rocks" community website. https://mps.rocks/
17. The page listing academic publications related to the MPS project. https://www.jetbrains.com/mps/publications
18. The source code repository of the MPS extensions project. https://jetbrains.github.io/MPS-extensions/
19. The JetBrains plugin repository for MPS. https://plugins.jetbrains.com/mps
20. The "Language repository" page listing the important third-party languages and language plugins. https://confluence.jetbrains.com/display/MPS/MPS+Languages+Repository

Part I
JetBrains MPS in Industrial Applications

Use MPS to Unleash the Creativity of Domain Experts: Language Engineering Is a Key Enabler for Bringing Innovation in Industry

Daniel Ratiu, Holger Nehls, Andreas Joanni, and Stefan Rothbauer

Abstract The work of domain experts is essential for the success of each company. Despite the fact that they have unique needs, many domain experts work with general purpose, low semantics tools, and ad-hoc-created tool chains. Generic domain agnostic tools force experts to fill a big encoding gap due to missing abstraction. The use of inadequate tools brings a large amount of accidental complexity, and instead of being productive and creative, experts spend a lot of time fighting against tools. Using appropriate domain-specific modeling languages (DSMLs) increases development efficiency and enables advanced tool support. In this chapter we present our experience gained over the last five years with instantiating domain-specific languages and tooling, built with MPS, in three different business domains within Siemens in order to enable innovative use cases, which releases domain experts from repetitive work and helps them focus on intrinsically complex domain problems and being more creative. We describe how we use MPS to allow experts to explore their domain and describe the MPS core features which made our work possible.

1 Introduction

Domain experts are the core assets of a company. Their work produces added value, which helps companies to differentiate the products and survive in an increasingly competitive environment which evolves at high speed. The creativity of domain

D. Ratiu (✉)
VW Car.Software.Org (previously with Siemens CT), Munich, Germany

H. Nehls
Siemens Healthineers, Forchheim, Germany
e-mail: holger.nehls@siemens-healthineers.com

A. Joanni · S. Rothbauer
Siemens Corporate Technology, Munich, Germany
e-mail: andreas.joanni@siemens.com; stefan.rothbauer@siemens.com

© The Author(s), under exclusive license to Springer Nature Switzerland AG 2021
A. Bucchiarone et al. (eds.), *Domain-Specific Languages in Practice*,
https://doi.org/10.1007/978-3-030-73758-0_2

experts is an essential key differentiation factor reflected in the performance of companies and the products they create. Not surprisingly, most domain experts have an educational background outside of the computer science domain, such as physicists, mathematicians, civil, mechanical, or electrical engineers, physicians, and economists.

1.1 Disconnect Between Domain Experts and Tool Providers

Tooling Needs of Domain Experts Many problems to be addressed by domain experts are highly specific, and off-the-shelf tools do not allow them to tackle these in an adequate manner. In such cases, general purpose tools often stay in the way of domain experts and produce frustration and friction loss. Letting valuable domain experts fight against accidental complexity introduced by general purpose or inadequate tooling leads to wasted "brain cycles" and missed opportunities.

- *Repetition:* People are notoriously inefficient when repetitive and monotonous work needs to be performed. Highly repetitive work takes away creative energy and kills motivation.
- *Inconsistencies:* Manually correcting low-level inconsistencies due to system evolution or requirement changes is slow, expensive, and error-prone. Manual reviews of long documents written in plain natural language text or using spreadsheets take a lot of time and many inconsistencies remain unaddressed.
- *Lack of Transparency:* Lack of communication among domain experts from different neighboring disciplines causes misunderstandings and frustration. Barriers to information flow lead to (communication) walls and thereby to sub-optimal approaches. Substantial resources are wasted on searching for local optima while low-hanging opportunities to find solutions closer to a global optimum are missed.

Influencing external vendors about what functions to implement is impossible for small teams of end-users. There is effectively no way for domain experts to influence the functionalities of upcoming versions of off-the-shelf tools which they use. The experts end up adapting themselves to the existing tools instead of using tools tailored to their needs. Off-the-shelf generic tools are often "tyrannical" and the experts have no choice but to use them.

> Empowering domain experts with domain-appropriate tools which minimize the encoding step between problem and solution domains boosts productivity, minimizes frustration, and increases quality. Domain experts can use their creative energy to solve intrinsically complex problems in the domain and explore innovative solutions.

Tooling Offerings by Tool Providers The discrepancy between off-the-shelf tool offerings and tooling needs of domain experts is often inherent due to the different interests. From the point of view of tool vendors, many of the abovementioned concerns have a very good reason:

- *Market Size*: Many use cases needed by domain experts are so specific that specialized tools are needed. There is simply no big market for such specific tools. Off-the-shelf tooling is often developed with a platform in mind—the target audience is kept as generic as possible such that the tool can be sold to many customers, thus increasing the profit while keeping the price per license low.
- *Specific Know-how*: Individual creativity of domain experts to solve specific categories of challenges requires deep domain experience and understanding, which is simply not available on the part of generic tool vendors. They lack understanding of the domain-specific needs.
- *Cutting-edge Innovation*: Some specific tasks of domain experts and the methods they use are so new that no tools exist yet. The release cycle of commercial tools spans several years—so when a tool release reaches a user, it contains functionality which has been around (conceptually) for many years. The competitive advantage of using new and fresh tooling disappears.

Domain experts think that building appropriate languages and tooling for their needs is something exotic and must be prohibitively expensive. This is wrong, since MPS makes it cost-effective to develop and evolve domain-specific tooling.

1.2 Intended Audience

The target audience of this chapter is (1) people outside of computer science who seek to understand how MPS can support domain experts to be innovative, and (2) computer science people who need to pitch the DS(M)L and MPS technology to non-computer scientists. In particular we focus on:

- *Technology scouts* who look for the costs/benefits of introducing new technologies in their organization
- *Domain experts* who look for better tools to help them in their daily work and want to understand the spectrum of possibilities
- *Managers* who aim to empower their teams with modern tooling and are continuously looking for new approaches which address their unique needs
- *Industrial researchers* who seek ways to operationalize their concepts such that they can get closer to practitioners

1.3 Structure of This Chapter

In this chapter, we report on our experience with developing and deploying DSLs built with MPS over the last five years in three different business domains and at

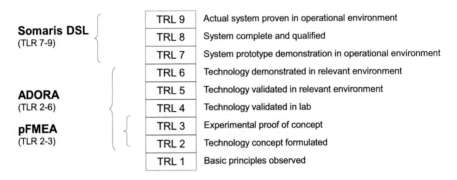

Fig. 1 Overview of different technology readiness levels and how our projects map onto them

several maturity levels. The status of the projects regarding their development phase and productive usage is described by so-called technology readiness levels (TRL)—illustrated in Fig. 1. We describe our experience with different scenarios where we successfully helped domain experts to improve the efficiency of their daily work by using domain-specific tools:

- **pFMEA**—is a DSL that enables explorative research and interaction with practitioners in the *smart factories* domain. The work has been done in the frame of a publicly funded research project and the goal was to realize a proof of concept and (partial) validation in laboratory conditions (TRL 2-4).
- **ADORA**—is a stack of DSLs to formalize *financial aspects of technical contracts* and their interaction with technical characteristics of systems. ADORA is an internal research transfer project. Different functionalities are at different various technology readiness levels from formulated concepts (TRL 2) up to demonstration in the relevant environment (TRL 6).
- **Somaris DSLs**—is a stack of DSLs aimed to boost productivity of physicists for defining parameters of computed tomography (CT) scanners. These DSLs are designed for productive but internal use and are built on experience accumulated over the years by domain experts within the *medical domain*. Aiming at production use, the TRL for various functions is thereby much higher (TRL 7-9).

In Table 1 we present at a glance the main motivation of the three projects.

Structure In Sect. 2 we present the pFMEA project and how we used MPS as a vehicle to realize prototypes and thereby to enable communication with project partners and experts. In Sect. 3 we present how we used MPS to build ADORA, a research transfer project which is focused on building a digital twin of contractual agreements and linking them to technical aspects of systems. In Sect. 4 we present our experience with deploying domain-specific tooling built with MPS into production as part of the SomarisDSL project. In Sect. 5 we retrospectively discuss our lessons learnt. Section 6 concludes the chapter.

Table 1 Overview of the motivation of our projects and the main pain points addressed. We gave between one and five stars to different motivation points: the more stars the more relevant a point is to motivating our work; '-' means that the specific point does not apply to the tool

Tool	pFMEA	ADORA	SomarisDSL
Explorative Research	*****	*****	**
Research Transfer	**	*****	**
Avoid Repetitive Work	-	***	*****
Enable Domain Formalization	***	****	*****
Enable Deep Analyses	****	*****	****
Generate Other Artifacts	-	***	*****
Improve Communication	**	*****	****
Integrate into Delivery Pipeline	-	-	*****
Shorten requirement feedback loop	-	-	*****
Speed-up Development	-	****	*****
No existing off-the-shelf tool	*****	*****	*****

2 Modeling Failures in Automated Production Lines

In the following we will present our experience with developing DSLs for modeling production failures in the industry automation domain. The work has been performed in the frame of a publicly funded German national research project called CrESt,[1] focused on development methods for collaborative embedded systems, such as autonomous production equipment within smart factories. The factory of the future will contain smart production equipment (e.g., robots) which is able to reconfigure itself and cooperate with other equipment to build complex products on demand. To achieve this, production processes, capabilities of factories, and recipes needed to assemble a certain product need to be described in a machine processable way. Complex analyses should be enabled to decide whether a smart factory can build a certain product and for what costs and what quality can be guaranteed. Different aspects of our DSLs have already been published in [6] and [4].

2.1 Ensuring Product Quality for Smart Automated Production

A production process is characterized along two directions. First, the production process has to meet the technical and functional requirements, e.g., if a production step is to be applied to a partly produced product, suitable equipment has to be available that meets all technical constraints, e. g., the capability to work with the involved material to the tolerances required or simply to process the partly finished product based on physical constraints (dimensions, weight, etc.). This aspect is

---

[1] https://crest.in.tum.de/.

usually dealt with in MES systems. Second, non-functional requirements of the products are also to be considered, e.g., an aspect that is especially important when highly reliable products are built is that the production errors are guaranteed to be within certain tolerances. The product not only needs to be produced, but also has to meet a certain quality grade, meaning, specifically, that possible errors in the production process, for example because of equipment failure, need to be detected and quality measures applied. This aspect is very important when highly reliable products are being produced, or products that will be used in a safety-critical environment.

Traditionally, the second aspect has been addressed in an experience-based and manual way. For a given production process a manual analysis has been performed by a panel of domain experts, potential failures evaluated, and quality measures imposed where necessary. The analysis technique commonly applied is a *Failure Mode and Effects Analysis (FMEA)*. When applied to a production process we refer to it as a *process FMEA (pFMEA)*. This approach has worked for production environments with very infrequent changes to product and production facilities. In a smart factory setting, where product variability is high and where the production process is deployed on machinery not known at product design time, the manual FMEA approach is no longer feasible.

2.1.1 Model-Based Approach to pFMEA

To enable flexibility in the description of models needed for the above-stated problems, we decided to develop a domain-specific language. The main driving force of the design of our DSL was to enable each stakeholder involved in the production process to describe his concerns in a modular manner. In this way, each partner would be able to contribute the information pieces he is responsible for, has control over, and knows best, while using what others have already defined from their scope. The approach should also help with modularization of the whole analysis process and support (semi-)automated optimizations.

In order to be able to disseminate our approach to practitioners, it was crucial to develop appropriate tooling which supports our methodology. Tooling support also becomes indispensable when the process should be automated in the end and when the products considered are of reasonable complexity. To cope with the large number of uncertainties and development iteration cycles expected, we searched for a language workbench that would allow the definition of our language and models in an agile and iterative manner and thereby support us to explore different options for modeling smart production processes. This flexibility is intrinsically required by the explorative nature of the research project.

2.1.2 Meta-Model for Automated pFMEA

In Fig. 2 we present a high-level view of the meta-model that enables multiple stakeholders to collaborate in defining the respective parts of the model. The definition of abstract services with their respective service properties and service failure modes needs to be agreed upon so that each stakeholder will be able to use this definition in their parts, i.e., definition of the production recipes for a certain product by the customer, the definition of services offered by different production equipment, the definition of severity classes or quantitative values, and detection possibilities for failure modes and mitigation approaches. A customer specifies the requirements for the new product to be assembled together with an available budget and non-functional requirements such as how severe (*Sev*) consequences of failures are for his product. The owner of a production facility specifies what equipment he has at his disposal, how likely individual failure modes are when a particular piece of equipment provides a required service (*Occ*), and how well each failure mode can be detected by a piece of quality equipment (*Det*). A concrete workflow and collaboration model for an eventual introduction at production sites has been out of focus of the research project. Careful thought has to be given to the possibility of adapting individual service instances in a concrete setting with, for example, very specific failure modes not relevant in most other contexts.

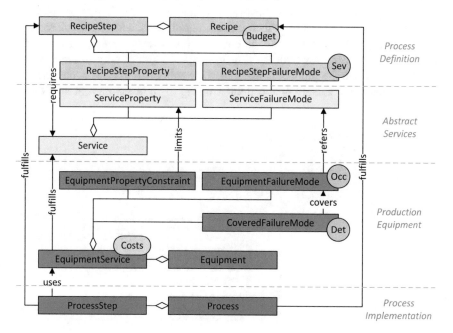

Fig. 2 The metamodel for automated pFMEAs decoupling different stakeholder domains

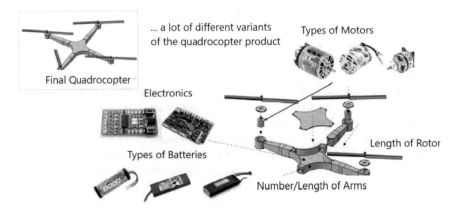

Fig. 3 An intuitive view of the most important parts of a quadrocopter and of the product variation points, e.g., different batteries, motors, electronics

2.2 Example: Assembling a Quadrocopter in a Smart Factory

As an example, we will present in the following the production of a quadrocopter in a smart factory. The customer has to specify a number of variation points of the quadrocopter and the smart factory, and then has to decide whether based on material needs and assembly skills it is able to produce the requested quadrocopter. The assembly process is illustrated in Fig. 3. In Fig. 4-left we present the definition of the skills required for building a quadrocopter together with different failure modes, e.g., when the product is assembled the robot can use the wrong parts, or assemble them too loosely or too tightly. In Fig. 4-right we present an example

```
skills catalogue: Production Skills    product: Quadrocopter-basic
  skill: Assemble part                   maximal risk: 10.0
    failure modes:                       BOP:
      Assembly of wrong part               id: Q-2 Assemble Motors
      Assembly too loose                   required material: Quadrocopter Motor basic
      Assembly too tight                   required skill: Assemble part
  skill: Provide basis                       maximum Risk: <no maxRisk>
    failure modes:                           failure modes:
      Provide wrong part                       failure mode: Assembly of wrong part severity: 5_Production
                                               failure mode: Assembly too loose severity: 5_ProductionStop
                                               failure mode: Assembly too tight severity: 5_ProductionStop
                                           id: Q-3 Assemble Electronics
                                           required material: Quadrocopter Electronics
                                           required skill: Assemble part
                                             maximum Risk: <no maxRisk>
                                             failure modes:
                                               failure mode: Assembly of wrong part severity: 5_Production
                                               failure mode: Assembly too loose severity: 5_ProductionStop
                                               failure mode: Assembly too tight severity: 5_ProductionStop
```

Fig. 4 Model of production skills of assembly robots including their failure modes (left). The skills are referenced from product definitions and this ensures the consistency of failure modes (right)

```
production schedule: Quadrocopter Basic Model Production
   factory: Quadrocopter Production Plant
   product: Quadrocopter-basic

Step 1 : map required skill Q-1 Provide Body (Provide basis) to equipment Assembly Station
   required material: Quadrocopter Body 2-arm to provided material: Quadrocopter Body 2-arm
Step 2 : map required skill Q-2 Assemble Motors (Assemble part) to equipment Assembly Station
   required material: Quadrocopter Motor basic to provided material: Quadrocopter Motor basic
Step 3 : map required skill Q-3 Assemble Electronics (Assemble part) to equipment Assembly Station
   required material: Quadrocopter Electronics to provided material: Quadrocopter Electronics
Step 4 : map required skill Q-4 Assemble batteries (Assemble part) to equipment Assembly Station
   required material: Quadrocopter battery normal capacity to provided material: Quadrocopter batter
Step 5 : map required skill Q-5 Assemble rotors (Assemble part) to equipment Assembly Station
   required material: Quadrocopter Rotor to provided material: Quadrocopter Rotor
```

Fig. 5 Example of a deployment definition for the production process of a certain product on the assembly units of a smart factory

definition of a quadrocopter product together with the severity associated with different failure modes. The product definition makes use of already defined skills, in this example listed in a catalogue of skills, which in practice could be provided by a library.

In Fig. 5 we present an example deployment of the production recipe for machinery of a small factory which will assemble the final product. After relevant models have been defined, an automated analysis can be performed to check whether certain quality aspects of the production process can be fulfilled. To this end, we generate a pFMEA table as shown in Fig. 6. The risk of introducing unwanted quality problems is computed and compared to an overall risk goal. In this example, the overall risk goal of the product is not met and this requires further production measures to address the most important contributors to the risk budget.

2.3 Conclusion

The advantages of a model-based approach to process FMEA generation have been confirmed within the research project. The decoupling of individual stakeholders artifacts has proven to be a key measure to support the modularization. Using MPS has helped immensely in iteratively shaping the language, as it provides a way to define and instantiate the meta-model with minimal effort. The fast development cycles for the meta-model (definition, application, redefinition) helped to clarify important requirements that were not obvious at the beginning.

We have been able to show the feasibility of the proposed approach to be used in an actual production setting. For actual use, a more thorough implementation targeting higher technology readiness levels would be needed. In addition, more effort would have to be spent on usability and integration aspects, which in the context of a research project for a proof-of-concept prototype have not been addressed so far.

F Quadrocopter Assembly pFMEA

```
FMEA: Quadrocopter Assembly pFMEA
  for schedule: Quadrocopter Basic Model Production
  product: Quadrocopter-basic

Process FMEA Table
sort Process FMEA Table by risk: □
```

Step	Production Step	Failure Mode	Occ.	QM	Det.	Sev.	Risk
Step : 1	Provide basis : Assembly Station : Body 2-arm	wrong part	0.10	None	0.00	9.00	0.90
Step : 2	Assemble part : Assembly Station : Motor basic	wrong part	0.10	None	0.00	9.00	0.90
Step : 2	Assemble part : Assembly Station : Motor basic	too loose	0.10	None	0.00	9.00	0.90
Step : 2	Assemble part : Assembly Station : Motor basic	too tight	0.10	None	0.00	9.00	0.90
Step : 3	Assemble part : Assembly Station : Electronics	wrong part	0.10	None	0.00	9.00	0.90
Step : 3	Assemble part : Assembly Station : Electronics	too loose	0.10	None	0.00	9.00	0.90
Step : 3	Assemble part : Assembly Station : Electronics	too tight	0.10	None	0.00	9.00	0.90
Step : 4	Assemble part : Assembly Station : Battery norm.	wrong part	0.10	None	0.00	9.00	0.90
Step : 4	Assemble part : Assembly Station : Battery norm.	too loose	0.10	None	0.00	9.00	0.90
Step : 4	Assemble part : Assembly Station : Battery norm.	too tight	0.10	None	0.00	9.00	0.90
Step : 5	Assemble part : Assembly Station : Rotor	wrong part	0.10	None	0.00	9.00	0.90
Step : 5	Assemble part : Assembly Station : Rotor	too loose	0.10	None	0.00	9.00	0.90
Step : 5	Assemble part : Assembly Station : Rotor	too tight	0.10	None	0.00	9.00	0.90

```
Process FMEA Risk breakdown by process step
sort Risk breakdown table by risk: □
```

Process Step	Risk for Process Step	Max risk allowed
Step : 1	0.90	10.00
Step : 2	2.70	10.00
Step : 3	2.70	10.00
Step : 4	2.70	10.00
Step : 5	2.70	10.00

```
Total risk: 11.70
Maximal risk allowed: 10.0
```

Fig. 6 Example of pFMEA analysis—based on the deployment definition, the assembly of a product might be influenced by different failures with associates probabilities. If the risk of failures in manufacturing is higher than allowed, then an error message is presented in the editor

3 Modeling Contractual Agreements

In this section, we present our experience gained over the last four years in a Siemens internal research project on modeling contractual agreements for making or servicing complex technical systems. Examples of such contracts are engineering, procurement, and construction contracts for industrial plants, or manufacturing and supply contracts for railway projects that may also entail service support contracts over several decades. Projects involving complex technical systems typically have a substantial financial volume and may involve contractual obligations of the contractor with many parties (customer and suppliers) over possibly long periods of time (sometimes even 20–30 years).

Frequently, the corresponding contracts for these kinds of projects stipulate so-called non-functional requirements (NFR) such as contractual due dates, or reliability, availability, and maintainability (RAM) targets, etc. Moreover, there are usually contractual agreements between the customer and the contractor on one hand, and between the contractor, several suppliers, or even consortium partners on the other, which may or may not allow for transfer or distribution of risks. Non-conformance with contractual RAM requirements may entail substantial costs for a contractor, for instance due to penalties, warranty costs, or compensation for damages, and therefore may impact the profitability of a project.

Hence, it is clear that efficient and transparent assessment of the potential financial impact of non-conformance with these requirements in the bid phase as well as during project execution is essential, and requires taking into account technical, contractual, and commercial aspects, typically also with quantification of uncertainties.

In practice, it can be observed that the technical, contractual, and commercial details of the abovementioned requirements are dealt with by different persons, who are specialists in their domains and each use different and disconnected tooling such as spreadsheets calculations or complex simulations in Matlab. This may lead to results that ignore the effects of dependencies of contractual consequences, thus over- or underestimating risk exposures, or to results that completely ignore the statistical distributions of risks. Moreover, state of practice approaches may not always offer modularity, reuseability, and abstraction.

3.1   ADORA: DSLs for Modeling Contractual Agreements

We propose a domain-specific modeling (DSML) approach that captures both contractual and commercial aspects and the technical characteristics of the system in an integrated manner (as illustrated in Fig. 7). These aspects should be modeled in a way such that they can be understood and evaluated by domain experts with various backgrounds: commercial and technical project managers, contract managers, but

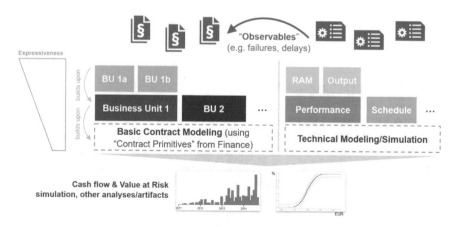

Fig. 7 Overview of the stackable modeling approach for contracts. ADORA features two stacks of DSLs: (1) financial models that describe the cash-flow (left) and (2) technical models describing the system (right). The financial and technical models are linked via so-called observables. Based on the models, we implemented simulations of cash-flows and of risk distribution. Both stacks of DSLs (financial and technical) can be made more specific for the needs of a certain business unit

also engineering experts. Furthermore, the nature of contracts varies between different business domains such as energy infrastructure projects, transportation, or factory automation.

Once these integrated models are built, they can be automatically generated into appropriate low-level computational models and then evaluated, thereby supporting more traceable and transparent decision making, eliminating inconsistencies, and offering a solid basis for quantitative optimizations.

3.1.1 Modeling Economic Aspects

For approximately two decades, research has been directed toward formalization of (business) contracts using formal models with precise semantics. The formalization of contracts brings about several benefits. First, a rigorous model provides a precise way to describe complex contracts, which may immediately reveal ambiguities of contracts expressed in a natural language. Second, semantically rich models provide the basis for analyzing and integrating complex analyses on contracts such as the simulation of cash-flows. Third, models are bases for more automation in contract management.

For the purpose of modeling business contractual aspects, we base our approach on the pioneering work on modeling of financial contracts by Peyton Jones et al. [9], who constructed a compact library of so-called contract primitives in Haskell (a functional programming language). We found a subset of the contract primitives to be useful and sufficient in the context of contractual requirements for technical systems. To us, a drawback of the proposed primitives is that they are at a very low abstraction level (a kind of "assembly language" for financial contracts), as are the models built with them. Effectively, they are verbose and difficult to write and read by domain experts. To address this, we decided to build a stack of DSLs on top of contract primitives, as presented in [5].

3.1.2 Integrating Technical Aspects

Our contracts reference technical behavior of systems (e.g., penalties needed to be paid if the availability of a system is under a certain threshold, or warranty clauses for failures in various subsystems). This is done by following the approach in [9] where contract primitives are supplemented by the concept of so-called observables, which determine how the meaning (and value) of a contract evolves over time. Observables, loosely speaking, are (potentially) time-varying quantities that are objectively measurable but may be uncertain in advance, i.e., they are essentially stochastic processes. Observables define when certain conditions become true that entail a certain payment at that time, or what the precise amount of a payment is.

For example, whether a given component of a technical system (e.g., a cooling pump) has failed or not at a given time may constitute an observable. Another example is the average availability of a module of an industrial plant over a given time period, or whether and when a certain milestone of the project schedule has been reached. From these examples, it is clear that observables are the very concepts that glue together the formal contract model and the model of the technical system, as illustrated in Fig. 7. Hence, for the purpose of contractual requirements for technical systems, the modeling of technical aspects is one source of observables that determines how the meaning (and value) of a contract evolves over time.

3.2 Evolution of ADORA

The development of ADORA started in 2016 as an internal research project. In our group, we have extensive experience with RAM analyses and the economic implications of RAM aspects through contractual agreements. The idea to use DSLs arose due to the need for reusability and automation that we had experienced when assessing financial risks originating from technical failures.

The *first phase* of the ADORA project spanned several months, where we first created prototypical DSLs comprising technical and financial aspects. Using these DSLs we performed demos and quickly gathered positive feedback from other domain experts and practitioners who expressed their potential interest. By the end of this phase, we had successfully reached TRL 3 (see Fig. 1 for a description of TRLs).

The *second phase* started in late 2016, spanning more than a year and focusing on refactorings to modularize the tool, implementing concepts for contract primitives and creating a stack of DSLs which could be instantiated for different business domains and use cases. At the end of this phase, we were confident that we could extend and adapt ADORA for different business units. By the end of this phase, we had successfully reached TRL 4.

The *third phase*, still ongoing, started in mid-2018 with the main goal of creating a working prototype applicable to real projects for a real customer. Via many iterations with our customer (commercial project managers), we had implemented a working prototype by end of 2019 capable of modeling, analyzing, and simulating a real project (TRL 6). In early 2020 our customers decided to start piloting the tool on a second project.

In summary, for the ADORA approach, the MPS technology proved to be a key enabler for starting and maturing the contract modeling approach. Early tooling allowed us to carry out many demos and engage in interactions with domain experts. The most important features of MPS for this project are the possibility of developing DSLs in an agile fashion, the possibility of creating modular stacks of DSLs, the notational freedom which increases engagement of domain experts, and language refactorings capabilities which allow us to easily evolve the languages.

4 Specifying Parameters of Computed Tomography Scanners Product Lines

In this section we present our experience over the last 5.5 years with developing and deploying domain-specific modeling languages for computed tomography scanners in a medical devices domain. Modern Computed Tomography (CT) scanners are highly complex machines, enabling radiologists to perform examinations of patients, such as trauma scans, evaluation of neurological abnormalities, detection of tumors, and diagnosis of heart diseases. While the x-ray beam rotates around the patient, the detector measures the attenuation, which represents the composition of the scanned object. Based on this volume data, it is possible to reconstruct slice images and calculate 3D visualizations of the human body and organs (Fig. 8). This data is the basis for applications that support the radiologist in the diagnosis process.

CT scanners are perfect examples of software-intensive cyber-physical systems—a large amount of software enables the realization of complex use cases and interaction with the real world. The system depends on a wide set of parameters that represent quantities from the physical world, such as dose parameters, geometric properties, and special scanner capabilities. In addition to the program code per se, the complexity of software is also due to the wide variability defined by these configuration parameters. Valid combinations of parameters reflect the physical capabilities of the devices and the desired clinical cases to be performed. *A central challenge that the scanner development teams need to address is keeping the parameters consistent for a wide variety of clinical cases, on different hardware and across product lines.* Inconsistencies of the parameter configurations can lead to low-quality imaging or even damage to the CT scanners.

4.1 Somaris DSL: Specification of CT Parameter Configurations

Traditionally (Fig. 9-top), experts from the CT domain (e.g., physicists) define the properties of a CT system and its behavior using a huge set of possible parameter configurations. The specifications are distributed in several documents. These docu-

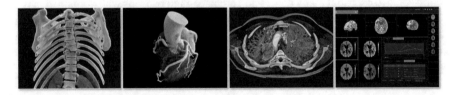

Fig. 8 CT image impressions. From left to right: CT acute care imaging, CT cardiovascular imaging, CT oncological imaging, CT neuro imaging

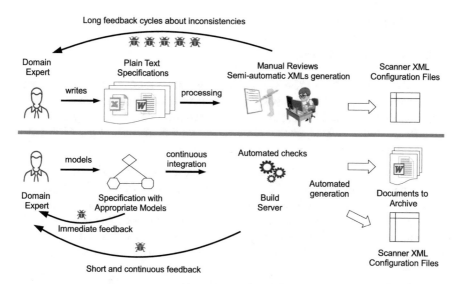

Fig. 9 Specifying parameters and their relations using plain text and Excel sheets requires a massive review effort for quality assurance and fragile semi-automatic generation of XML files (top); model-driven specification of parameters enables deep and automatic consistency checks and automatic generation of XML-based configuration files to be loaded on the server (bottom)

ments are written in Microsoft (MS) Excel or MS Word using plain natural language and have a moderately defined structure. Quality assurance of these specification documents is realized exclusively through manual reviews and the users receive feedback at integration time of the software. Once the valid configurations are defined, a semi-automatic process involving manual transformations and different scripts is employed to generate configuration files in XML format which can be loaded by the scanner software. This manual process of creating the specifications is slow, is prone to inconsistencies, and reaches its limits due to the complexity of modern CT scanners. To cope with the complexity of the CT domain, we have built a set of domain-specific languages and tooling (in the following called *Somaris DSL*) which we use to specify the configurations of parameters for CTs (Fig. 9-bottom). These rich models allow a wide range of consistency checks and automated generation of configuration files in XML format which are subsequently loaded in CT scanners. In addition to XML, for process compliance reasons we also generate PDF documents which are subsequently archived. Different aspects of our DSLs have already been published in [8, 10].

4.2   Project Timeline

4.2.1   Language Engineering

Initial Exploratory Phase   The exploratory phase was started in 2014 as a research cooperation project between Siemens Healthcare and a university chair and took approximately one year. During this period, a proof of concept (TRL 3) was realized by a Ph.D. student, which made it clear that it could be feasible to use MPS-based DSLs for the specification of the parameters space of our CT scanners.

Initial Prototype   In autumn 2015 a prototype phase started for about 6–9 months. An ad-hoc composed team of three to four people, working sporadically on that project, produced a first prototype which contained the essential core functionalities. The total effort was approximately 3 months split among four developers. In interviews with an author of a very central specification document, we further clarified the domain. Based on these requirements all core scenarios were exercised to make sure that the use cases could be addressed by the MPS technology. We re-wrote the code freshly and reached an advanced prototype (TRL 5).

Advanced Prototype   From mid-2016, the target switched to developing a production-ready tooling and thereby a core team was built up. A part-time developer (40%) was allocated to the project and together with another individual from Siemens Research (20%), continuously supported by the software lead architect, the project reached a higher speed. Additionally, we involved the first end-user to get early feedback on needed functionalities and UI design. In a few months we managed to model the first two CT scanners and generated the first documents (TRL 7). By the end of this phase, the language engineering team was ramped up and able to work independently, and the first domain expert wrote the scanner specification document with the MPS based tooling (Rich Client Platform, RCP).

Productization   Within the last 3 years (beginning of 2017 to 2020), the team has grown from one part-time developer to currently a head count of four with effectively 2.5 developer resources. Early in 2017 we got an experienced developer in UI design on board and this let us also focus on styling and creating a common look and feel. In addition, the end-user space has grown from one stakeholder, writing his specification with an MPS-based RCP, to currently seven physicists, distributed between Germany and China. The tooling evolved to a standalone RCP with company-specific branding and styling, and the checking rules were extended successively. User feedback regarding missing and helpful editor functions was always welcome and we reserved a dedicated buffer for this. Currently, we have nine scanner model instances in the model and are prepared for new complexity, given by the evolving CT scanner innovations.

4.2.2   Involving Domain Experts

When moving the natural language specifications into formalized models, MPS helped a great deal to move from an initial concept to a working language definition which can be validated by domain experts. Thereby, the language engineering team quickly obtained results that were helpful for domain experts.

Ramping-Up After realizing the key functionalities in 2016, we were able to switch from MS Word as editor for the specification to an MPS-based domain-specific modeling approach. Even if not all consistency checks or generators existed yet, it proved to be a good idea to add new content to the model right from the start. Our first end-user has had a very good tolerance level regarding missing comfort functionality in the editor or sporadic bugs. The enablers of this collaboration are very close communication and short feedback loops. We focused on the end-user's wishes and identified improvements such as UI design, editor actions, and consistency checks.

Production Use In 2017 and 2018, our end-users added several more scanner instances. At the end of 2018, we had three end-users on board. All of them learned how to operate the new tooling and use the git repository to share their work. In 2019, two users joined who are located at different development sites. These two Chinese colleagues received a short training on how to use the tooling. This training was already provided by an experienced end-user and this showed us that our users community has its own dynamic.

We are still in close contact with our users. Personal support is provided all the time. This creates a win-win situation: We can help them without any delay, which would block them in their daily work. On the other hand, we receive direct feedback and they are open for all our callbacks about new domain content.

4.2.3   Somaris DSL in Numbers

Currently we have 24 languages that contain 725 concepts. Behavior aspects and utility classes contain approximately 39,000 statements. Model consistency is ensured by 160 checking rules and 210 concept constraints and scoping rules. Language aspect functionality such as typesystem checks and constraints as well as editor actions are currently validated by 1500 test cases. On the model instance side, all our users work in a single MPS project with two solutions and 14 models. The models contain 195 root nodes and 86,000 node instances.

4.3   Examples of Models

In the following figures, we illustrate examples of DSLs that we developed. These examples of course only contain dummy data due to confidentiality constraints.

Please note that our languages make heavy use of tabular notation and many models look rather "like forms" and not "like code." Most table cells have constraints associated with them which check the validity of the data. Often the cell values are in fact references to already defined parameters and rules. At the core of our models we have the definition of parameters (see Fig. 10) with a unique name, data type, and possible value range. For readability and understandability the user can add free description text about the intended meaning of a parameter. Concrete scanner model instances can use only the parameters that have already been defined. We have different families of scanners and in order to support them we follow a platform approach. The top level (Fig. 10-top) defines the full set of available value range and then these are further specialized in a hierarchical structure using "restriction catalogues" (Fig. 10-bottom) in order to support concrete scanner models.

Figure 11 illustrates the definition of valid value combinations of parameters, defined with tabular notation. Each row of a table describes a valid set of parameter values for a list of corresponding use cases; for example, the top row of the first table (Fig. 11-top) defines that for "Regular" analyses, the "Tube Voltage" parameter can have values of 10 or 12; and the "Number of rotations" is set to be 2. In cases where a parameter has many possible values, we developed a new language abstraction called "mutual combination table" which can be used to specify allowed/forbidden sets of parameters (Fig. 11-center). We also illustrate the definition of complex formula, using mathematical notations, which reference existing parameters (Fig. 11-bottom).

More advanced abstractions enable the user to define aspects with a very low level of granularity (so-called value combinations). The tool combines the aspects and creates the resulting combinatorics automatically. To enable the definition of possible scan modes for several use cases, the domain expert can extend the data by tags. A query language is provided for this purpose. Figure 12 gives an impression of the look and feel.

4.4 Development Infrastructure and Process

4.4.1 Repository and Build Infrastructure

With the advanced prototype phase, we moved the git repository to our regular SW development environment—a Microsoft Team Foundation Server (TFS). TFS hosts several git repositories for language development and model definition. It also enables continuous integration (and delivery) with automated builds triggered by pushed commits to the git branches. In Fig. 13 we present at a glance the build chains defined for the language engineering and language use workspaces.

Language Engineering Figure 13-left shows the DSL-engineering workspace. We share our development increments and use common branch models. Approximately

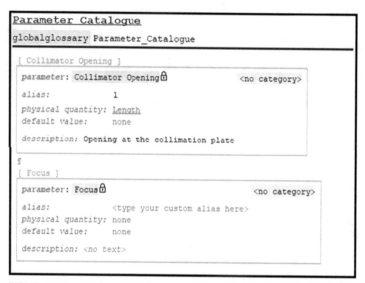

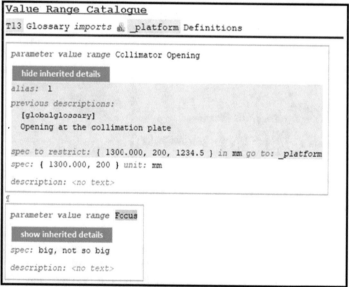

Fig. 10 A glossary with defined parameters (top) and a corresponding restriction catalog for a concrete system (bottom)

three RCP major releases per year are deployed to our end-users. Hotfix versions are created on demand.

Language Use Side Our end-users also benefit from a version control system and build automation (Fig. 13-right). A git repository enables history reviews and they

tabular rule Mode Parameters

		Number of Rotations	Spectral Filtration	Tube Voltage [kV]	platform_Clinical_Cases
▲ ▼	1	2	None	10, 12	Regular, Topogram
▲ ▼	2	7	Mg	8, 22	Case8, Topogram, Case4, Case6, Case5
▲ ▼	3	4711	AgMg	7, 9	Case6

Error: Value '4711' for Number of Rotations does not match the (restricted) parameter specification: (instance of RangeParamSpec)

mutual combination table allowed combinations

for Parameter with list of values

description: <no text>

Update Table

	option 1	option 2	option 3	option 4	option 5
option 1					
option 2	▣				
option 3	☐	☐			
option 4	☐	▣	▣		
option 5	▣	☐	▣	☐	

▣ Allowed
☐ Forbidden

f

formula Formula with Parameter References

alias: S_1

usage: Default (Regular)
description: This is a text to decribe the formula.

$$S_1 = \text{SliceWidth} * 4 + \sum_{i=3}^{s_{\text{set}}} \left(\frac{\text{Slice}}{3} \right) + \left(\cos \left(\text{SliceWidth} \right) + \text{kV} \right)$$

Fig. 11 Valid parameter combinations, defined with tabular notation (top), specifying allowed/forbidden combinations of parameter values (center) and complex formula which reference existing parameters (bottom)

can share their increments among each other. Furthermore, access rights are granted on different repositories in order to ensure the required confidentiality level of the data. The user's git repositories are also stored on our development TFS server. Each push of user-side commits results in an automated build which performs our customized consistency checks and—in case of successful assessment—creates the resulting SW artifacts (XML file bundles). The assessment performs all typesystem and constraint checks, extended by computation-intensive custom consistency checks. When checks fail, users get immediate feedback about the failure (their build fails) and have the chance to fix inconsistencies before any specification-consuming SW developer is involved.

The use of models enables domain experts to directly contribute to the delivery pipeline of the scanner software.

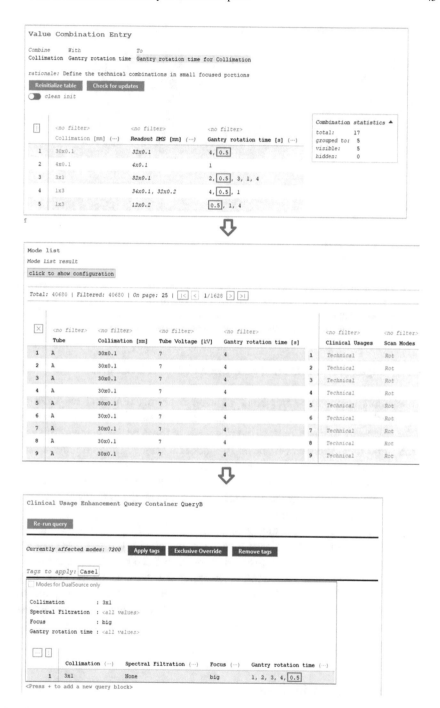

Fig. 12 Atomic value combinations (top) with the resulting combinatorics (center) and a query to extend this data by tags (bottom)

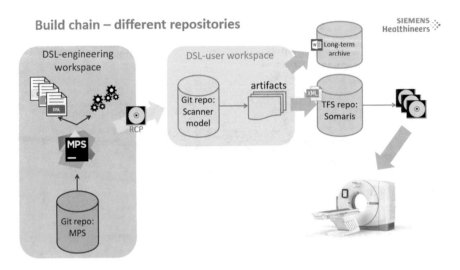

Fig. 13 Continuous delivery chains. On the left side the delivery chain for the developed languages is presented. When a release happens, it is taken by the domain experts whose models are themselves integrated in a continuous integration chain. Generated artifacts (XMLs) are automatically taken by the continuous integration pipeline of the scanner software

4.4.2 Language Evolution and Migration of Model Instances

The scanners' complexity has been growing over this time and we have been continuously extending our domain knowledge. New generations of scanners require new modeling approaches and this leads to the need for language evolution. At the same time, the users work on the model instance. Thus, migration scripts ensure that no data is lost between two language versions. This is challenging, because users might have local changes. The origin branch is migrated centrally by the language development team, but local changes on the user client side lead to the merging of issues from time to time.

For maintenance reasons, model updates, based on former model content, are needed. For a scanner SW release milestone, we branch out the model content. Maintenance work leads to a discussion regarding backward compatibility. In theory, it is possible for languages by keeping the old concept versions or just by migration of old concept instances. But it is hard to maintain for generators, especially because schema and scanner SW API breaking changes occur in between. Hence, finally we host an RCP instance with language versions, matching each model release branch.

4.4.3 Validation and Verification

We strive for test-driven development. Typesystem checks and scoping need at least a sandbox model for live verification of the functionality. Thus it was only a small step to move the sandbox instance into a NodesTestCase that can be reused for automated regression tests later on. The same argument is valid for editor actions.

For testability reasons, editor code is largely paged out to util classes. End-to-end tests, based on editor actions, are not yet automated as this requires the definition of a matching test strategy and the identification of adequate tooling. Here, we face the same challenges as known from common SW development processes.

Artifact generators are validated by baseline tests, while complex util classes, used in the generators, are tested on unit test level by JUnit tests. Baseline tests cover the range from different simple input data for isolated tests on simple transformations, up to real-world representative input data.

We have made use of many of the MPS capabilities for automated testing of DSL implementations, which were described in [12]. Comprehensive support for testing of DSLs proved to be essential for us in order to reach a production-level domain-specific tooling, and at the same time to embrace the changes due to new stakeholder requirements and the new versions of the infrastructure.

4.5 Conclusion and Outlook

The DSML approach has proven to help domain experts to specify the parameters of a very complex system. An adequate and specialized tooling enables short and direct feedback. Our end-users appreciate the RCP features with their automation regarding editing atomic definitions and creating specific views on the resulting complex combinatorics. We decided to introduce the new approach in small iterations. There are so many ideas for additional and new aspects of our scanner model to be added to the model. But we are focusing incrementally on one specification document after another. This ensures that we can handle the effort to support end-users and fulfill their needs, understanding the domain and delivering a formalized and consistent model structure with generators for corresponding SW artifacts.

In the midterm future we strive for fully automated integration tests of the generated artifacts. Additionally, we are going to add a system/feature model on top of the parameter combination rules. For the long term, more and more former MS Word-based specifications that are based on the parameter combination rules will be added. The domain experts will therefore benefit from automated consistency checks. The goal is for any definition of a scan mode to be immediately checked in terms of its validity for the system. At the same time, the monotonous and error-prone manual transformation from textual specifications into SW readable artifacts will be automatized as much as possible. Domain experts will be able to generate a set of consistent configurations by themselves and use it for prototype integration without involving the SW teams. We are aware that this is limited to non-concept-breaking changes that do not impact implemented domain logic in the several SW components.

5 Lessons Learnt

In this section we summarize the lessons learnt from building and deploying DSMLs with MPS inside Siemens and interacting with domain experts over the last five years. We discuss topics related to the adoption of DSMLs, using MPS to toolify research concepts in order to facilitate their dissemination among practitioners, and the MPS features which helped us (language engineers) and are appreciated most by our users (domain experts).

5.1 Adoption

Economic aspects of developing, maintaining, and evolving domain-specific tooling are very important for decision makers in order to make informed decisions. There are many sources of costs when developing and maintaining DSLs [2]. In order to be successful, the cost/benefits for developing new tools must be favorable. We can achieve this both by minimizing the costs of tools development and by maximizing the benefits brought by domain appropriate tools. In a case where the new tooling functions allow domain experts to focus their creative energy on intrinsic domain problems instead of struggling with tools that do not support the tasks well, then this is a good argument for developing DSLs and tooling. In Fig. 14 we illustrate intuitively the aimed added value, which is two to three times or more.

As presented in numerous earlier publications, [3, 14–16], the flexibility of MPS allows for its deployment in various domains. Our experience from Siemens confirms the fact that MPS enables an extremely efficient development of DSLs capable of addressing the needs of domain experts with different backgrounds. This allows minimization of DSLs development costs up to the point that creating new DSLs constructs or evolving existing ones can be done in a matter of hours, and this drastically improves the economic balance. Our finding on the importance of the economic aspects of DSLs development for their adoption is aligned with other works from the literature [13].

Domain know-how in the language engineering team is a huge benefit for development. Communicating with domain experts and speaking their language in order to elucidate their requirements is essential. This can be either a language

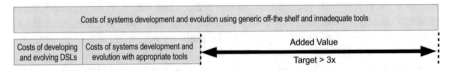

Fig. 14 Economic arguments for developing DSLs: the efforts of developing DSLs and then using them by domain experts to build systems should be substantially lower than the costs of systems development with general off-the-shelf tools

engineer or a domain expert who is an early adopter and in permanent contact with the language engineering team. Domain experts acting as multiplicators are highly efficient when the DSLs are to be rolled out. It is more efficient when domain experts (users) train their colleagues with the DSLs.

Language engineering know-how is a new skill that must be learnt by software engineers. Experiences with training software engineers to build MPS-based DSLs are presented in detail in [11]. Once a language engineering team is bootstrapped, integrating new members is much easier. Awareness of domain experts about possibilities opened up by MPS in terms of creating new DSLs, evolving existing ones, using different notations, creating consistency checks, enabling workflow automation, and generating other artifacts proved to be very useful in order to scale their expectations as to what can be achieved, in what time period, and with which effort.

Notation is extremely important. It turned out that languages on a very high level of abstraction that present the models in the form of tables or high-level templates have a higher chance of becoming accepted. It is worth investing effort in making editors look better by using colors or icons for root concepts. In summary, it can be stated that it pays off to spend some effort on usability and user experience from the beginning, in order to lower the barrier for those who are less familiar with language engineering approaches. This finding is aligned with other works on the importance of notations for domain experts to increase the usability of DSMLs [1, 7].

Strong arguments for developing DSLs are cases in which one or more of the points below are applicable:

- Domain experts do a lot of repetitive manual work.
- There is a lot of copy-paste of generic parts and small modifications.
- There is a lot of work to assess the impact and implement small changes; the knowledge is implicit and shared among several people.
- Different stakeholders have (slightly) different understandings of the same content.
- The content produced often contains "dummy" inconsistencies.
- Often the needed functionality is cutting edge and so novel that it is at the edge of the technology and no other tools exist.

> Above all, the uniqueness of core tasks of domain experts in the critical parts of the business is what motivates investing in building domain-specific tools. These tools relieve domain experts from additional burden and let them focus on the essential parts and on producing value.

5.2 Tooling-Driven Research

A portion of the projects was done at Siemens Corporate Technology, a central research unit of Siemens. We successfully used MPS to toolify the methods and concepts we developed and this proved to be a key aspect which enabled the transfer into production. Practitioners need to see examples of toolified research concepts in order to understand how research ideas can be put into practice and gain confidence about the degree to which the research concepts can address their concrete needs. Innovation requires experimentation, and having domain experts in the loop and allowing them to evaluate and validate toolified concepts is essential.

5.3 Mostly Used MPS Features

In Table 2 we present at a glance the most important features of MPS which allowed us to efficiently engineer DSL and tooling. As can be noted, the DSLs development speed and agility in language development enabled by MPS are key factors for all our projects. The closer the project is to production and larger-scale deployment, the more important the features of MPS related to continuous integration, reuse of language fragments via building modular DSLs stacks, distributed development of languages, or automatically migrating models to new versions of the language.

In Table 3 we present the core MPS features which allow domain experts to boost their productivity. In all of our projects, domain experts highly appreciate the notation freedom and the agile way of discovering the domain and creating DSLs constructs in a close loop. The more complex the built user models, the more important the automation support, continuous integration, and distributed development.

Table 2 Overview of different MPS features and their importance for our **language engineering** work. We gave between one and five stars to different points: the more stars the more relevant a point is to motivating our work; '-' means that the specific point does not apply to the tool

Tool	pFMEA	ADORA	SomarisDSL
DSLs Development Speed	*****	*****	*****
Notation Freedom	**	*****	*****
Modular Stackable DSLs	***	*****	*****
Agile DSLs Development	****	*****	*****
Language Refactorings	***	****	*****
Models Migration	*	****	*****
Continuous Integration	-	**	*****
Distributed Development	-	***	*****
Support for Testing DSLs	-	**	*****

Table 3 Overview of different MPS features and their importance for our **users**. We gave between one and five stars to different points: the more stars the more relevant a point is to motivating our work; '-' means that the specific point does not apply to the tool

Tool	pFMEA	ADORA	SomarisDSL
Editor Automation	**	****	*****
Notation Freedom	**	*****	*****
Online Consistency Checks	**	****	*****
Agile Domain Discovery	***	*****	*****
Models Migration	*	****	*****
Continuous Integration of User Models	-	-	****
Distributed Development on User's Side	-	**	*****
Generation of Other Artifacts	-	***	*****
Support for Deep Analyses	**	*****	*****
Deployment of Standalone Tool	-	*****	*****

6 Conclusions

In addition to increasing the productivity of domain experts, domain-specific modeling languages enable them to unleash their creativity by supporting new use cases which directly address cutting-edge developments within a business. In this chapter we presented the experience we gained with three projects addressing the needs of domain experts from three different domains: factory automation, management of technical contracts, and medical devices. Two of these projects (ADORA and SomarisDSL) passed the research phase and are currently piloted and used in production.

The language engineering features of MPS helped us to develop appropriate domain-specific languages and tooling to address the needs of domain experts and thereby make them more productive. In all three projects we developed unique tools which help domain experts avoid accidental complexity and use their creativity to deal with the intrinsic complexity of their business domain. MPS proved to be an enabler of efficient building of domain-specific tools, thereby supporting domain experts working in innovative projects.

References

1. Abrahão, S., Bourdeleau, F., Cheng, B.H.C., Kokaly, S., Paige, R.F., Störrle, H., Whittle, J.: User experience for model-driven engineering: Challenges and future directions. In: 20th ACM/IEEE International Conference on Model Driven Engineering Languages and Systems, MODELS. IEEE Computer Society (2017)
2. Cabrita, H., Barišic, A., Amaral, V., Goulao, M.: Towards a cost model for domain-specific language engineering. Preprint (2020). Available at https://www.researchgate.net/publication/332910210_Towards_a_Cost_Model_for_Domain-Specific_Language_Engineering. Accessed October, 2020

3. Fowler, M.: Language workbenches: The killer-app for domain specific languages? June 2005
4. Höfig, K., Klein, C., Rothbauer, S., Zeller, M., Vorderer, M., Koo, C.H.: A meta-model for process failure mode and effects analysis (PFMEA). In: 24th IEEE International Conference on Emerging Technologies and Factory Automation (2019)
5. Joanni, A., Ratiu, D.: Modeling and valuation of contractual RAM requirements using domain-specific languages. In: Annual IEEE Reliability and Maintainability Symposium (RAMS) (2018)
6. Koo, C.H., Rothbauer, S., Vorderer, M., Höfig, K., Zeller, M.: SQUADfps: Integrated model-based machine safety and product quality for flexible production systems. In: Model-Based Safety and Assessment: 6th International Symposium (IMBSA) (2019)
7. Moody, D.: The "physics" of notations: Toward a scientific basis for constructing visual notations in software engineering. IEEE Trans. Software Eng. **35**(6), 756–779 (2009)
8. Nehls, H., Ratiu, D.: Towards continuous delivery for domain experts – using MDE to integrate non-programmers into a software delivery pipeline. In: 1st International Workshop on DevOps@MODELS (2019)
9. Peyton Jones, S., Eber, J.-M., Seward, J.: Composing contracts: An adventure in financial engineering (functional pearl). SIGPLAN Not. **35**(9), 280–292 (2000)
10. Ratiu, D., Nehls, H., Michel, J.: Taming the software development complexity with domain specific languages. In: Schaefer, I., Karagiannis, D., Vogelsang, A., Méndez, D., Seidl, C. (eds.) Modellierung 2018, pp. 281–292. Gesellschaft für Informatik e.V., Bonn (2018)
11. Ratiu, D., Pech, V., Dummann, K.: Experiences with teaching mps in industry: Towards bringing domain specific languages closer to practitioners. In: Proceedings of the ACM/IEEE 20th International Conference on Model Driven Engineering Languages and Systems, MODELS '17, pp. 83–92. IEEE Press (2017)
12. Ratiu, D., Voelter, M., Pavletic, D.: Automated testing of dsl implementations–experiences from building mbeddr. Software Quality J. (2018)
13. Tolvanen, J., Kelly, S.: Effort used to create domain-specific modeling languages. In: Proceedings of the 21th ACM/IEEE International Conference on Model Driven Engineering Languages and Systems, MODELS (2018)
14. Voelter, M.: Fusing modeling and programming into language-oriented programming. In: Leveraging Applications of Formal Methods, Verification and Validation. Modeling, pp. 309–339. Springer International Publishing, Cham (2018)
15. Voelter, M., Ratiu, D., Schaetz, B., Kolb, B.: Mbeddr: An extensible c-based programming language and ide for embedded systems. In: Proceedings of the 3rd Annual Conference on Systems, Programming, and Applications: Software for Humanity, SPLASH '12, pp. 121–140. Association for Computing Machinery, New York, NY, USA (2012)
16. Voelter, M., Warmer, J., Kolb, B.: Projecting a modular future. IEEE Software **32**(5), 46–52 (2015)

JetBrains MPS as Core DSL Technology for Developing Professional Digital Printers

Eugen Schindler, Hristina Moneva, Joost van Pinxten, Louis van Gool,
Bart van der Meulen, Niko Stotz, and Bart Theelen

Abstract To address the challenges of efficiently performing continuous innovation with sustainable quality, Canon Production Printing envisions the exploitation of models during the complete lifecycle of printer variants. The design of professional digital printers involves several engineering disciplines ranging from software and electrical and mechanical hardware to physics and chemistry. All these engineering disciplines already exploit various models in diverse tools to support their design activities. Apart from exploiting commodity modeling tools that are used in domain-specific ways, specialized domain-specific modeling tools are also developed. At the time of writing, Canon Production Printing had selected JetBrains MPS as one of the core technologies to interconnect the diverse range of models at the specification level. Such models are, for example, used for configuring virtual printers for analysis (e.g., by means of simulation), generation of documentation, and automating synthesis in some engineering disciplines. To allow for automated processing, MPS is also used for capturing domain-specific knowledge in models that has not yet been formalized. At the time of writing, approximately 10 people at Canon Production Printing develop domain-specific languages using MPS and approximately 40 people use these as part of their daily printer development activities. This chapter gives an overview of some of the applications of MPS at Canon Production Printing and how it is changing the way-of-working to achieve efficient continuous innovation with sustainable quality.

E. Schindler · H. Moneva · J. van Pinxten (✉) · L. van Gool · B. van der Meulen · N. Stotz ·
B. Theelen
Canon Production Printing Netherlands B.V., Venlo, The Netherlands
e-mail: eugen.schindler@cpp.canon; hristina.moneva@cpp.canon; joost.vanpinxten@cpp.canon;
louis.vangool@cpp.canon; bart.vandermeulen@cpp.canon; niko.stotz@cpp.canon;
bart.theelen@cpp.canon

53

1 Introduction

Canon Production Printing develops high-end professional digital printers in three categories: (1) industry-leading continuous-feed printers for massive print volumes and fast, high-quality results in full color or black & white; (2) highly efficient, high-volume printers for in-house printing or publishing; and (3) large-format printers for stunning display graphics and high-quality CAD/GIS applications. These products serve the professional print market with suitable trade-offs between multiple system Key Performance Indicators (KPIs) such as productivity, perceived image quality (i.e., how good does the printed image look), print robustness (e.g., how well does the ink stick to the medium), and cost. Figure 1 highlights some example printer families with an indication of their productivity capabilities and physical sizes.

The printers in Fig. 1 exploit an inkjet print process, which covers steps such as image processing, positioning the jetted ink on media, and spreading & solidification of the ink. How each print process step is realized has an impact on the various system KPIs. A multitude of engineering disciplines (software, electrical and mechanical hardware, physics, and chemistry) is involved in the development of print processes and printers, and hence in realizing competitive values for all the system KPIs.

Development within Canon Production Printing exploits several model-based approaches in all engineering disciplines to cope with the ever-increasing complexity. The complexity of professional digital printers is nowadays fairly comparable to that of high-end cars. At Canon Production Printing, model-based approaches have already proven to be essential for efficiently performing continuous innovation with sustainable quality in a highly competitive market.

125000 Personalized Magazines

200 Signs

100000 Brochures

6000 Books

3000 m² Billboards Banners

425000 Direct Mail Packages

Each Day

Fig. 1 Examples of professional digital printers developed by Canon Production Printing

An important ingredient of model-based development at Canon Production Printing is to have good tool support to do the actual modeling. Architects, designers, and engineers often rely on tools that are to some extent targeted for addressing specific aspects of a printer. For example, the mechanical design relies on using a CAD tool, which is, however, an unfamiliar development environment for a software designer. Nevertheless, the mechanical and software designer are working on the same printer, and hence part of the knowledge captured in their models must be the same to ensure that together they come to a design that will actually work. Exposing (the knowledge captured in) models to a wider audience than the original context from which they originated is an essential ingredient of achieving consistent designs within and across engineering disciplines. Instead of teaching the wider audience to use the tool in which a model was originally created, it can be more appropriate to introduce a (meta)tool that allows for automated exchange of the knowledge captured in various domain-specific models (which are developed in a diversity of tools). This allows for much better reuse of models within and across engineering disciplines. In summary, the benefits of using a (meta)tool include:

- Users don't have to learn the quirks of numerous tools.
- Within one (meta)tool, multiple models can be integrated much more intimately.
- Integrating and maintaining one (meta)tool in development (and automated build) environments is less work than integrating and maintaining multiple tools.

MPS is a core (meta)tool that is used extensively within Canon Production Printing. However, it is not only used for realizing consistent exchange of knowledge captured in models developed in more domain-specific tools (such as the CAD tool example). It is also being used as the main tool for creating models to capture knowledge that has not yet been formalized. This allows computer-based processing for more automated printer development as essential extensions to the capabilities of consistent exchange of knowledge between domain-specific tools. This chapter highlights several modeling efforts that emerged within Canon Production Printing and how MPS played a role in these efforts. Figure 2 gives a high-level impression

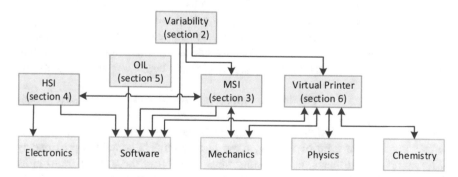

Fig. 2 Relations between the DSLs in this chapter and domain models in various engineering disciplines. In reality, several additional DSLs are involved to cover some of the expressed relations

of the main relations between the different DSLs discussed in this chapter and knowledge captured in domain models for the involved engineering disciplines.

Section 2 describes how MPS is deployed for coping with the variability that is the result of supporting many product variations within a single piece of software. Section 3 shows how knowledge about mechanical properties previously encoded in C++ was lifted to models, enabling effective and consistent communication between different stakeholders. Section 4 treats a similar abstraction effort in the context of hardware-software interfaces. Where Sect. 2 shows how we used and slightly extended an existing "horizontal" DSL to address a specific aspect of our software development, Sect. 5 presents a "horizontal" DSL that was entirely developed at Canon Production Printing for the description of control behavior. In contrast to these two "horizontal" languages, Sect. 6 presents a real "vertical" (print domain-specific) effort to model several aspects of our print process. Section 7 discusses some meta-level efforts that should help us to make the power of domain-specific modeling available to a larger user community. Finally, Sect. 8 summarizes some lessons learned from applying modeling, and in particular MPS.

2 Product Variability

Canon Production Printing encounters variations in different contexts: between products, within shared platforms, by used or supported hardware, or depending on settings or purchased licenses. Historically, these variations are maintained on an ad-hoc basis within our software. This has typically led to locally optimal solutions to determine which features are supported for a specific configuration. However, this evolution also led to issues such as different information sources in different modules for the same variation point, an incomplete overview of applicable variations and their dependencies, and higher testing and maintenance effort.

We started to migrate our variations from various contexts to an MPS-based feature model, based on the sound theory of Product Line Engineering [2, 16, 17]. The feature model language was implemented by *itemis* as a result of the IETS3 project [14]. *itemis* also provided a complementary extension language to support our specific use case with named constraints and feature flags. We further leveraged MPS's language extensibility by attaching additional validations to the feature model language, and implementing a generator to target our specific run-time environment.

Some of our ad-hoc variations (expressed as conditions in regular source code) have already been successfully migrated to MPS-based feature models. The source code artifacts generated from these feature models have also been deployed to production. At the time of writing, these feature models contain approximately 70 features, 30 attributes, and 30 constraints. We expect these numbers to grow by at least one order of magnitude. We indeed observe the expected benefits to our code structure, such as less code duplication, single source of information, and clearer dependencies between variations. Hence, we intend to continue the migration process.

Currently, our feature model comprises (rather low-level) technical features expressing variability from a technical implementation perspective, which we can therefore migrate directly to implementation code, for example. Due to their technical nature, these models are used by developers. In the future, we want to explore combining different technically minded feature models, or relate them to more abstract domain-focused feature models. Such domain-focused feature models express variability from the customer perspective when buying or using our printer systems.

Introducing MPS to our software developers also came with some hurdles. A first hurdle was usability-related: especially the unconventional editing experience and the abundant warnings required a change in mindset. Second, we missed editor-related features such as triggering transitive model updates and amending the inspector view of existing concepts for our extension language. A final hurdle relates to our generation target being a programming language that is not yet available through a DSL model within MPS. Our solution was to exploit the external extension PlaintextGen [8] to generate plain text instead of using a model-to-model transformation.

2.1 Variability at Canon Production Printing

Within Canon Production Printing, we handle variations in different contexts and at different points in the product lifecycle. Some of these variations only concern our own development, while others are visible to the market or to a specific customer. Examples of internal variations include the specific hardware components within a printer and products based on the same platform. To the market, variations might be different products or versions of the same product family, supported so-called finishing equipment (e.g., third-party staplers or stackers), and available optional features. Specific customers can vary in their purchased licenses, product environment, and individual printer settings. We need to consider platform-related variations very early on when designing a shared platform. Variations between printer products, supported equipment, or optional features are part of product design, but might change with subsequent versions of the same product. Variations based on installed finishers, purchased licenses, or individual settings are only known at run-time.

2.1.1 Designing for Variability

Handling variations ad-hoc leads to a range of design challenges. It is not easily visible which variation can occur in which combination, and whether we covered all relevant combinations. We might have variations without any actual difference, leading to code duplication and higher effort for testing and issue fixing.

Many variations depend on each other: a specific kind of ink might be available only on some product releases, and can only be used if the customer purchased the appropriate license. Tracking such dependencies is infeasible if they are only expressed as part of the software source code.

At each variation point within the software, we have to decide whether some variation is valid or not (think of "Is glossy media[1] supported?" as an example). In one software module (e.g., built-in UI of the printer), we might decide depending on the installed hardware revision. In another module (e.g., printer driver), the same decision might be based on an internal code name, because the code name changes with the hardware revision, and reading the revision directly might be cumbersome. Assume for a new product that the installed hardware revision stays the same, but the internal code name changes. This leads to potential discrepancies: the former module decides the variation is valid (based on the hardware revision), but the latter module decides the same variation is invalid (based on the internal code name). Thus, the user could select glossy media directly on the printer, but not in the printer driver.

2.1.2   Development Effort and User Base

The internal extensions to the Variability language are supported by one language engineer. The same engineer develops the run-time environment. At the time of writing, the total effort amounted to less than 10 weeks. Most of the language development is tasked to *itemis*. We extended their languages with approximately 20 concepts, checking rules, and intentions. The generator toward our run-time environment constituted the bulk of in-house development.

At the time of writing, the language is used by approximately one dozen users. In total, we spent roughly 1 week on training; general MPS education took the largest share of this effort. We expect the majority of our software engineers to use this tool chain.

2.2   Product Line Engineering

The problem of variations has been thoroughly researched in Computer Science under the term *Product Line Engineering* [2, 16, 17]. Fundamentally, they describe *features* as boolean variables (i.e., each feature might be enabled or disabled); at each *variation point*, we query the appropriate feature and act accordingly. The dependencies between features are described with *constraints*. Product Line

---

[1] A type of paper .

Feature model

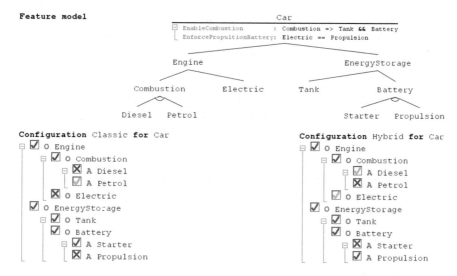

Fig. 3 A *feature model* and two *configurations* in MPS (see footnote 2) Each node in the tree represents a *feature*. Lines represent *constraints* between features. Additional *constraints* are expressed in predicate logic. The configurations denote *enabled* features with a check-mark and *disabled* features with a cross

Engineering research came up with an easy-to-understand, tree-based notation for the most common constraints; more complex constraints are expressed with predicate logic. A *feature model* contains all features and their constraints. One set of values, i.e., enabled or disabled state for each feature in a feature model, is called a *configuration*. A configuration is *valid* if it fulfills all constraints. Figure 3 shows a simple example.[2]

2.2.1 Solution Outline

We aim at migrating any ad-hoc variation into unique features. All variation points that relate to the same variation should query the same feature; this ensures consistent effects of enabled or disabled features throughout the system. Each variation point should query as few features as possible; any kind of dependencies on other features should be modeled as constraints. This removes all dependency logic from the code, and ensures that the same source of information is used.

To cater for our needs, we augment the feature model with feature-specific *flags*. These allow extra information to be captured, such as *derived*, *plain*, or *run-time*. The value of a *derived* feature is determined by constraints: only this

---

[2]We use a car-based example here because of the more generally known concepts, in contrast to lesser known concept variations in the printing domain.

amendment allows constraints to actively enforce dependencies between features. A *run-time* feature can change its value at run-time - contrary to *plain* features that are configured at design-time. This allows us to model features such as installed finishers or printer-specific settings.

We need to access the feature model at run-time to query for the relevant feature at each variation point. Resource limitations prohibit us from deploying MPS on a printer. Furthermore, accessing MPS models from the existing system would require considerable additional engineering effort. Thus, we generate source code from the feature model. The generated code holds all the knowledge from the feature model (i.e. all defined features, constraints, and attributes), and ties in with our manually implemented run-time framework. In combination, this code ensures that only features flagged *run-time* can be changed on the printer, and all features flagged *derived* are updated accordingly. This means that we reuse the same constraints to check for valid configurations at design-time and run-time.

2.2.2 Example

Assume the legacy code contains the pseudo-code fragments shown in Listings 1 and 2 for the UI module and job control module respectively. At both conditional expressions (i.e., the variation points), we have to make a decision based on product variant, available hardware revision, and whether glossy media (see footnote 1) is licensed. productCode is set based on product variant and hardware revision. The code exhibits several of the listed issues: different sources of information for the same decision, difficult to correlate both variation points, hard-coded dependencies to other variations.

Listing 1 Legacy UI
```
if (productCode == "nextGenPrinter" and isLicensed (GlossyMedia)) {
    glossyMediaCheckbox.visible = true
} else {
    glossyMediaCheckbox.visible = false
}
```

Listing 2 Legacy job control
```
if (job.media.type == Glossy) {
    if ( productVariant != Versatile
        or hardwareRevision < 2
        or not isLicensed (GlossyMedia)) {
        refuseJob ("glossy not supported or not licensed")
    }
}
```

After introducing the feature model in Fig. 4, we can replace both conditions by a simple query for feature MediaGlossy.

2.3   Advantages of MPS

Our feature model is implemented in MPS, based on a generic feature modeling language provided by *itemis*, who integrated a constraint solver with their feature model language. This constraint solver provides instant feedback on inconsistent models or contradicting constraints within the model. On our request, *itemis* implemented an accompanying language to support the feature flags. We further leveraged MPS's language extensibility to add custom validations on top of the existing feature model language. We exploit this, for example, to ensure unique feature names and that feature names adhere to the rules of the target language. As MPS allows additional generators without changing the source model's language, we have implemented our own generator based on the language stack developed by *itemis*.

The MPS projectional editor integrates seamlessly both the graphical feature tree and the textual constraint expressions. Modeling and reasoning about all features and their dependencies is quite challenging. However, the integrated rendering and seamless editing allow the focus to be placed on the inherent complexity, rather than dealing with inadequate or split up editors (i.e., tooling issues).

2.4   Shortcomings of MPS

As we are replacing the logic with variation points throughout our code base, team members regularly encounter MPS for the first time when they adopt our feature model. Being developers, this user group is not discouraged by MPS's IDE

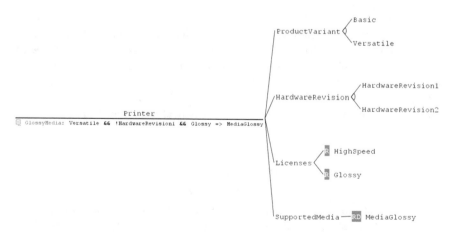

Fig. 4 Example feature model in MPS deriving the supported media from design-time features (product variant and hardware revision) and run-time feature (license) *R* and *D* on dark background represent the feature-specific flags Runtime and Derived

appearance. However, they still have difficulties in working with the tool without close guidance. The main usability issues include the separation between context menu and intention menu, the unfamiliar keyboard navigation and selection scheme.

The feature modeling language consists of two main aspects: the feature model and configurations. After every change to the feature model, the user has to explicitly adapt each configuration to the changes by triggering an intention. This could be avoided if MPS would provide language developers with an easy mechanism to propagate changes to other parts of the model, while keeping manual changes on the propagation target untouched. MPS supports generic language extension through *node annotations* and accompanying amendments to the projected main editor. However, a language extension cannot easily amend the projected inspector editor.

The target programming language of our custom generator is not available as MPS language, and is too complex to easily implement. MPS's TextGen is not well suited to generate large amounts of text, especially if the generated structure differs from the input model. We resolved this issue by leveraging the PlaintextGen extension [8].

2.5   Status and Outlook for Product Variability Modeling

At the time of writing, we migrated approximately one dozen software variation points to the feature model and successfully delivered products based on this development into production. We are continuing the migration of ad-hoc variation points to the feature-based approach. In this process, we extend the internal user base of MPS-based modeling. Several other areas, including hardware variations, are being prepared to leverage feature modeling in MPS (see also next sections).

In a first step, the feature models on the software and hardware side are expected to stay independent. Combining these models might lead to additional insights on dependencies and reuse-benefits. We intend to investigate this direction in the future.

As we migrate source code to feature models, these models are very detailed and technical. However, most features stem from domain, product, or business variations (similar to what is described in Sect. 2.1). It would be interesting to model these more abstract features and relate them to the technical feature models.

3   Mechanics-Software Interface

The Mechanics-Software Interface (MSI) is a collection of DSLs that are used together to describe how sheets of paper are transported through the paper path of a printer. The *paper path* is a mechanical system described using three-dimensional components that exist in the mechanical sub-domain of printers, such as *transport belts*, metal *sheet guides*, (movement) sensors, and actuators such as *pinches* and *deflectors*.

Canon Production Printing developed the MSI DSLs to support the HappyFlow model-based design approach for sheet movement in so-called cut-sheet printers. This *HappyFlow* approach is *"the conscious simplification of the model, where only the desired behavior of a sheet and the ideal movements of all parts are modeled"* (for more details, refer to [12]). HappyFlow decouples the low-level (non-ideal) physical behavior from the high-level scheduling of the sheets. The scheduling defines for each sheet when it is released and when it comes back for the second (duplex) printing. Scheduling is not trivial due to the large return loop and the run-time media variations and corresponding constraints between subsequent sheets. The *HappyFlow* approach allows reasoning regarding the effectiveness of a paper path to transport individual sheets as well as the impact of timing requirements on streams of sheets. Such timing requirements are imposed so that certain actions can be performed on a sheet. Examples of these actions include deflecting a sheet,[3] fixating the image onto a sheet using heaters, and subsequently cooling the sheet.

This section describes part of the evolution of the *HappyFlow* model-based design approach since its initial publication in [12] and what role MPS played in adopting a continuous-integration approach. Since the original *HappyFlow* approach was introduced, paper paths have become significantly larger and more complex. The complexity of the sheet transport for the printing domain requires a broad understanding of physical properties, as well as an in-depth understanding of scheduling and interaction of software components. It is therefore beneficial to alleviate the mental burden of the paper path designers by capturing reusable domain knowledge. Capturing this knowledge also allows automatic generation of software artifacts, as well as automated verification and optimization techniques.

This section presents how MPS has been used to capture the cut-sheet printer-specific mechanics and software domains and how it interfaces between these domains. We specifically highlight how MPS helped to achieve or improve:

- **Modularity** of the paper path in relation to product variability (see also Sect. 2)
- **Communication** between interdisciplinary teams
- **Continuous Integration** of model-based design artifacts

Figure 5 illustrates how the paper path (mechanical CAD models), parts, sheet timing, and sheet scheduling constraints are connected in MPS and how the generated software artifacts relate to each other. We use this overview throughout the remainder of this section.

---

[3]For example, a sheet needs to enter the duplex loop only if it needs to be printed again.

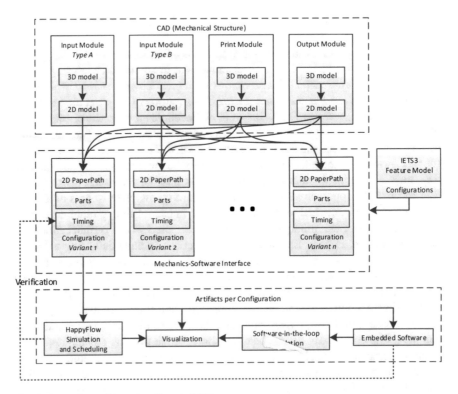

Fig. 5 Example models and artifacts in MSI

3.1 Paper Paths

The three-dimensional paper path layout is constructed in a CAD environment. A two-dimensional definition of the paper path is exported as an XML file, which is in turn imported by MPS. The 2D paper path model is most naturally displayed as a graphical model (see also Fig. 6). This allows easy communication between the mechanical engineers and the engineers defining timing requirements. The *segments* (lines) contain annotations on *points-of-interest* (POIs), which refer to locations of, e.g., sensors, pinches, and synchronization points. Different *routes* are defined based on these segments for sheets that need to be printed once (simplex) or twice (duplex). Each route describes which POIs are encountered during transportation of a sheet.

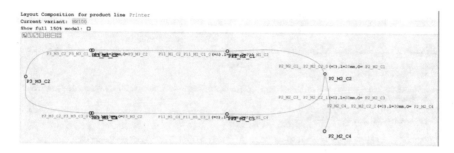

Fig. 6 Example paper path layout in MPS consisting of multiple *segments* between *points-of-interest* (the small circles). Such a paper path layout is a composition of paper path building blocks (such as input, process, and output) that are instantiated (and connected at points-of-interest that allow such connections) as a result of an instance of the product variability model explained in Sect. 2

3.2 Parts

The software that reads the sensors of the paper path and controls its actuators requires information about the physical properties of the motors (type, torque, maximum acceleration, or velocity), sensors, and pinches (circumference), for example specifying whether a motor in the paper path is realized through a stepper-motor or a brush-less direct-current motor. In addition, these motors are connected through different gears to one or multiple pinches or belts in the paper path.

This mechanical information is not provided in the CAD export, and is described by means of *parts* in the MSI DSLs. A part typically has multiple stakeholders in different engineering disciplines and, as such, different representations. The most detailed representation contains all required and optional attributes of a part, whereas the high-level overview of logical connections between motors, gears, and pinches can be shown best as a graphical diagram. MPS allows us to switch effortlessly between the different representations, which eases communication and verification.

3.3 HappyFlow Sheet Timing

The sheet timing model defines at what speed and acceleration a sheet should ideally move at any position in a route. This has traditionally been engineered by coding such behavior directly in C++. The sheet timing DSL started out as a C++ API, which meant that a significant amount of detail needed to be programmed, which is not directly relevant to the conceptual definition of the sheet timing. Lifting the C++ API to a proper DSL in MPS means that the designer responsible for sheet timing can focus on the definition of this timing behavior without being distracted by any C++ peculiarities. The timing-related instructions are typically physical

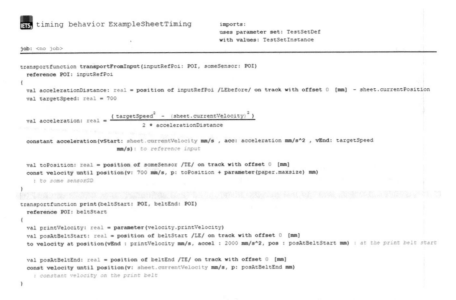

Fig. 7 Example functionality used in the sheet timing model in MPS. The focus is on the sheet's actions and mathematical computations, with connections to its movement through the printer

computations regarding the velocities and accelerations of the sheet. For such computations in our domain, we have used the general-purpose functional kernel called KernelF [20]. Integrating KernelF through MPS's language composition into our own DSL constructs immediately enabled sufficient support for computational expressions used in the domain. The result is that the sheet timing model is more easily captured using general statements and mathematical notation instead of C++. Figure 7 gives an example of the succinctness of the sheet timing model. These sheet timing models are used to generate the information on where the sheet should be at what time. Figure 8 shows an example inline graph with the position (i.e., displacement in the sheet track) of a sheet versus time for two sheets, one simplex, one duplex.

A benefit of using MPS for the sheet timing definitions is that particular details can be hidden, depending on the level of detail that is required to present the functionality to involved stakeholders. Such information can be hidden either in the MPS Inspector window or in different projections of the same model. This greatly enhances the conciseness and readability of certain parts of the sheet timing calculation.

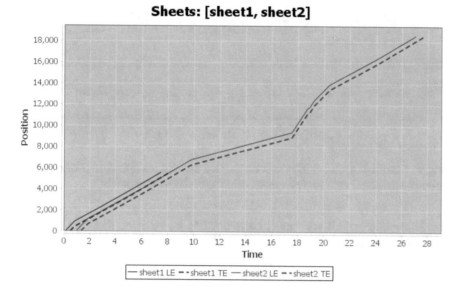

Fig. 8 Sheet position (displacement) vs time diagram

3.4   Sheet Scheduling Constraints and Verification

The sheet timing model imposes constraints on the transportation of each individual sheet. In this section, we describe how we deal with the scheduling constraints that impose constraints between subsequently transported sheets. The value of these constraints depends on the media properties and functional requirements to ensure that the image is transferred correctly onto the sheet; i.e., the time between two sheets at the print head must be sufficient, and no sheets should collide with each other at the merge point. A timing designer needs to develop, check, and optimize the sheet timing as well as the timing constraints so that the displacement of sheets is sound and complete. In addition, the productivity KPI is influenced directly by the design of the sheet timing and sheet constraints.

The demand for higher productivity has led to larger and more complex paper paths, as mentioned at the start of this section. The numerous timing requirements that arise due to this additional complexity are harder to manage than when *HappyFlow* was originally developed [12]. Whereas previous printers had up to 10 simultaneously moving sheets, paper paths of current printers may hold 100 moving sheets simultaneously. The variety of media types (such as sheet dimensions and material type) has also increased. The interactions between the sheets can therefore no longer be optimized or analyzed without advanced tool support.

The definition of these scheduling constraints was lifted from C++ constructs. Similar to in the sheet timing models, the KernelF expression language was embedded to allow sufficient expressiveness without having to create our own

```
Inter-sheet constraints
inter-sheet constraint HFDeflectorConstraint(prev: Sheet, next: Sheet) on Loop
   TE (prev) = OCMDEF1(1) ----- parameter(sec.switchTime) s ----> LE(next) <= OCMRPI1(1)
      CG ref POI: ITMSREULPI

Initial sheet constraints
initial-sheet constraint WarmUp(s: Sheet)
   LE(s) <- ITMIN(1) for at least: max(parameter(sec.DrumWarmUp), parameter(sec.HeadWarmUp)) s

Distance constraints
[ Code gen: DISABLED ]
distance constraint Test(prev: Sheet, next: Sheet) on segment Input
   TE(prev) - LE(next) >= 0 mm
```

Fig. 9 Example sheet constraints in MPS showing how the minimum time/distance constraints are computed and how these relate to the sheets as well as the layout of the printer

implementation of all arithmetic, corresponding interpreters, and type checkers. This has made it possible to write down timing requirements succinctly, as shown in Fig. 9. Each timing constraint is generated into dozens of lines of C++ code. These sheet scheduling constraints are the input for heuristic online schedule optimization algorithms [18, 19, 21].

We have also added algorithms to perform automatic verification of sheet movement schedules. Lifting the models from C++ to MPS has also allowed us to implement an automatic verification technique. This verification technique can determine the *robustness* [6, 7] of a schedule of sheets with respect to the sheet scheduling constraints that were defined. The results of the verification can be shown directly in the model editor, due to the inline integration of graphs.

The position time diagrams resulting from the models in Sect. 3.3 can be interpreted as STL[4] signals for which we can write logic to check them for functional correctness, such as shown in Fig. 10. In this example constraint, the trailing edge of sheet 2 violates the constraint that it needs to arrive on a belt 0.2 s after the leading edge arrives on that same belt. The robustness is negative between $t = 15$ and $t = 16$, indicating that the constraint is violated at those time instances.

3.5 Product Variants and Modularity

Section 2 discussed the increasing variation in printer configurations. We have already illustrated that the models for a particular configuration benefit the printer designers. However, due to the large number of possible configurations, we have also used modularity in the design to avoid repetitions. The modules imported from

---

[4]The extension of Signal Temporal Logic (STL) [6, 7] for constraints validation is developed by the Embedded Systems Institute (ESI) at the Netherlands Organisation for Applied Scientific Research (TNO) in the Octo+ research program with Canon Production Printing as carrying industrial partner.

`plot LEFollowedByTEOnBelt`

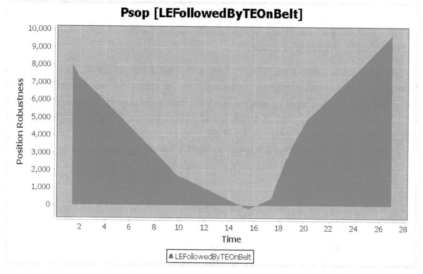

```
STL[ LEafterStartBelt ]: sheet2 LE >= 7200
STL[ LEbeforeEndBelt ]: sheet2 LE >= 8500
STL[ TEafterStartBelt ]: sheet2 TE >= 7200
STL[ TEbeforeEndBelt ]: sheet2 TE >= 8500
STL[ LEOnBelt ]: LEafterStartBelt && LEbeforeEndBelt
STL[ TEOnBelt ]: TEafterStartBelt && TEbeforeEndBelt

STL[ TEOnBeltWithinInterval ]: G( TEOnBelt ) between [ 0.2 , 5.2 ]

STL[ LEFollowedByTEOnBelt ]: LEOnBelt => TEOnBeltWithinInterval
```

Fig. 10 Example sheet constraint robustness using sheet displacement as STL signal

mechanical CAD drawings are enriched with other models regarding parts, timing, routes, etc. The paper paths and parts are composed from these enriched modules, in accordance with the information in the variability model, as shown in Fig. 5. This has led to a cleaner and smaller definition of the product lines than is possible without the variability models.

3.6 Continuous Integration of Model-Based Design Artifacts

The MSI language set described in the previous sections is used for generating packages of embedded software, simulation, and visualization artifacts. We have integrated the MPS command line build tool in our DevOps environment to achieve Continuous Integration. This is done in a three-stage approach:

1. The language engineers create and update the languages, which are built to the (MSI) DSL plugins.

2. The domain experts use these DSL plugins to create and update (MSI) models, which are generated into artifacts such as (C++) source code and XML files.
3. The generated artifacts are integrated into the embedded software repository to compile the final implementation.

The generated software packages therefore become immediately available to the embedded software developers. The versions are stored as build artifacts that can be referenced by multiple projects. The automated testing of languages (as part of step 1) and models (as part of steps 2 and 3) has ensured that multiple developers can work on the same code base (both models and languages) with the same conveniences as Continuous Integration allows for normal software development.

3.7 Concluding Remarks on MSI

We are using the projectional editor of MPS to combine textual, graphical, and tabular notations into a single editor experience. Combined with the modularity of MPS, i.e, the composability of languages that is possible due to the projectional nature, languages can quickly adopt existing solutions, such as mathematical notations for expressions, and inline integration of graphical editors and computed graphs.

4   Hardware-Software Interface

The Hardware-Software Interface (HSI) is a collection of DSLs for describing the available input and output (I/O) ports in the embedded system (electronics) boards of a printer. Such boards include, among others, an embedded processor and Field Programmable Gate Arrays (FPGA) that are to be programmed with embedded and control software. The top part of Fig. 11 illustrates that the HSI combines the

- Hardware domain to cover the I/O available in the embedded processor
- Hardware Description Language (HDL) domain for the I/O on the FPGAs
- Software domain for configuring the I/O

into a single domain-specific model. Each domain expert uses the respective projection to view and edit the part of the model that matches his/her domain. This allows the exclusion of the details of other domains, which are typically irrelevant for him/her.

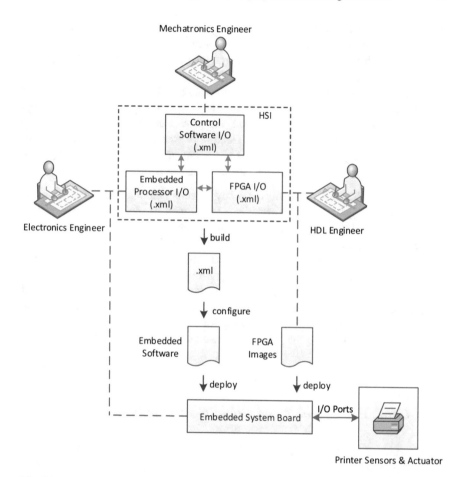

Fig. 11 Initial XML-based version of the HSI bridged three domains at design-time

4.1 Initial Version of HSI

The HSI was initially developed as DSLs described in XML files (see also Fig. 11). It relied on XSD and XSLT for syntax and sanity checking. Engineers in each of the domains would create their own set of files and the information in these files was combined *during build time* into one configuration file to be used on the printer. Three reasons were key to starting the approach with DSLs in MPS:

- **Model Size** Our projects use more and more I/O, which leads to an increase in model size and model connections. It became error-prone and too complex to keep the XML files consistent; the unique keys used to combine the specified information may not contain typos. Such typos were only detected at build time.

- **Modularization** The I/O is implemented by FPGAs and corresponding electronics in modules. The embedded system boards were modularized to allow for reuse, which avoids duplication of I/O modules and with it the risk of incorrect modifications.
- **Product Variability** Due to the product variability described in Sect. 2, the I/O that actually needs to be instantiated is no longer statically known at design and build time of the printer. Instead, the printer configuration is determined dynamically at run-time. The actual I/O that is used is thus only known at run-time. This means that with the initial setup, the super-set of all I/O that can be instantiated for each configuration needed to be available.

The complexity resulting from these key reasons amounted to increased complexity for the engineers. More complex files as well as more complex checking rules were needed to ensure that files used on the target (i.e., the embedded systems board) were still valid. Note that errors that occur in the I/O at run-time are hard to debug and in the worst case even lead to broken mechanical hardware that is expensive to replace. More complex designs in the FPGA were also needed to incorporate all the I/O, which in turn led to the need for bigger FPGAs and thus a higher cost price. The initial approach was not scalable for product lines that are increasing in complexity, while striving for a price-competitive product for the customer. To address these challenges, we created a new version of the HSI in MPS (see Fig. 12).

4.2   Combined Domains and Domain-Specific Editing

MPS enabled the combining of all the domain-specific knowledge and information covered in several DSLs into a single source of information. This means that MPS guards the consistency of the model on the fly, while still allowing the engineers to edit the information with the same domain-specific editing experience as before, by making use of projections. While the whole system has become more powerful and more complex, the editing of the HSI information has been kept simple.

4.3   Harnessing Modularization

While the modularization of the embedded system board introduced more complexity to the HSI, it also enabled the exploitation of the generation power of MPS. The HSI specification now generates the actual HDL content that is used to create FPGA images. In the initial version of Fig. 11, these FPGA images were made by hand for each specific situation and the HSI was written manually. This approach was cumbersome and error-prone in view of guaranteeing the consistency between the FPGA image and the HSI. With the new version of MPS shown in

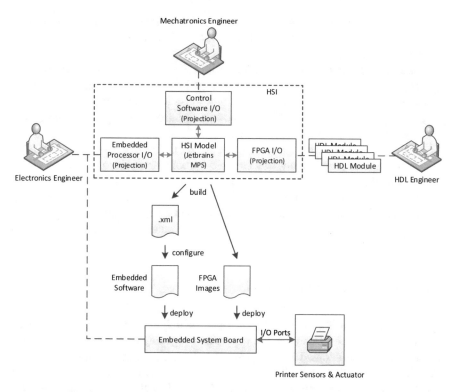

Fig. 12 MPS version of the HSI

Fig. 12, this process was reversed. The HSI now uses standard building blocks, each corresponding to an HDL module. The specification of such blocks leads to generating HDL code and thus to generating FPGA images that are consistent with the HSI.

Because MPS is also able to show the HSI in a simplified way, the new HSI version also enables non-HDL engineers to easily create an FPGA image just by specifying which I/O they need for their functionality or test setup. This automation frees up HDL engineers to work on novel design solutions instead of having to spend a lot of time on manually creating FPGA images for various printer and test setups.

4.4 Coping with Increased Complexity

The demand for modularity in our embedded systems board increased the complexity of the initial version of the HSI to a point where it made sense to migrate to a language workbench. The increase in complexity was tackled in multiple ways (see Fig. 12):

- **Projecting the same model in different ways** Different experts can now view and edit the same source of information without being bothered by the specifics of other domains.
- **Error reporting and quick-fixes/intentions** The initial version of the HSI had very limited error checking, and no way of helping an end user with solving detected errors. The HSI DSLs in MPS now make it possible for an inexperienced user to create an HSI instance, and if an error is introduced the editor can be used to help the user to resolve such errors.
- **First-class support for language testing** In the initial version of the HSI, the end-to-end functionality was checked by comparing the output for a set of predefined input files against a reference output. Such a check is still in place to validate the generators of the HSI DSLs in MPS, but now the editor experience and checking rules are also tested. Such a mature regression test allows new functionality or redesigning to be added without much risk on regression.

4.5 Status and Outlook for HSI

The development of the HSI has taken approximately one man year of effort over a period of 4 years by one domain expert/language engineer. During this period the HSI has been adopted by the projects within Canon Production Printing as functionality has become available. At this moment it is used in all main projects for the expansion and maintenance of the HSI and VHDL development. The total user base is approximately one dozen engineers, while the maintenance and new development is done by one language engineer.

The exploitation of MPS has automated ensuring the consistency across different engineering disciplines. Other information sources that include information about I/O needs is captured by other DSLs in MPS, such as the sensors and actuators in the Mechanics-Software Interface (see Sect. 3). Such information can be used to further facilitate the definition of an HSI instance. On the other hand, it would also be possible to use the HSI with all its information on the I/O as the input for diagnostics software to support service engineers. Finally, the information could be used to automatically create I/O tests for development purposes.

Mechatronics engineers at Canon Production Printing use Matlab Simulink for model-based development of the control software to be run on the embedded system boards. They use the available simulation facilities of Matlab Simulink to validate the model against possible inputs. In the past, these models were manually rewritten into C or VHDL (depending on the deployment). This meant that the validation had to be redone to ensure that the C or VHDL code was correct. Nowadays, automatic generators are used when targeting C code. It is also possible to generate VHDL code from the Matlab Simulink models. However, such generated VHDL code does not integrate straightforwardly with the VHDL code already generated by our MPS-based version of the HSI. Hence, some standardization on the interface with Matlab Simulink models to generate the required glue VHDL code is being investigated.

5 Domain-Specific State Machine Specification

As in many high-tech companies, control behavior ("state machines") is an important aspect of the software that we develop at Canon Production Printing. In our software development process, many different approaches have been and are being used to implement such behavior. This ranges from switch-case statements in general-purpose languages, standard state machine libraries, in-house built state machine libraries, in-house built state machine DSLs and tools (implemented using either generic scripting languages or language workbenches), to the use of advanced commercial tools such as RSARTE [13]. Having such a multitude of different approaches to tackle the same challenge is not desirable. We therefore aim toward preferably one standard state machine approach and tool.

5.1 Yet Another State Machine Language

The concept of state machine is "horizontally" domain specific in the sense that it is not specific to a particular "vertical" business domain like printing. One would expect to be able to buy a perfectly suitable off-the-shelf tool. We have, however, not been able to find a tool that fits all our needs in the different contexts where control software plays a role. We therefore took up the challenge to create a DSL that does suit our needs. Together with several of our experts in control software development, we thought about how we would want to specify some of our most complex control components. In parallel, we developed a DSL that enabled us to write down such specifications.

5.2 Open Interaction Language (OIL)

An important requirement on the DSL was that it should enable us to compactly and intuitively express the complex control behavior that we face. A crucial factor was the ability to separate the behavior into multiple concerns, each describing a specific aspect of the behavior. Furthermore, next to a compact and intuitive textual representation, it should also allow for compact and intuitive graphical representations, all of which should be semantically consistent and complete. The language should have a well-defined formal semantics and allow for behavioral verification and fully automatic generation of efficient executable code. The resulting language was called OIL, which stands for Open Interaction Language.

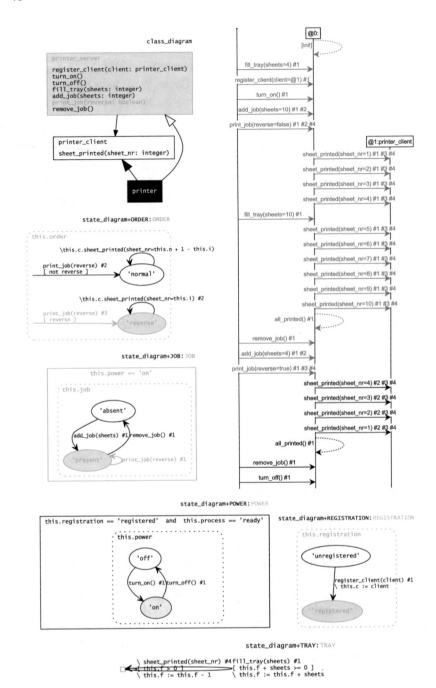

Fig. 13 Some views of a toy OIL specification in the Python/XML-based prototype

5.3   Prototype Tool

To develop and use OIL, we created a prototype tool that can generate various views of a specification such as class diagrams, state diagrams, sequence diagrams, implementation code, and model-checking code. The prototype was implemented with generic technologies such as Python and XML/HTML. An intricate interplay of parsers and code generators enables aspect-based views and simulation of traces (Fig. 13).

5.4   Behavioral Verification

To enable behavioral verification of OIL specifications, a PhD project was started in which a transformation from OIL to the formal language mCRL2 was developed [3, 9]. Using the mCRL2 model-checking tools, several behavioral aspects such as absence of deadlock, liveness, and confluence can be automatically verified. Using simulation, counterexamples can be analyzed at the level of the specification.

5.5   Usability and Maintainability

Although the prototype tool for OIL has quite advanced capabilities, it is just a prototype, and its usability and maintainability are mediocre. To tackle this issue, but also to extend our knowledge on domain-specific modeling and application of formal methods in general, two PhD students and a masters student have together studied OIL in depth, one focusing on syntax, one on semantics, and one on code generation. The language workbench Spoofax was used to create a more maintainable implementation of OIL, including generators to several target languages [4, 5, 10].

Although Spoofax is a good tool for implementing textual DSLs and transformations between DSLs, many of our engineers prefer a tool that enables them to directly define and manipulate state machines in their graphical form. This is where MPS came in. Based on the OIL language, an MPS implementation including textual and graphical projections was constructed. Thus, instead of having a textual DSL from which graphical representations were generated, we now have an integrated tool in which both textual and graphical projections can be directly edited (Fig. 14).

example_printer_tray_super state_diagram+PROTOCOL: PROTOCOL

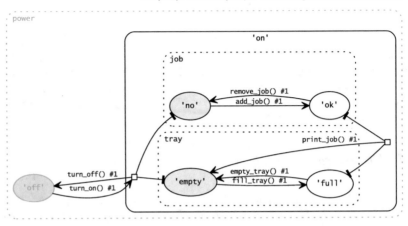

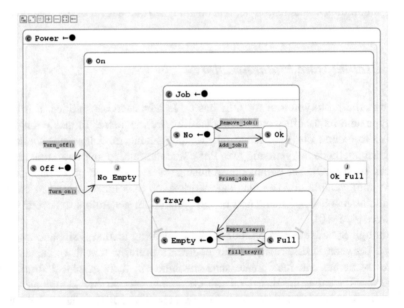

Fig. 14 An OIL specification in the Python/XML-based tool (top) and MPS-based tool (bottom)

5.6   Conclusion for OIL

There is still quite some work to do. The current MPS implementation only supports a subset of OIL, lacking several features that are essential to keep specifications of complex behavior compact. The reason for this is that the currently implemented code generator in MPS generates code that uses an in-house developed C++ state machine library. This library lacks several features of OIL and is also approximately one factor 10 slower than the low-level C++ code that is generated by the prototype.

We also implemented an OIL specification text generator in MPS, enabling use of the prototype tooling and code generator. However, being a prototype, this code generator is not something we want to maintain. The work carried out by the PhD students and master's students resulted in a flexible code generator architecture. This architecture uses several intermediate representations to ease adding code generators for different target programming languages such as C++, C#, and Java. As mentioned, this was implemented in the Spoofax language workbench. It remains an open question how easy it is to implement this in MPS, or whether we perhaps should resort to a combination of MPS as editing front-end and Spoofax as code generator back-end.

Overall, MPS enabled us to create a state machine tool that our engineers value for its capabilities. Especially the idea of not having separate code and design, but code *generated from* the design, combined with the ability to model graphically was well-received. Full integration of the tool into our development environment was also an important factor for its acceptance, although properly integrating it took quite some effort. There are still open challenges, like a proper approach to code generation and integration of behavioral verification. Most of the conceptual challenges were, however, already tackled in the prototype, and thus creating our one standard state machine approach and tool should be a matter of (hard...) work.

6   Virtual Printer Configuration

Canon Production Printing is creating various virtual printer environments to support the development of novel printer systems. The Virtual Printer Configuration DSLs define simulation specifications that allow the evaluation of trade-offs in aspects such as *productivity*, *print quality*, and *cost* of a printer. We describe how MPS helps us to manage simulation configurations and show two examples of simulation specification DSLs specific for our virtual printer environment that supports development of novel print processes: *Print Head* and *Carriage Motion* specifications.

6.1 Specifying Simulation Configurations

Figure 15 highlights our virtual printer environment that supports the development of novel print processes. It processes a *source image* through various simulation models that represent the steps in the print process such as *image processing*, *positioning* of the print heads and medium (e.g., paper), and *jetting* ink onto the medium. After ink droplets have been jetted, they (potentially) *interact* with other droplets and the medium. *Solidification* of the ink (i.e., the ink turns from a liquid into a solid substance by applying, for example, heat or UV light) is the last step in creating a *virtual print*. Subsequently, relevant properties of the virtual print can be evaluated. This includes *image quality aspects* (e.g., how good the printed image looks), *print robustness* (e.g., how well the ink sticks to the medium), and *media deformation* (e.g., how well the printed medium keeps its shape after being wetted by the ink and dried by heat). *Design-space exploration* can be applied to find suitable parameter settings for the desired balance between the mentioned properties of the virtual print.

The Virtual Printer in Fig. 15 exploits several simulators and models, which each has a value on its own. Together, they allow for evaluation of a complete print process for different types of printer systems. The Virtual Printer Configuration DSLs allow the specification of what printer system type is being investigated and what further parameter settings to use during the simulations. This also means that different simulators or models are, for example, used for *single-pass* latex-inkjet printers such as the Canon VarioPrint iX product family,[5] which print sheets of paper in a single pass, and *multi-pass* UVGel-inkjet printers such as the Canon Colorado product family,[6] which use a similar multi-pass print principle to commodity desktop printers. A concrete configuration expressed in the Virtual Printer Configuration DSLs results in instantiating the relevant chain of simulators with the desired parameter settings. Instantiated simulator chains are typically a variation of the following example:

- Select/generate input image.
- Process the input image for a selected print strategy.
- Compute media/print head movement trajectory to position ink droplets.
- Simulate nozzle activation, ink spreading, and solidification.
- Evaluate image quality aspects.

We aim to make the simulation models usable for both experts and novices. This can be achieved by mixing high-level and low-level detail in the configuration of each of the simulators. For novices, we use MPS to show only those abstractions that are required from the printer design point of view. The remaining parameters are then auto-generated or have default values. Experts can use either their familiar

---

[5]https://www.canon-europe.com/business-printers-and-faxes/varioprint-ix-series/.

[6]https://www.canon-europe.com/business-printers-and-faxes/colorado-1640/.

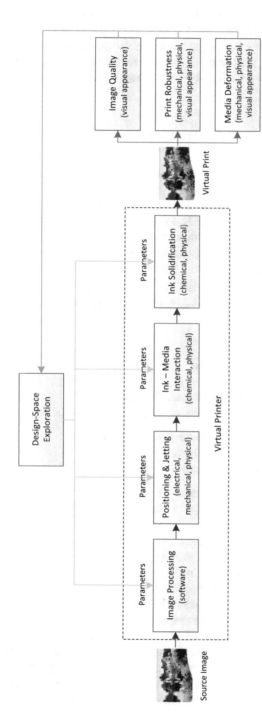

Fig. 15 Virtual printer supporting evaluation of print quality aspects during print process design

interface to the simulation tool or model directly, or use the more detailed configuration facilities provided with the Virtual Printer Configuration DSLs. MPS allows
us to present the configuration models via table/text-based editors and a graphical
editor using a similar view to that shown in Fig. 15, showing the various simulation
models (with ability to edit their parameters) and their interconnections.

6.2   Example Virtual Printer Configuration DSLs

Several parts of a printer need to be specified to allow for simulation of its print
quality and productivity. The placement and activation of *nozzles* in a *print head*
have a significant impact on where the ink droplets can be jetted, and on the
resolution and accuracy of droplet positioning. This also largely determines the
productivity or throughput in terms of, for example, printed sheets or area per time
unit. Given a model of the ink spreading behavior and the behavior of interaction
with the medium, the ink droplets jetted from print head nozzles simulate how
ink layers are formed on the medium [22, 23]. This is essential for evaluating the
print quality of the final print (i.e., its image quality, print robustness, and media
deformation; see Fig. 15).

6.2.1   Print Head Specifications

The first example of our Virtual Printer Configuration DSLs concerns the specification of print heads. Such *print head specifications* include the following aspects:

- Ideal (designed) position of nozzles in print heads
- Mapping of image lines onto the nozzles to activate
- Imperfections in nozzle positions and jetting conditions

Due to the large number of nozzles inside a print head, it is not desired to specify
each individual nozzle separately. In addition, specifying each nozzle separately
would hide the overall structure of nozzles in a print head. Hence, we use MPS
to define logical structures of nozzles and give immediate feedback to the user in
terms of correctness and derived properties of the nozzle structure definitions. We
also interactively visualize the effective placements of nozzles, so that the end user
can verify the interpretation of these logical structures as illustrated in Fig. 16.

After defining the ideal nozzle locations for all print heads, the user can
specify how the image lines are mapped onto nozzles. These mappings rely on
a synchronization between the Image Processing step and the nozzle activation
simulator in the Positioning & Jetting component shown in Fig. 15. The third aspect
of the Print Head Specification model, i.e., nozzle position and jetting imperfections,
is defined on top of the ideal nozzle locations. Such imperfections can be *structural*
or *dynamical*. Structural imperfections include misplacement of nozzles, and scaling

```
virtual printer configuration Examples using Scanning coordinate system
{
   staggered nozzle plate ExampleChip {
     10 nozzles at 75 npi in x
     Stagger width: 1 mm
   }
   nozzle group ExampleHead {
     placed ExampleChip at (x, y) = (0, 0)
   }
   Print Carriage 4xExampleHead @ 32 kHz {
     2 drop sizes

     Ink Channels: C M Y K
     Slot 1 : ExampleHead at (x, y) = (0, 0) using C
     Slot 2 : ExampleHead at (x, y) = (4, 0) using K
     Slot 3 : ExampleHead at (x, y) = (8, 0) using M
     Slot 4 : ExampleHead at (x, y) = (12, 0) using Y
   }
   Print Carriage 8xExampleHead @ 21 kHz {
     2 drop sizes

     Ink Channels: C M Y K
     Slot 1 : ExampleHead at (x, y) = (00, 0.000000000) using Y
     Slot 2 : ExampleHead at (x, y) = (02, 0.169333333) using C
     Slot 3 : ExampleHead at (x, y) = (04, 0.000000000) using M
     Slot 4 : ExampleHead at (x, y) = (06, 0.169333333) using K
     Slot 5 : ExampleHead at (x, y) = (08, 0.000000000) using K
     Slot 6 : ExampleHead at (x, y) = (10, 0.169333333) using M
     Slot 7 : ExampleHead at (x, y) = (12, 0.000000000) using C
     Slot 8 : ExampleHead at (x, y) = (14, 0.169333333) using Y
   }
}
```

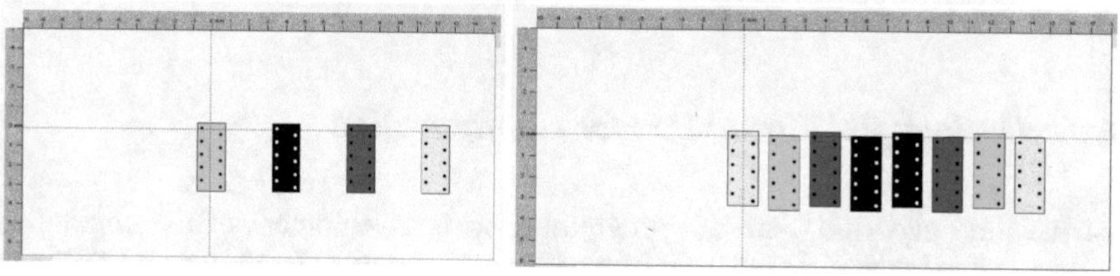

Fig. 16 Example printer configuration and visualization of 4 × ExampleHead and 8 × ExampleHead in MPS

or rotation of nozzle structures. Dynamical imperfections include *droplet volume deviations*, definition of so-called *satellite droplets*, and *jetting speed variations*.

Separating the specification of the ideal (designed) print head properties from possible imperfections enables the configuration of the simulator models in a way that would not be straightforward when configuring the simulators directly. This is because imperfections need to be combined with the ideal (designed) situation before configuring the simulators. For example, some imperfections may end up as an addition or multiplication for a single parameter of a simulator. Furthermore, MPS helps us in guiding the users in understanding constraints when configuring the simulators. Certain imperfections can, for example, not occur together (i.e., they conflict with each other), and that information is presented to the user while editing.

6.2.2 Carriage Motion Specification

The nozzles defined in the Print Head are either placed in a *Print Carriage* in case of multi-pass printer systems or in a *Print Station* in case of single-pass printer systems. Multi-pass print systems move their carriage(s) over the same piece of media multiple times to create the result image. This approach requires fewer of the costly print heads, and allows for much larger and a much wider range of media to be printed, at the cost of additional time to print the resulting image (lower productivity).

To properly simulate the forming of ink droplets, the relative timing between droplets needs to be accurately modeled. Section 3.3 describes our approach to modeling how a piece of paper flows through single-pass cut-sheet printer systems. In such systems, the sheet moves at a constant velocity when the image is being printed. This is actually a very small part of the overall sheet movement from the *paper input modules* to the (printed) *paper output modules* of such printer systems.

For multi-pass printer systems, the carriage motion needs to be described. The motion of the carriage(s) is not necessarily with constant velocity and has a significant impact on the relative timing between droplets. We describe the synchronization points of the carriage(s) together with the minimum and maximum physical constraints (acceleration, velocity, time) imposed on each of the trajectories. The timing and trajectories of each cycle are automatically computed by the simulator. MPS again allows us to mix convenient notations for the synchronization points, parameters, and visualization of the carriage motion trajectory (Fig. 17).

6.3 Outlook for Virtual Printer Configuration

At the time of writing, we are progressing with development of the simulation infrastructure, as well as creating several domain-specific simulators and DSLs to configure these simulators. Only recently, two language engineers started developing the DSLs described in this section. Hence, they are still in an early prototyping phase. We are, however, already deploying these DSLs together with the simulation infrastructure in production contexts. Currently, we are broadening the scope of users from mostly software developers, model creators, and simulator experts to application specialists. At the time of writing, there are about five application specialists that exploit the Virtual Printer in Fig. 15 in daily printer development activities.

Looking at maturing the DSLs described in this section, variability modeling would allow us to specify which combinations of simulation models are allowed, and give the user a convenient interface to define a virtual printer configuration for their experiment. This will allow for the easy interchanging of, for example, the print heads and the inks, the lamps in the curing carriage, as well as certain image processing steps. Hence, we intend to exploit feature models as described in Sect. 2.

```
timing notebook ExampleMotion (media width: (25.4 * 5) mm) {
  val headHeight = 127 / 225 * 25.4
  val headWidth = 10
  val headSpacing = 12

  val mininmalTurnTime = 0.700

  carriage geometry PrintingCarriage : # AEAEAE {
    PrintHeads(x: 0, y: 0, w: 4 * headSpacing, h: headHeight) at 0 , 0
    Y(x: 0 * headSpacing, y: 0, w: headWidth, h: headHeight) relative to top left of PrintHeads
    C(x: 1 * headSpacing, y: 0, w: headWidth, h: headHeight) relative to top left of PrintHeads
    M(x: 2 * headSpacing, y: 0, w: headWidth, h: headHeight) relative to top left of PrintHeads
    K(x: 3 * headSpacing, y: 0, w: headWidth, h: headHeight) relative to top left of PrintHeads
    PinCureR(x: 15, y: 0, w: 10, h: headWidth) relative to top right of K
  }
  carriage geometry CuringCarriage : # FFFFFF {
    PostCure(x: 0, y: 0, w: 100, h: 50) at 0 , 0
  }

  repeated motion SomeMotion {
    carriages: PrintingCarriage
    situations:
      BoS L2R {
        PrintingCarriage { right of PrintHeads is aligned with left of PrintMedium @ 1000 mm/s }
        CuringCarriage   { left of PostCure is aligned with left of PrintHeads      @ 1000 mm/s }
      }
      EoS L2R {
        PrintingCarriage { left of PrintHeads is aligned with right of PrintMedium @ 1000 mm/s }
      }
      BoS R2L {
        PrintingCarriage { left of PrintHeads is aligned with right of PrintMedium @ -1000 mm/s }
      }
      EoS R2L {
        PrintingCarriage { right of PrintHeads is aligned with left of PrintMedium @ -1000 mm/s }
      }
    trajectories:
      constant speed for PrintingCarriage : BoS L2R -> EoS L2R
      constant speed for PrintingCarriage : BoS R2L -> EoS R2L
      turn trajectory for PrintingCarriage : EoS L2R -> BoS R2L
        /max accel: 10000, max jerk: <no maxJerk>/
      turn trajectory for PrintingCarriage : EoS R2L -> BoS L2R
        /max accel: <no maxAccel>, max jerk: 1000/
    timing constraints:
      EoS L2R -> BoS R2L { time >= mininmalTurnTime }
      EoS R2L -> BoS L2R { time >= mininmalTurnTime }
  }
}
```

Fig. 17 Example carriage motion definition and corresponding situation visualization in MPS

We make use of the different projection capabilities of MPS, as well as the typical language engineering aspects such as error handling and type checking. We do not expect typical (non-software developer) users, i.e., application specialists exploiting the Virtual Printer in Fig. 15, to become comfortable with the user interface of MPS. Even with a stripped down RCP application, the user interface remains too focused on being a software IDE and language workbench. Another concern is model management. Typical application specialists may have some Matlab or Python programming experience, but most are not familiar with Git or other software version control systems. Avoiding or resolving version conflicts early is, however, an important aspect of model management. An approach to both avoid the use of complicated version control systems and improve on user interface aspects is the Modelix solution direction for collaborative modeling described in the next section.

7   Collaborative Domain-Specific Modeling

MPS comes with a high-end Integrated Development Environment (IDE) that is well suited for the development and exploitation of Domain-Specific Languages (DSL) in an industrial context. This IDE is a stand-alone desktop application. Its users include *DSL engineers* developing DSL models with accompanying functionalities and *DSL users* that create and exploit instances of such DSL models. The appearance of the IDE can be customized to ease usage for DSL users (e.g., as RCP). This helps in reducing the learning curve that is often experienced and in only covering the specific functionality relevant for DSL users. Exploitation of MPS at Canon Production Printing has, however, revealed the need for some additional capabilities:

- **Collaborative modeling**: DSLs at Canon Production Printing often represent domain-specific interfaces between models from different engineering disciplines, as also exemplified with the DSLs in Sects. 3 and 4. Such interfaces would benefit from the ability to collaboratively update DSL instances in a similar fashion to Google Docs and Microsoft Office 365 support for office documents. Collaborative modeling would benefit from a web-based front-end for, in particular, DSL users. A server-based deployment would also ease version control for DSL users unfamiliar with traditional software technologies and terminology for version control. In addition, it eases updating any involved tools (e.g., for automated code generation, build, and test tool chains) in case of DSL evolution.
- **Integration in larger GUI applications**: Canon Production Printing has various existing development environments that could benefit from exploiting DSL technology. Such environments may rely on custom Graphical User Interfaces (GUI) for which it is often not easy or even infeasible to (completely or partly) replace them in a gradual or disruptive step by the IDE for MPS. Such situations

would benefit from the ability to integrate the DSL technologies provided by MPS into the existing development environments as DSL widgets.

- **Domain-specific customization of look-and-feel**: Canon Production Printing positioned model-driven development as crucial for timely development of novel printer systems. Engineers of all engineering disciplines are expected to exploit DSLs for which tooling is realized using MPS. However, engineers with little or no affinity for software development have many difficulties in adopting the IDE (even as DSL users). It would be beneficial to provide DSL technology as part of highly customized GUIs with a domain-specific look-and-feel that is much closer to that of domain-specific tools currently used by such engineers.

This section[7] peeks into the future direction Canon Production Printing is considering for a widespread exploitation of MPS throughout the organization, which covers not only research & development but also, for example, sales and service.

7.1 Blended Collaborative Domain-Specific Modeling

A fundamental concept underlying MPS is the use of a *model-view architecture*. This is exposed by the DSL model instance being *projected*, possibly even with multiple different syntaxes at the same time, to a DSL user. The DSL user can change the DSL model instance via any of these projections or *views* in traditional model-view architecture terminology. This results in the DSL model instance changing, and hence all projections of the DSL model instance update consistently. This principle is also suited for collaborative modeling since it is irrelevant whether the projections are to a single DSL user or to multiple DSL users. Such projections may concern different syntaxes for the same DSL model instance. Note that *blended collaborative domain-specific modeling* as described here requires the one DSL model instance to be (simultaneously) accessible for all involved DSL users.

itemis is experimenting with generating all that is needed to support blended collaborative domain-specific modeling based on a DSL model defined in the IDE that comes with MPS [1]. Figure 18 shows a high-level overview of *itemis'* initiative called *Modelix* [15]. It relies on the DSL model instance being accessible on a central server. Based on a plugin, the DSL model instance can be accessed with the existing IDE of MPS. The DSL model instance can, at the same time, also be accessed via a web-based front-end in a DSL user's web browser. The idea is that execution of DSL facilities such as model transformations and code generation runs on the server.

itemis' Modelix approach shown in Fig. 18 has the major benefit that existing DSL models defined with MPS like those highlighted in previous sections can

---

[7]The work described in this section is partially supported by ITEA3 project 18006 BUMBLE.

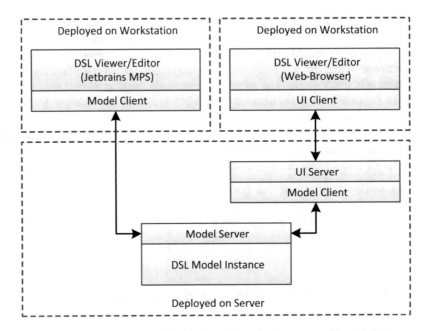

Fig. 18 A model-view architecture for blended collaborative domain-specific modeling

be used in a blended collaborative way without restarting their development in a different technology such as Javascript. In addition, the existing IDE can still be used by DSL users that are already familiar with it as it integrates seamlessly. Based on these advantages, Canon Production Printing intends to use *itemis'* technology to extend the applicability of DSL technology throughout a larger part of the organization.

7.2 DSL Widgets in Custom GUIs

Next to the Graphical User Interfaces (GUIs) made available to print professionals (customers of Canon Production Printing) as part of the Professional Digital Printer product families, several tools to develop and maintain these product families are also being created for use within Canon Production Printing. Application of DSL technology to formalize the domain-specific knowledge underlying both such Graphical User Interfaces has major benefits. However, existing DSL technology does not (yet) provide the customization flexibility that traditional software technology provides to develop GUIs. With the introduction of *itemis'* Modelix, Canon Production Printing envisions the use of Modelix to create DSL widgets as part of traditional GUIs applications realized with traditional web technology such as Google's Angular [11].

MPS and Angular use a similar component-based approach to compose complex views on a collection of related data items from simple views on individual data items. On the other hand, the concepts underlying a model-view architecture can be realized fairly easily in Angular. In the Angular context, the controller concept of a model-view architecture, which is responsible for converting (raw) data into a form that can be displayed to users via a view, is often denoted as *ViewModel*. Given the similarities, Canon Production Printing envisions that Angular applications can be partly DSLified with Modelix-based components, bringing together the strengths of MPS's DSL technology and the customization flexibility of Angular.

7.3 *Outlook for Collaborative Modeling*

Canon Production Printing intends to investigate how the combination of Modelix and Angular can serve the creation of blended collaborative domain-specific modeling as part of (possibly existing) larger GUI applications with domain-specific customization and look-and-feel. This future direction is expected to vastly increase adoption of MPS's DSL technology at Canon Production Printing.

8 Conclusions and Lessons Learned

Engineers can spend countless hours discussing a design aspect of a printer system, both within and across engineering disciplines. It is hard to overestimate the time spent on discussing printer-specific details while (sometimes unconsciously) speaking different languages to explain such details to each other. Commodity tools used for capturing printer-specific knowledge in models do not necessarily allow for domain-specific customization. Hence, when sharing knowledge, engineers still spend a lot of time on interpreting the models in such tools. At Canon Production Printing, technology for domain-specific languages has proven to provide a suitable means to bridge this domain-specific interpretation gap between models in commodity tools.

Moving to a model-based way-of-working is mostly a no-brainer at Canon Production Printing. However, choosing MPS as core technology to bridge domain-specific interpretation gaps certainly is not. It is also not straightforward to introduce it as core technology for formalizing printer knowledge to enable automated processing. As highlighted in previous sections, the main challenges with MPS have been as follows:

- *Steep learning curve* of MPS, both for DSL engineers and DSL users: The projectional editing experience is unlike any commodity tool, which therefore requires adapting to a different way of user interaction. In addition, the vast amount of already available languages and their interrelations is challenging to overview. These foundations are, however, key to the strengths of MPS. They enable language modularity and seamless editing of different views with one and the same underlying model. We believe that the direction of *itemis'* Modelix can substantially reduce the steepness of the learning curve for DSL users.

- *Lack of full-fledged DSL models in MPS for commodity languages* such as C++, C# and VHDL: As exemplified in Sects. 4 and 5, such languages are generation targets from specification models at Canon Production Printing. Instead of being able to exploit model-to-model transformations to full-fledged DSL models that rely on fully engineered model-to-text transformations in a final code generation step, we resorted to creating our own model-to-text transformations. This approach hampers maintainability, also in view of remaining compatibility with libraries for such target languages. Hence, we intend to exploit future DSL model solutions that the (open-source) MPS community may develop.
- *Existing parsers or grammar rules* commonly available in alternative technologies *are not immediately reusable* in MPS. Integrating existing textual languages, for example, tends to require more effort than just integrating an existing parser technology. We believe that extending MPS with a means to also allow traditional text-based parsing would ease adoption considerably.
- We experienced that *the performance* of (chains of) (model-to-model) transformations *can be undesirably low*. This is, however, not only experienced for MPS but also for alternative DSL technologies, including Eclipse Xtext/Sirius.

Despite the above, more and more people within Canon Production Printing are taking up the challenge to learn MPS or will be empowered by user-friendly interfaces toward a consistent and coherent set of domain-specific models (e.g., by exploiting *itemis'* Modelix). The key advantage over other DSL technologies to pursue this direction are the architectural foundations of MPS easing supporting (1) multiple syntaxes (views) for a DSL model (including having one source of information) and (2) composability or modularity of DSL models (including the availability of meta-languages like KernelF). This enables DSL engineers to focus on the DSL model itself instead of on resolving low-level, often tool-related, challenges that tend to arise in other DSL technologies. DSL users benefit primarily from the ease of using multiple syntaxes and of course the well-known general benefits of using DSL technology (e.g., the early while-you-type validation and auto-completion facilities).

References

1. Birken, K.: MPS Applications in the Browser: Cloud MPS (2020). https://blogs.itemis.com/en/mps-applications-in-the-browser-cloud-mps
2. Bosch, J.: Design and Use of Software Architectures: Adopting and Evolving a Product-Line Approach. ACM Press/Addison-Wesley, New York (2000)
3. Bunte, O., Willemse, T.A.C., van Gool, L.C.M.: Formal Verification of OIL Component Specifications using mCRL2 (2020)

4. Delft University of Technology: Spoofax. https://www.metaborg.org
5. Denkers, J., van Gool, L., Visser, E.: Migrating custom DSL implementations to a language workbench (tool demo). In: Proceedings of the 11th ACM SIGPLAN International Conference on Software Language Engineering (SLE), pp. 205–209 (2018)
6. Donzé, A., Maler, O.: Robust satisfaction of temporal logic over real-valued signals. In: Formal Modeling and Analysis of Timed Systems, pp. 92–106. Springer, Berlin (2010)
7. Donzé, A., Ferrere, T., Maler, O.: Efficient robust monitoring for STL. In: International Conference on Computer Aided Verification, pp. 264–279. Springer, Berlin (2013)
8. DSLFoundry: PlainTextGen. https://jetbrains.github.io/MPS-extensions/extensions/plaintext-gen/
9. Eindhoven University of Technology: mCRL2. https://www.mcrl2.org
10. Frenken, M.: Code Generation and Model-Based Testing in Context of OIL (2019)
11. Google: An Application Design Framework and Development Platform for Creating Efficient and Sophisticated Single-Page Web-Apps (2010–2020). https://angular.io
12. Heemels, W., Muller, G.: Boderc: Model-Based Design of High-Tech Systems; A Collaborative Research Project for Multi-Disciplinary Design Analysis of High-Tech Systems. Embedded Systems Institute (2006)
13. IBM: Rational Software Architect Real-Time Edition. https://www.ibm.com
14. itemis et al.: IETS3. https://github.com/IETS3
15. Lißon, S.: A Next Generation Language Workbench Native to the Web and Cloud (2020). https://github.com/modelix/modelix
16. Metzger, A., Pohl, K.: Software product line engineering and variability management: achievements and challenges. In: Future of Software Engineering Proceedings, pp. 70–84 (2014)
17. Pohl, K., Böckle, G., van Der Linden, F.J.: Software Product Line Engineering: Foundations, Principles and Techniques. Springer Science & Business Media, Berlin (2005)
18. van der Tempel, R., van Pinxten, J., Geilen, M., Waqas, U.: A heuristic for variable re-entrant scheduling problems. No. 2 in ES reports. Technische Universiteit Eindhoven (2018)
19. van Pinxten, J., Waqas, U., Geilen, M., Basten, A., Somers, L.: Online Scheduling of 2-re-entrant flexible manufacturing systems. ACM Trans. Embed. Comput. Syst. **16**(5s) (2017). https://doi.org/10.1145/3126551
20. Völter, M.: Kernelf: An Embeddable and Extensible Functional Language (2017). http://voelter.de/data/pub/kernelf-reference.pdf
21. Waqas, U., Geilen, M., Kandelaars, J., Somers, L., Basten, T., Stuijk, S., Vestjens, P., Corporaal, H.: A re-entrant flowshop heuristic for online scheduling of the paper path in a large-scale printer. In: Proceedings of the Conference on Design, Automation and Test in Europe (DATE 15), 9–13 March 2015, Grenoble, France, pp. 573–578 (2015)
22. Wijshoff, H.: The dynamics of the piezo inkjet printhead operation. Phys. Rep. **491**(4–5), 77–177 (2010)
23. Wijshoff, H.: Drop dynamics in the inkjet printing process. Curr. Opin. Colloid Interface Sci. **36**, 20–27 (2018)

A Domain-Specific Language for Payroll Calculations: An Experience Report from DATEV

Markus Voelter, Sergej Koščejev, Marcel Riedel, Anna Deitsch, and Andreas Hinkelmann

Abstract We review our experience developing a domain-specific language at DATEV, a large payroll service provider. The language enables business programmers to efficiently implement, test, and validate payroll calculations independent of downstream deployment considerations. It is fundamentally functional and addresses core domain challenges such as versioning of calculation rules and data and the processing of temporal data. We evaluate the language regarding reduction of complexity in payroll programs, the impact on quality, its suitability for use by domain experts, as well as the integration into the IT infrastructure. The chapter concludes with general learnings about building business DSLs.

Keywords Business DSLs · Domain-specific languages · End user programming · Case study · JetBrains MPS

1 Introduction

Over the last 3 years, DATEV, a leading German payroll services provider, has been developing a domain-specific language (DSL) for expressing the calculation logic at the core of their payroll systems. The goal is to allow business programmers to express and test the calculations and their evolution over time in a way that is completely independent of the technical infrastructure that is used to execute them in the data center. Business programmers are people who are experts in the intricacies of the payroll domain and its governing laws and regulations (LaR), but not in software development. This leads to interesting trade-offs in the design of the DSL. The specific set of challenges that motivated the development of

M. Voelter (✉) · S. Koščejev
Independent/itemis, Lünen, Germany
e-mail: voelter@acm.org; sergej@koscejev.cz

M. Riedel · A. Deitsch · A. Hinkelmann
DATEV e.G., Nuremberg, Germany
e-mail: marcel.riedel@datev.de; anna.deitsch@datev.de; andreas.hinkelmann@datev.de

© The Author(s), under exclusive license to Springer Nature Switzerland AG 2021
A. Bucchiarone et al. (eds.), *Domain-Specific Languages in Practice*,
https://doi.org/10.1007/978-3-030-73758-0_4

the DSL is given in Sect. 3.2. Payroll might seem dull and not too complicated ("just a bunch of decisions and some math"). However, the need to work on data that changes over time, to follow the evolution of the LaR, and to keep the language understandable for non-expert programmers makes it interesting from a language design perspective. The need for execution independent of the deployment infrastructure in the data center and on other devices plus the required flexibility in terms of service granularity and packaging into user-facing applications add interesting non-functional challenges.

In this chapter we evaluate the development of a real-world, non-trivial DSL targeted at business programmers. We describe the language and tool support in Sect. 5. The specific research questions we address are given in Sec. 4.1, and we answer them in Sect. 6. We also list general learnings from this language development project in Sect. 7 and briefly discuss validity (Sect. 8) of our experience report as a case study. We end the chapter with related work in Sect. 9 and a conclusion (Sect. 10).

2 Terminology

Business Programmers Business programmers understand the (payroll) domain very well but have no formal computer science training. They do not necessarily have a thorough understanding of advanced computer science concepts, such as polymorphism, inheritance, separation of concerns, or interface vs. implementation. Nor do they aspire to: they consider themselves experts in the business domain, not in software engineering. They are more than analysts though, because they use (domain-specific) languages to develop a formal, executable representation of the business logic in the domain, and not just (more or less) informal requirements documents.

Domain-Specific Languages We assume that the reader is familiar with domain-specific languages and their productivity benefits (if not, check out [5, 6, 18, 22–24, 26, 27, 46, 49]). Many DSLs are built for developers; several examples are given by van Deursen et al. in [40]. DSLs targeted at domain experts and business programmers are less common and less well documented. This is probably because they are targeted at narrower domains and often considered non-publishable intellectual property, so the companies that use them successfully consider them as a competitive advantage. The language discussed in this chapter is one of these. We discuss others in Sect. 9.

Modeling vs. Programming The style of DSLs described in this chapter can best be seen as a mix between modeling and programming. This is why we use the terms *model* and *program* interchangeably. From modeling we borrow high-level domain-specific concepts, while we also use low-level, more generic expressions (e.g., for arithmetics, comparisons, or decisions) that are traditionally associated with programming. We also mix tabular and diagrammatic notations (modeling) with textual syntax (programming). Finally, we rely on non-trivial type systems, another feature that is not typically associated with modeling. See [43] for a more detailed discussion of this perspective.

3 Context

3.1 Business Context

DATEV is one of Germany's largest software companies and IT service providers with over 8000 employees and a yearly revenue of more than 1.1 billion EUR. As Germany's leading provider of payroll services for small- and medium-sized businesses, DATEV's software and services process more than 13 million payroll slips each month.

DATEV has been developing payroll applications for decades; traditionally the applications ran on a Windows PC, accessing data stored centrally in a data center; we describe some details in Sect. 3.3. Recently, DATEV has decided to make the application available as a web service, shifting the business logic into the data center and using the browser as the UI. Because the existing implementation cannot be retargeted easily, this decision prompted a rewrite of the whole system.

3.2 Business Challenges

In addition to bringing the payroll system to the cloud, the overall goal is to increase development efficiency (the effort to implement new features, the effort to maintain the software, and the time to market) in order to keep up with business needs and the market. More specifically, DATEV faces the following business-critical challenges:

C1 **Externally Driven Evolution** Every year, changes in the applicable laws and regulations prompt changes to calculations and data structures. Keeping track of these versions reliably is key for business success: versions for previous years remain valid and must remain executable to reproduce old payroll calculations; avoiding duplication of unchanged code sections and the ability to reliably identify and then remove now unnecessary code is important to keep maintenance efforts low.

C2 **Business Agility** The current payroll application is general purpose: it comes with forms that allow users to enter *all* the data required by the LaR. Several simpler, more use case-specific applications exist as well, with *separate* implementations of (parts of) the same business logic. As DATEV expects an increasing variety of such applications in the future, it becomes crucial that the core calculation logic can be reused (and modularly extended) in new contexts, giving more flexibility to DATEV as to how to make their core assets available to the market. Several of these applications require that calculations are precise to the day instead of using the month as the smallest distinguishable unit of time; the current infrastructure cannot provide this granularity.

C3 **Deployment Flexibility** DATEV expects technology changes to be more frequent in the future. By default, calculations will run as a set of microservices in the data center, implemented in Java. In addition, parts will also have to be run in the browser for quick validation and to improve UX, which requires an implementation in JavaScript. And some of the new use case-specific applications mentioned in **C2** might be implemented in Swift, for execution on iOS.

3.3 The Legacy System

The original, to-be-replaced system, which has been in use for 20+ years, consists of 25,000 data field definitions and 2.5 million lines of COBOL code. Some of that code is generated from a declarative specification that describes how to load and prepare the data necessary for each calculation. In particular, it describes how to handle the temporal changes of the data, because in the calculation itself, the data is pre-aggregated per month. So if, for example, an employee's salary changes from 5000 to 6000 EUR in the middle of a month, the calculation code sees only one number, in this case the latter one. This is a fundamental limitation of the legacy system that must be removed with the new system; we referred to this as "calculations must be precise to the day" above. The implementation of the business logic comprises around 200,000 of the 2.5 million LoC and is expressed using a restricted, easier-to-understand subset of COBOL that relies mostly on MOVE, COMPUTE, IF...ELSE, and DO...UNTIL, plus the aforementioned specifications for data loading. The specification is around ten times less code than the "expanded" COBOL.

Throughout this chapter, and in particular in Sect. 5 where we describe the new DSL, we compare to the old system in paragraphs labeled with **LEGACY**.

3.4 Why a DSL

In 2017 DATEV started developing a Java prototype for the new system based on Java EE technology. However, this prototype focused on the calculation logic and the deployment into microservices; it did not convincingly address the core challenges of the domain given in Sect. 3.2. As a consequence, and influenced by DATEV's history with code generators and DSLs (such as the COBOL specifications mentioned above), DATEV management commissioned a prototype DSL as a potentially more efficient path. 22 days were spent on the DSL prototype by itemis. It successfully demonstrated that the key complexity drivers, temporal data, precision to the day, and versioning (see Sect. 5) can be significantly simplified using a DSL; this result prompted the development of the full DSL.

3.5 Language Development

Tools The DSL is implemented with the JetBrains MPS language workbench[1] and makes use of utilities from the MPS Extensions repository[2] and the mbeddr.platform.[3] The language is based on KernelF [42], a functional programming language implemented in MPS for the express purpose of being embedded in (and extended for) DSLs. All ingredients—except the final payroll DSL—are open-source software.

Scope In order to manage the overall risk and organizational impact, the DSL's scope was limited to the core domain logic; in particular, the automation of the integration with the execution infrastructure (beyond the generation of Java code that implements the business logic) was out of scope. However, this decision will likely be revisited in the future, because some related artifacts (such as service interfaces or database schemas) are closely related to the structure of the calculations described with the DSL and could presumably be generated easily.

Size of the Language The overall solution for DATEV is split up into several MPS-level languages, some of them reused from KernelF. Table 1 shows the sizes of these languages. The total of ca. 282 custom language concepts[4] (402 minus those reused from KernelF) makes it a typical DSL in our experience. For example, the PLUTO language described in [49] is in the same ballpark. Our style of language design [43] leads to a relatively large number of first-class concepts.

Effort During the initial development period, four developers, one product owner, and a scrum master were involved from DATEV. itemis supplied three language engineers. In total, we spent around 3 person-years for analysis, discussions, language design, development and testing of the languages, interpreter, generators and IDE, knowledge transfer on MPS from itemis to DATEV, as well as project management. The overall effort of the project (analysis, processes, deployment, management) was more than one order of magnitude larger than this—so building a DSL was not perceived as an outlandish investment (but did require persuasion, because the investment would amortize only over time).

---

[1] https://www.jetbrains.com/mps/.

[2] https://github.com/JetBrains/MPS-extensions.

[3] https://github.com/mbeddr/mbeddr.core.

[4] A concept in MPS is similar to a metaclass in MOF/EMF or a non-terminal in grammar-based systems.

Table 1 Size of the languages developed for DATEV

Kind	Language	# of concepts
DATEV proprietary	`payroll.dsl.core`	166
	`payroll.dsl.test`	32
	`payroll.dsl.institution`	26
	`payroll.dsl.migration`	7
Developed for DATEV	`kernelf.datetime`	27
and then open sourced	`kernelf.temporal`	24
Use as is from KernelF	KernelF	120
	Total	**402**

Process We used scrum with 2-week sprints. Code was maintained in Git, issues were tracked in GitLab. The DATEV and itemis teams worked at separate locations but met regularly every few weeks.

3.6 System Architecture

The DATEV IT organization has a clear architecture strategy for new applications. They rely on microservices, each with a well-defined business context, developed by applying the domain-driven design [14] practices to focus on the domain logic while keeping deployment as simple as possible. To ease operations in DATEV's data center, applications are required to choose from selected technology stacks. The new payroll application is built on Java within the Spring Cloud ecosystem hosted on a Cloud Foundry Platform-as-a-Service (PaaS) environment. We discuss the details of the architecture and the consequences for the DSL in Sect. 6.4. As we have said before, we do not generate infrastructure integration code from the DSL to limit the scope; we generate Java classes which are then manually integrated into services.

3.7 Current Status of the System

The first production use of the DSL was in late 2018, as part of a simple online payroll calculation tool: this is one of the aforementioned new apps that packages parts of the overall calculation logic into a use case-specific application. Twenty business areas (such as wage tax, social insurance, and church tax) have been implemented for 2 years (2018 and 2019), making use of key language features such as temporal data and versioning.

As of early 2020, all microservices that make up the evolving software-as-a-service payroll application have their core calculation logic generated from DSL models.

Five business programmers currently use the DSL productively, supported by the language development team. Over time, as the legacy application is rewritten step by step, dozens of business programmers are expected to work with the language routinely.

The language continues to evolve to reflect the changing requirements, typically, a new language version is released to the end users every 14 days, based on 14-day scrum sprints.

Today, development is done mostly in-house at DATEV with occasional support by itemis, especially if and when extensions or fixes of KernelF are required, or when special skills regarding internals of MPS are needed.

4   Case Study Setup

4.1   Research Questions

Experts in any domain typically point out how complex their domain is; the payroll domain is no exception. The authors hypothesize that much of this perceived complexity is accidental because of a language that is unsuitable to the domain or is induced by too much dependency on the implementation technology: if the right abstractions were used, most of this accidental complexity would vanish, revealing the core of the domain to be much simpler. Our metric for the total complexity (essential + accidental) in this context is the size of programs as well as the amount of work/time required to make typical evolutionary changes to programs; if we can reduce this metric while still solving the domain problem, we have successfully reduced accidental complexity. This leads us to the first research question:

RQ1 Is a Suitably Designed DSL Able to Significantly Reduce the Perceived Complexity in the Payroll Domain?

The alignment of the DSL with the domain, improved analyzability and tool support, plus the reduced (accidental) complexity of the business logic, should make the models easier to test and validate than code, reducing the potential for errors. The automation through code generation should reduce low-level coding errors. On the other hand, using a DSL introduces additional components into the developer tool chain that could introduce bugs: language workbenches, language definitions, interpreters, and generators.

RQ2 Does the Use of DSLs and the Associated Tools Increase or Decrease the Quality of the Final Product?

Key to increasing flexibility and speed as described in **C1** and **C2** is to empower the business programmers to express and validate executable versions of the LaR that govern payroll calculation. Once the tests written by the business programmer are green (and assuming they have enough coverage, which we measure), no downstream engineer will ever have to look at the domain logic expressed by business programmers to ensure the business logic is correct.[5]

However, for the quality assurance based on tests written by the business programmers to work, the business programmers have to understand the (semantics of the) DSL. This is perceived as a challenge because, in the experience of many engineers, DATEV's business programmers have to learn using abstractions: they prefer small-step, imperative programs. Instead of

```
var entitled = listOfBusinessTrips.distance.sum > 3000
```

they prefer to write

```
var entitled = false
var tripSum  = 0
foreach t in listOfBusinessTrips
   tripSum += t.distance
end
if tripSum > 3000
   entitled = true
end
```

because it is "easier to understand." Clearly, if the very minor step of abstraction involved in the first alternative is "too much," then a DSL with even higher-level abstraction is a challenging proposition.

RQ3 Can a DSL that Reduces Complexity be Taught to the Business Programmers with an Effort that Is Acceptable to Them?

The code generated from models has to exist in the context of a data center architecture and other deployment platforms in the future (C3 and Sect. 3.6). Building, testing, and packaging the models and the generated code have to fit with the development processes and technology stacks used for the data center and must also be future-proof.

RQ4 How Well Does the DSL and Its Use for Application Development Fit with Established IT Development Processes and System Architecture?

In this chapter we do not analyze the effort of building the language because we have shown in previous papers [46, 49] that the effort for language development based on MPS is in the same ballpark as the development of many other software artifacts and can be carried by development projects; the efforts for the current project were comparable.

---

[5]Of course they look at the code as part of their maintenance of generators, libraries, and frameworks, but not for routine domain development work.

4.2   Data Collected

For this case study, we collected numbers and statistics from the code base at the time of writing. We revisited the commit history and the issues in our bug tracker to remind us about the evolution of the languages. The personal recollections of the development team were an additional input.

5   The Language and Tooling

In this section we describe the core features of the DSL.[6] These features have been designed to reduce the complexity of the programs to the essential core of the domain (RQ1) and to reduce the risk of particular kinds of errors (RQ2), while at the same time being accessible to business programmers (RQ3) and keeping the models independent of a particular execution paradigm or target platform (RQ4); in the rest of this section, we do not highlight this connection for each specific feature.

5.1   A Functional Language

The language is functional: values are immutable and variables are assigned exactly once. The individual calculations are small. This fits well with a domain that is heavy in calculations and decisions, programs are easy to analyze, and it allows us to reuse many low-level non-DSL component that orchestrates calculations (decide what to calculate in which order) and handles state (supply data and context). Figure 1 illustrates this structure.

LEGACY   The COBOL system was imperative (making local analysis harder), allowing read-and-write access to a catalog of global data from everywhere. Understanding which data was modified where was hard, and the execution order was fixed.■

An additional drawback of the functional approach is that it was not easy to teach it to the business programmers, especially treating values as immutable and assign-once semantics for local variables. The challenge was particularly pronounced for those who have extensive experience in the old COBOL system, a fully imperative world.

---

[6]The language uses German keywords; in the screenshots, we have translated them to English to ease understanding.

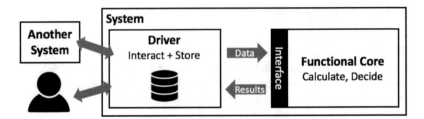

Fig. 1 Overall architecture of the calculations and the driver

5.2 Execution

A continuous integration (CI) pipelines generates the DSL programs (and all tests) to Java code, packages it, stores it in a Maven repository for deployment, and also runs all tests. End users never invoke this generator; they work with an interpreter that is directly integrated into the IDE (see Fig. 6).

5.3 High-Level Structure

DATEV's payroll domain comprises several dozen business areas such as `tax`, `health insurance`, or `company car`. The DSL uses these as its top-level structure. Business areas then contain `versions` (see Sect. 5.9), and versions contain `modules` (think of them as files), which in turn contain the declarations for types, data structures, and calculations.

5.4 Domain Data Types

In addition to the usual primitive types, the language supports dates, currency, and percentages as built-in types, in terms of syntax, type system, operators, and IDE support.

```
val taxRate   : %%%  = 20%              // type explicitly given
val minIncome : EUR  = 2000 EUR
val minTax           = 200 EUR          // type inferred
val deadline         = /2019 01 01/

fun calcTax(income: EUR, d: date)
  = if d > deadline                     // compare dates
      then if income > minIncome        // compare currency
            then (taxRate of income)    // work with percentages
            else minTax + 10 EUR        // calculate with currency
        else 0 EUR
```

Users can define record-like data that serves as input and results for calculations (see data and result in Fig. 3).

LEGACY Data was defined in a GUI tool called Datenkatalog; COBOL structures were generated from these definitions. A changing requirement for the business logic required coordinated changes in the Datenkatalog, in the COBOL code, and in the user-facing Windows UI, which made implementing straightforward requirements cumbersome and error-prone.■

5.5 Tables

The calculations in our domain are characterized by lots of special cases that are the result of years of (not always systematic) evolution of the LaR. Capturing these concisely is infeasible with the if-then-else or switch-case constructs commonly found in general-purpose languages. Instead we have developed various forms of decision tables (Fig. 2).

LEGACY The requirements documents created from analyzing the law already contains decision tables. However, there was no direct way to represent them in the COBOL sources.■

5.6 Temporal Data

Most data changes over time: employment contracts begin and end, salaries vary, and a person's marital status changes. The language has types for temporally evolving data, and the operators (+, -, *, /, &&, ||, >, >=, <, <=, ==, !=) are overridden to work as expected but returning temporal values as well (see Fig. 4). There is also support for reducing a temporal type TT<U> to a value of type U, for example, by selecting the last value in a month or by computing a monthly weighted average.

```
fun base(area: GerPart, gross: EUR, spec: boolean)
```

area	gross	spec	base: EUR	rebate: %%
EAST		true	bbgRvEast	20%
EAST	> bbgRvEast	false	bbgRvEast	10%
WEST	> bbgRvWest		bbgRvWest	0%
			gross	0%

Fig. 2 A decision table in a function. Decision tables have one or more columns to match (here: columns 1 through 3) and return one or more values (4th and 5th column). Note the use of "abbreviated expressions" for comparison (2nd column) and the implicit equality comparison (columns 1 and 3). They are executed top-down in order to allow a special case to preempt a more general one

```
data EmployeeData [EM] {
  religion : TT<religion> reduce LAST
}

data EmploymentRel [EM] {
  salary   : TT<EUR> reduce WEIGHTED
  endDate  : date
}

result [monthly] TaxReport [EM] {
  salaryInMonth   : EUR
  incomeTax       : EUR
  relTax          : EUR
} where [ incomeTax + relTax < salaryInMonth ]
```

```
calculation for TaxReport
  depends emp : EmployeeData
          rel : EmploymentRel
    where rel.endDate >= increment.begin
as [monthly] {
  salaryInThatMonth := rel.salary@
  incomeTax := salaryInMonth * INCOME_RATE
  val mustpay = emp.religion@.isIn(cath, prot)
  relTax := alt [ mustpay   => rel.salary@ * REL_RATE ]
               [ otherwise => 0€                      ]
}
```

Fig. 3 Data definitions, results, and calculation rules. EmployeeData is a data structure that is indexed with the built-in domain entity EM (short for employee). It has one attribute whose type is a temporal type whose default reduction rule is to use the last value a given period. EmploymentRelationship is similar, but the salary of an employment, when reduced to a simple value, is weighted over the period. TaxReport is a result data structure, which means it is calculated by a rule. That rule is shown next, its signature expressing that it consumes the two data entries and produces the TaxReport. The rule is tagged monthly, which means that during execution, there's an implicit context parameter, referred to by increment, that is of type month. When the default reduction operator @ is invoked on a temporal value, it is this month that is used as the period within which the default reduction is applied

Consider the following example. The function takes two temporal values salary and religiousAffil; "temporal" means that each argument represents a value that varies over time. In the first line, the function reduces this temporal value to a primitive value of type EUR by grabbing the last entry in the month m in the time series represented by TT<religion>. It then checks if that value is catholic or protestant. If so, it computes the weighted average of the salary within m.

```
fun churchTax(salary: TT<EUR>, religiousAffil: TT<religion>, m: month) =
  // last religious affiliation reported in any month m is relevant
  if religiousAffil.reduce(LAST in m).isIn(catholic, protestant)
    // use weighted average salary in that month
    then salary.reduce(WEIGHTED in m) * 0.15
    else 0 EUR
```

Some language constructs, such as calculation rules, define an implicit temporal context (typically the month for which a result is calculated; see Fig. 3). At such program locations, the @ shortcut invokes the default reduction that is declared for the data (see the datas in Fig. 3). Temporal data, and the shortcut syntax in calculation rules, are a major enabler for the day-specific calculations mentioned as part of C2 (Fig. 4).

LEGACY All temporal aspects were handled in the generated data access layer. The smallest granularity of data was "one number per month"; a day-granular treatment of data, as described above, was not supported. ∎

A Second Dimension of Time At its core, the system is bitemporal [21]: the first temporal dimension D_1 captures the points in time where values change; it is represented by the TT types discussed above. A second dimension D_2 represents the point in time from which we look at the data. For example, in May 2019 (D_2), a user enters that on April 1 2019 (D_1) the salary changes to 6000 EUR. However,

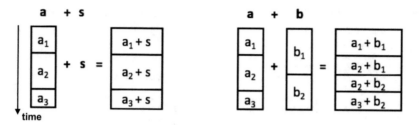

Fig. 4 Adding a scalar s to a temporal value a means that the s is added to each of the slices. Adding two temporal values a and b "reslices" the result and adds the components. Similar for other arithmetic operators

in June (D_2), this is corrected to 5500 EUR. So, depending on whether we look at the data from May or June (D_2), the salary changes on April 1 (D_1) to 6000 or 5500 EUR. To keep complexity under control, we have decided that D2 will be handled outside the language, as part of the driver application that runs the calculation and supplies the data. We do not cover the driver or D_2 in the chapter.

5.7 Indexing

Many data items are indexed with a particular employee or client. Similarly, lots of data is time-indexed. Indexing means that they are implicitly associated with one or more keys such as the employee or month. The DSL provides direct support for indexing; for example, in Fig. 3, TaxReport is indexed with the built-in abstraction employee ([EM]) and time-indexed ([monthly]). This means that each employee in the system has one instance of TaxReport per month.

In the calculation rule (right part of Fig. 3), the created TaxReport is automatically associated with the current month and the context employee, both implicitly provided by the driver application. Together with the @-notation that invokes the default reduction, this makes for a notably compact syntax.

Understanding the difference between temporal data (a *continuous* value that changes at arbitrary points in time) and time-indexed data (exactly one instance *per* month or year) was a major conceptual breakthrough during the development of the language.

5.8 Declarative Dependencies

Calculations specify the input data and upstream results they depend on (see the depends clause in Fig. 3). For indexed data, the dependency implicitly refers to data with the same indexes (in Fig. 3, the current month and employee). It is also

possible to "navigate" time explicitly by using special operators (such as –1or
allInCurYear) in square brackets; these unify simple dependencies with temporal
aggregation.

```
calculation for TaxStatistics
  depends thisMth : TaxReport              // TaxReport from this month (
    implicit)
          lastMth : TaxReport[-1]          // TaxReport from last month
          rest    : TaxReport[allInCurYear] // list of reports
as [monthly] { ... }                       // from all prev. months
```

LEGACY Dependencies were indirect by accessing the same global data. While analysis tools
could extract business area dependencies through analysis of global data access, this required a
separate tool and was cumbersome. Unintended dependencies resulted.■

5.9 Versioning

The versioning described in the remainder of this section covers the domain-related
evolution of the models, mostly driven by changing LaR. However, currently, during
development, much of the evolution of the code for a business area is driven by
changing technical requirements and the increase of domain coverage, where, for
example, a data structure now has additional attributes because the business area
covers additional special cases (e.g., the wage tax for people who are both employed
and have a freelance side business). This often leads to breaking changes in the data
structures and the need for downstream business areas to adapt. To manage these
changes, all our models are of course versioned in Git. To coordinate semantically
dependent changes, we use organizational mechanisms (discussing and planning
changes with all involved business areas) supported by the IDE, for example, by
highlighting those data structures that are in fact shared by different business areas.

Domain-Related Versioning Challenge C1 states that programs must evolve with
the LaR, but previous models and their tests must remain valid to reproduce old payroll calculations. Using the version control system to represent this evolution does
not work because several versions would have to be checked out simultaneously.
Instead, the DSL supports the notion of a versionof a business area. A version
specifies the date at which it becomes valid.

Version Kinds Ideally, the code written for the various business areas can evolve
independently from others. While internal changes to calculations do not affect other
business areas, interface changes requires coordination. To make this explicit, the
language supports two kinds of versions that are distinguished by how they differ
from its predecessor: a calculationversion may change parameter values and the
logic inside calculations. And an interfaceversion differs in the structure of
the data that is exchanged with other business areas.

The kinds also govern how new versions affect the versions of downstream
business areas and the requirement for redeploying generated code. A

`calculation`version requires regeneration and redeployment because the code that performs the calculation of the result changes. However, since the data structures (which act as the interface between business areas) remain stable, downstream business areas are unaffected, structurally, and no redeployment is required. In addition, since calculations depend on data and not on the particular rule that computes it (e.g., the dependency on `TaxReport`above), calculations that span different `calculation`versions are automatically dispatched; we explain how this works below.

An `interface`version is more invasive. The new version can completely remove a data or result entity and optionally declare a new one that (semantically) replaces the deleted one. Downstream business areas then have to create a new version as well to make use of this new data structure. Alternatively, entities can also evolve. For one, new members can be added; in addition existing members can be deleted. A deleted member can no longer be accessed in the new version, but it is retained in the physical data structures that serve as the technical interface to external clients in order to retain backward compatibility. Renaming or changing the type is not supported, because the impact would be harder to track, both for the tool and also for humans.

Note that the IDE knows about these versions and their start dates: code completion and type checking will exploit the information statically to provide version-aware IDE support.

Inter-version Reuse A new version inherits all contents (parameters, data structures, calculation rules) from its predecessor; the new version can then selectively override. Parameters replace similarly named parameters; a parameter can also be deprecated, which means that it cannot be used in the new (and even newer) versions. For `data`and `result`structures, the new version can choose whether to add fields to or remove fields from the old one, as we have explained above.

To understand the automatic dispatch of rule invocations for a version, let's consider the following example. It shows three successive versions of some business area, with several rules for a particular result data structure `Res`.

```
version 1 (from 2018)        version 2 (from 2019)              version 3 (from 2020)
-----------------------      ---------------------------
        -------------------------------
add r1(Res, c1)  {...}       change r1(Res, c1) {...}
add r2(Res, c2)  {...}
        {...}                                                   change r2(Res, c2New)
add r3(Res, c3)  {...}       delete r3
                                                                add r4(Res, c4) {...}
add default(Res) {...}       change default(Res) {...}
```

As we have said before, the language supports several rules for the same result data structure (`Res`) as long as they have different applicability conditions (`c1`, `c2`, . . .); this can be interpreted as several functions with the same signature but different preconditions. The default rule is executed if none of the conditions of the other rules applies. Let's understand this logic by figuring out which rules apply for each year in the example above.

From the perspective of a calculation that applies to 2018, it is rather obvious, because only version 1 is visible. So v1.r1, v1.r2, v1.r3, and v1.defaultrule are candidates for execution; the decision which one actually runs is based on the conditions.

From the perspective of 2019, the effective set of rules is v2.r1(because this one has been overridden in version 2), v1.r2(it is inherited), and v2.default(also overridden). v1.r3is not available; it has been deleted in version 2.

From the perspective of 2020, the following rules are candidates for execution: v3.r4(added in version 3), v3.r2(changed in version 3), v2.default(inherited from version 2), and v2.r1(also inherited).

To aid understanding which rules are relevant for each particular point in time, the IDE shows the effective set of rules for each version. It is the task of the developer to make sure that the conditions are complete and overlap-free for each year; an integration of an SMT solver to verify this analytically has been a goal for a long time but has not yet been realized.

The exact semantics of overriding rules in successive versions took time to get right. In an earlier phase of development of the DSL, the set of rules for a given result in a version was not named. A new version did not explicitly override a discrete version; it only added another rule with a particular condition; if that condition was similar to a condition in the previous version, the rule with that condition would be effectively replaced. But conditions were also allowed to overlap partially, effectively overriding a rule only for a special case. However, this was too complex for our users to understand, especially considering the lack of SMT support. We have thus moved to the slightly less flexible but easier to understand approach described above.

Removal of Unneeded Code The LaR require DATEV to be able to reproduce payroll calculations for 5 years. As a corollary, DATEV wants to be able to remove code that is no longer needed for the versions of the preceding 5 years. Because dependencies are explicit and the type system takes versions into account, the respective analysis can be performed statically and "old" code can be removed with confidence.

LEGACY No language-level abstraction for versions was available, which led to a lot of accidental complexity. One consequence was very little systematic reuse between the code for subsequent "versions," driving up maintenance effort. Systematic detection and removal of unneeded code were not supported, which means that (presumably) dead code was still actively maintained.■

5.10   Data Validation

Before the system can make any calculations, it has to ensure that the input data is valid relative to user-defined rules. The DSL supports validation of single fields (generated to browser-side UI code), of record-style data structures, as well as validations that span multiple records. For the validation of fields and records, the lexical location for the respective validation condition is obvious: at the field and record declarations (see the where-clause on TaxReportin Fig. 3). For validations that span multiple records, it is less obvious where to write them down. We decided on the following two locations. For records that have relationships (Employment --[1..*]--> Car), the referencing record can navigate into the target as part of its own validation conditions. The other case occurs when a calculation rule uses several structurally unrelated inputs (so we cannot navigate from one to the other) but still needs to constrain the data relative to each other. In this case, the respective condition is expressed as a precondition of the particular rule (similar to the one in the where-clause of the calculation in Fig. 3).

LEGACY Data validation was mostly duplicated in the client application and the COBOL backend, synchronized manually. This was tedious and error-prone.■

5.11 Testing Support

To reach the goal of enabling business programmers to fully validate the domain logic, specific test support has been built on top of KernelF's generic support for unit tests; Fig. 5 shows an example.

Repository The repository specifies the "universe" of data upon which a set of tests are executed using a compact table notation. It contains instances of dataitems (optionally indexed) as well as instances of results. Since the execution semantics of the language is functional and incremental, the engine only calculates those results that are not in the repository; a result that is put into the repository as part of the test setup is effectively a mock for a calculation.

Checks Checks query the system for calculated data. They specify a point in time that determines the applicable version as well as the expected result (e.g., TaxReport(500 EUR, 100 EUR)). Multiple checks can be run against a single repository.

Deltas and Vectors Often, a set of checks use only slightly different repository setups. The language supports two ways of avoiding the duplication resulting from separate repositories: (1) a check can specify a delta repository that overwrites some of the data in the test-wide repository, and (2) the data in the repository as well as the queried data can contain variables (e.g., TaxReport(i, c)). Values for these variables form a test vector. A check can then specify a list of such vectors as a table and run all of them.

LEGACY Because of the sequential nature of the programs and the reliance on global data, unit testing was cumbersome and the developers relied on integration-level tests. Data was supplied through CSV files without tool-supported checking against the required input. It relied on COBOL code, so accidental complexity was higher and the turnaround time was slower.■

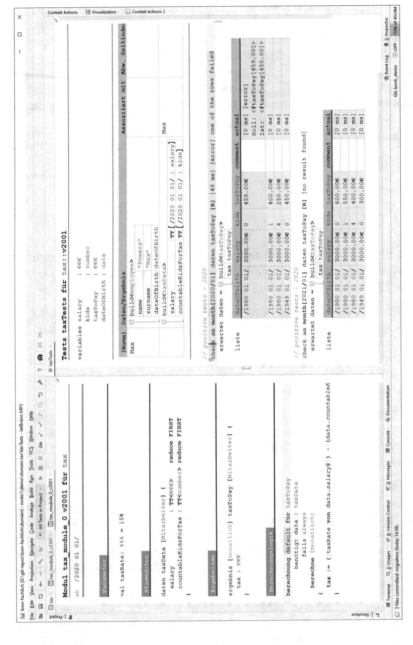

Fig. 5 A screenshot of the MPS IDE with the languages developed for DATEV. On the left you see data and rule definitions, and on the right you can see a corresponding test case

5.12 External Components

Although the system described in this chapter is a complete redevelopment, it does not live in isolation, and integration with external components is necessary. We give two examples here.

External Logic The core of the wage tax calculation in Germany is complicated. Luckily, the German Ministry of Finance provides this calculation as a specification[7] plus an associated XML file. DATEV has developed a generator that transforms this XML file to Java and packages it into a JAR file. To access it from DSL programs, we have implemented a language concept that allows to call this generated library like a built-in function to perform the calculation. This language concept also performs static-type checking, based on the type specifications in the XML. The same library is also used in the generated microservice, albeit without the DSL wrapper.

External Data To calculate the salary slip, we need access to lots of data that is not maintained in our system but provided to us as JSON files with a known schema; examples include the list of municipal tax offices and the health insurance providers in Germany. We have developed a language extension that allows us to map the JSON structures to data entities declared in models. Based on this mapping, the data is accessible from within DSL programs as if it were native to our system. The mapping exploits advanced features of our language, such as temporality, so even external data that changes over time is accessible to DSL models using the convenient native support for temporal data. And like any other data, we can mock the data in (interpreted) unit tests. Once deployed to the data center, the data is retrieved in real time via REST calls and made available to the generated implementation of the business logic. In line with the general goal of the DSL, this approach decouples the domain developer from the technical concerns while at the same time leading to minimal integration effort for the backend developer.

5.13 IDE Features

MPS provides the usual **editor support** for the DSL. Several domain-specific refactorings are available. To visualize the big picture, the **IDE** provides shortcuts for common operations, for example, to navigate to all rules for a particular result, or to the corresponding declaration in previous and future versions. For a test, the IDE shows the transitive closure of the versions of the accessed business areas applicable for the point in time specified in the test. There is a customized project view that

---

[7] https://www.bundesfinanzministerium.de/Content/DE/Downloads/Steuern /Steuerarten/Lohnsteuer/Programmablaufplan/2019-11-11-PAP-2020-anlage-1.pdf ?__blob=publicationFile&v=2.

shows the hierarchy of business areas, modules, versions, tests, and declarations. Several PlantUML[8]-based **visualizations** help illustrate relationships and highlight circular dependencies. The in-IDE **interpreter** allows users to execute tests with zero turnaround time and effort; the checks are color-coded red/green to show success or failure. Tests can also be analyzed step by step using a **tracer**; every expression execution is shown in a tree, and values of program nodes (usually expressions) can be overlaid over the program code. The infrastructure also supports the measurement of three kinds of **coverage** for a set of test cases: (1) language concepts and the relationships between them; (2) the interpreter implementation; and (3) test subject program nodes. The data is collected by the interpreter and then visualized in the IDE. Finally, various reports help understand the big picture; for example, there are reports for all validation messages used in the system. For a visual impression of IDE the see Fig. 5 and this video: https://vimeo.com/339303255.

LEGACY No meaningful IDE support is available. No coverage measurement was available, so the code was manually analyzed to design test cases in a way they would cover the code.■

6 Evaluation

6.1 RQ1 *Is a Suitably Designed DSL Able to Significantly Reduce the Perceived Complexity in the Payroll Domain?*

Comparison to the Old System Specific differences that led to accidental complexity have been pointed out in the chapter already using the **LEGACY** label. We will not repeat them here.

Three-Layer Separation A first look at the payroll domain suggests that it is mostly about complex decisions and calculations. And indeed, these are a problem worth addressing. For example, Sect. 5 shows how we use decision tables and domain-specific data types to reduce complexity and increase readability. However, most of the domain complexity comes from temporal data, dependencies between business areas, and the variability between different versions; hence most language features relate to those. Addressing these complexities directly in the language allowed us to reduce the perceived complexity significantly. At the beginning of the project, we heard statements like "this looks simple—why do we need a DSL?" from some of the engineers at DATEV. Of course it is only simple *because* of the DSL. We have seen this three-layer structure—surface logic, hidden complexities, and technical aspects—in other domains, too [45].

Debugging The ease of locating and understanding errors is a major factor for productivity and a major pain point in the **LEGACY** system. The DSL brings three

---

[8]http://plantuml.com.

improvements: (1) The execution of a calculation collects explanations and end user relevant messages that explain a potentially non-intuitive result ("The church tax rate is 9% instead of the standard 8% because the person lives in Bad Wimpfen."). (2) The tracer mentioned above that shows the complete calculation tree with values overlaid over the program. Those two approaches allow the business developer to track down errors without considering technical aspects. Case (3) is different: if a calculation succeeds in the interpreter but fails in the generated Java code, then there is either an error in the interpreter or in the generator; debugging the interpreter implementation or the generated code, together with an engineer, is necessary. But once the infrastructure is tested, this third step is rare, and most of the debugging can be done with methods 1 and 2.

Post-mortem Debugging If the calculation is correct in the interpreter but then fails in the generated Java, the error must lie in the generator, and the problem must be debugged by a technical developer. However, sometimes a corner case might occur in a real-world calculation for which no test exists, leading to a faulty result. To understand this, users can let the tracer create a test case which debugs the calculation in the IDE. Depending on how often this will occur in practice (it shouldn't, with sufficient test coverage!), we will add functionality to collect the data at runtime and automatically construct a corresponding test case.

6.2 RQ2 Does the Use of DSLs and the Associated Tools Increase or Decrease the Quality of the Final Product?

Reuse of a Mature Language Reuse is a proven means of reducing development effort and increasing quality. There is lots of research into language modularity and composition [12], and it works robustly in MPS [47]. A low-level functional language is a good candidate for reuse because most DSLs include expressions for arithmetics, comparison, and logical operations. KernelF [42] is such as language, and the payroll DSL uses it as its core. KernelF and its interpreter has been used in several other projects, and it is therefore stable and mature. In particular, its test suite achieves 100% branch coverage regarding the semantics definition in the interpreter. The payroll DSL benefited significantly; we found only one major semantic bug in KernelF and fixed a few minor issues.

Redundant Execution The duplication of execution semantics in the interpreter and the generator adds complexity, and it took some time to align the semantics of the two by ensuring all tests succeed in both environments. On the other hand, the relatively simpler interpreter acts as a kind of "executable specification" for the more complex generator. Aligning the two was simplified by the fact that both are ultimately Java, so they could share runtime classes (such as BigInteger, BigDecimal, or Date), avoiding discrepancies in small-step semantics. We are confident in the approach, because we have used it before in healthcare [49], where the redundancy was essential to the safety argument.

Generated Low-Level Code Because the mapping to the execution infrastructure is generated, it is very easy to achieve consistency in the implementation. A change in the use of the infrastructure, a bug fix, or an optimization requires only a change in the generator to update the whole code base. This approach increases agility regarding the technical aspects of the system. Of course, the generator can also be a source of errors: a mistake in the generator spreads into the code base as well. However, such errors are usually relatively easy to find, because lots of things break simultaneously. Based on our experience in this and other projects, the trade-off works: once the generator is tested reasonably well, overall stability increases, and the time to roll out improvements decreases.

Reuse of QA Infrastructure We were able to reuse the KernelF infrastructure for testing, including the ability to run interpreted tests on the CI server as well as the facilities for measuring various aspects of coverage for the language implementation.

Multi-step QA A goal of the DSL is to allow business programmers to express and test the payroll logic without caring about technical aspects (C3). To this end, we separate functional and technical concerns: models contain only business logic; the generators, runtimes, and frameworks take care of the technical aspects. Our development process (see Fig. 6) adds concerns step by step, which means that a failure diagnoses precisely where a fault lies. Step (1) concerns and tests the functional correctness. A failing test indicates an error in the business logic or in the interpreter (in early phases of the project while the interpreter is not yet mature). Step (2) translates the business logic to Java and thus concerns performance. We run the same set of tests, and if one fails, either the generator or the interpreter is faulty; likely it is the generator, because it is more complex, and the test has already been considered correct in the previous step. Step (3) adds the infrastructure to make the system scale. A failure after this step indicates a problem with frameworks or the platform.

Documentation and Communication Because the DSL programs are free of technical concerns and use domain-relevant abstractions and notations, the need for documentation (beyond comments that explain rationales) is greatly reduced. This prevents the documentation from diverging from the code. The language definition and the tests cases also serve as a formalized interface between the business programmers and the technical teams, which puts their communication and coordination efforts on a more solid foundation, reducing the risk of misunderstandings and other inefficiencies.

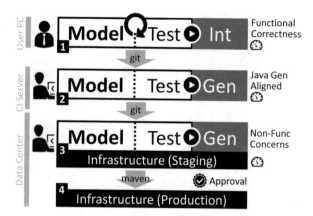

Fig. 6 The process from modeling to deployment. (1) Iteratively model the business logic, test it with the interpreter ("Int" in the figure), and measure coverage; (2) generate ("Gen") to Java on the CI server, run the same tests, and measure Java coverage; (3) embed "domain.jar" into the microservices infrastructure and run the same tests in a distributed environment; (4) after final QA and management approval, move the new version from staging to production

6.3 RQ3 Can a DSL that Reduces Complexity be Taught to Domain Experts in a Reasonable Amount of Time?

IDE Support Users wanted tool support beyond the MPS defaults. For example, they expected buttons to insert data, enumor calculationdeclarations into a (new version of a) module, intentions to selectively copy declarations inherited from a previous version into the current one for subsequent change, or menu items for creating a test case for a module. While many of these make sense because they bundle repeated multi-step changes, others were *exact* duplicates as the default code completion. For example, typing calcand then using code completion produce

```
calculation for <result>
        depends <dependencies>
as [] {
  <code>
}
```

which is what our users wanted a button to do. Once users got familiar with code completion (as opposed to buttons known from classical applications), the requests for these fine-grained UI actions subsided.

Error Checking The quality of analyses and associated error messages is important for the acceptance of the DSL with its users. We put a lot of effort into a precise wording of error messages and into making sure they are reported at the correct locations(s); many error messages come with quick fixes that automatically fix the problem when triggered by the user.

Liveness Short turnaround times help developers stay "in the flow." In addition, for people with limited experience with abstraction such as our users, it is very useful to be able to execute programs immediately and reduce the gap between the program and its execution—which is one of the motivations for live programming [29]. In our architecture, this rapid turnaround is facilitated by the in-IDE interpreter: users iteratively create models, play with them, and then write tests to verify the behavior (see (1) in Fig. 6).

The Big Picture Reuse between versions was a contested issue: a new version v4 selectively overwrites the declarations from previous versions, requiring the user to look through v1..v3 to understand the effective contents of v4. End users did not appreciate this need to mentally assemble "everything" from parts to achieve reuse. To resolve this tension, we exploit MPS' projectional editor to optionally show inherited declarations in the new version: "everything" can be seen in one place, optionally. In addition, we integrated automatically rendered UML-style diagrams to show the relationships between the declarations in a module, as well as a tree view that shows the applicable versions and their effective declarations for a calculation that spans several business areas. Since each business area can have a different set of versions that might start on different dates, it is not trivial to understand which versions of which business area are applicable for a calculation on some particular date.

End User Involvement During initial development, involvement of domain experts was difficult. The team worked on the core language abstractions without focusing on usability. User feedback would have been negative for "superficial" reasons; we wanted to avoid such negative first impressions. In addition, many future users struggle with formulating the requirements for the DSL because they are not aware of the design space for the language and IDE. Instead, the DATEV language developers, themselves former "payrollers," acted as proxies for our users. Once the language started to mature, future users were integrated more broadly through demo sessions, screencasts, and workshops. The feedback loops were shortened, and we focused on more and more detailed aspects of the language and the IDE.

Teaching The best way to teach the DSL is to let future users experience the language. We did this in four steps: (1) language developers create sample models that address common problems in the domain; (2) these samples form the basis for tutorials, demos, screencasts, and how-tos that illustrate language and tooling in a way that connects with future users; (3) user/developer pairs implement the examples; and (4) gradually, users try to independently implement further examples, supporting each other. Language developers are available as second-level support. Initially the last step was harder than expected; our users told us that routine work didn't allow them to spend time "playing around with the DSL." Now, after some time of learning, the approach works really well, and the business programmers "experiment" with the language as they try to implement new requirements.

Git Most business programmers had not used a version control system before. To keep the complexity of using Git low, we taught the users the basics using the built-in IDE features of MPS, avoiding the command line. In addition, developers try to avoid merge conflicts (perceived as especially cumbersome) by using a development process that avoids parallel work on the same parts of the system by different developers in the first place.

Infrastructure A crucial ingredient to limiting the complexity for the end users is that they are not required to deal with *any* part of the deployment stack; once they get their tests running in the IDE and have pushed the changes into Git, they are done (see Fig. 6).

LEGACY Developers were required to deal with multiple components of the overall stack, increasing complexity.∎

6.4   RQ4 *How Well Does the DSL and Its Use for Application Development Fit with Established IT Development Processes and System Architecture?*

Layered Architecture The DSL was specifically scoped to cover only the business logic of the domain; integration with the deployment infrastructure is done on the level of the generated code using agreed interfaces. Before considering a DSL for the business logic, DATEV had already decided to use a microservice architecture and to apply domain-driven design [14]. Each service would be layered like an onion (compare [37]), with outside-in dependencies. Figure 7 illustrates the current architecture of a microservice focusing on DSL integration. The domainlayer contains the generated business logic. It relies on libraries that form the DSL runtimethat are shared among services for the generated DSL code. The apilayer exposes the service functionality to the outside and, in our case, also contains the Driverthat provides the current employee, the current date, and access to reference data as well as to the (calculation results of) other services. Finally, the infrastructurelayer contains technology adapters (database, UI, middleware).

Generating the technology-independent domainlayer from models was a natural integration point for the DSL. The first test of this approach was to remodel, and then regenerate, a manually written domainlayer for a prototype microservice. Agreeing on the DSL runtimeinterfaces and those implemented by the generated domain layer took a couple of iterations. In particular, building a common understanding of the relation between versions, their impact on deployment, and an the API that supports cross-version polymorphism for calculationversions took time.

Flexible Deployment From corporate architecture guidelines, it was clear from the start that the calculations would run in a distributed, microservice architecture. However, the allocation of functionality to services was open because of the different trade-offs regarding performance, scalability, stability, and service management

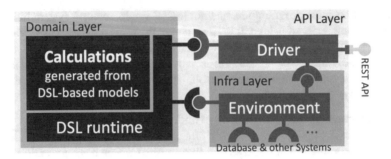

Fig. 7 The adaptation of the onion architecture integrating the DSL approach

overhead: (i) every version of every business area in a separate service; (ii) all versions of a business area in one service; (iii) multiple business areas with all their version in one service; and (iv) all business areas and versions in one service.

It was useful that the DSL can accommodate all four options by adapting generators or build scripts. In addition, the development of business logic could proceed without deployment decision in the architecture team, which helped to "unblock" the teams. Ultimately option (iii) was chosen for the initial deployment. A different trade-off might lead to choosing different options in the future. For now, the mapping of business areas to services is performed outside of the DSL, as part of the build process.

LEGACY The monolithic COBOL architecture could not be broken up easily into different deployment units, making the trade-offs harder to reevaluate.■

Technology Change Even during the development of the system, the execution infrastructure was changed from JEE to Spring; this required changes to method signatures and annotations in the generated POJOs and the persistence layer. Those changes could be achieved by modifying the generators. No modification of the business logic was necessary. Overall, the integration effort into the new technology stack was low, in line with our expectations and the "promise" of model-driven development, DSLs, and code generation.

Execution Paradigm Another technical aspect concerns the execution of the computation. Initially it was not clear whether, when data changes, computations would recalculate everything for a particular employee and month or whether they would store intermediate results and use the dependencies to incrementally recalculate the transitive closure of the changed data. The functional nature of the language allows both, after generators and runtimes are adapted. Currently, we use the simpler from-scratch approach.

More generally, future optimizations in terms of scalability or resource consumption will very likely be implementable in the generators and frameworks, without invasive changes to the DSL programs.

LEGACY   The monolithic COBOL architecture relied on a hard-coded, imperative execution paradigm.∎

Technology-Independent Testing   A natural consequence of the onion architecture is that the domain layer can be run without infrastructure, by mocking the infrastructure interfaces. This is an important ingredient of our QA approach, as illustrated by step 2 in Fig. 6.

Generator Complexity   Developing the generator to Java was more effort than expected. One reason was that the functional language had to be mapped to Java's imperative style. This led to excessive use of closures in the generated code as well as long, hard-to-debug chained dot expressions. For the latter we have implemented a transformation that splits the chains into sequences of variable declarations before generation. For example,

```
val v = aContext.longExpr.anEvenLongerOne
        .andAHigherOrderOne(|it.withSomething|)
```

is transformed to

```
val __t1 = aContext.longExpr
val __t2 = __t1.anEvenLongerOne
val v = __t2.andAHigherOrderOne(|it.withSomething|)
```

The generated Java code will then also use a sequence of variable declaration statements, making it easier to read and debug.

DATEV initially wanted the generated code to look exactly as if it were handwritten, partly to simplify debugging, partly to preempt those engineers who were skeptical about code generation, and partly to make the integration with the existing infrastructure, frameworks, and programming guidelines easier. We were required to respect naming conventions and use strongly typed APIs even behind the interfaces to the generated black box. This led to larger, more complex generators (we developed an intermediate language to deal with versioning of strongly typed APIs) as well as to a significantly bigger (generated) codebase compared to a solution that relied on more generic APIs inside the generated code.

Over time, as more and more of the microservices contain generated business logic and the trust in the generator-based approach increases, DATEV realized that the hard requirements for strongly typed data structures and readable generated code decreases. As of now, the first microservices process the data structures as JSON and do not rely on strongly typed Java classes internally. This significantly reduces the complexity of the generator. Another example is that necessary checks, if a new version of a business object still has a value for a deleted field, doesn't lead to a "compilation error" anymore—we now report this as an error the validation of the model (as opposed to a compile error on code level), which is fully accepted by the users.

Build Process   The automated build shown in Fig. 6 had to be integrated into DATEV's CI infrastructure. In principle this is not a problem with MPS—it can be used in headless mode to check, generate, and test models. However, the (partially reusable) build infrastructure of KernelF relies on gradle and DATEV required the use of Maven. Also, setting up an MPS headless build is generally tedious and error-prone (see [47]). This led to a few weeks of additional effort.

MPS Distribution MPS is a Java application that runs on the desktop. It does require infrastructure for deploying the tool to the (virtualized) PCs of the users. The effort to set this up was higher than expected.

Language Updates Like most other IDEs, MPS relies on a plugin system; the languages and IDE customizations used by business programmers are such plugins. The integration server builds these plugins for every commit, and at the end of each sprint, these are made available to the MPS installations via a Cloud Foundry web server. The MPS installations prompt the user to download the new plugins and potentially run model migrations.

7 General Learnings

Specific and Generic A well-designed general-purpose programming language has a small number of orthogonal and composable language concepts that allow users to define their own abstractions. For DSLs, in contrast, it is less important that users can define their own abstractions; instead, users expect the DSL to come with predefined abstractions for the use cases relevant to the domain (which partially explains the large number of language concepts in Table 1).

However, if a DSL is designed in this rigid way, it cannot grow towards more expressive power over time without expensive structural refactorings. An extensible functional language like KernelF, together with MPS' capabilities, provides an elegant middle ground. Structurally, everything is an `Expression`. However, initial iterations of the language only ship with use case-specific, high-level expressions that are easy for the end users to understand (an example is the Boolean `list l1 and l2 do not share data` used in a constraint). As users become more experienced, one can add more expressive constructs (`l1.intersect(l2).isEmpty`) without changing the fundamental architecture of the language.

A second example: in several cases, our end users asked us to remove genericity in favor of a more specific approach (with better, less generic tool support); for example, when assigning to an `enum`-valued result variable in a calculation, users suggested code completion to propose only the enum literals ("it is too complex otherwise"), not realizing that they might want to *compute* the value. Instead of changing the structure of the language, we used MPS' capability for constraining language concepts at particular locations to only show/allow enumliterals when computing enum-typed values. However, once people realized they did indeed want to compute them, we added them back in without any significant change to the language. Potentially, this filtering can be user-specific, catering to both newbies and more experienced users.

We have since found a great compromise: when assigning to enum-valued variables, we customized the MPS code completion menu to show the enumliterals at the top and in bold and all the other expressions further down; this will highlight the "simple" approach while still allowing more expressive, generic expressions.

There's a saying in the computer science community: "Every DSL will eventually evolve into a general-purpose language." We think this is wrong—this DSL and other similar ones are not a replacement for Java or C. However, most DSLs, as they evolve, will need more (mostly lower level) features that make it Turing complete. But these languages still have lots of domain-specific concepts in them as well, so they are not general-purpose. However, when selecting the tooling to build the language, make sure you chose one that is expressive enough to be able to handle this evolution.

Functional Programming The functional approach is very useful for lots of technical reasons—such as easy extensibility and relatively simple analyzability—and to provide lots of end user-relevant features with acceptable implementation effort. However, many business programmers, especially those who have extensive imperative experience, consider it a challenge. We mitigated this by providing high-level declarative abstractions for things that are ubiquitous in the domain, so that "low-level functional algorithmic programming" is required rarely. The approach is (half jokingly) called "funclerative programming" in [42].

The Price of Reuse Language reuse comes at a price: an existing language concept might be 100% what is needed in a DSL. For example, a keyword might be English instead of German, one might prefer a different default (e.g., does the type number without a specification of decimal digits denote an integer or a real?), or one might prefer the first operation on a list<T> to be of type T instead of opt<T> because the reusing language does not use option types. In practice, we usually start a new DSL by reusing (potentially non-ideal) language constructs from KernelF to get the project going quickly and proof its viability. In later phases, once we know the investment will not be wasted, we replace (some of) them with more ideal, custom-developed constructs.

We have also reused the KernelF-to-Java generator; the low-level abstractions, such as the basic expressions, worked in the DATEV context without problems. The higher level the reused language construct, the more likely it is that the choices made by the original generator developer do not fit with the project-specific context. For example, the generator for messages, a facility for collecting and reporting errors and warnings to the user, did not fit directly. Luckily, MPS provides mechanisms to override the existing generator in such situations.

SMT It turns out that many analyses that are expected by our business programmers require abstract interpretation [9, 10] on an SMT [3] domain. An example is checking a set of Boolean expressions (in a switch-like expression or distributed over several calculations) for completeness and overlap. However, users do not necessarily understand why this is so much more complicated than some of the other error checking performed by the IDE. We have observed the same in other

DSL projects [49]. To make such analyses possible, we would have to translate all of KernelF to solvers like Z3 [11] and build this transformation in a way that is easily extensible towards constructs from DSLs that extend or embed KernelF. This is a major task; itemis has been working on for the last few years but has not yet finished.

This can be seen as a negative consequence of reusing KernelF: our language is now so expressive that it is prohibitively expensive to translate it into SMT. However, the domain does require this expressiveness, so *not* reusing KernelF would not make it better. However, what we *can* learn from this is that we should develop a successor to KernelF which is integrated with—meaning: translatable to—an SMT solver right from the start.

Attention to Detail There is different emphasis between end users and language engineers regarding detail. Examples abound. We had to allow leading zeros in date and month literals as well as German umlauts and § signs in identifiers. We developed an infrastructure to manage abbreviations of name components (a central list of allowed name components, component-wise code completion of multi-part names based on the list, checking rules, refactorings to extract name components, showing names in abbreviated and expanded form). We spent a lot of time on the exact rounding rules for currency types. We worked on tool infrastructure to support internationalization for messages and integration with external translation tools. And we were required to use German-language keywords for DATEV-specific language concepts, which leads to a curious mix of German and English, because the keywords of KernelF-concepts cannot easily be changed to German due to an MPS limitation. When initially estimating the overall effort for the project, we did not take such requirements into account.

Pros and Cons of the Projectional Editor A projectional editor is a good fit for DSLs like the current one because of its support for non-textual notations such as tables; the ability to use non-parseable, natural language-like syntax; and its support for more highly structured, text-template-like notations such as the one for `calculation`shown in Sect. 6.2. And since grammar cells [48] have been available, the "feel" of the editor is close enough to a text editor for it to be acceptable to most users. The projectional editor is also an important enabler for the versatile support in MPS for language extension and composition [41], because one never runs into parsing ambiguities.

However, we did run into a few limitations. For example, insertion into the headers of decision tables took a while to get smooth. And the `/yyyy mm dd/`syntax for dates is a non-convincing compromise: `dd.mm.yyyy`would be preferred, but it is ambiguous with decimal number literals because a projectional editor has no look-ahead to be able to distinguish the two.

MPS Limitations More generally, we encountered a few limitations of MPS, including (1) keywords in multiple languages, (2) projecting nodes in places other than their location in the AST, (3) execution of expensive global validations, and (4) execution of a single set of tests both using the interpreter and the Java generator.

For (2), (3), and (4), we developed workarounds; (1) is unresolved. For a thorough discussion of the "good, bad, and the ugly" of MPS regarding the development of large-scale DSLs, we refer to [47].

MPS for End Users From an end user perspective, MPS looks and feels too much like an IDE (even though everything that is not needed for the payroll DSL has been removed from the UI). The requirement to install it locally on the users' PCs is also not a plus. An ideal tool would run in the browser and feel more like a modern web app while still supporting all the language engineering available in MPS. However, as far as the authors know, such a tool is currently not available, even though various communities have started to develop prototypes; examples include JetBrains' WebMPS[9] and itemis' modelix.[10]

MPS Learning Curve Learning to be a productive MPS *language developer* is hard, for many reasons: most developers do not have *language* development experience in the first place, MPS is a powerful tool and has many facets, not everything is as consistent within MPS as it could be, and the documentation is not as thorough and far-reaching as it should be. While the focus of this chapter is not the mechanics of building the DSL (we refer the reader to [47]), it is worth pointing out that it took longer than expected for the new language developers to become productive with MPS.

Resistance to Change? It is often said that domain experts and business programmers resist change, such as when moving to a DSL. We have heard it too in this project. Upon closer inquiry we have found that what they are really saying is something like: "last time we had to change, the new system was not ready yet, bugs were not fixed fast enough, we were not taught how it works, our feedback was not taken seriously, and, during the period of changing to the new system we were expected to be as productive as during the time before the change." Avoid these things, and you will encounter much less resistance.

8 Validity

Internal Validity The authors were involved in the development of the DSL, which might lead to bias regarding its success. However, we think that we have provided enough evidence in this chapter to allow readers to judge the success of the project for themselves. At the very least, the chapter should be useful to raise concerns that can be considered when starting a new DSL project.

---

[9]https://confluence.jetbrains.com/download/attachments/145293472/WebMPS.pdf?version=1&modificationDate=1571311862000&api=v2.

[10]https://modelix.org.

External Validity Can the findings be extrapolated to outside the payroll domain? We think yes. Our experience, and the experience of others [34] with projects in the healthcare [49], finance, tax, and public administration domain, suggests that domains that have to handle complex decisions and calculations generally benefit from DSLs.

How specific are the results to MPS? The core approach of using DSLs to capture business logic does not depend on MPS; for example, the German federal employment agency uses a set of Xtext-based DSLs to model their enterprise application data, validation, business rules, and processes [19]. However, limitations might apply. For example, reusing an existing expression language such as KernelF requires support for modular language composition; there is significant variability among language workbenches as to how robustly this is supported [13]. Similarly, MPS' support for non-textual notations is crucial for reducing accidental complexity (consider the decision tables). Other language workbenches, such as Xtext, do not directly support mixed notations. However, in the case of Xtext, they could be built with other Eclipse-based UI technologies, albeit with higher effort and less seamlessly integrated. Summing up, it is less obvious how language workbenches other than MPS could be used to build DSLs like the one discussed in this chapter, though it is definitely possible. For a more general comparison of language workbenches, see [13].

Are the results specific to DSLs in general? We compare the DSL approach to a decades-old legacy system. A more meaningful comparison might be with a modern implementation using state-of-the-art programming languages and technologies. Such a comparison is not available. However, there are several indications that a DSL will still come out favorably. First, we showed already during the 22 day proof-of-concept that the DSL can better handle the complexities of the domain such as temporal data and versions. Second, considering the attention to (domain-specific) details by our end users, it is hard to see how a general-purpose language could fulfil them. Third, the enforced separation in the software architecture improved the collaboration of the business programmers and the software developers due to the focus. Finally, the flexibility regarding infrastructure, execution paradigm, and performance is hard to achieve without a "custom compiler" that decouples the business logic from its implementation on a particular platform.

Conclusion Validity and Risks An important factor for the success of the new DSL and tooling is the long-term maintenance effort. Obviously, at this point in the life cycle of the DSL, we have only very limited data to draw conclusions about this. However, we can say the following: Regarding the maintenance of the business logic expressed with the DSL, there is reason to be optimistic regarding long-term maintainability, because the language has been designed specifically to address maintenance challenges through its support for versions, temporal data, and garbage collection, driven by specific previous experience at DATEV.

Regarding the maintenance of the language implementation itself, the situation is comparable to every other reusable assets, such as a framework or a tool: ongoing effort has to be spent in order to avoid "code rot." A related risk is the dependence on MPS. In the past, DATEV had used proprietary tools and COBOL preprocessors. It turned out to be a challenge to maintain the tools and technologies over time, leading to a maintenance backlog and thus reduced acceptance of the technology itself. However, DATEV considered this risk acceptable for MPS.

9 Related Work

Business DSLs The closest related work is the use of DSLs for specifying public benefit payments and tax rules by the Dutch Tax Agency [34]: they also target non-programmer users, deal with temporal data, and use MPS. Their language uses a syntax that is more natural language-like. The language is in production for specifying the whole Dutch public benefits system and is being introduced in the tax domain. In personal conversations the team reported significant savings in efforts and much shortened time to market; unfortunately, no comprehensive case study has been published to date.

The stated goal of Intentional Software [36] was to allow non-programmers to participate directly in the creation of software using DSLs with mixed notations, very much like MPS. Kolk and Voelter [25] give a high-level overview of its prototypical use in an insurance. No detailed case study is available, and, although promising, the system never went into production. Intentional Software has since been acquired[11] by Microsoft, and as far as we know, the team is no longer working on DSLs and language workbenches.

Risla [39] is a DSL for implementing financial instruments (loan, swap, future). It targeted at engineers, but a questionnaire-style frontend allows financial experts to define new products as well. The paper reports a speedup from 3 months to 3 weeks per product, as well as significant increases in readability and portability. Compared to our case, this language is smaller in scope, does not come with IDE support, and is used to describe much smaller/simpler programs.

Rebel [38] is used to specify algorithms used in banks (such as money transfers) and then use model checking to verify correctness. The emphasis is on the verification of correctness, and indeed, prototypical used at ING found errors in existing algorithms. However, they also found that the programming-language style syntax was not accessible to non-programmers. This explains why lots of effort goes into syntax of DSLs when targeting non-programmers.

Peyton-Jones introduces a DSL for financial contracts [30, 35]. The language allows the concise expression of contracts: "only 10 combinators are required." However, its reliance on advanced functional programming techniques, its embedding in Haskell, and the resulting syntax and limited tool support make it hard to use for non-programmers. In addition, temporality and versioning were not in scope. A

---

[11]https://techcrunch.com/2017/04/18/microsoft-acquires-intentional-software-and-brings-old-friend-back-into-fold/.

similar language is described in [33], with similar findings. The Actuarial Modeling Language [8] is not implemented in Haskell, but its design makes it clearly targeted at mathematicians, who are used to formal languages and abstraction; the challenge is different to ours.

BPM and Workflows Classical workflow and business process management languages such as Barzdin et al. [4], Faerber et al. [15], or OMG's BPMN [7] capture business processes: which party performs which activity with which data, under which conditions. They do not address the core business logic of, for example, insurance products, tax calculations, or payroll. More recently, the OMG has defined the Decision Model and Notation (DMN) [32]. It contains an expression language not unlike KernelF and incorporates various forms of decision tables to make complex decisions more amenable to non-programmers. We could not find published case studies about the use of DMN in industrial practice. Also, the standard (and existing tools) are not extensible to allow adding domain-specific abstractions such as temporal data or versioning. Implementing DMN in MPS in order to allow such extensibility would be an interesting exercise.

Spreadsheets Many business problems are attacked with Excel. However, when seen through the lens of DSLs, spreadsheets lack a data schema, type checking, the ability to generate code, and a language-aware IDE. While spreadsheets are a good source to mine knowledge that goes into DSLs, we do not consider sophisticated spreadsheets a DSL and therefore do not compare further.

Other Non-programmer DSLs Several DSL target healthcare: the languages described in Voelter et al. [49] and Florence et al. [17] allow healthcare professionals to describe therapies and dosing medicines; those discussed in Kendrick [1] and Ronald [2] help healthcare researchers simulate epidemiological models and understand the spread and treatment of malaria, respectively. All papers report increased productivity and better integration of business programmers into the development process; this is in line with our findings.

A wide range of DSL-like languages target engineers in non-software domains; many examples are listed on the MetaCase website [31]. Tools like Simulink, ASCET, or SCADE are widely used in control-heavy domains. However, their abstractions are so general and low level (state machine or dataflow graphs) that it is a stretch to call them domain-specific; they are better thought of as general-purpose languages for a particular computational paradigm. Their main contribution is a graphical notations (which seems to be liked by engineers) and that they can generate code that has particular safety or performance characteristics (which is relevant in automotive or aerospace).

Teaching Languages Several languages have been designed specifically to teach programming, especially to children; the most well-known are LOGO [16] and Scratch [28]. Obviously, they cannot be used directly in our context because they lack the domain-specific abstractions needed for the payroll domain.

Should these languages be seen as DSLs? LOGO could be seen as a DSL for line drawing. But Scratch is better seen as a general-purpose language that uses a particular notation (the nested shapes). More generally, the design decisions that make these languages accessible to novice programmers are not applicable the same that make them good DSLs: they emphasize generic simplicity and learnability over domain specificity and productivity. However, these languages could be used to teach the domain experts and business programmers the basics of programming needed to use the DSL effectively.

Other similar initiatives exist, including some teaching programming from scratch [20] and some that assume basic knowledge of Excel [44] and in the context of computational thinking [51]. There are also "domain-specific teaching languages," which help novices to learn programming *in a particular domain*. For example, CoBlox [50] does this for industrial robots. However, CoBlox and similar languages do not attempt to cover the whole domain and scale to real-world problems, which is in contrast to the payroll DSL described in this chapter.

DSLs for Programmers DSLs are widely used as a tool for software developers; as we have mentioned in the introduction, most report significant productivity boosts. However, since the constraints regarding complexity, syntax, IDE support, and infrastructure are very different from those targeted at non-programmers, we do not compare further in related work.

10 Conclusions

Summary We have described the development of a domain-specific language for payroll applications at DATEV. The DSL reduces complexity in terms of the core domain and infrastructure dependencies (RQ1); increases quality by simplifying testing, immediate feedback, and a stepwise build process (RQ2); is accessible to non-expert programmer end users (RQ3); and integrates with existing architectures and build pipelines while keeping deployment options flexible (RQ4). This way, the language helps DATEV address core business challenges including keeping track with evolving law (C1), the need to develop new and innovative products faster (C2), and running those on a wide variety of platforms (C3). While not everything was smooth sailing, the DSL is now in productive use.

Conclusions At a more general level, all involved parties agree that the goals set out for the DSL-based development process have largely been reached, as far as we can tell after a few years of development and use. Both the business programmers and the infrastructure developers recognize the value of separating the domain and technical concerns. Business programmers who have been overheard saying that "we really don't care about the technical implementation in the data center" are happy that they can implement, test, and deploy (!) new functionality reliably within a single sprint, something that was not feasible before. The infrastructure developers are also happy because they "don't have to care about the complexity of payroll calculation" and that they are able to ship cross-cutting optimizations in the generated code with relative ease. The pain-free migration from JEE to Spring also drove home this benefit.

The Future Based on the positive experience with the DSL, it will be expanded in the future. As of now, two major extension of the scope of the DSL are currently being addressed. The first is data transfer to external consumers (such as government agencies) where we are working on language features to specify the respective data mappings. The second extension is the creation of reports and lists, where the DSL will support query and aggregation of data.

Acknowledgments We thank Bastian Kruck and the reviewers of the book for detailed and very useful feedback on this chapter. Our thanks also goes to the anonymous reviewers of the MPS book.

References

1. Anh, B.T.M., Stinckwich, S., Ziane, M., Roche, B., Vinh, H.T.: Kendrick: A domain specific language and platform for mathematical epidemiological modelling. In: The 2015 IEEE RIVF International Conference on Computing & Communication Technologies-Research, Innovation, and Vision for Future (RIVF), pp. 132–137. IEEE, Piscataway (2015)
2. Antao, T., Hastings, I.M., McBurney, P.: Ronald: A domain-specific language to study the interactions between malaria infections and drug treatments. In: BIOCOMP, pp. 747–752 (2008)
3. Barrett, C., Tinelli, C.: Satisfiability modulo theories. In: Handbook of Model Checking, pp. 305–343. Springer, Berlin (2018)
4. Barzdins, J., Cerans, K., Kalnins, A., Grasmanis, M., Kozlovics, S., Lace, L., Liepins, R., Rencis, E., Sprogis, A., Zarins, A.: Domain specific languages for business process management: A case study. In: Proceedings of DSM, vol. 9, pp. 34–40 (2009)
5. Broy, M., Kirstan, S., Krcmar, H., Schätz, B., Zimmermann, J.: What is the benefit of a model-based design of embedded software systems in the car industry? In: Software Design and Development: Concepts, Methodologies, Tools, and Applications: Concepts, Methodologies, Tools, and Applications, p. 310. IGI Global, Pennsylvania (2013)
6. Bruckhaus, T., Madhavii, N., Janssen, I., Henshaw, J.: The impact of tools on software productivity. IEEE Softw. **13**(5), 29–38 (1996)
7. Chinosi, M., Trombetta, A.: BPMN: An introduction to the standard. Comput. Stand. Interfaces **34**(1), 124–134 (2012)
8. Christiansen, D.R., Grue, K., Niss, H., Sestoft, P., Sigtryggsson, K.S.: An actuarial programming language for life insurance and pensions. In: Proceedings of 30th International Congress of Actuaries (2013)
9. Cousot, P., Cousot, R.: Abstract interpretation: A unified lattice model for static analysis of programs by construction or approximation of fix points. In: Proceedings of the 4th ACM SIGACT-SIGPLAN Symposium on Principles of Programming Languages, pp. 238–252. ACM, New York (1977)
10. Cousot, P., Cousot, R.: Abstract interpretation frameworks. J. Logic Comput. **2**(4), 511–547 (1992)
11. De Moura, L., Bjørner, N.: Z3: An efficient SMT solver. In: International Conference on Tools and Algorithms for the Construction and Analysis of Systems. Springer, Berlin, (2008)
12. Erdweg, S., Giarrusso, P.G., Rendel, T.: Language composition untangled. In: Proceedings of the Twelfth Workshop on Language Descriptions, Tools, and Applications, p. 7. ACM, New York (2012)

13. Erdweg, S., Van Der Storm, T., Völter, M., Boersma, M., Bosman, R., Cook, W.R., Gerritsen, A., Hulshout, A., Kelly, S., Loh, A., et al.: The state of the art in language workbenches. In: International Conference on Software Language Engineering, pp. 197–217. Springer, Berlin (2013)
14. Evans, E.: Domain-Driven Design: Tackling Complexity in the Heart of Software. Addison-Wesley Professional, Boston (2004)
15. Faerber, M., Jablonski, S., Schneider, T.: A comprehensive modeling language for clinical processes. In ECEH, pp. 77–88. Citeseer (2007)
16. Feurzeig, W., Lukas, G.: LOGO - a programming language for teaching mathematics. Educat. Technol. **12**(3), 39–46 (1972)
17. Florence, S.P., Fetscher, B., Flatt, M., Temps, W.H., Kiguradze, T., West, D.P., Niznik, C., Yarnold, P.R., Findler, R.B., Belknap, S.M.: POP-PL: A patient-oriented prescription programming language. In: ACM SIGPLAN Notices, vol. 51, pp. 131–140. ACM, New York (2015)
18. Hermans, F., Pinzger, M., Van Deursen, A.: Domain-specific languages in practice: A user study on the success factors. In: International Conference on Model Driven Engineering Languages and Systems, pp. 423–437. Springer, Berlin (2009)
19. Huber, G., Wälzlein, R.: Problem und lösung beschreiben. Java Mag. **2017**(1) (2017)
20. Iu, M.-Y.: Programming basics: A website teaching people how to program. http://www.programmingbasics.org/en/ (2018)
21. Johnston, T.: Bitemporal Data: Theory and Practice. Newnes (2014)
22. Jürgens, E., Feilkas, M.: Domain Specific Languages (2006)
23. Kärnä, J., Tolvanen, J.-P., Kelly, S.: Evaluating the use of domain-specific modeling in practice. In: Proceedings of the 9th OOPSLA Workshop on Domain-Specific Modeling (2009)
24. Kieburtz, R.B., McKinney, L., Bell, J.M., Hook, J., Kotov, A., Lewis, J., Oliva, D.P., Sheard, T., Smith, I., Walton, L.: A software engineering experiment in software component generation. In: Proceedings of the 18th International Conference on Software Engineering, pp. 542–552. IEEE Computer Society, Washington (1996)
25. Kolk, H., Voelter, M.: Democratizing software creation. Presentation at OOP 2008 Conference http://voelter.de/data/presentations/KolkVoelter_IntentionalSoftware.pdf, (2008)
26. Liebel, G., Marko, N., Tichy, M., Leitner, A., Hansson, J.: Assessing the state-of-practice of model-based engineering in the embedded systems domain. In: International Conference on Model Driven Engineering Languages and Systems, pp. 166–182. Springer, Berlin (2014)
27. Liggesmeyer, P., Trapp, M.: Trends in embedded software engineering. IEEE Softw. **26**(3), 19–25 (2009)
28. Maloney, J., Resnick, M., Rusk, N., Silverman, B., Eastmond, E.: The scratch programming language and environment. ACM Trans. Comput. Education (TOCE) **10**(4), 16 (2010)
29. McDirmid, S.: Usable live programming. In: Proceedings of the 2013 ACM International Symposium on New Ideas, New Paradigms, and Reflections on Programming & Software, pp. 53–62. ACM, New York (2013)
30. Mediratta, A.: A generic domain specific language for financial contracts. PhD Thesis, Rutgers University-Graduate School-New Brunswick (2007)
31. Metacase Consulting. DSM examples. https://metacase.com/cases/dsm_examples.html (2019)
32. Object Management Group. Decision model and notation specification version 1.2. https://www.omg.org/spec/DMN (2019)
33. Pace, G.J., Rosner, M.: A controlled language for the specification of contracts. In: International Workshop on Controlled Natural Language, pp. 226–245. Springer, Berlin (2009)
34. Pepels, B., Zanten, G.V.v.: Model driven software engineering in the large: Experiences at the Dutch tax and customs service (industry talk). In: Proceedings of the 1st Industry Track on Software Language Engineering, ITSLE 2016, pp. 2–2. ACM, New York (2016)
35. Peyton Jones, S., Eber, J.-M., Seward, J.: Composing contracts: An adventure in financial engineering (functional pearl). In: ACM SIGPLAN Notices, vol. 35, pp. 280–292. ACM, New York (2000)
36. Simonyi, C., Christerson, M., Clifford, S.: Intentional software. In: ACM SIGPLAN Notices, vol. 41, pp. 451–464. ACM, New York (2006)

37. Stenberg, J.: Domain-driven design with onion architecture. https://www.infoq.com/news/2014/10/ddd-onion-architecture (2014)
38. Stoel, J., Storm, T.v.d., Vinju, J., Bosman, J.: Solving the bank with rebel: On the design of the rebel specification language and its application inside a bank. In: Proceedings of the 1st Industry Track on Software Language Engineering, pp. 13–20. ACM, New York (2016)
39. van Deursen, A.: Domain-specific languages versus object-oriented frameworks: A financial engineering case study. In: Smalltalk and Java in Industry and Academia, STJA 97, pp. 35–39. CiteSeer (1997)
40. Van Deursen, A., Klint, P., Visser, J.: Domain-specific languages: An annotated bibliography. ACM Sigplan Notices **35**(6), 26–36 (2000)
41. Voelter, M.: Language and IDE development, modularization and composition with MPS. In: GTTSE 2011. Lecture Notes in Computer Science. Springer, Berlin (2011)
42. Voelter, M.: The design, evolution, and use of KernelF. In: International Conference on Theory and Practice of Model Transformations, pp. 3–55. Springer, Berlin (2018)
43. Voelter, M.: Fusing modeling and programming into language-oriented programming. In: International Symposium on Leveraging Applications of Formal Methods, pp. 309–339. Springer, Berlin (2018)
44. Voelter, M.: Programming basics: How to think like a programmer. https://markusvoelter.github.io/ProgrammingBasics/ (2018)
45. Voelter, M.: The hidden layer between the fachlichkeit and the -ilities. https://medium.com/@markusvoelter/the-hidden-layer-between-the-fachlichkeit-and-the-ilities-7d850fde00bf (2019)
46. Voelter, M., van Deursen, A., Kolb, B., Eberle, S.: Using c language extensions for developing embedded software: A case study. In: OOPSLA 2015 (2015)
47. Voelter, M., Kolb, B., Szabó, T., Ratiu, D., van Deursen, A.: Lessons learned from developing mbeddr: A case study in language engineering with MPS. Softw. Syst. Model. **18**, 585–630 (2017)
48. Voelter, M., Szabó, T., Lisson, S., Kolb, B., Erdweg, S., Berger, T.: Efficient development of consistent projectional editors using grammar cells. In: Proceedings of the 2016 ACM SIGPLAN International Conference on Software Language Engineering, pp. 28–40. ACM, New York (2016)
49. Voelter, M., Kolb, B., Birken, K., Tomassetti, F., Alff, P., Wiart, L., Wortmann, A., Nordmann, A.: Using language workbenches and domain-specific languages for safety-critical software development. Softw. Syst. Model. **18**, 1–24 (2018)
50. Weintrop, D., Afzal, A., Salac, J., Francis, P., Li, B., Shepherd, D.C., Franklin, D., Evaluating coblox: A comparative study of robotics programming environments for adult novices. In: Proceedings of the 2018 CHI Conference on Human Factors in Computing Systems, p. 366. ACM, New York (2018)
51. Wing, J.M.: Computational thinking. Commun. ACM **49**(3), 33–35 (2006)

FASTEN: An Extensible Platform to Experiment with Rigorous Modeling of Safety-Critical Systems

Daniel Ratiu, Arne Nordmann, Peter Munk, Carmen Carlan, and Markus Voelter

Abstract The increasing complexity of safety-critical systems and the shorter time-to-market requires a high degree of automation during all development phases from requirements specification to design, implementation, verification, and safety assurance. To make this feasible, we need to describe different system aspects using appropriate models that are semantically rich and, whenever possible, formally defined such that they are verifiable by automated methods. At the same time, they must be easy to understand by practitioners and must allow them to capture the domain concepts with minimal encoding bias. In this chapter, we describe FASTEN, an open-source research environment for model-based specification and design of safety-critical systems using domain-specific languages. FASTEN enables the experimentation with modeling abstractions at different levels of rigor and their integration in today's development processes. We present an overview of the currently available domain-specific languages (DSLs) used to formally specify requirements, system designs, and assurance arguments. These DSLs have been developed and used in technology transfer projects by researchers from different organizations—Siemens, Bosch, fortiss, and itemis. Last but not least, we discuss lessons learned from implementing the languages and interacting with practitioners

D. Ratiu (✉)
VW Car.Software.Org (previously with Siemens), Munich, Germany

A. Nordmann
Robert Bosch GmbH, Stuttgart, Germany
e-mail: arne.nordmann@de.bosch.com

P. Munk
Robert Bosch GmbH, Stuttgart, Germany
e-mail: peter.munk@de.bosch.com

C. Carlan
fortiss, Munich, Germany
e-mail: carmen.carlan@fortiss.org

M. Voelter
Independent/itemis, Stuttgart, Germany

131

and discuss the language engineering features of MPS that enabled our approach and its open challenges.

1 Introduction

It is common knowledge that software-intensive systems in general are becoming larger, more complex, and more relevant to crucial tasks in our society. Due to the high impact of malfunctioning, we must have a high degree of confidence that the systems cannot harm people or expensive equipment [14].

Testing Is Limited Testing is a well-known approach to building trust. Systems are "tried out," unit tests and integration tests are written and automatically executed for the software parts, hardware-in-the-loop tests verify aspects of the hardware, and red teams try to attack the system to uncover vectors for malicious attacks. However, usually, testing can only show the presence of bugs and not prove their absence. Phrased differently, testing suffers from the coverage problem, which means that you can only be sure that your system is "correct" if you test it completely. "Completely" is a high bar that is often not reachable in practice for complex systems.

Formal Methods Formal methods can be an important ingredient in an engineer's toolset to build trust in critical systems. Depending on the particular formalism, formal methods either can help with systematically improving the coverage of tests or can even proof the *absence* of certain classes of errors such as runtime errors (e.g., overflows) or conformance of a client's implementation with a API. Some formal verification tools (e.g., cbmc [9]) work directly on source code; however, most require a model expressed in a particular language on which to operate. While this can be seen as a disadvantage (if you are a code-centric developer), it has the important advantage that models cannot just represent software—they can also represent aspects of the system implemented in hardware, or even aspects of the environment. Models—for example, of interfaces, protocols, or state-based behavior—can also be defined in earlier stages of development where hardware or source code is still elusive. This way, engineers can experiment with various design alternatives *early* in the development, building trust in their work *early*, and avoid expensive rework during later stages of development.

Bringing Formal Methods Closer to Practitioners However, formal methods are hard to use by practitioners for several reasons. First, some of the formalisms are conceptually hard to understand [21]; they often encode nontrivial mathematical ideas that are not familiar to engineers [31]. The input languages of verification tools contain low-level abstractions that are targeted toward verification, which forces engineers to bridge a large abstraction gap when they encode system-level concepts. Second, these formalisms are by necessity general—they are not specific to the engineer's domain, which makes the transformation of the engineering model to the tool's input and the lifting of the results even harder. Third, there is often no robust tool support (IDEs) for verification engines; and common software IDE services such as auto-completion, refactorings, or debugging the models are nonexistent. Fourth, using real-world verification requires the use of *multiple* formalisms for the definitions of state transitions or constraints, requiring multiple encodings of the engineering model and/or fusion of the results. Fifth, the interpretation of the results of the verification tools, such as understanding the witnesses for verification failures in terms of the engineering model, is often not trivial either. In safety-critical contexts, formal verification results may be used as evidence supporting assurance arguments that demonstrate that the system meets critical goals. Finally, not everything that is needed to make an argumentation for the system's safety can be formalized [13, 34]. In these cases, unstructured or semi-structured artifacts (such as the original textual requirements, SysML diagrams) must be integrated with formalized models, both conceptually and technically.

Our Vision We envision an integrated modeling and verification platform that deeply integrates models for requirements, design, verification, and assurance at increasing levels of formality as illustrated in Fig. 1. Our platform has the following characteristics: (1) The user interacts with a limited number of models whose structure and notation are meaningful to the user's engineering domain. Informal parts of the system such as textual requirements or safety arguments can be incrementally formalized and combined with other formal specifications. (2) The languages used to define these models allow the user to express properties that they want to verify; again, these properties are expressed with a language that is close to the user's domain. (3) These models, together with the properties they must satisfy, are then automatically translated into one or more verification formalisms, and (4)

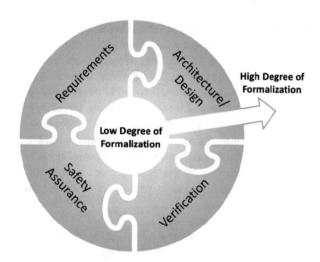

Fig. 1 FASTEN Vision: Deeply integrated models for requirements, design, verification, and safety assurance. The models support transition from informal to formal system representation

existing verification engines are executed to verify the properties. (5) The low-level verification results are lifted back to the level of the engineering model; potentially, the results from multiple verification tools are semantically integrated. (6) Using references and other model-level mechanisms, the formal models can be connected to informal or semiformal content, (7) integrating system and safety engineering models in a semantically rich assurance case to ensure consistency between design and safety models. Last but not the least, the tool should be built as an open platform to make it extensible with new formalisms or user-facing languages, and its user experience should be on par with modern IDEs in terms of editor features, type checking, and error reporting.

How to Get There We rely on language workbenches [12], tools that support the efficient implementation of languages, type systems, model transformations, and IDEs. We use a layered approach that delivers early benefits even while only a part of our overall vision is implemented. As foundational language workbench, we chose JetBrains MPS[1] due to its powerful support for language engineering (Sect. 7.2).

We start with the implementation of several input languages of verification tools in our language workbench—e.g., we implement the language SMV, the input language of the NuSMV [7] model checker, or Promela, the input language of Spin [15] model checker. This step does not give us improvements in terms of semantic abstraction, but it results in a robust IDE for writing models in the notation of the formalism that has the usual modern front-end features such as syntax coloring, code completion, type checking, and reporting of the verification results. Based on JetBrains MPS' support for modular language extension, we incrementally add discrete extensions to these low-level input languages to make idiomatic use simpler. These extensions are still generic but useful for less mathematically minded users.

Next, we implement an integrating language based on the component-instance-connector paradigm; such languages are well-known to many engineers, provide good support for hierarchical breakdown of systems, and are reasonably generic (as evidenced by SysML [27]). Furthermore, we develop extensions to the component language that allow the user to annotate properties relevant for verification. A chain of model-to-model transformations converts this model, including the properties to verify, into the input language of one of the integrated verification tools. After the verification is run, we provide lifting of verification results back to the users such that they can easily understand what went wrong and perform fixes. This integrated language for modeling and verification is the first major goal of our vision.

To enable a transition from textual requirements to formal models, we have developed a set of DSLs for specifying requirements by using increasingly semantically rich models. The requirements models range from plain natural language text to requirements templates (aka. boilerplates) or formal models written, e.g., using temporal logics. The richer the models, the more rigorous verification is possible.

---

[1] https://www.jetbrains.com/mps/.

The results of verification can be further used in safety assurance arguments that we integrate via another set of DSLs specialized for safety engineering.

Are We There Yet? FASTEN[2] is an open-source[3] platform that enables experimentation with modeling abstractions amenable for verification on the way to our vision. It supports exploration of the idea, in a bottom-up manner by combining informal and increasingly formal models, and verifies the degree to which it is realistic. FASTEN is built on JetBrains MPS, which has been used successfully in a safety-critical context [37]. While FASTEN is not a production-ready tool, it has been used to verify realistic systems in industrial settings. To validate the extensibility with regard to verification formalisms, we present various extensions shipped with FASTEN itself. In addition to these open-source extensions, we also discuss closed-source extension, developed independently at Bosch. To validate the extensibility for a particular domain, we demonstrate a more extensive case study developed at the Corporate Research department of Bosch.

Contributions The main contribution of this chapter is FASTEN, an open-source platform based on JetBrains MPS, for safety-critical systems development. FASTEN allows experimentation with adequate and domain-specific modeling abstractions to capture different aspects of safety-critical systems from requirements, design, verification, to safety assurance. The part focused on safety assurance is referred to as FASTEN.Safe. For each of these aspects, we provide DSLs that enable the transition from informal to formal descriptions. We present a novel architecture for building model-driven engineering tooling around modular and extensible stacks of DSLs that leverage on the language engineering capabilities of the Jetbrains MPS language workbench. FASTEN has been built over the last 3 years by industrial researchers from three companies (Siemens, Bosch, itemis) and a research institute (fortiss). Last but not least, this chapter presents our experiences and lessons learnt with developing and using FASTEN in research transfer projects inside our organizations.

Structure In Sect. 2, we present the FASTEN platform, which is the infrastructure that serves as a basis for our DSLs. Section 3 presents DSLs for modeling requirements at different levels of rigor from natural language text to boilerplates or formal models. Section 4 presents DSLs for design and specification developed on top of SMV, the input language of the NuSMV model checking engine. Section 5 presents DSLs for modeling safety assurance arguments and linking them with other system models to enable automated consistency checks. Section 6 presents extensions and applications developed by Bosch. We conclude this chapter by presenting our lessons learned in Sect. 7 and conclude it in Sect. 8.

---

[2]https://sites.google.com/site/fastenroot/home.

[3]https://github.com/mbeddr/mbeddr.formal.

2 The FASTEN Platform

To enable an efficient implementation of our vision, we have modularized recurring functionality in a set of DSLs and libraries that make up the *FASTEN Platform*. Figure 2 shows an overview of the FASTEN architecture. FASTEN integrates external analysis engines (see bottom of the figure) as black boxes—NuSMV [7], Spin [15], and Prism [22] are integrated as external binaries, and Z3 [10] is integrated via its Java API.

Foundational Libraries All languages and functionalities are developed on top of JetBrains MPS plus languages and libraries provided by the *MPS-extensions*[4] and *mbeddr-platform*[5] projects. We use these language libraries for diagrammatic, tree, and tabular notations, for improving editor usability (via grammar cells [36]) and

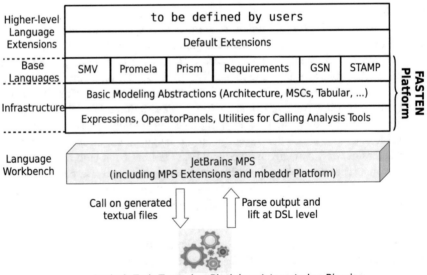

Fig. 2 FASTEN architecture features layers of DSLs (top) built on the JetBrains MPS language workbench (middle). External analyses tools (bottom) are integrated at binary level. At its base, FASTEN provides itself a platform of reusable DSLs (FASTEN Platform) that contains an implementation of an expressions language, utilities for generic modeling abstractions (e.g., for modeling architecture, MSCs), and, based on these, the implementation of standard modeling languages (e.g., GSN, STAMP) and of base languages of analysis engines (e.g., SMV, Promela). On top of the platform, FASTEN provides a set of extensions as presented in the following sections

---

[4]https://github.com/JetBrains/MPS-extensions.

[5]http://mbeddr.com/platform.html.

for generated code review. From an implementation perspective, this infrastructure proved to be crucial to our approach.

Our Infrastructure: The FASTEN Platform In order to facilitate the development of DSLs and the integration of formal analysis tools, FASTEN comes with a set of basic languages and functionalities that can be grouped as follows:

1. *Infrastructure:* commonly used DSLs such as an expressions language; support for calling external tools, displaying analysis results in the IDE,
2. *Basic modeling:* base DSLs for the definition of modeling languages such as architecture, message-sequence-charts or tabular specifications,
3. *Input languages of existing analyses tools:* the implementation of input languages (e.g., SMV, Promela, SMTlib, Prism) of the integrated analysis tools.
4. *Standard languages:* the GSN [18] modeling language for creating assurance cases, the STAMP [23] modeling language for performing hazard analysis, and a base language for the specification of textual requirements.

On top of the *FASTEN platform*, we have created DSL extensions to enable more comfortable modeling and verification. In the following sections, we present selected examples of higher-level abstractions and functionalities that have been built so far.

3 Modeling of Requirements

As presented in the introduction, one of the essential ingredients of our vision is to enable a seamless transition from informal to formal specifications. This is especially crucial for requirements, because in the industry, they are usually written as mostly plain natural language. To enable this, we defined a set of DSLs that allow users to write requirements in an increasingly rigorous manner, starting from plain natural language up to formal models. In Fig. 3, we illustrate our current stack of DSLs for requirements modeling.

Textual Requirements (Natural Language) At its lowest level, requirements are specified using plain natural language text and pictures. Traces can be created

Formal Specification	Temporal Logics		SMV Models
Semi-formal Specification	Tracing to Models		Sentence Templates
Informal Specification	Requirements Base Language (Natural Language)		

Fig. 3 Stackable DSLs for modeling requirements and enabling transition from informal to (semi-)formal specifications

Req 010.01 : Airbag functionality overview
created by: john kind: functional

An airbag shall protect the passengers of a car in case of impact. The figure below illustrates intuitively the deployment of airbags. Requirement @req(010.02) contains the specification of the interface between the car sensors and the airbag system.

    press enter to add sub-requirement

Fig. 4 Example of textual specification of requirements. Besides the text, a requirement might contain pictures or references to other requirements

between requirements or other models. In Fig. 4, we present an example of textual specification of an airbag function that references other requirements.

Semiformal Specification (Sentence Templates) A lot of work has been done on structuring requirements by expressing them in controlled natural language (CNL) [33]. There, requirements are expressed as a set of boilerplates (natural language sentence templates) which are instantiated for a given system. FASTEN provides boilerplates for properties over traces (aka. temporal patterns). In Fig. 5, we present examples of templates mixed with natural language text for specifying an airbag.

Formal Specification This allows the specification of requirements using formal models with a mathematically defined meaning. FASTEN allows users to write requirements using temporal logics by providing DSLs for commonly recurring patterns [11], as illustrated in Fig. 6. Furthermore, FASTEN allows referencing formal models from within requirements specifications, as exemplified in Fig. 7, which defines the activation logic of the airbag. Using the editor capabilities of MPS, fragments of formal models can be displayed (projected) where the textual

Req 020.01 : Airbag high-level functions
created by: john kind: functional

Airbag requirements are specified below using sentence boilerplates for temporal patterns

temporal logics specification {
  Globally, it is always the case that %airbag is ready to deploy in case of imapct% holds.
  After %impact was detected%, it is always the case that if %impact severity is high% holds
    , then %the airbag will be deployed% eventually holds.
}
    press enter to add sub-requirement

Fig. 5 Example of specification of requirements using boilerplates mixed with unstructured text

| Req 030.01 : Airbag protects the passengers in accidents
| created by: dan kind: interface
___

The input port collision_detected is TRUE when sensorts detect a collision.
The airbag should explode whenever a collision is detected - as formalized in the following.
¶

in scope airbag **the following properties hold {**
  Globally, collision_detected **eventually holds.**
  After collision_detected, **it is always the case that** airbag_explode_command **holds.**
}

press enter to add sub-requirement

| Req 030.02 : A deactivated airbag shall not explode
| created by: dan kind: interface
___

The input port deactivete_airbag is TRUE when the airbag was deactivated by the driver.
After an airbag is deactivated it shall not explode - as formalized in the following.
¶

in scope airbag **the following properties hold {**
  Globally, deactivate_airbag **eventually holds.**
  -- this requirement is in contradiciton with the one from above;
  After deactivate_airbag, **it is always the case that** !airbag_explode_command **holds.**
}

Fig. 6 Example of specification of requirements using temporal logics patterns defined by [11]. The patterns formalize the textual requirements and thereby enable automated consistency checks

| Req 050.01 : Airbag basic function
| created by: dan kind: interface
___

If not in a deactive state, the airbag shall explode whenever a collision
is detected - as formalized in the following.
¶
>> Traced-node spec: **airbag**

```
MODULE airbag(deactivate_airbag, collision_detected) {
  DEFINE {
    output airbag_explode_command := explode_state;
  }
  VAR {
    deactivated_state : boolean;
    explode_state : boolean;
  }
  ASSIGN {
    init(deactivated_state) := FALSE;
    next(deactivated_state) := deactivated_state | deactivate_airbag;

    init(explode_state) := FALSE;
    next(explode_state) := explode_state | (!deactivated_state & collision_detected);
  }
```

Fig. 7 Example of tracing formal models from requirements. In this example, we present the activation logic of the airbag specified as an SMV module. The traced nodes can be projected directly in the requirements document

requirements are defined. By displaying the formal model in the proximity of the textual requirement from where it originates, we ease the validation of the model.

4 Formalizing System-Level Designs with SMV-Based DSLs

In this section, we present how we formalize system-level designs by using DSLs built on top of SMV, the input language of the NuSMV [7] model checker. Compared to the other verification engines integrated in FASTEN (e.g., Spin and

Higher-level Modeling	Contracts	Contract-based Design	Verification Cases	Generalized Tests
"Simple" Extensions	Architecture	State-Machines	Tabular Spec	Scenarios	Tests
Convenience	SMV Convenience Extensions (e.g. adding types to module parameters, typedef)
Base	SMV Base Language

Fig. 8 On top the SMV language, there are layers of DSLs to facilitate the specification of architectures (e.g., contracts), behavior (e.g., state machines, tables), or properties (e.g., scenarios, generalized tests, temporal logic patterns)

Prism), the integration of NuSMV is the most advanced both in terms of tooling and in terms of higher-level DSLs. Figure 8 shows an overview of the stack of DSLs developed on top of SMV. At the bottom of our stack is an implementation of SMV itself. Thus, in its most basic usage scenario, FASTEN could be seen as a front-end for developing SMV models. On top of SMV we have been "growing" layers of DSLs that are at higher abstraction levels to make systems' modeling easier. A detailed discussion of the SMV extensions available in FASTEN is presented in [29].

Basic Extensions To conveniently work with SMV models, we have developed extensions for (1) adding types to module parameters, (2) defining structured types, and (3) declaring user-defined types (aka. typedefs). In Fig. 9, we illustrate examples of these extensions. The annotated types are used for IDE-level checks and automation but are removed when textual SMV code is generated (SMV does not support the definition of types for parameters of modules). Despite the fact that

```
typedef 0..100 as Time ;
typedef 0..100 as Speed ;

struct Position {
  x : 0..100;
  y : 0..100;
}

MODULE emergency_braking(crt_speed_x : Speed, car_pos : Position) {
  VAR {
    old_car_pos : Position;
  }
  ASSIGN {
    next(car_pos.x) := car_pos.x + crt_speed_x;
    next(crt_speed_x) := car_pos;
  }
}       Error: type Position is not a subtype of Speed
```

Fig. 9 Example of SMV-basic extensions (marked in figure with red). We have added support for user-defined types, structured types, or explicitly specifying types of module parameters

test case: test_1 for module: counter {

#	Inputs		Outputs	
	stop_cmd	step	out_valid	out_value
1	FALSE	1	TRUE	0
2	FALSE	2	TRUE	1
3	TRUE	3	TRUE	3
4	FALSE	1	FALSE	3
5	FALSE	5	FALSE	3

}

test case: test_2 for module: counter {

#	Inputs		Outputs	
	stop_cmd	step	out_valid	out_value
1	FALSE	1	TRUE	0
2	FALSE	2	TRUE	1
3	TRUE	*	TRUE	#
4	*	*	FALSE	#
5	*	*	FALSE	#

}

```
MODULE main
 VAR
  __crtStep : 0..100;
  cnt : counter(stop_cmd,step);

 DEFINE
  stop_cmd := ((__crtStep = 0) ? FALSE:
               (__crtStep = 1) ? FALSE: ...;
  step := ((__crtStep = 0) ? 1: (__crtStep = 1) ? 2: ...
 ASSIGN
 init(__crtStep) := 0;
 next(__crtStep) := ((__crtStep + 1) < 5) ?
                    (__crtStep + 1):(5);

 LTLSPEC ((cnt.out_valid=TRUE & cnt.out_value=0)) &
  (X (cnt.out_valid = TRUE & cnt.out_value = 1)) &
  (X X (cnt.out_valid = TRUE & cnt.out_value = 3)) ...
```

```
MODULE main
 VAR
  __crtStep : 0..100;
  cnt : counter(stop_cmd, step);
  stop_cmd_nondet : boolean; step_nondet : 0..10;
 DEFINE
  stop_cmd := ...(__crtStep=3) ? stop_cmd_nondet: ...;
  step := ... ((__crtStep = 2) ? step_nondet: ...
 
 ASSIGN
 init(__crtStep) := 0;
 next(__crtStep) := (((__crtStep + 1) < 5) ?
                    (__crtStep + 1):(5));

 LTLSPEC ...
  (X X (cnt.out_valid=TRUE & cnt.out_value=3)) &
  (X X X (cnt.out_valid = FALSE))...
```

Fig. 10 FASTEN features classical tests (left) or generalized tests which have ranges for certain inputs (right). On the lower part of the figure is exemplified the translation of these DSLs to SMV

both Time and Speed are reduced to SMV as interval types, variables with speed type cannot be assigned to those with time type.

(Generalized) Tests The most commonly used verification method by practitioners is testing. Thus, we have implemented DSLs extensions for writing tests for modules as illustrated in Fig. 10-left. In this example, the system under test is a counter module that has two inputs (stop_cmd and step) and two outputs (out_valid and out_value); if the input stop_cmd is true, the counter will stop counting and set its output out_valid to FALSE.

On the lower part, we illustrate the translation of test cases to SMV. We provide a counter (__crtStep) representing the current step in the execution of the test. Based on the current step, we select the inputs of the module (as illustrated by the stop_cmd and step defines) and the expected outputs.

A test case represents a single run of a system with specific inputs—the coverage of the input space by simple test cases is very limited. To increase coverage efficiently, we have extended the testing language with *generalized* tests (Fig. 10-right) that contain "*" (stars) as inputs. These mean that the value of the input in a certain step is taken from an interval. This way, each generalized test describes a family of test cases that cover an input space equivalent to thousands or even millions of tests. For the cases in which the value of an output is irrelevant, users can write "#" (meaning "Don't care" or "Discard"). We implement the "asterisk" using special SMV variables generated for the corresponding inputs that

```
allowed scenario: pedestrian allow
```

#	Inputs	Outputs
	ped request	ped signal
1	FALSE	DontWalk
2	TRUE	DontWalk
3	FALSE	DontWalk
4	FALSE	DontWalk
5	FALSE	DontWalk
6	FALSE	DontWalk
7	FALSE	DontWalk
8	FALSE	Walk

}

```
MODULE harness
 VAR
   __crtStep : 0..100;
   tlc : traffic_lights_controller(ped_request);

 DEFINE
  ped_request := ((__crtStep = 0) ? FALSE:
                     (__crtStep = 1) ? FALSE: ...;
 ASSIGN
  init(__crtStep) := 0;
  next(__crtStep) := (((__crtStep + 1) < 9) ?
                     (__crtStep + 1):(9));

 LTLSPEC !(tlc.ped_signal = DontWalk &
             (X (tlc.ped_signal = DontWalk)) & ...
```

Fig. 11 Examples of a high-level model that describes allowed scenarios and the translation of scenarios to SMV. The actual parameter values of the module under test, tlc, are set based on the value of the __crtStep; the LTLSPEC checks on the output ped_signal of the tlc module

are "unconstrained," meaning that they can take all values allowed by their type. An example is shown in Fig. 10-right.

Allowed/Disallowed Scenarios When the system under verification contains non-determinism, using tests to check its behavior does not make sense since due to the non-determinism for certain input values, various output values are possible. For these situations, FASTEN supports the definition of allowed/disallowed scenarios. Figure 11 illustrates a scenario definition for a traffic lights controller—when the signal ped_request is true, the ped_signal will eventually allow walking across the street. Note that the translation of scenarios to SMV is similar to the translation of tests, but with a different property specification: because a scenario is a *possible* trace through the system (which due to non-determinism might or might not happen), in order to fully check the feasibility of a scenario, we negate the entire formula in SMV. If the verification with NuSMV is successful, then the property (specifying the allowed scenario) fails since there is no trace with the given values.

Architecture, Contracts The basic modularization mechanism of SMV are modules. A SMV module has input parameters, a set of (typed) internal state variables, and a set of definitions (DEFINEs) which represent aliases for expressions. A module can be used as the type of state variables (Fig. 12-top presents three variables with type controller and one with type voter_2oo3). SMV does not specify outputs of modules, all variables of modules, and DEFINEs can be accessed globally, which breaks encapsulation. In order to describe the architecture, we extended the SMV language with special kinds of define that are outputs of modules. We also specialized the VAR section with a new concept WIRING. All variables inside a WIRING can take only module types. A WIRING thus defines a composite component that can be projected as a diagram. In Fig. 12, we exemplify the definition of a three-channel architecture for a braking controller both in textual and in diagrammatic notation.

```
MODULE system(speed1, dist1, speed2, dist2, speed3, dist3) {
  DEFINE {
    output break_cmd := v.break_cmd;
  }
  WIRING {
    c1 : controller(speed1, dist1);
    c2 : controller(speed2, dist2);
    c3 : controller(speed3, dist3);
    v : voter_2oo3(c1.break_cmd, c2.break_cmd, c3.break_cmd);
  }
}
```

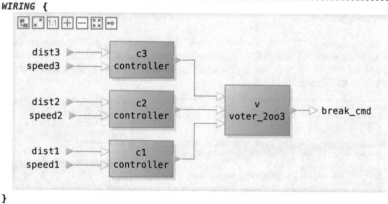

Fig. 12 Examples of a WIRING section for modeling the architecture (textual notation on top and diagrammatic notation on the bottom). The example presents a three-channel architecture for an emergency braking controller—the voting component issues a braking command only when at least two out of three controllers issue this command

Once we have defined the syntactic interface of components (inputs and outputs), the next step is to add semantics via contracts written using temporal logics or a higher-level extension (e.g., temporal logics patterns). In Fig. 13-top, we exemplify how FASTEN users can attach contracts to modules—in the example, the contracts refer to the conditions for the explosion of an airbag. The contracts are subsequently translated to SMV as LTL formula (LTLSPECs)—Fig. 13-bottom.

Contract-Based Design FASTEN also supports contract-based design by providing languages to define interfaces and assemblies. The interfaces can carry contracts (pre-/post-conditions), and their compatibility and refinement can be checked by reducing them to SMV. If the verification fails, NuSMV gives a witness (aka. counterexample) which represents a set of values for input ports which lead to the property violation. Once the counterexample is produced, it is lifted at the abstraction level of the DSL, and values of various ports can be projected on the diagram. In Fig. 14-left, we illustrate an example of interface definitions and an assembly for modeling a simplified airbag system containing an instance of a SensorPlausibilization and an instance of AirbagController. The semantics of these interfaces and of the assembly is expressed via contracts (the

```
pre(1) collision_pre : G (collision -> X collision);
post(1) exploded_only_by_collision : G (explode_cmd -> O collision);
post(2) explode_when_collision : G (collision -> F explode_cmd);
MODULE airbag_controller(collision) {
  DEFINE {
    output explode_cmd := explode;
  }
  VAR { ... }
}
```

```
MODULE AirbagController(collision)          LTLSPEC G (collision -> X collision);
  DEFINE                                    LTLSPEC G (explode_cmd -> O collision);
    explode_cmd := ...;                     LTLSPEC G (collision -> F explode_cmd);
```

Fig. 13 Examples of contracts attached to modules definitions (upper side) and their straightforward translation to SMV as `LTLSPEC` specifications (lower part). Using the contracts annotation, the intent of the formulas (being a pre-/post-condition) is preserved; when these formulas are translated to SMV, their intent is lost

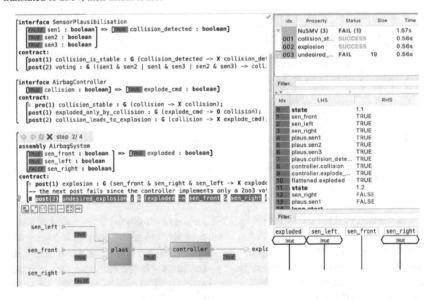

Fig. 14 Examples of the definition of architectures via semantically rich interfaces and attached contracts. Once the contracts are defined, semantic compatibility and refinement can be checked using NuSMV. If a contract fails, the counterexample can be projected in the editor, or selected variables displayed as a Message-Sequence-Chart (bottom-right)

`pre` and `post` in the code). When the verification is run, the results are lifted to the abstraction level of the input DSL—Fig. 14-right. When counterexamples are long and complex containing hundreds of entries, they can be difficult to understand. We address this by allowing different visualizations of counterexamples (such as Message-Sequence-Charts, Fig. 14-right-bottom) or by projecting the values directly in the editor—e.g., the values are presented with a red background in Fig. 14-left.

5 Modeling Safety Aspects

When developing systems operating in safety-critical applications, safety standards such as ISO 26262 [16] in the automotive domain prescribe the execution of a safety lifecycle. A safety lifecycle describes a set of activities that should be performed to support the safety assurance of a system, such as (1) hazards and risk analysis and the definition of safety goals, (2) development of functional and technical safety concepts, and (3) verification and validation that the system meets the defined safety goals. Further, the corresponding outputs of these activities, namely, the safety work products, are also described. The execution of the safety lifecycle is today mostly a manual process, and therefore time-consuming and resource demanding. This hinders the development of safety-critical systems in an agile way. This is especially problematic now when, given the current speed of technology advancements, the move toward agile development becomes a necessity [6].

Agile development of safety-critical systems calls for automation [39]. To enable automated checks on the safety work products generated by the execution of the safety lifecycle, these work products must be formally defined. We tackle this by defining a set of DSLs, called *FASTEN.safe* [5], which capture safety work products. To achieve a high degree of automation, the safety models have to be deeply integrated with the system models such as requirements and design. In *FASTEN.safe*, we experiment with the integration between safety and system engineering models.

In Fig. 15, we present an overview of the current set of DSLs for modeling safety cases and outputs of safety analysis (e.g., Hazards and Risk Analysis (HARA), or Systems Theoretic Process Analysis (STPA)). In its most basic usage scenario, *FASTEN.safe* can be seen as a front-end for modeling safety work products like hazards, control structures using STPA, or safety cases using the Goal Structuring Notation (GSN) [32]. To support automatic checks on safety case models, we extend the safety languages with semantically rich specializations of GSN constructs which are at higher abstraction level and which are integrated with other system models and verification engines. In Fig. 15, we highlight in blue the parts that belong to *FASTEN.safe*. Specialized GSN constructs reference system models such as requirements specifications or architectures annotated with contracts.

DSLs Extensions	Extensions of GSN which Integrate Formal Models					
	SMV-based Req. Spec.	Contract-based Design		Patterns		
Core	Requirements	SMV	Architecture	HARA	STPA	GSN

Fig. 15 Overview of the *FASTEN.safe* stack of DSLs. In blue, we highlight the parts that belong to *FASTEN.safe*—they comprise models to support the execution of HARA and STPA, an implementation of GSN language, and a set of GSN patterns. Specialized GSN constructs reference formally specified elements of system models such as requirements specifications written with the SMV language or contracts annotations on architecture and components

5.1 Modeling Support for Hazards and Risk Analysis

Modeling Accidents and Hazards The objective of the hazard analysis and risk assessment phase in the safety lifecycle is to identify and categorize the hazards of the *system under assurance* (also known as "item"). From each of the identified hazards, goals for its prevention or mitigation are derived. A hazard is defined as a state or set of conditions of a system that, together with other conditions in the environment of the system, could lead to an accident. An accident is an undesired or unplanned event that results in a loss, including loss of human life or human injury, property damage, environmental pollution, or mission loss [19]. As such, before starting a safety analysis, its purpose should be decided by answering the question "What kinds of losses (also known as 'accidents') will the analysis aim to prevent?" [24]. In *FASTEN.safe*, those losses are modeled explicitly, each loss having an identifier and a name (see Fig. 16-top). The safety engineer can also model the hazards list, also with an identifier and a name (see Fig. 16-bottom). Further, each hazard may be traced to one or more losses. To support the specification of hazards for systems that must demonstrate compliance to ISO 26262, the safety engineer can add ISO 26262-specific properties, i.e., severity, probability of exposure, and estimation of controllability.

Modeling Support for STPA There are several techniques that can be used for a systematic identification of the hazards and safety goals of the item. The one supported by *FASTEN.safe* is the System-Theoretic Process Analysis (STPA) [24]. After identifying the system-level hazards, a safety engineer identifies the operational and functional hazards. To this end, STPA recommends modeling a control structure, which is defined as a system model that is composed of feedback control loops. An effective control structure enforces constraints on the behavior of the overall system. A controller may provide control actions to its actuators or to a controlled process. Further, a controller may receive feedback from its sensors or

Losses model

Loss ID	Loss Name
L01	Loss of life or serious injury to people
L02	Electrical damage (economic loss)

Hazards model

Hazard ID	Hazard Name	Severity	Exposure	Controlability	Associated loss
H01	Electrical hazard	S2	E2	C2	L01
H02	Explosion of the car	S2	E3	C2	L01
H03	Cable temperature too high	S0	E0	C1	L02
H04	The cable catches fire	S1	E2	C2	L02
H05	Smoke comes out of the cable	S1	E1	C1	L02
H06	Tripping	S2	E2	C1	L01

Fig. 16 Models of possible losses (accidents) due to malfunctioning of a charging cable for electric vehicles (top) and models of hazards and their connection to losses (bottom)

STPA model – Control Structure

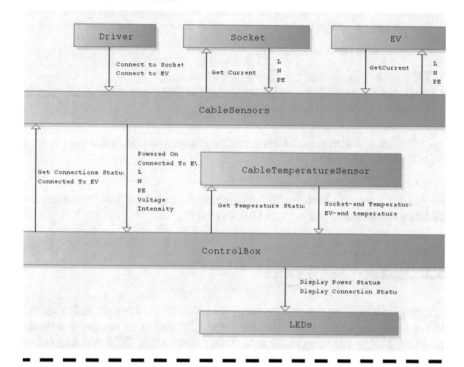

STPA model – Unsafe Control Actions

Source Controller	Action	Not Providing Causes Hazard	Providing Causes Hazard
CableSensors	Voltage	N/A	The @controller (CableSensors) provide a voltage outside the expected range while the ControlBox is powered on

Fig. 17 Models of the control structure for a charging cable for electric vehicles (top) and the analysis of possible unsafe control actions (bottom)

from another process (see Fig. 17-top). Based on such a control structure, during STPA, safety engineers can specify unsafe control actions. An unsafe control action (UCA) is an action of one of the controllers that, in a particular context and worst-case environment, will lead to a hazard (see Fig. 17-bottom). In *FASTEN.safe*, the system engineer can model UCAs as tables, as proposed in the STPA Handbook [24]. Each UCA shall be traced to at least one system-level hazard.

Modeling Safety Requirements Based on the identified hazards, safety requirements are then specified. In *FASTEN.safe*, we extended the requirements base

```
Req FSR01 : Over-current protection
created by: IEC 61581 kind: functional safety - addressed hazards H01

Disconnect EV from mains in the case of residual currents exceeding the defined limit
¶
  press enter to add sub-requirement

Req FSR02 : Disconnect because of miswiring
created by: Hannes kind: functional safety - addressed hazards H01

Disconnect EV from mains in case of miswiring
¶
```

Fig. 18 Examples of safety requirements defined for a charging cable for electric vehicles that are linked to already defined hazards

language presented in Sect. 3 with safety requirements, which have the particularity that they must trace to one or more hazards (see Fig. 18).

5.2 Modeling Safety Cases

A safety case is an argumentation about the satisfaction of system safety requirements based on all the outputs of the safety lifecycle (i.e., assurance artifacts). In *FASTEN.safe*, engineers can model safety cases using GSN and higher-level extensions. GSN contains a small number of constructs to capture an argument. It supports the graphical representation of the logical flow between safety claims, depicted as *goals*, *strategies* for decomposition of the claims in sub-claims, and evidence for the truth of the claims, depicted as *solution* elements. GSN can also represent contextual information via *context* and *assumption* elements as well as the rationale behind the arguments with the help of *justification* elements. Further, *FASTEN.safe* supports the creation and usage of safety case patterns. Similar to design patterns, safety case patterns describe solutions for how to argue the satisfaction of certain system properties, in a certain context, based on certain type of evidence. Patterns are described as templates entailing placeholders for system-specific information, which have to be filled when the pattern is instantiated in a safety case model.

GSN provides rules for connecting GSN elements among each other in order to obtain a syntactically correct argumentation. However, there are no rules defined for ensuring the semantic validity of an argumentation. In *FASTEN.safe*, we explore ways in which safety cases can be made checkable, yet easy to understand by practitioners. To this end, we define specialized GSN constructs that may be connected to each other only via special types of connections. A set of interconnected high-level safety case constructs forms a checkable safety case fragment. The use of semantically rich specialized constructs, integrated with other engineering models, allows for three types of automated checks: (1) intrinsic consistency of safety case models, i.e., checks regarding the validity of the argumentation structure, (2) consistency checks between safety case and system models, and (3) verification of safety claims within safety case models by using external verification tools. In the following paragraphs, we present these categories of checks in more detail, together with small examples.

1. Intrinsic Consistency The fact that specialized GSN constructs may only be connected to each other via specialized GSN connections constrains the argumentation structure so that only valid arguments may be constructed. For example, in Fig. 19, an instantiation of the *Argument over Hazards* checkable pattern is presented. The *Argument over Hazards Strategy* references a hazard list. This type of strategy can only be supported by goals of type *Hazard Mitigation Goal*, *Eliminated Hazard Goal*, *Negligible Hazard Goal*, and *Hazard Substitution Goal*, which reference individual hazards. Once such a goal supports an *Argument over Hazards Strategy* referencing a certain list of hazards, the goal can only reference hazards from that particular list, implemented via (static) scoping rules. If not all hazards of the list referenced by the strategy are referenced by refining goals, then an error is displayed in the editor signaling that the argument is incomplete.

2. Consistency with System Models The integration of specialized constructs extending GSN elements with different types of system models (e.g., hazards, requirements, architecture models) created in the same tool allows safety case models to be aware of changes in the referenced models. Further, we annotate each specialized construct with consistency criteria, which enables automatic identification of inconsistencies between models. For example, given an addition or deletion of an item in the requirements document referenced by the *Argument over Requirements Strategy*, an error will be triggered in the safety case model (see Fig. 20). If a new requirement is added, the consistency checks will announce that there is no argument about the satisfaction of the newly added requirement (i.e., the *Argument over Requirements Strategy* is not supported by a *Satisfied Requirement Goal* referencing the newly added requirement). If a requirement is deleted, an error will appear stating that a certain goal references a missing requirement.

3. Verification of Safety Claims Specialized Solutions can be connected with verification tools, and these verification tools can be started directly from within FASTEN. These solutions automatically integrate new verification results as evidence whenever the evidence needs to be updated. The verification results are lifted up to the safety case level, the solution entities being aware if the verification has been successful or not. Further, given a change in the verified system, the evidence is annotated as outdated (see Fig. 20), prompting the user to rerun the verification.

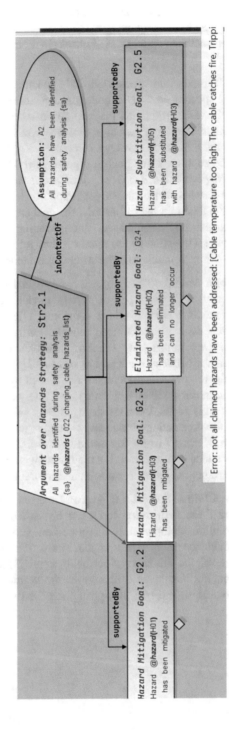

Fig. 19 Instantiation of the *Argument over Hazards* checkable pattern. A special strategy called *Argument over Hazards Strategy* references a list of hazards and can only be supported by specialized goals (e.g., *Hazard Mitigation Goals*) that reference hazards from the list. If not all hazards in the list have a corresponding goal, then an intrinsic check will fail, and an error is displayed

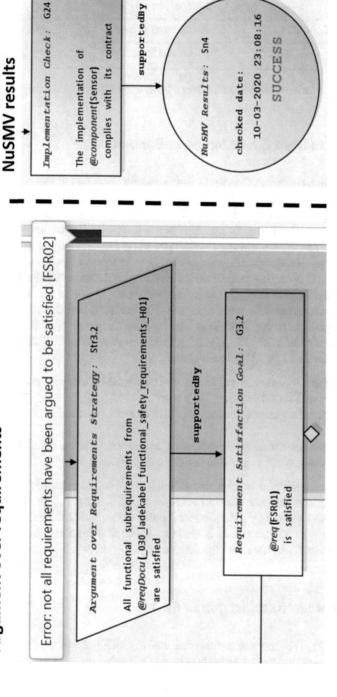

Fig. 20 On the left-hand side, it is depicted the instantiation of the *Argument over Requirements* checkable pattern for arguing about the satisfaction of all safety requirements identified for the mitigation of hazard **H1** of the charging cable system. A special strategy called *Argument over Requirements Strategy* references a list of requirements and can be linked only to goals of type *Requirement Satisfaction Goal*, which references individual requirements. If not all requirements have a corresponding goal, then a consistency check will fail, and an error is displayed in the editor. On the right-hand side, an instantiation of the *Argument based on NuSMV results* checkable pattern is presented. The specialized solution lifts up the NuSMV results, so that it describes that the verification has been successful, but the verification results are outdated

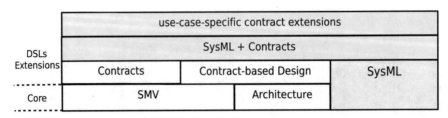

DSLs Extensions	use-case-specific contract extensions		
	SysML + Contracts		
	Contracts	Contract-based Design	SysML
Core	SMV	Architecture	

Fig. 21 Bosch-specific extensions to FASTEN (blue), based on SysML (green) and the FASTEN SMV extensions

6 Experiences from the Automotive Domain

An internal research project at Corporate Research of Robert Bosch GmbH works on providing tailored safety-oriented model-based systems engineering solutions to handle incomplete and imprecise specifications for safe autonomous systems. The project builds on the FASTEN platform as a research vehicle to drive toward this vision. In particular, we leveraged FASTEN to develop DSLs that allow the definition of safety-relevant specification as contracts on top of a system model. In the context of this chapter, the project serves as an example and evaluation of the approach proposed by FASTEN. Our solution must be applicable to industrial use cases from the various business units of Bosch. This required that the tool is built around models specified in the OMG Systems Modeling Language (SysML), which we have implemented in MPS [25] (Fig. 21, green). Our extensions to FASTEN are depicted as blue boxes in Fig. 21. They include:

1. Translation of the SysML language to the according SMV extensions (Sect. 4), especially contracts-based design (CBD)
2. A contract pattern language according to [2, 20] as another extension of the CBD extensions
3. Domain-specific extensions to SysML port and contracts to be able to verify certain properties specific to and relevant for some business units

These extensions allowed prototyping of different, use-case-specific contract *dialects* and notations that we will introduce in the following. All of them get transformed to FASTEN's SMV extensions and verified with NuSMV. The FASTEN platform together with our extensions is made available as stand-alone RCP client, referred to as *SASOCS Workbench* in the following.

6.1 System Model Specification in SysML

We use our SysML MPS implementation described in [25, 26] to specify the system model. In addition, we created a contracts language following the contract definition

```
block Primary_Device {
  port has_data_in flows in boolean
  port torque_request_from_sd flows in boolean
  port has_power_in flows in boolean
  port torque_out flows out boolean
  port torque_request_to_sd flows out boolean

  contract InSlaveNominal
    assume     true
    guarantee globally [(self.state == Slave &&
                          self.has_power_in &&
                          self.torque_request_from_sd)
                          => next [(self.state == Slave && self.torque_out)]]
```

Fig. 22 Textual definition of a SysML block with one of its contracts from our EPS use case introduced in Sect. 6.3

by [3, 8] that allows specification of formal assumptions and guarantees for SysML blocks in the form of SMV; see Fig. 22.

The SysML system model and the contracts can be translated to the CBD extensions introduced in Sect. 4. Generators translate architectural elements like SysML blocks to their corresponding SMV extensions like component interfaces and assemblies; ports with complex types are translated to multiple simple-typed ports of the SMV extension. Additional generators translate our contract specifications to the corresponding SMV extensions such as pre-conditions (our assumptions) and post-conditions (our guarantees). These translations are lightweight and are therefore performed instantaneously and continuously as the user edits the model with the help of the Shadow Models transformation engine [38].

6.2 Contract Specification Patterns

To enhance writability, readability, as well as adoption by practitioners, we allow expression of the contract's assumptions and guarantees in structured English. Our language extension follows the specification patterns by Autili et al. [2]. These patterns are already in use and known within Bosch business units (see Post et al. [28]) which eases adoption of the *SASOCS Workbench*. The top contract in Fig. 23 shows an example of a guarantee formulated as a pattern. The grammar for these patterns is well-specified [2, 20], as is their translation to NuSMV. This made implementation in MPS fairly straightforward.

A further separate language extension provides a different notation of safety contracts that is closer to domain experts, i.e., an explicit distinction of *strong* assumptions and *weak* assumptions as suggested by Kaiser et al.: "*Weak assumptions are used to describe a set of possible environments in which the component guarantees different behaviors. This separation is only methodological, and does*

```
contract safety
  assume     true
  guarantee Globally, it is always the case that                    _
               if self.pedestrian_lights == WALK holds then
               self.traffic_lights == RED holds as well
safety contract safety
  assume     true (hard, invariant, always has to be true)
  under the condition  (weak assumption) self.pedestrian_lights == WALK
               guarantee self.traffic_lights == RED
  guarantee: (self.pedestrian_lights == WALK => self.traffic_lights == RED)
```

Fig. 23 Two contract specifications with similar semantics, but different notations. The *safety contract* on the bottom explicitly distinguishes between *strong* assumptions and *weak* assumptions. The light gray text shows its translation to the *classical* contract notation

not affect the semantics of the definition of the original contracts" [17, Sect. 2.2]. The second contract in Fig. 23 shows an example of how our safety contracts look in the notation proposed by Kaiser.

6.3 Case Studies

We highlight two industrial case studies built in cooperation with Bosch business units: a redundant steering system for highly automated driving and a map-based extension to automatic cruise control (ACC).

Electronic Power Steering Electronic power steering (EPS) is used in highly automated driving vehicles. It supports the driver in steering and also can steer the vehicle without any input from the driver by receiving steering commands from a vehicle bus. Hence, the EPS system has high safety, reliability, and availability requirements.

We focus only on the electronic control unit (ECU), which is schematically depicted in Fig. 24. It includes two separate channels, named *primary* and *secondary*. Each channel has its own independent power supply and is connected to an independent vehicle bus. Both channels can communicate with each other via redundant intra-ECU communication channels. Each channel contains a lock-stepped microcontroller with an external watchdog and is able to drive two electric motors that actuate the steering. The lock-stepped microcontroller contains two cores that compute the same instructions in parallel. At each cycle, a comparator circuit inside the controller compares the state of both cores. The microcontroller exhibits fail-silent behavior, so in case the two core states are not equal, no result is output, and the directly connected motors are unlocked. In order to check whether the comparator is working correctly, an external watchdog sends challenges to the comparator and checks the correctness of the response. If the challenge is answered incorrectly or if a timeout error occurs, the entire microcontroller including the comparator is reset while maintaining fail-silent behavior.

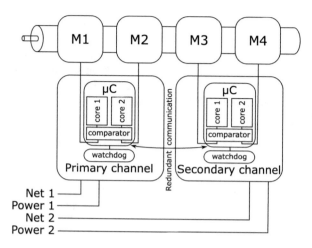

Fig. 24 Schematic overview of the ECU with two redundant channels [4]

Each channel is in one of three modes at any given time: *master, slave,* or *passive*. In master mode, the channel calculates the torque for its two motors and sends a request to the other channel in slave mode to set the same torque to its connected motors, so all four motors provide the same torque. If the torque request is not received, the channel in slave mode has to assume that the other channel has failed silently; hence, it becomes master and calculates the required torque itself. Since one channel and its directly connected two motors are sufficient to steer the vehicle, the EPS system is still available even if one channel fails. In case a channel does not receive any input from its connected vehicle bus or it detects an internal failure, it switches to passive mode and exhibits fail-silent behavior.

A qualitative analysis of the EPS case study has been carried out by Abele [1] using a fault tree analysis (FTA). In a fault tree analysis, the atomic *basic events* leading to a *top event* are identified through deductive reasoning. The causes of the top event are broken down iteratively by combining them with logical AND and OR gates. As a result of the FTA, a *minimum cut set*, i.e., the smallest possible combination of basic events that trigger a top event, can be computed and used to reason about the risk of the top event. The author performed this FTA by manually inspecting all possible states and transitions. He demonstrated that the order of events causing the mode transitions can be neglected, and thus an FTA is applicable. However, such manual analysis is error-prone and does not scale up when additional channels or faults must be considered.

Bozzano et al. [4] propose a new formal method, based on minimal cut sets, to generate explanations for operational mode transitions, in terms of causes defined as combinations of basic events and recovery actions. This method was applied on the same EPS system and showed its ability to replace the manual analysis. However, the system was modeled in plain-text SMV code, and command-line tools that require lots of expert knowledge to be used correctly were applied.

While we have not yet included the analysis method proposed by Bozzano et al. [4] in our tool, we were able to model the system and analyze its behavior for manually injected basic events. In order to do so, the contract pattern language had to be extended to be able to express the order of events. Five additional operators were added to the pattern language introduced in Sect. 6.2, which can be easily translated to the corresponding SMV expressions:

X The "*next*" operator

Y The "*yesterday*" operator is the temporal dual of X and refers to the previous time instant

Z The Z operator is similar to the Y operator, only differing in the way the initial time instant is dealt with: at time zero, Y_φ is false, while Z_φ is true

O The "*once*" operator is the temporal dual of F (sometimes in the future), so O_φ is true iff φ is true at some past time instant (including the present time).

H The "*historically*" operator is the past-time version of G (always in the future), so that H_φ is true iff φ is always true in the past

Figure 22 shows an excerpt of the SysML blocks modeling the primary channel including its ports and the internal attribute indicating the state of the channel. The contract shown in Fig. 22 describes that the primary channel starts in master mode and stays in this mode unless energy or input data is lost. Similar contracts describe the behavior in other modes, the secondary channel, as well as the components. Using FASTEN's contract-based design extensions (Sect. 4), we first verified that the modeled behavior is indeed correct, i. e., the primary channel stays in master mode indefinitely. Next, we modified the contracts of individual components to manually inject faults, e. g., the power supply does not provide power at some point in time (*finally*). In a contract assigned to the subsuming component (the EPS block), we specified that one channel in master mode is sufficient for the system to function correctly. With the contract refinement check, we were able to check that this specification is indeed valid even if one of the power supplies fails. By manually injecting more faults in other components, e. g., modify the contract of a network connection to eventually not deliver data anymore, we finally reached a point where the contract of the subsuming component is not valid anymore. In other words, we injected a (not necessarily minimal) cut set of basic events. In order to automate this fault injection process, we plan to integrate approaches such as the method presented by Bozzano et al. [4] into the FASTEN framework, which allows us to specify a fault model externally and automatically extend the system model by these faults. Furthermore, the integration with FASTEN.Safe (Sect. 5), especially the assurance case in Goal Structuring Notation, is on our roadmap.

Automatic Cruise Control (ACC) Extension The purpose of the Automatic Cruise Control (ACC) Extension system is to optimize the energy consumption of a vehicle by operating its powertrain at best efficiency based on additional navigation data. For example, the vehicle is allowed to pick up a bit of speed when driving downhill and use the resulting energy to use less power when driving the following

```
safetyPort Curvature flows in boolean ASIL = ASIL-A
                                      FTTI = 500ms
                                      cycleTime = 100ms
                                      valueRange =[0|1023]
                                      End2EndProtection = true
```

Fig. 25 *Safety Port* extension to SysML, allowing additional safety properties to be used within contracts [30]

```
Contract    EMO_cycleTime
assume      It is always the case, that the property cylceTime of all Input-Ports
            is greater equal than the property of the connected Output-Port.
guarantee   It is always the case, that specified Property cycleTime of all Output-
            Ports is guaranteed.
```

Fig. 26 Case-study-specific contract notation that refers to the safety properties of the introduced safety ports [30]

uphill section. The required road geometry is taken from map data and includes road types, slopes, curvature, and speed limits for the most probable path ahead.

Within this use case, we want to verify the component integration based on a model of safety properties of their interfaces. To allow verification with the FASTEN framework, the SysML language was extended to support the specification of safety-relevant properties per port [30]; see Fig. 25. These parameters include the automotive safety integrity level (ASIL), the fault-tolerant time interval (FTTI), cycle times of periodic real-time tasks, value ranges, and end-to-end protection being available or not. The chosen properties aim at having a wide range of data types and also represent important characteristics for vehicle software development, so that the approach is proven to be able to cope with the widely used data types found in power train development. These properties can be referred to in a domain-specific contract pattern extension that is translated to FASTEN SMV extensions as well. Thereby, these safety properties are included in the model checking process. Figure 26 shows an exemplary contract that specifies the relation of input port cycle times and output port cycle times.

7 Discussion and Lessons Learned

We started with the FASTEN project by focusing solely on extensions of SMV in October 2017, and then we gradually extended to other verification engines. Bosch started their use in late 2018, and researchers from fortiss actively contributed to FASTEN since late 2019. We estimate the total language development effort to roughly 3 person years, split mainly across the three organizations. In addition to language development, considerable effort was invested to come up with the present set of abstractions by continuously learning from our interactions with practitioners and the research community. FASTEN is still actively developed and subject to significant extensions. In the following, we present a discussion and summarize the lessons learned from developing and using FASTEN in our research and technology transfer projects.

7.1 Discussion

Maturity FASTEN is a research tool. Different functionalities are at various Technology Readiness Levels (TRLs) spanning from TRL4 (*validated in a lab*) to TRL6 (*demonstrated in industrially relevant environment*). FASTEN is currently not intended to be used in production. Our main audience are tool builders, tech leads, technology scouts, and people responsible for processes, methods, and tools who are looking for ways to improve on the status quo and address new challenges caused by the complexity increase of the products. Domain experts have the chance to test hands-on how different aspects of their systems could be modeled, tools builders get inspired about new tooling functions and how they can be integrated, and technology scouts get to know how DSLs can help increase the automation degree of the safety-critical systems development.

Extensibility The FASTEN approach relies on development and integration of modeling languages, in a bottom-up fashion by using stacks of DSLs. The multitude of DSLs presented in this chapter (developed at Siemens, Bosch, and fortiss) show that it is feasible to create domain-specific environments on top of FASTEN. As shown in Sect. 6, the FASTEN framework enables rapid prototyping for the integration of domain-specific languages with formal methods. Its modularity and extensibility allows to quickly connect other DSLs such as SysML. We could easily experiment with different language dialects for representing architecture and contracts.

Tool-Driven Research Transfer The set of functionalities provided by FASTEN exceeds the state-of-practice technologies used in the industry: today's practice is dominated by loosely coupled tool chains. Each aspect from FASTEN (requirements, architecture, design, safety analyses, safety argumentation, verification) is covered by one or more tools, each providing informal specification and modeling means (plain text for requirements, SysML for design or spreadsheets, and plain text for safety analyses and argumentation). The loosely coupling of tools leads to information loss at the boundaries and introduce accidental complexity; their informal content is preventing automation.

We have extensively used FASTEN for interacting with systems and safety tech leads to demonstrate advanced concepts related to model-driven engineering, model-based safety engineering, and formal methods. FASTEN allowed us to create demos and verify the usefulness of different modeling and specification approaches for concrete industrial problems. Being able to play with models and analyze them directly in the tool has shown to be extremely useful when presenting to respective business units and other stakeholders.

7.2 MPS Features Supporting Our Work

MPS is a key enabler for the development of FASTEN as we discuss in the following.

Language Development Productivity MPS enables highly efficient definition, extension, and refactoring of languages. The time taken between an idea and its implementation as DSLs and subsequent creation of user-level models is very short (often only a few hours or days), which allows us to perform many iterations over a short time span. This, in turn, enabled us to evolve the languages based on practitioner feedback and to experiment with new modeling concepts or their combination. In the end, this stimulates co-creation of tooling hand in hand with domain experts or fellow researchers.

Support for Modular, Extensible, and Stackable DSLs MPS' mechanisms for language modularization proved to be essential for our project, because they allow independent creation of DSLs by different organizations. For each of the integrated tools, we have implemented its input language as an MPS language. The extensions are "grown" as stacks of DSLs in a modular fashion with higher-level abstractions, similar to what mbeddr does for the C base language [35]. DSLs addressing different aspects of safety-critical systems' development (i.e., requirements, architecture, design, safety engineering) are integrated with each other, and seamless workflows beyond the boundaries of single disciplines are enabled.

Notation Freedom In FASTEN we heavily use combinations of notations: textual, diagrammatic, tree, or tabular. MPS allows easy definition of editors and provides multiple notations for the same language concepts, drastically improving usability. We learned that domain-specific or even application-specific notations are key for tool adoption by domain experts, e. g., safety engineers [25]. Sometimes, this might even require replicating the look and feel of established tools in shape and color to ease adoption.

Editor Automation and Auto-Completion MPS provides several means for increasing the automation of model authoring—context-sensitive auto-completion being the most important. This reduces to some extent the effort of learning new syntax of the verification tools—when auto-completion is used, many gotchas can be avoided.

Syntax-Driven Editing and In-Editor Errors The projectional editor of MPS guides the users to create meaningful models and prevents them upfront to make mistakes. With MPS, it is easily possible to define extensible sets of context-sensitive constraints and display errors in the editor when they are violated. Users get immediate feedback about errors, and thereby many inconsistencies can be fixed right away, allowing domain experts to focus on essential things.

Model Annotations We have used nodes attributes to annotate design models with information of variables values (e.g., the values of counterexamples are projected in the IDE as illustrated in Fig. 14). This proves to be very useful when users need to debug their models.

7.3 Open Challenges with MPS-Based Tooling

Projectional Editing While MPS' projectional editing allows maintaining different, domain- and/or stakeholder-specific notations, the projectional editor comes with its own challenges. When used with the expectation of a classical text editor or graphical editor, the resulting editing experience might lead to a lot of frustration when editors are not designed with great care and significant effort. Specialized DSLs like the "grammar cells" [36] ease the creation of editors and partially increase their usability by offering a behavior closer to the textual editors. Despite this, the users still need to be aware that they are not working with a classical textual editor.

IDE Errors Hard to Understand There is a quite steep learning curve for non-programmers to get accustomed with MPS. Many errors of the IDE seem cryptical to domain experts. Several of these errors are not even meant to be seen by non-programmers, and thereby they easily get confused. We consider these situations to be bugs in MPS.

IDE Footprint The sheer size and resource-consumption of the IDE also tend to hinder adoption. It is hard to argue why a >500 MB IDE is the right choice for working with small domain-specific artifacts that may sometimes look like simple text snippets. Developing a lightweight MPS-based IDEs is still an open challenge. Recently, there has been highly promising work done to deploy MPS on a server and access its models via web browsers in the *modelix*[6] project. We plan to leverage on this in order to make our DSLs more accessible by occasional users and thereby make experimentation by domain experts easier.

Deployment While MPS does provide support for deployment of languages as plug-ins or stand-alone IDE, this support is still fragile and requires patching jars for advanced customizations. Furthermore, integration into CI pipelines requires handling of a significant technology stack (such as ant, maven, and gradle)— automation and maintenance of the builds remains challenging.

---

[6]www.modelix.org.

8   Conclusions and Future Work

In order to tackle the complexity of safety-critical systems, increase trust, and enable agile development, we need semantically rich and deeply integrated models about different aspects of the system from requirements, design, and safety engineering. Currently, the industry is using ad hoc and loosely coupled tool chains, featuring informal models, and they cannot cope with today's challenges. In this chapter, we presented FASTEN, an extensible platform based on JetBrains MPS, developed and used by researchers from three organizations over the last 3 years, both from industry and academia. We presented a set of requirement DSLs that enable the transition from informal requirements to formal models, DSLs for the formal specification of architecture and system-level behavior, and DSLs for safety engineering and assurance. We successfully used the DSLs to model two industrial systems from the automotive domain.

MPS is a key enabling technology for the FASTEN system. *On tools building side,* MPS empowered us to efficiently build extensible stacks of DSLs; to integrate independently developed modular DSLs; to provide most appropriate notations; to equip language constructs with rich and extensible sets of semantic rules; to implement advanced editing support for creating models; and, last but not least, to integrate external analysis tools and present the analysis results at the abstraction level of the DSL. *On research and technology transfer side,* MPS enabled us to experiment with adequate abstractions, to prototype new ideas in closed-loop interactions with domain experts or fellow researchers, as well as to cooperate beyond the borders of a single company. FASTEN is an open-source and open-innovation platform for research and technology transfer in the field of safety-critical systems.

Future Work   FASTEN can be easily extended with new DSLs in order to experiment with higher-level modeling abstractions. FASTEN is still under development both at the platform level and regarding the higher-level modeling languages. We are extending and fine-tuning the DSLs based on the feedback from domain experts such as requirements, system, or safety engineers. We plan future work along three directions: enabling new modeling Abstractions, integration of existing abstractions to enable higher-level workflows, and better integration of tooling.

Examples for directions for modeling extensions are boilerplate patterns for the specification of timing/reliability aspects of requirements, integration of failure models and formal models for robustness analysis of the design, or enriching the semantics of safety argument structures to enable more automated checks. Furthermore, we plan to integrate model-based fault injection approaches similar to [4].

Regarding directions for modeling integrations, we are looking at the integration of the modeling languages developed by Bosch with more functionality from FASTEN.Safe, especially the assurance case in GSN, or the integration of system models with the software or hardware aspects.

Finally, examples of better integration of tooling in modeling workflows are to further improve the lifting of analysis results, to enhance the existing interaction with analysis engines and to integrate new engines.

References

1. Abele, A.: Transformation of a state description into a qualitative fault tree. In: Praxisforum Fehlerbaumanalyse & Co. (2019)
2. Autili, M., Grunske, L., Lumpe, M., Pelliccione, P., Tang, A.: Aligning qualitative, real-time, and probabilistic property specification patterns using a structured english grammar. IEEE Trans. Software Eng. **41**(7), 620–638 (2015)
3. Benveniste, A., Caillaud, B., Nickovic, D., Passerone, R., Raclet, J.B., Reinkemeier, P., Sangiovanni-Vincentelli, A., Damm, W., Henzinger, T., Larsen, K.G.: Contracts for systems design: Theory. Tech. rep., INRIA (2015)
4. Bozzano, M., Munk, P., Schweizer, M., Tonetta, S., Vozárová, V.: Model-based safety analysis of mode transitions. In: Proc. of SAFECOMP (2020)
5. Cârlan, C., Ratiu, D.: FASTEN.Safe: A model-driven engineering tool to experiment with checkable assurance cases. In: Proceedings of the International Conference on Computer Safety, Reliability, and Security (SAFECOMP), LNCS, vol. 12234, pp. 298–306. Springer (2020)
6. Cawley, O., Wang, X., Richardson, I.: Lean/agile software development methodologies in regulated environments - state of the art. In: Proceedings of First International Conference on Lean Enterprise Software and Systems - LESS, Lecture Notes in Business Information Processing, vol. 65, pp. 31–36. Springer (2010)
7. Cimatti, A., Clarke, E.M., Giunchiglia, E., Giunchiglia, F., Pistore, M., Roveri, M., Sebastiani, R., Tacchella, A.: NuSMV 2: An opensource tool for symbolic model checking. In: Proceedings of the 14th International Conference on Computer Aided Verification, CAV '02, pp. 359–364. Springer, Berlin, Heidelberg (2002)
8. Cimatti, A., Tonetta, S.: A property-based proof system for contract-based design. In: 38th Euromicro Conference on Software Engineering and Advanced Applications, SEAA 2012, Cesme, Izmir, Turkey, September 5–8, 2012, pp. 21–28 (2012)
9. Clarke, E., Kroening, D., Lerda, F.: A tool for checking ANSI-C programs. In: Tools and Algorithms for the Construction and Analysis of Systems (TACAS 2004), Lecture Notes in Computer Science. Springer (2004)
10. De Moura, L., Bjørner, N.: Z3: An efficient smt solver. In: Proceedings of the Theory and Practice of Software, 14th International Conference on Tools and Algorithms for the Construction and Analysis of Systems, TACAS'08/ETAPS'08, p. 337–340. Springer, Berlin, Heidelberg (2008)
11. Dwyer, M.B., Avrunin, G.S., Corbett, J.C.: Patterns in property specifications for finite-state verification. In: Proceedings of the 21st International Conference on Software Engineering, ICSE '99, p. 411–420. Association for Computing Machinery, New York, NY, USA (1999)
12. Erdweg, S., Van Der Storm, T., Völter, M., Boersma, M., Bosman, R., Cook, W.R., Gerritsen, A., Hulshout, A., Kelly, S., Loh, A., et al.: The state of the art in language workbenches. In: International Conference on Software Language Engineering, pp. 197–217. Springer (2013)
13. Graydon, P.J.: Formal assurance arguments: A solution in search of a problem? In: 2015 45th Annual IEEE/IFIP International Conference on Dependable Systems and Networks, pp. 517–528 (2015). https://doi.org/10.1109/DSN.2015.28
14. Hatcliff, J., Wassyng, A., Kelly, T., Comar, C., Jones, P.: Certifiably safe software-dependent systems: Challenges and directions. In: Future of Software Engineering Proceedings, FOSE 2014, pp. 182–200. Association for Computing Machinery, New York, NY, USA (2014)

15. Holzmann, G.: Spin Model Checker, the: Primer and Reference Manual, 1st edn. Addison-Wesley Professional (2003)

16. ISO: 26262: Road vehicles-Functional safety, vol. 26262. International Organisation for Standardization (ISO) (2018)

17. Kaiser, B., Weber, R., Oertel, M., Böde, E., Nejad, B.M., Zander, J.: Contract-based design of embedded systems integrating nominal behavior and safety. Complex Syst. Inf. Model. Q. (CSIMQ) **4**, 66–91 (2015)

18. Kelly, T., Weaver, R.: The goal structuring notation – a safety argument notation. In: Proc. of Dependable Systems and Networks 2004 Workshop on Assurance Cases (2004)

19. Knight, J.: Fundamentals of Dependable Computing for Software Engineers. CRC Press (2012)

20. Konrad, S., Cheng, B.H.C.: Real-time specification patterns. In: 27th International Conference on Software Engineering (ICSE 2005), 15–21 May 2005, St. Louis, Missouri, USA, pp. 372–381 (2005)

21. Kossak, F., Mashkoor, A., Geist, V., Illibauer, C.: Improving the understandability of formal specifications: An experience report. In: Salinesi, C., van de Weerd, I. (eds.) Requirements Engineering: Foundation for Software Quality, pp. 184–199. Springer International Publishing, Cham (2014)

22. Kwiatkowska, M., Norman, G., Parker, D.: PRISM 4.0: Verification of probabilistic real-time systems. In: Gopalakrishnan, G., Qadeer, S. (eds.) Proc. 23rd International Conference on Computer Aided Verification (CAV'11), LNCS, vol. 6806, pp. 585–591. Springer (2011)

23. Leveson, N.: Engineering a Safer World, 1st edn. MIT Press (2012)

24. Leveson, N.G., Thomas, J.P.: Stpa Handbook. Cambridge, MA, USA (2018)

25. Munk, P., Nordmann, A.: Model-based safety assessment with SysML and component fault trees: application and lessons learned. Software Syst. Model. **19**, 889–910 (2020)

26. Nordmann, A., Munk, P.: Lessons learned from model-based safety assessment with SysML and component fault trees. In: Proceedings of the 21th ACM/IEEE International Conference on Model Driven Engineering Languages and Systems, MODELS 2018, pp. 134–143. ACM (2018)

27. OMG: OMG Systems Modeling Language (OMG SysML), Version 1.3 (2012). http://www.omg.org/spec/SysML/1.3/

28. Post, A., Menzel, I., Hoenicke, J., Podelski, A.: Automotive behavioral requirements expressed in a specification pattern system: a case study at Bosch. Requirements Engineering **17**(1), 19–33 (2012)

29. Ratiu, D., Gario, M., Schoenhaar, H.: FASTEN: An open extensible framework to experiment with formal specification approaches. In: Proceedings of the 7th International Workshop on Formal Methods in Software Engineering, FormaliSE '19, pp. 41–50. IEEE Press (2019)

30. Rauhut, J.: Safety assurance of open context systems. Master's thesis, University of Applied Science Esslingen (2020)

31. Spichkova, M., Zamansky, A.: Teaching of formal methods for software engineering. In: Proceedings of the 11th International Conference on Evaluation of Novel Software Approaches to Software Engineering - Volume 1: COLAFORM, (ENASE), pp. 370–376. SciTePress (2016)

32. The Assurance Case Working Group: Goal structuring notation community standard version 2 (2018). https://scsc.uk/scsc-141B

33. Tommila, T., Pakonen, A.: Controlled natural language requirements in the design and analysis of safety critical i & c systems. Tech. rep., VTT, Finland (2014)

34. Viger, T., Salay, R., Selim, G.M.K., Chechik, M.: Just enough formality in assurance argument structures. In: Computer Safety, Reliability, and Security - 39th International Conference, SAFECOMP 2020, Lisbon, Portugal, September 16–18, 2020, Proceedings, Lecture Notes in Computer Science. Springer (2020)

35. Voelter, M., Ratiu, D., Kolb, B., Schaetz, B.: mbeddr: Instantiating a language workbench in the embedded software domain. Automat. Software Eng. **20**(3), 339–390 (2013)

36. Voelter, M., Szabó, T., Lisson, S., Kolb, B., Erdweg, S., Berger, T.: Efficient development of consistent projectional editors using grammar cells. In: Proceedings of the 2016 ACM SIGPLAN International Conference on Software Language Engineering, SLE 2016, pp. 28–40. ACM (2016)
37. Völter, M., Kolb, B., Birken, K., Tomassetti, F., Alff, P., Wiart, L., Wortmann, A., Nordmann, A.: Using language workbenches and domain-specific languages for safety-critical software development. Software Syst. Model. **18**, 2507–2530 (2018)
38. Voelter, M., Birken, K., Lisson, S., Rimer, A.: Shadow models: Incremental transformations for MPS. In: Proceedings of the 12th ACM SIGPLAN International Conference on Software Language Engineering, SLE 2019, pp. 61–65. ACM (2019)
39. Vuori, M.: Agile development of safety-critical software. Tech. rep., Tampere University of Technology. Department of Software Systems. Report 14 (2011)

Migrating Insurance Calculation Rule Descriptions from Word to MPS

Niko Stotz and Klaus Birken

Abstract Zurich Insurance used to specify their calculation rules in form-based prose and pseudo-code, which was subsequently implemented by an external party. The resulting long turnaround time seriously affected Zurich's time-to-market. Zurich and itemis replaced these specifications with the *FuMo* DSL. Its productive usage has been ongoing for more than 2 years now.

Due to MPS' projectional editor, the DSL closely resembles both the previous forms and the well-known pseudo-code. The language's generator removed the external party from the development round-trip. Consequently, the turnaround time went down by several orders of magnitude.

This project imported existing calculation rules from their C implementation and lifted them to FuMo DSL. We hid the complexity of C while lifting, so the end-users can focus on domain aspects. MPS' language integration enabled a clean design of the FuMo DSL, while edge cases could be handled with special concepts or in embedded C blocks.

We split the import process into small steps that could be validated independently. We assured all steps could be executed by the development team. By annotating the execution with trace logging and comparing the trace logs of the original source code with the generated one, we could handle large batches of similar import issues efficiently.

N. Stotz (✉)
Canon Production Printing Netherlands B.V., Venlo, The Netherlands
e-mail: niko.stotz@nikostotz.de

K. Birken
itemis AG, Stuttgart, Germany
e-mail: klaus.birken@itemis.de

1 Introduction

This chapter reports on a project at Zurich's [11] life insurance branch in Germany. Zurich and itemis [3] started this project to shorten time-to-market by improving the product implementation process. We achieved this goal by migrating technical product descriptions from Microsoft Word to an MPS-based domain-specific language (DSL). To ease adoption, we leveraged MPS' projectional editor by rendering the DSL very similar to the original Word documents. Originally, the Word documents were implemented in C by an external service provider. We superseded this process step by a generator from the DSL to C code, cutting down the turnaround time for each change from days or weeks to seconds.

> **Info**
> This chapter focuses on the implementation side of Zurich's project with itemis. Organizational aspects are out of scope; domain-specific details are only mentioned insofar as they affect technical decisions.

Section 2 introduces Zurich, key aspects of the insurance industry, and the project's context. It provides an overview of the way of working in Zurich's relevant departments prior to this project, describes participants and artifacts, and explains the challenges Zurich was facing. The participants include the *IT department* to translate requirements to technical descriptions and an *external service provider* for implementation. They worked with artifacts for data model definition, functional specification, implementation in C, and functional and regression tests.

Section 3 points out how this project met its challenges. These challenges can be categorized as follows: (1) tooling challenges, including ad hoc version control, unstructured pseudo-code in Word-based technical product descriptions, and inaccurate searches; (2) implementation challenges, like memory allocation based on different libraries, inconsistencies between technical product descriptions and implementation, and coarse test result granularity; (3) process challenges, including required C language knowledge for nonprogrammers, duplicated implementation effort, test execution only available on mainframe systems, high communication effort, and long turnaround time. This section furthermore motivates technological choices and design decisions, including MPS and key language characteristics.

Section 4 describes the project's results and delves into issues during its implementation. The section discusses MPS' benefits and shortcomings for such a migration project. It describes in detail both our first—ultimately failing—attempt to import the existing code base and the key differences that turned the second attempt into a success.

Section 5 summarizes the advantages and disadvantages of the MPS platform for this project and evaluates the project's results.

2 Project Description and Challenges

Zurich is an international insurance company offering a wide range of insurance products. An *insurance product* is one specific insurance a customer can buy. One example might be *term life insurance with constant sum insured*. They continuously develop new products or evolve existing products, for reasons such as changing regulatory requirements, technical innovation, and business innovation. These products are core assets to every insurance company. As such, they need to be maintained on the highest level of quality.

The industry faces specific challenges for their products. Insurances operate in a mature market, so there is always an alternative insurance provider with a similar offering. With such fierce competition, time-to-market is a critical success factor.

Especially for life insurance, single insurance policies might run for a long time (i.e., decades): think of a term life insurance taken out by a young mother in her 20s. Old policies must keep working as they were agreed upon, while new policies of the same product must adhere to changed laws or updated risk assessments. Thus, the IT systems must support different versions of the same product in parallel.

Prior to this project, the development process for a new or changed product consisted of these high-level steps (see Fig. 1):

1. *Product modelers* specified all domain-related details. They are experts on insurance maths and devised all calculation rules. The results are documented in a Microsoft Word *specification* document.
2. The *IT department* analyzed these documents and derived technical descriptions called *FuMos* (*Funktionenmodelle*, function models). FuMos are rigidly structured Microsoft Word documents, written in German. Conceptually, a FuMo resembles a programming language function. In the *Versicherungsanwendungs-datenmodell* (insurance application data model, VADM), the IT department described the data structures shared among all FuMos.

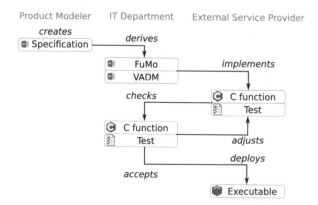

Fig. 1 Flow diagram of the original product development process before the start of this project

3. An *external service provider* received the FuMos, implemented them in C code, and wrote tests.
4. The IT department checked the implementation. In case of issues, the IT department advised the external service provider; they adjusted the implementation. These steps were repeated until all issues were resolved. Each round-trip took days to weeks—an obvious bottleneck for swift development.
5. The external service provider moved the changes into production.

> **Info**
> The remainder of this section discusses the relevant artifacts (e.g., VADM, FuMo, C sources) and participants of the product development process in detail.

2.1 Data Model Definition with VADM

The *Versicherungsanwendungsdatenmodell* (insurance application data model) is a global data structure shared among all FuMos. It was written manually in Word in tabular form, one row per element. It contains all parameters referred to by FuMos (see Fig. 2). Each parameter is assigned to a top-level structure (*Struktur vertrag*, structure contract). Next to columns *Bezeichnung* (description) to denote the nesting level and technical name, and column *Typ* (type) to specify the C data type, the table contains proprietary Zurich information not relevant to this chapter. References to other parts of VADM are denoted by an asterisk in the description column. Some references are kept for technical reasons, especially performance optimization (e.g., 2 *hmr_ptr). Note the strong technical influence on this domain-level artifact—none of C data types, pointer notation, or performance optimizations are domain specific. Composite attributes use bold formatting and only provide a description and attribute of VADM. Attribute names are unique within their parent composite structure, but not globally. Composite structures could be embedded in more than one parent composite structure, or—with different names—more than once in the same parent composite structure.

VADM also provides static input data such as mortality tables (not depicted). This data was written in Word in the obvious table form: one table per structure, one column per attribute, one row per entry.

Bezeichnung	Typ	Attribut des VADM	Entität des VADM	Proj.Code
1 vertrag		Vertragsdaten		
2 pd_id	char[]	Kenn-Produkt	LV-VERTRAG	
2 lvbegt	Long	Beginn-Termin-technisch	LV-VERTRAG	
2 ruewbeg	Long	Rueckwirkender-Beginntermin	LV-VERTRAG	
2 ~~~	Long	Beginn-Termin-Sta~	LV~~	D~
2 kz_bfr	short	Kz-f-Beitragsfreistellung	LV-VERTRAG	CH0007.53
2 kz_bfr_mahnl	short	Kz-f-Beitragsfreistellung-Mahnlauf	LV-VERTRAG	CH0010.12
2 bfr_termin_stufe	long	BFR-Termin-Stufe	LV-VERTRAG	D0023.34
2 kz_rkw_gar	Short	Kz-f-RKW-Garantiert	LV-VERTRAG	CH0007.70
2 alpha_z	double	Abschlusskostensatz-Zulagen	LV-VERTRAG	D0014.08в
2 *hmr_ptr	Void	techn. Verweis auf produkttypspez. Hoch- und Modellrechnungen	UNTYP. POINTER	
2 *bvd_ptyp_ptr	Void	techn. Verweis auf produkttypspez. Beschreibende Vertragsdaten	UNTYP. POINTER	
2 *hochrechnung_ad_ptr	Void	techn. Verweis auf Hochrechnungs-Struktur AD	UNTYP. POINTER	
2 *vk_liste	VK	techn. Verweis auf VK	POINTER	
2 vbtg		Gesamtbeitrag		
3 zw	Short	Kenn-Zahlweise	INKASSO-ZAHLWEISE-VEREINBARUNG	
3 zw_anf	Short	Kenn-Zahlweise-anfaenglich	INKASSO-ZAHLWEISE-VEREINBARUNG	VVG
3 vzb	Double	Zahlbeitrag-V-ratierlich	LV-VERTRAG	
3 vzb_vst	Double	Versicherungssteuer-Zahlbeitrag-V	LV-VERTRAG	
3 btrabgl	Double	Beitragsabgleich	LV-VERTRAG	
3 btrabgl_rea	Double	Beitragsabgleich-f-Reaktivierung	LV-VERTRAG	

© Release 18.1   gespeichert: 14.10.2015   3-4

Fig. 2 Example of a Word VADM (*Versicherungsanwendungsdatenmodell*, insurance application data model). It describes the global data structure all code is operating on. Only the first three columns are relevant to this chapter[1]

Info

In this chapter, we use the term *attribute* for one VADM member. The term *parameter* is used when a FuMo uses a VADM attribute to exchange data with the FuMo's caller. This reflects Zurich's terminology.

---

[1] Figures 2, 3, 5, 6, and 10 depict original artifacts from the customer's business domain and the corresponding DSLs. This encompasses not only the content but also the German language. In order to convey the domain as original as possible, we decided against translating the artifacts and keep them in German.

2.2   Functional Specification in FuMo

A FuMo (*Funktionenmodell*, function model) describes the technical implementation of domain functionality. From a programmer's point of view, a FuMo is a function with side effects.

2.2.1   Description

The roughly 1000 FuMos were written manually in Word, following a rigid structure (compare to annotations in Fig. 3):

1. Technical meta-information, like function name (*Funktion*), containing C source file (*Programmquelle*), VADM attributes used as parameters (*verwendete Attribute*), and other FuMos used by this one (*aufgerufene Funktionen*)
2. Domain meta-information, like product type (*Produkt-Typ*) and product category type (*PK-Typ*)
3. Administrative meta-information, like current version (*Status*) and version history (table)
4. Functionality described in German prose text (*Verarbeitungen*), interspersed with references to VADM attributes (light gray rectangle) and math formulas (medium gray rectangle)
5. Functionality described in pseudo-code (remainder of document), containing references to VADM attributes (bold) and calls to other FuMos (italics, dark gray rectangle)

The function name and source file were used by the external service provider's implementation. The referenced VADM attributes and other FuMos were maintained manually. The file's version history was kept inside the document. During active development of a FuMo, Word's *track changes* functionality was used regularly. All descriptions and names were written in German language. Inside the prose text and the pseudo-code, formatting was used to refer to parameters or used FuMos.

The pseudo-code leveraged the usual concepts of a structured, procedural programming language. It was not specified formally or informally, but used by *common sense*. Blocks were denoted by indentation and/or block end statements (Falls kz_rw_param = 12 ... sonst ... Ende Falls kz_rzw_param = 12, *if... else... end* block). References to VADM attributes were implicit, i.e., only distinguishable from local variables by formatting—if applied correctly. VADM attribute references were implicitly scoped: whether the attribute was a member of a composite type, and of which instance of the composite type, was inferred from the context. Think of a nested dot notation with only the rightmost part actually written. Parameter passing semantics (pass-by-value vs. pass-by-reference) was implicit.

Funktionenmodell

Formale Beschreibung

a	**Funktion:**	berbwvekFF		
a	**Programmquelle:**	vmsctfa1.c		
b	**Produkt-Typ:**	FONDS	**PK-Typ:**	KAPITAL-KONTO
		Name	Verw.	Entität
a	**verwendete Attribute:**	lkm_akt_param	E	PARAMETER
		lkm_faell_param	E	PARAMETER
		ber_zweck_param	E	PARAMETER
		kz_rzw_param	E	PARAMETER
		bwvek	A	RETURN
a	**aufgerufene Funktionen:**	berbweinzelFF VTRKermbtgfaellFF		
c	**Status:**	18.1		

c zuletzt geändert von ... am ...	Joachim Kaiser, 09.10.2014

d **Verarbeitungen**

Die Funktion liefert den Barwert per lkm_akt_param des vorschüssigen Zahlungsstroms der Höhe 1 von Monat lkm_akt_param bis lkm_faell_param – jeweils einschließlich. Zahlungszeitpunkte sind jeweils die Monatsbeginne, also **lkm_akt_param** -1 bis **lkm_faell_param – 1.**

Der Parameter **kz_rzw_param** steuert die zu berücksichtigende Zahlweise des Zahlungsstroms. Möglich sind zur Zeit nur die Ausprägungen 0 (Zahlungen zu den Beitragsfälligkeiten) und 12 (monatliche Zahlungsweise).

e Schleife über lkm_faell_hilf = **lkm_akt_param** bis **lkm_faell_param**

Falls **kz_rzw_param** = 12

kz_bf_hilf = 1

sonst

kz_bf_hilf = *VTRKermbtgfaellFF*(lkm_faell_hilf)

Ende Falls **kz_rzw_param** = 12

bwvek = bwvek

+ kz_bf_hilf * *berbweinzelFF*(**lkm_akt_param**, lkm_faell_hilf - 1, **ber_zweck_param**)

Ende Schleife

return **bwvek**

berbwvekFF.docx 14.10.15 19:14 Seite 1/1

Fig. 3 Example of a Word FuMo (*Funktionenmodell*, function model). It describes the technical implementation of domain functionality. The annotations correspond to Fig. 6[1]

In theory, the prose text and pseudo-code would be equivalent and geared towards different audiences: prose text to explain the FuMo to domain experts, and pseudo-code to enable programmers to implement the FuMo. In most cases, this pseudo-code was detailed enough to be executed by a computer.

2.2.2 Challenges

Version Control The FuMo and VADM documents were kept on a shared network drive without formal version control, leading to well-known issues: any cooperative or conflicting change to a document had to be coordinated manually; keeping a change log was up to each developer's discipline.

FuMo Structure FuMos were written manually in Word, i.e., without any formal consistency check. The pseudo-code was effectively a programming language, but written without any programming tools: neither syntax check nor named reference resolution or type compatibility check was available to the authors.

Without syntax check, block boundaries might be ambiguous. FuMos used both indentation and block end statements to denote block boundaries. They might be inconsistent or ambiguous (e.g., "Does this statement belong to the `if` statement or the outer loop?").

As references had been updated manually, inconsistencies were inevitable: the lists of attributes and used FuMos had not been updated to changes in the functional description, and name changes had not been propagated to all references. The formatting of references to VADM attributes and used FuMos had not been applied in all cases. To start a new FuMo, the developer had copied a similar existing one. This practice had increased the likelihood of outdated references.

Implicit scoping of VADM attribute references was prone to omitted intermediate steps in the attribute access chain. Think of a nested dot notation with missing segments in between. As VADM attribute names are not globally unique, references could be ambiguous.

Due to the missing language specification, different authors used different wording to describe the same concept, e.g., both *Schleife über x = ... bis ...* (loop over x = ... until ...) and *Schleife von x = ... zu ...* (loop from x = ... to ...). The lack of specification leads to undefined semantic details: in the above example, will the upper limit value be contained within the range of the loop?

2.3 Executable Implementation in C

FuMos and VADM structures were implemented in the C programming language.

2.3.1 Description

The C implementation consisted of about 200,000 lines of code. It was compiled for verification with Microsoft Visual Studio by the IT department and for production on a mainframe with the system's own compiler. In most cases, one FuMo was implemented by one C function; it was up to the implementer to split the implementation in more functions, if necessary. VADM composite attributes mapped to C `structs`, with simple VADM attributes as members. The implementation leveraged an extensive library of insurance-specific functions, like depreciation or life expectancy.

The source code files were stored on a shared network drive, similar to FuMos. A basic version control scheme kept old versions of C source files by renaming the old version of the file and appending a version number. The version number loosely related to the *Status* field in FuMo.

The code base evolved alongside the executing system. Thus, a lot of different engineers worked on the code over time, leading to inconsistent style and patterns. Most notably, the code base contained three different APIs for memory allocation.

The run-time environment initialized one complete VADM structure. FuMos had access to this complete structure, read and/or wrote parts of the structure, and returned to the caller. The caller implicitly knew which attribute would contain the expected results. Other attributes would be used to store intermediate results or to transfer intermediate results between multiple FuMos participating in the same processing chain. Value function parameters rarely passed domain-related information; mostly, they were used to provide temporary values like counters or array indices.

2.3.2 Challenges

Version Control The basic version control scheme led to similar issues as mentioned in Sect. 2.2.2: it requires lots of manual coordination and complicates tracking changes.

Memory Allocation During this project, we had to unify the memory allocation to one API. This process revealed typical issues related to this topic like use-after-free, duplicate memory usage, or mismatches between the APIs used to allocate and free the same chunk of memory.

Global VADM Structure One global structure for passing around input and output parameters removes all locality from single functions; thus, the system effectively has only one global scope. Two functions can only work in the same context if they *happen* not to use the same VADM attributes. Without a formal declaration which VADM attributes are used by each function for input, output, or temporary storage, there is no way to assure correct results besides individual inspection.

2.4 Functional and Regression Tests

The calculation rules implemented by FuMos constituted core business value for Zurich. Appropriately, extensive functional and regression tests were in place.

2.4.1 Description

The test data accumulated to about 1.5 terabytes; a complete test run on a mainframe took several days. The test setup integrated tightly with VADM processing. Each test loaded a specific state of the VADM structures, ran the FuMo under test, and binary compared the VADM structures afterwards with the expected result. Members of the IT department created the test data during development.

2.4.2 Challenges

Execution Environment As both test setup and expected result consisted of all values of the complete VADM structure, they were tightly coupled to the mainframe execution environment. They could not be executed on a PC. Thus, the mainframe staging system that ran tests became a bottleneck.

Test Result Granularity The test output was binary compared with the expected result. This way, we could only determine automatically whether a test succeeded or failed; we could not provide a reason for failure. Any failing test required detailed analysis of the test output data and thus considerable manual effort.

2.5 IT Department Team Authoring VADM and FuMo

The members of the involved team in the IT department possessed thorough insurance domain knowledge, gained through years of experience. They leveraged their expertise to translate insurance specifics from the specification documents into technical FuMo documents. The IT department also verified the C code created by the external service provider by means of manual code inspection.

2.5.1 Description

The team consists of five engineers and one team lead. One team member had a formal computer science background. Their prior experience with version control was limited. None of them had worked with modeling tools before.

IT department staff regularly searched through all existing functionality. Rationales to do so included finding all contexts a FuMo is used in or assuring the interpretation of an attribute's value.

The IT department had to assure the correct implementation of FuMos by the external service provider. Thus, the team members needed to be proficient in understanding C source code. Due to the domain's complexity, simply reading the C source code was not sufficient; they also needed to execute, debug, and experiment with the C implementation.

The team members sometimes prototyped parts of a FuMo for validation in C, before sending it to the external service provider.

2.5.2 Challenges

Search Through C Code Base The staff could not use their primary artifacts, the Word files containing VADM and FuMos, for global searches. Word's search capability had proven to be insufficient in both flexibility and performance. Thus, the team members regularly used the C implementations as search corpus. Only the C implementations guaranteed correct named references to parameters, functions, etc. Correct names were crucial, as most searches looked for function or parameters usage—similar to *find all references* functionality in an *integrated development environment* (IDE).

C Language Knowledge For all of searching, prototyping, and assuring the correct implementation, team members had to know C. Thus, each member of the team had to understand both the domain (to interpret the specification documents) and the intricacies of the C language. These diverse requirements seriously limited staffing options.

Duplicated Implementation Effort As the only available executable environment was C code, team members could only validate a FuMo via a C prototype implementation. However, implementing C should have been the responsibility of the external service provider. Thus, team members had to delve into tasks that were more suitable to other parties, and the external service provider had to spent effort into reworking or re-implementing the prototype.

2.6 External Service Provider Implementing Executable C and Tests

The external service provider accounted for all implementation, testing, performance, monitoring, scalability, and security.

2.6.1   Description

Only the external service provider's engineers were allowed to change the C implementation or tests. The majority of the involved engineers were located overseas and did not speak German as their native language.

2.6.2   Challenges

Inconsistencies Between FuMo and C Implementation   A FuMo and the corresponding C implementation were maintained by different parties. Also, they were updated without any strong feedback mechanism or notification, especially during iterative issue resolution. Thus, they often grew apart.

Two different FuMos, or even two parts of the same FuMo, might have been implemented by different software engineers. Even though the FuMo used the same pseudo-code, it might have been translated to C in different ways.

High Communication Effort   The IT department and the external service provider were from different corporations, native languages, and professional backgrounds. This setup increased communication overhead, posed the chance of misunderstandings, and potentially added commercial aspects to the discussion.

Long Turnaround Time   The IT department assured correct functionality of the implementation, but only the external service provider could apply changes. Any time IT department members spotted incorrect functionality, they had to describe the issue, hand it over to the external service provider, wait for the implementation, and could verify the change only then. The round-trip could cause the IT department members wait for a long time (days to weeks) until they would know the definitive result of any change.

3   Proposed Solution

We proposed to migrate VADM and all FuMos to MPS models and generate the C implementation. The revised product development process is depicted in Fig. 4. It removed the *implement–check–adjust* cycle between the IT department and the external service provider.[2] The test creation process remained the same. The IT department continued to define FuMos and VADM, but in MPS instead of Word. The MPS models were stored in the *Subversion* [1, 7] version control system. All non-domain aspects were moved to support libraries. This approach removed most of the identified shortcomings.

---

[2]Close cooperation is still required to ensure nonfunctional requirements and infrastructure enhancements.

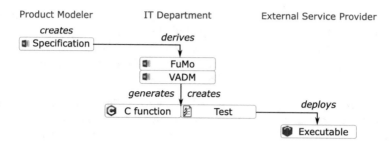

Fig. 4 Flow diagram of the revised product development process, as resulted from this project

Version Control FuMo models are versioned like any other development artifact. The versioning system provides proven diff/merge support, completely integrated into MPS. C implementations do not need to be versioned any more, as they can be regenerated at any time.

FuMo Structure By formalizing the FuMo DSL, we provide all the regular IDE tooling: entering invalid or inconsistent syntax becomes impossible by design, auto-completion supports the user with available choices, named references are replaced by technical references and guarantee consistency, and model validation provides instant feedback. We have implemented a generator, so inherently each construct has defined semantics. Of course, all technical meta-information listed in the FuMo header is implicit: we automatically collect the lists of parameters and used FuMos from the FuMo DSL.

Memory Allocation The FuMo DSL does not provide direct access to memory management; it is handled by the generator. We use the same memory allocation API throughout the generator.

Global VADM Structure We do not change this fundamental software design choice. For once, the approach has been chosen for a good reason: it minimizes data copying and enables high performance. Also, such a change has been out of the scope of the project, and it would not have been wise to combine such a fundamental implementation change with the technology migration at hand. However, due to the FuMo DSL, we know exactly which FuMo (or function) accesses which VADM attribute. This offers a sound basis for future changes, if desired.

Test Execution Environment Although not initially planned, we had to enable test execution on PCs to finish the migration to MPS (see Sect. 4.4). Based on this work, Zurich now runs tests in an automated nightly build.

Test Result Granularity For our migration efforts, we semiautomated more granular failure reports through trace logging (see Sect. 4.4). However, this required invasive changes to the production code and would hamper performance seriously. Thus, these changes were only temporary.

Enable Accurate Searches Most searches look up named references. By providing first-class technical references, we replaced these searches by straightforward linking and *find all references* commands. FuMo models become the definitive source, and generation guarantees consistency of FuMo and C implementation. Thus, we cannot miss any reference from the model.

C Language Knowledge and Duplicated Implementation Effort IT department staff writes FuMos in FuMo DSL and can immediately generate, compile, and execute the resulting implementation—prototyping and implementing a FuMo uses the same tool. This means searching and prototyping does not require detailed knowledge of the C language any more. Programming skills are still required for debugging purposes.

Inconsistencies Between FuMo and C Implementation All C implementations are generated from the FuMo models. Therefore, we cannot have any inconsistencies. As we use the same generator for all FuMos, all C implementations for one FuMo DSL concept must be identical.

High Communication Effort With code generation, writing FuMos and implementing them in C happen at one place by one party, thus removing any communication overhead. The external service provider stays accountable for nonfunctional aspects of the system. They can focus on support libraries and operational aspects. Of course, both parties need to stay in close alignment.

Long Turnaround Time Code generation delivers the C implementation of every FuMo within seconds, i.e., several orders of magnitude faster than the previous process. This provides the IT department with immediate feedback and direct control of the outcome.

3.1 Solution Technologies

We proposed MPS as implementation technology for several reasons. To ease adoption, we kept a form-like user experience similar to the existing FuMos. This is easily feasible with projectional editors. Similarly, projectional editors support VADM's tabular style. Intermixing prose text in FuMos with formal math expressions and links to parameters would be hard or even impossible with parser-based systems.

MPS' language extension mechanism supports clean language design decisions while providing an escape mechanism for edge cases in legacy code. We could design the FuMo DSL on its existing level of abstraction. Edge cases like irregular pointer access were handled by language concepts unavailable to the end-user, while performance optimizations like pointer arithmetic could be represented by embedded C code.

itemis knows MPS very well, rendering this technology the obvious choice. We could leverage our experience with *mbeddr* [2, 4, 10] as MPS-based C implementation and generator to C source code. Our internal importer from C source code to mbeddr C models enabled the import of existing FuMo implementations. Zurich tasked itemis with maintenance, migration, and further development, relieving them from MPS development.

We proposed Subversion as a version control system, as it was available within Zurich. It is less complex than git, lowering the initial threshold especially for users unfamiliar with version control systems. MPS supports Subversion out of the box.

3.2 VADM

The Word variant of VADM was represented as a set of tables with one row per attribute (see Sect. 2.1). Static input data like mortality tables was also maintained as Word documents containing tables.

3.2.1 Language Design

Our MPS language followed the same table-based approach for both parameters and input data (see Fig. 5). Optionally, we showed known references to this attribute from both VADM and FuMo (not depicted).

3.2.2 Language Implementation

The VADM language is straightforward. The concepts were translated one-to-one from the semantics of rows and columns in Word, with *slisson tables*[3] we could implement the editors easily.

At first, we tried to keep exactly the same kind of granularity as in Word, i.e., one root node for each Word document. Some of these root nodes became too large to render performantly in MPS. We split them up at the first nesting level. Due to automatic references, the additional effort for the end-user was negligible: They can follow references similar to hyperlinks or *find all references* to navigate in the opposite direction.

We tried to simplify this kind of navigation even further by listing all usages of each VADM attribute in an additional column. However, this means running *find all references* for each attribute. This only performs well for small VADM documents or not heavily used attributes. Thus, we hid this column by default.

3.3 FuMo

The visual design of our language tried to follow the Word representation closely (see Fig. 6). We used the same layout for domain and technical meta-information.

---

[3] Editor extension for advanced table structures [5].

VADM–Hauptstruktur rg_kk

		Bezeichnung	Typ	Attribut des VADM	Entität des VADM	Proj.Code
	1	rg_kk		nur zur Übung		
💡	2	fo_____tz	Ganzzahl	Attribut-Langname	\<no entity\>	\<no project\>
	2	___tz	Kommazahl	Attribut-Langname	\<no entity\>	\<no project\>
	2	ko_ra_id	Zeichenkette	Attribut-Langname	\<no entity\>	\<no project\>
	2	kz_zus_gar	Bool	Attribut-Langname	\<no entity\>	\<no project\>
	2	zm	Ganzzahl	Attribut-Langname	\<no entity\>	\<no project\>
	2	_____akt	Kommazahl	Attribut-Langname	\<no entity\>	\<no project\>
	2	zw	Kommazahl	Attribut-Langname	\<no entity\>	\<no project\>
	2	vtrk_zb	Ganzzahl	Attribut-Langname	\<no entity\>	\<no project\>
	2	kz_mandant	Zeichenkette	Attribut-Langname	\<no entity\>	\<no project\>

Fig. 5 Example of an MPS VADM (partially blurred for confidentiality)[1]

Funktionenmodell berbwvekFF

Formale Beschreibung

- **Funktion:** berbwvekFF
- **Programmquelle:** vmsctfa1.c
- **Produkt-Typ:** Fonds   **PK-Typ:** Kapital-Konto
- **Status:** 18.1

- **Parameter-Attribute**
  - lkm_akt_param
  - lkm_faell_param
  - ber_zweck_param
  - kz_rzw_param

- **Verwendete VADM-Attribute**
  - Keine verwendeten VADM-Attribute, werden automatisch hinzugefügt

- **Rückgabe-Attribut**
  - *bwvek*

- **aufgerufene Funktionen**
  - *VTRKermbtgfaellFF* (a)
  - *berbweinzelFF* (a; b; c)

- **Beschreibung**
  - Die Funktion liefert den Barwert per @lkm_akt_param des vorschüssigen Zahlungsstroms der Höhe 1 von Monat @lkm_akt_param bis @lkm_faell_param – jeweils einschließlich. Zahlungszeitpunkte sind jeweils die Monatsbeginne, also #lkm_akt_param – 1# bis #lkm_faell_param – 1#. Der Parameter @kz_rzw_param steuert die zu berücksichtigende Zahlweise des Zahlungsstroms. Möglich sind zur Zeit nur die Ausprägungen 0 (Zahlungen zu den Beitragsfälligkeiten) und 12 (monatliche Zahlungsweise).

  Hilfsvariablen
  - kz_bf_hilf

- **Verarbeitungen**

```
    Schleife über lkm_faell_hilf = lkm_akt_param bis lkm_faell_param
      Falls kz_rzw_param = 12
        kz_bf_hilf = 1
      sonst
        kz_bf_hilf = VTRKermbtgfaellFF (lkm_faell_hilf)
      Ende Falls kz_rzw_param = 12
      bwvek = bwvek + kz_bf_hilf * berbweinzelFF (lkm_akt_param; lkm_faell_hilf - 1; ber_zweck_param)
    Ende Schleife über lkm_akt_param bis lkm_faell_param

    return bwvek
```

Fig. 6 Example of an MPS FuMo (the annotations denote the same elements as in Fig. 3)[1]

3.3.1 Language Design

Our solution automatically derived the technical meta-information from the FuMo DSL: the language contains first-class concepts for calls to other FuMos or parameter references; we listed such references in the appropriate section. Subversion managed the administrative meta-information.

We amended the prose text descriptions with explicit references to parameters (light gray rectangle in Fig. 6) and other FuMos (dark gray rectangle). Math formulas could be written in an embedded variant of the FuMo DSL (medium gray rectangle) [9]. Contrary to the Word version, we prefixed all references and formulas with specific characters akin to at-mentions (@) or hashtags (#) in social media. We applied the text formatting familiar from Word.

The original pseudo-code used some interesting depictions for typical control structures. We implemented them also for the FuMo DSL. They might inspire similar design for other languages. `switch`-like statements are shown as a table (see Fig. 10). The table header contained the condition. Each row represents one `case`. The condition fills the first column, the body is in the second column, and the third column contains a description or comment.

The end of a block repeated a rendering of the relevant details, e.g., the condition in an `if` (e.g., "Ende Falls *kz_rw_param = 12*" in Fig. 6).

We tried hard to shield users from technical details of the C implementation. Ideally, the generator should handle them. mbeddr takes care of some parts, e.g., generating an arrow or dot member access operator. For cases we could not handle automatically, we followed two approaches:

- Create a FuMo DSL concept, but do not allow the users to enter it. These concepts would only be used by the importer, e.g., explicit pointer de-referencing, explicit type casts, and explicit memory allocation.
- Use a generic *escape to C*: allows entering any mbeddr C code. Obviously, this code is completely in the responsibility of the user and outside any guarantees by the system. Examples include performance optimizations via pointer arithmetic and calls to undesired deprecated functions.

An internal accessory model provided stubs[4] for all library functions that need to be called by FuMo DSL code (see Sect. 2.3.1).

3.3.2 Language Implementation

We implemented prose text with embedded references and math by using *richtext* language.[5] We introduced specific characters (@ for references, # for math) as we had to switch into the appropriate context and show the correct auto-completion entries to the user. This turned out to be very helpful, as the users could directly type these symbols, and did not have to invoke any special action to switch context.

itemis has lots of experience with implementing procedural languages like Zurich's pseudo-code. Thus, the basic language implementation did not pose serious challenges. We spent some time inventorizing all pseudo-code concepts, as there was no formal definition. In discussions with the IT department, we clarified

---

[4]Referenceable placeholders for objects outside the model.
[5]Editor extension for arbitrary text intermixed with other elements [6].

ambiguous semantics. During *pattern recognition* (see Sect. 4.2.4), we identified additional domain-specific concepts and added them to the language.

Initially, we wanted to infer types in FuMo. After the first experimental import of the old code base, this turned out to be infeasible: in some cases, we could not assure the "direction" of type inference. As an example, a function parameter type should only be inferred from the function's body, not from its callers. Especially with the unsolved issue of function parameter type inference, any change to the code would trigger the typesystem to re-evaluate major parts of the code base. This overwhelmed MPS' typesystem implementation and would have rendered the editors unusable. However, the end-users were acquainted with explicit types anyway—they read them in C on a daily basis. Thus, explicit typing was acceptable; it was required in VADM in any case. Type checking could draw lots of inspiration from mbeddr and was implemented without notable hurdles.

4 Evaluation and Lessons Learned

MPS proved to be a good choice for this project. Projectional editors combined the familiar look to the end-users with semantically structured models. In combination with language extensibility, the editors enable new ways of dealing with imported legacy code. Generators assured consistent output.

We could mitigate MPS-related issues regarding editor and typesystem performance. We faced the biggest hurdles in the project with the import of the original code base. They were not specific to the MPS platform, but a mixture of generic legacy transformation and code-to-model challenges. The project's total effort amounted to roughly 40 person months.

4.1 Language Implementation

For both VADM and FuMo, projectional editors enabled a visual design very close to the original Word forms. Their implementation did not pose considerable challenges. MPS' language composition features enabled clean language design without too many compromises for backward compatibility, as we could defer edge cases to special constructs not accessible to end-users, or even to plain C models. Standard MPS features like technical references with forward and backward navigation, Subversion integration, and plain text intermixed with model elements contributed tremendously to the final result.

We experienced platform limitations in two areas: large editors tend to perform sluggishly, and we were not able to implement type inference as we planned. The table-heavy VADM editors posed the biggest editor performance issue. These editors barely interacted with the type-checking system, thus excluding it as potential performance issue. The original VADM was kept in few and large Word files.

Thankfully, the top-level VADM structures provided semantic borders to break the documents into several root nodes. The resulting editors performed reasonably. Regarding the typesystem issue, we abandoned the idea of heavy type inference. It might be possible to implement, but we decided not to spend the required effort. The impact on the result was acceptable, as our end-users were familiar with typed languages.

4.2 Import and Generation

Importing the original code was by far the most difficult part of the project. Even our original approach took way longer than anticipated (see Sect. 4.3), before we concluded it to be infeasible because of too long feedback loops. We eventually succeeded with the second approach (see Sect. 4.4), but again had to overcome unforeseen hurdles like running mainframe-targeted tests on a PC and semiautomatically analyzing test failures.

We suspected most of these issues to be typical of automated application modernization projects; the team had only limited experience in this field. Using domain-specific languages presumably did not add huge additional effort to the fundamental problem. On the contrary, the flexibility of language composition and interactive *pattern recognizers* (see Sect. 4.2.4) opened up new possible ways to deal with application modernization issues.

4.2.1 Import Source

We quickly concluded that we had to use the C code as base for the import: the C code was executed, so only this artifact was known to be correct. The IT department members knew a multitude of examples where the Word FuMo was outdated with respect to the implementation in C.

Another argument was technical: Word is hard to read programmatically, especially as we would need to preserve formatting (to identify parameter references) and indentation (for control structures). Zurich used advanced Word features like tables and track changes; this would require a very solid library to reliably access the document's contents.

The original Word VADM/FuMos contained also a prose text description. In some cases, this description was copied into the C source code as comments; in these cases, we could import the description. For others, we had to copy them by hand from Word. As a one-off action, this would take an acceptable effort of a couple of days.

4.2.2 Big Bang vs. Incremental Transformation

A *big bang* transformation processes the complete source at one point in time in its entirety. Before the transformation, only the source is used; afterwards, the complete source is discarded and the transformation outcome is the only usable artifact.

With an *incremental* transformation approach, parts of the source are transformed step by step. The source artifacts are valid for non-transformed parts, whereas the outcome is the only valid artifact for already processed parts.

We opted for a big bang approach to import for several reasons. The mbeddr C importer was responsible for importing the C source files into mbeddr C models. It had to resolve all references prior to import. The code base turned out to be highly coupled. There were no simple ways to cut the code base in independent sub-slices that would not reference each other. So we either had to import all at once or import overlapping sub-slices and merge them afterwards. We deemed merging to be much harder than an all-at-once import.

Both the IT department and the external service provider kept working on the source code during the project. This implies that in an incremental transformation approach, the C source files might have changed between the import of different sub-slices—rendering any kind of merge even harder. Moreover, it would have been very hard to synchronize changes in the C source files to already imported mbeddr C models, let alone FuMo DSL code. Applying some parts of a change in already imported models, and other parts in the C source files, does not seem feasible either.

The big bang approach implied we would never change imported models manually (besides development trials). All the improvements were applied to the original C source code. This provided some investment safeguard for Zurich: even if this project would have failed, they could still profit from the source code improvements.

4.2.3 Cleaning Up Sources

The C source code had been developed over several decades. Naturally, it accumulated technical debt like different implementation styles or workarounds that have never been fixed. One particular area to clean up was memory management: the source code used three different APIs to allocate and free memory. Zurich, itemis, and the external service provider unified them to one API. This revealed memory management issues like use-after-free or duplicate memory usage. Analyzing and resolving these issues took considerable effort.

The abovementioned cleanups are independent of targeting a DSL environment. More specifically to this target, we had to unify different ways to implement the same FuMo DSL construct in order to automatically recognize it. For example, the pseudo-code contained a `foreach`-loop concept. This can be implemented in C with a `for` loop and index variable, or a `while` loop and pointer arithmetic. If both patterns had been used a lot, we would recognize both. However, if it had been implemented mostly with a `for` loop and the source had contained only a handful of `while`-loop variants, we would rewrite the latter.

4.2.4 Lifting from C to FuMo DSL

Lifting[8] describes the process of transforming rather low-level C code to semantically richer, more domain-specific language. Most of the concepts are very similar in C and FuMo DSL. A simple tree walker would process the C AST and create the corresponding FuMo DSL model. The tree walker would wrap any unrecognized element in an *escape to C* FuMo DSL concept.

Through manual inspection and interviews with IT department staff, we identified typical patterns in the C sources and how they mapped to FuMo DSL. We were very keen on matching domain-specific patterns, like formulas typical to insurance math, mortality table lookups, or access to Zurich-specific subsystems.

We implemented *pattern recognizers* to find these patterns during the C to FuMo DSL transformation. The tree walker incorporated the reliable (i.e., no false positives or negatives) recognizers. Less reliable recognizers were available as MPS intentions on the FuMo DSL. This combined the required manual assurance with easy application. It allowed continuous improvement both during our project and future development. Examples for pattern recognizers include `foreach` loops (see Fig. 7), VADM access, memory allocation, or pointer (de-)referencing.

The logical inverse of pattern recognizers are FuMo DSL to C generators. We developed them alongside the pattern recognizers.

4.2.5 Handling VADM Access

The actual VADM structures were expressed as C `struct`s; importing them was straightforward. Importing their usage, however, was much more difficult. The runtime environment initialized one complete VADM structure (see Sect. 2.3.1). We spent serious effort to identify these access patterns and provide good abstractions in FuMo DSL. We did not want to expose the end-users to the intricacies of C pointer handling—they should be concerned about insurance business logic.

We found quite a few cases where we could not reliably recognize, lift, and generate the correct pointer access scheme; especially performance-optimized loop handling turned out to be problematic. There were even too many of them to be treated as edge case with an *escape to C*.

We resorted to explicit FuMo DSL constructs for pointer handling *for existing cases*: We created these concepts in the importer, but did not provide the end-user with a way to instantiate them. If future changes require performance optimizations, they need to be provided through support libraries.

```
public class ForEachStatementMapper extends AbstractFumoMapper {
  protected Pattern<BaseConcept> getPattern() {
    <ForStatement(condition: NotEqualsExpression(right: NullExpression()))>;
  }

  public node<> map(node<ForStatement> input) {
    node<Iterator> iterator = input.iterator;
    node<Expression> init = null;
    if (iterator.isInstanceOf(ForVarRef)) {
      node<ForVarRef> forVarRef = iterator:ForVarRef;
      init = forVarRef.init;
    } else if (iterator.isInstanceOf(ForVarDecl)) {
      node<ForVarDecl> forVarDecl = iterator:ForVarDecl;
      init = forVarDecl.init;
    }

    node<ForEachStatement> result = <ForEachStatement(
      body: # mapRecursive(input.body):StatementList,
      collection: # mapRecursive(init):Expression,
      variable: # mapRecursive(iterator):IVariableDefinitionOrReference
    )>;

    putInTrace(input, result);
    return result;
  }
}
```

Fig. 7 Screenshot of the pattern recognizer for `foreach` loops. *getPattern()* describes eligible partial C language models for this pattern recognizer; in this case, `for` loops with a condition of `...!= null`. *map()* converts the input pattern to the output. It handles both variable references (`if` clause) and variable declarations (`else` clause) in the loop's initializer. Finally, it constructs the partial FuMo output model and descents recursively into subtrees

4.3 First Importing Approach

Our original approach to import the existing C code base into FuMo models relied on Zurich's exhaustive test coverage. We expected fast turnarounds for each import–lift–generate–compile–test cycle. We anticipated issues in the transformation chain to be found by the C compiler and relied on test coverage to catch implementation differences.

The major steps were (reflected in Fig. 8):

1. Use mbeddr C importer to import the original C source code to equivalent mbeddr C models. This step should be a one-to-one transformation. Where needed, we would improve the importer iteratively.
2. Lift mbeddr C models to FuMo models, as described in Sect. 4.2.4. We expected to learn about new patterns and edge cases during development. They would be resolved by improving the FuMo lifter or replacing edge cases in the original source code (see Sect. 4.2.3).

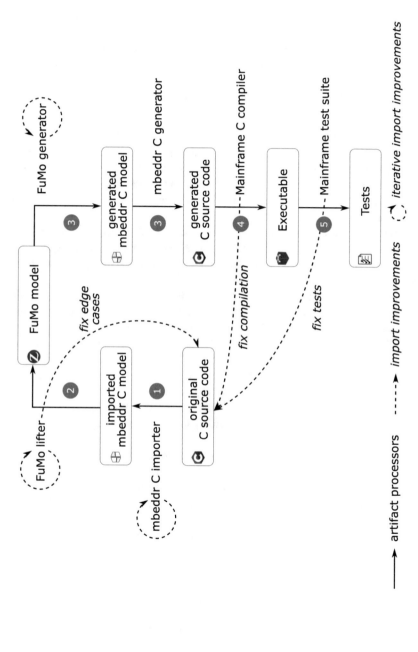

Fig. 8 Flow diagram of the first importing approach. Note the long feedback loop

3. Use the FuMo generator to transform FuMo models into mbeddr C models, and directly generate to C source code with the mbeddr C generator. The mbeddr generator has been used extensively in different contexts, so we expected little issues on that part.
4. With the help of the external service provider, compile the generated C source code on a mainframe. For any issues found by the compiler, we would adjust the original source code or the relevant processor along the transformation chain. We would iterate through these steps until the generated code can be compiled.
5. Execute the tests on a mainframe, as they relied on architecture specifics (see Sect. 2.4.2). We would apply the same fixes and iterations as for compiler issues until all tests pass.

This approach seems very naive in hindsight; we gained a lot of the experience presented here only after we had devised this approach. Based on our initial information, we assumed way faster processing times for almost every step. We anticipated a lot of similar errors at the beginning and assumed to converge quickly to edge cases—due to the highly automated processing chain. We ran into serious issues and ultimately failed with this approach.

The mbeddr C importer had been used in other projects before. However, C is very flexible. We encountered more parsing issues than anticipated, leading to more adjustment work. The importer took a lot longer to process the complete code base than we expected.

Originally, we expected to reuse the same PC-based C compiler as the IT department. This would have allowed us to compile the generated code ourselves, avoiding coordination overhead with the external service provider. Unfortunately, this compiler was unavailable outside Zurich, and setting up a usable development environment turned out to involve major effort. The PC-based C compilers were used to receive a lot more advancements than the mainframe C compiler. Thus, the compiler's error messages were not as helpful as we hoped.

The itemis development team lacked some advanced C knowledge. Even with some support by the external service provider, analyzing the compiler issues took some time.

During development, we did directly adjust mbeddr C models to analyze issues. But to assure our fixes would solve the problem, we had to adjust the original source code and rerun the complete import. At the beginning, a complete import took a weekend; later, we improved it to a night. In any case, the assurance took considerable time.

The test setup was not available outside Zurich's mainframe environment. Thus, a test cycle included shipping the generated code to Zurich, transferring it to the test system, running the tests, and getting the results back to the developers—not exactly a fast turnaround.

To summarize, this approach failed because it relied on fast turnarounds and checks in the model, or at latest by the compiler, to point out the majority of issues. We could not achieve the required turnaround speed and could recognize the issues only too late within an iteration.

4.4   Second Importing Approach

After having learned the lessons about turnaround speed and early issue recognition the hard way, we adjusted our approach. We could not reduce the turnaround time by splitting up the import in several sub-slices due to high coupling and the continued work by users, as described in Sect. 4.2.2.

Thus, we split up the single steps as far as possible and assured earliest possible feedback (steps are reflected in Fig. 9):

1. Make sure C import, generation, and test work (light gray background). After this step, we can trust the import processing chain from original C source code to mbeddr C model, and the generation processing chain from mbeddr C model via generated C source code, compiled with the mainframe compiler, to pass the mainframe test suite.

    a. Use mbeddr C importer to import the original C source code to equivalent mbeddr C models, and improve the mbeddr C importer where needed. This step stayed the same compared to the first importing approach.
    b. Directly generate the mbeddr C model to generated C source code, and compare the result with the original C source code. As the mbeddr C generator was quite mature, the only variable in this feedback loop was the mbeddr C importer. We adjusted the importer and, if required, the original C source code, until we encountered no meaningful differences between the original C source code and the generated one.
    c. Compile generated C source code on a mainframe. The generated C source code was *equivalent*, but not *identical* to the original one. The C language is very flexible, and especially compilers with a long history interpret details differently. With this feedback loop, we assured the mbeddr C generator and mainframe C compiler agreed on the same interpretation of C.
    d. Execute tests on a mainframe based on the generated C source code. Even if the mainframe C compiler had not flagged any issues with the generated C source code, it might still interpret the code differently than the original C source code. We eliminated that possibility by running the existing test suite on a mainframe based on the generated C source code.

2. Get faster, more expressive test results (medium gray background). This step aimed at decoupling the test execution from the external service provider, and provide more detailed insight why a test failed.

    a. Get tests running on a PC. We already managed to set up the PC-based C compilers during the first importing approach. However, we still depended on both the external service provider and a mainframe execution environment to run the test suite. With considerable effort, we found a way to run the test suite on a PC. Eventually, it produced the same test results as on a mainframe.
    b. Improve test results by trace logging. The test results did not provide any details on the failure reason, as explained in Sect. 2.4.2. Individually

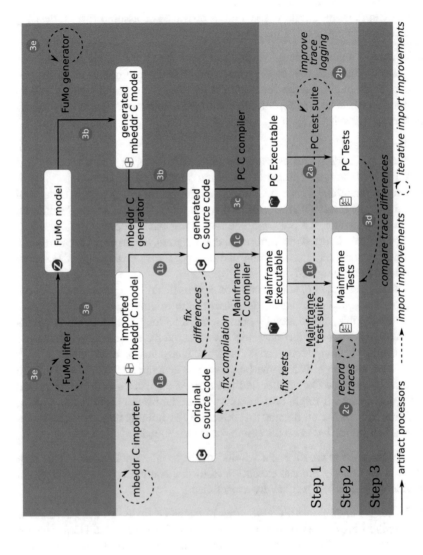

Fig. 9 Flow diagram of the second importing approach. Different background shades denote steps. Note separate, short feedback loops in each step

analyzing each test failure was completely unfeasible. Thus, we devised a semiautomated analysis: we wrote scripts that added trace logging statements to the C source code (refer to Sect. 4.5 for details).

c. Record traces from executing tests based on the original source code. With the trace logging scripts in place, we could apply them to the original C source code and record a *known good state* of trace logs. These logs formed the baseline to analyze deviations from running the test suite based on the generated C source code.

3. Get lifting and FuMo generation right (dark gray background). This step would add the missing parts of the processing chain compared to the first importing approach.

a. Lift mbeddr C to FuMo DSL. Based on the validated mbeddr C model, we could focus on fine-tuning the FuMo lifter. Similar to the first importing approach, we extended and adjusted our pattern recognizers or fixed up edge cases in the original C source code.

b. Generate to C. After the work on step 1b, we were sure the mbeddr C generator would produce the desired output. Thus, we only had to get the FuMo generator up to par.

c. Run tests based on the generated code. Leveraging the effort of step 2a, we could run the test suite in a PC environment based on the generated C source code. We amended the generated C source code with the trace logging scripts.

d. Compare traces with recorded traces to point out problematic parts. From step 2c, we had a baseline of trace logs. We compared this baseline with the trace logs from step 3c.

e. Iteratively improve FuMo lifter and generator. At this point, the only source for trace log deviations could be the FuMo lifter or the FuMo generator. Thus, we adjusted both of them as necessary. We could execute all steps locally and iterate quickly. Finally, we met one of our original assumptions: We started with a lot of similar trace deviations and quickly converged on a rather small list of singular issues.

4.5 Analyzing Test Failures at Scale

We were fortunate enough to have a good test coverage to begin with, spanning thousands of tests. However, the test setup would only tell us *which* tests failed, with little hints on *why*. Due to the amount of tests and their execution time, it was infeasible to debug them one by one. Based on the available *known good* version of the source code, we devised a more efficient solution.

We wrote some scripts to automatically inject trace logging code at function calls, if branches, and other key points in the source code. We applied these scripts on both the original source code and our generated code. After running the tests with the original source code, we knew the desired execution path.

Simple text comparison of the desired execution path's trace logging with the one from our generated code revealed the places of concern. We could also cluster similar issues, as they would deviate from the desired execution path at the same point. This way, we reduced the number of required turnarounds by fixing the whole cluster at once and thus our total time to process all issues.

It turned out a lot of the failing tests were false failures. As described in Sect. 4.2.3, we streamlined different implementation styles. As a side effect, this changed how VADM attributes were used to store intermediate results. So after executing the FuMo under test, the resulting VADM structure contained different values than expected, and the test failed—but the differences only concerned insignificant attributes! Identical trace logs in a failing test proved to be a strong hint for those cases.

5 Conclusion

5.1 Technical Advantages and Shortcomings

MPS provided the means to go for a fully structured DSL while keeping the familiar document appearance (see Fig. 10). Language composition allowed well-designed and fine-grained decisions on first-class language concepts vs. backward-compatible compromises or low-level constructs. Intentions provided an easy way to integrate user-controlled pattern recognizers to higher-level language concepts.

We encountered performance issues if MPS showed big root nodes in the editor. Even more useful editors would have been possible if MPS provided cached access to *find all references* results. We did not succeed with implicit type inference, because we could not strictly separate scopes that should infer types from scopes that should only check type compliance.

Importing the existing code base posed the biggest challenge by far. We succeeded with a multistep approach that ensured early feedback on import issues. We strongly recommend short feedback loops for any large-scale model import, as processing time grows exponentially with every additional step, and the complexity even of simple transformations gets out of hand quickly.

Both non-incremental C source code import and insufficient model merge technologies forced us to only change the original C sources and reimport the complete code every time. Improvements in both fields would considerably simplify similar challenges.

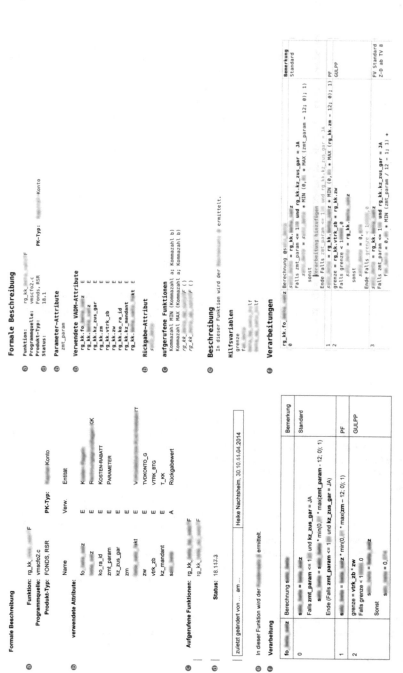

Fig. 10 Comparison of Word (left) and MPS FuMo (right), including *track changes* marks in Word, and a switch-like statement. The annotations point out equivalent contents on both sides. (Partially blurred for confidentiality)[1]

5.2   Project Results

The users in the IT department are very satisfied with the MPS-based solution. We consider their early involvement, continuous feedback during development, and early training for both MPS and Subversion vital for the success of the project.

The users profit from guaranteed consistency of the FuMo DSL code they are working with and the executed code. The turnaround time between a change in a FuMo and testable code is reduced by several orders of magnitude—from days or weeks to seconds.

Complete version control of all artifacts through Subversion assures safe processing and storage of changes. It streamlines collaboration, both within the IT department and with the external service provider.

Shorter turnaround time and reduced communication overhead lead to higher efficiency and fewer misunderstandings, ultimately speeding up time-to-market and lowering the defect rate.

Both the IT department and the external service provider can focus on their field of expertise: insurance domain knowledge and operational/nonfunctional aspects, respectively.

The MPS-based FuMos are in production for more than 2 years. Zurich and itemis continue to improve the system, migrate it to new MPS versions, and adjust it to new requirements.

References

1. CollabNet Inc., et. al.: Apache Subversion (2021). https://subversion.apache.org/
2. Grosche, A., Igel, B., Spinczyk, O.: Exploiting modular language extensions in legacy c code: An automotive case study. In: I. Schaefer, D. Karagiannis, A. Vogelsang, D. Méndez, C. Seidl (eds.) Modellierung 2018, pp. 103–118. Gesellschaft für Informatik e.V., Bonn (2018)
3. itemis AG: MPS Extensions (2021). https://www.itemis.com/
4. itemis AG, et. al.: mbeddr (2021). http://mbeddr.com/
5. itemis AG, et. al.: mbeddr Platform (2021). http://mbeddr.com/platform.html
6. JetBrains s.r.o., et. al.: MPS Extensions (2021). https://jetbrains.github.io/MPS-extensions/
7. Pilato, C.M., Collins-Sussman, B., Fitzpatrick, B.W.: Version control with subversion: next generation open source version control. O'Reilly Media, Inc. (2008)
8. Tomassetti, F., Ratiu, D.: Extracting variability from c and lifting it to mbeddr. In: Proceedings of the International Workshop on Reverse Variability Engineering (2013)
9. Voelter, M.: Integrating prose as first-class citizens with models and code. In: MPM@ MoDELS, pp. 17–26. Citeseer (2013)
10. Voelter, M., Ratiu, D., Schaetz, B., Kolb, B.: mbeddr: an extensible c-based programming language and ide for embedded systems. In: Proceedings of the 3rd Annual Conference on Systems, Programming, and Applications: Software for Humanity, pp. 121–140 (2012)
11. Zürich Beteiligungs-Aktiengesellschaft (Deutschland): Zurich Versicherung (2021). https://www.zurich.de/

Part II
JetBrains MPS in Research Projects

Projecting Textual Languages

Mauricio Verano Merino, Jur Bartels, Mark van den Brand, Tijs van der Storm, and Eugen Schindler

Abstract One of the strengths of the Jetbrains MPS projectional language workbench is that it supports mixing different kinds of notations (graphical, tabular, textual, etc.). Many existing languages, however, are fully textual and are defined using grammar technology. To allow such languages to be used from within MPS, language engineers have to manually recreate the syntax of a language using MPS concepts. In this chapter, we present an approach to automatically convert grammar-based languages to MPS languages, by mapping context-free grammars to MPS concept hierarchies. In addition, parse trees of programs in those languages are mapped to MPS models. As a result, MPS users can import textual languages and their programs into MPS without having to write tedious boilerplate code. We have implemented the approach in a tool, Rascal2MPS, which converts grammars in the built-in grammar formalism of Rascal to MPS. Although the tool is specific for the Rascal context, the underlying approach is generic and can be instantiated for other grammar formalisms. We have evaluated Rascal2MPS by generating an importer for a realistic programming language (ECMAScript 5). The results show that useable MPS editors for such languages can obtained but that further research is needed to improve their layout.

M. V. Merino (✉) · J. Bartels · M. van den Brand
Eindhoven University of Technology, Eindhoven, The Netherlands
e-mail: m.verano.merino@tue.nl; j.bartels@student.tue.nl; M.G.J.v.d.Brand@tue.nl

T. van der Storm
University of Groningen, Groningen, The Netherlands
e-mail: storm@cwi.nl

E. Schindler
Canon Production Printing, Venlo, The Netherlands
e-mail: eugen.schindler@cpp.canon

1   Introduction

Language workbenches [1] (LWBs) are IDEs that support engineers in the design and development of software languages [2]. These tools are aimed to improve and increase the adoption of Language-Oriented Programming (LOP). LOP is a technique for solving software engineering problems through the use of multiple domain-specific languages (DSLs) [3]. DSLs are small and simple languages tailored to solve problems in a particular application domain [4]. There are two types of DSLs, internal and external [3]. The first one reuses the concrete syntax of the host language and its parser, much like a stylized library. An external DSL, however, typically requires the implementation of a parser and compiler.

Jetbrains MPS is a projectional language workbench that obviates the need for parsing and, as a result, allows the engineer to define DSLs with a multiplicity of notations, varying from textual, and tabular, to diagrammatic, or prose-like. MPS provides editor support that allows users to directly edit the abstract syntax structures of a language rather than reconstructing such structure from the linear sequences of characters entered in text editors.

Nevertheless, many existing languages are defined purely textually. For instance, all mainstream programming languages are textual (e.g., Java, C#, Javascript etc.). But many DSLs, like GNU Make, Graphviz, SQL, etc., are strictly textual languages too. To make such existing languages available for (re)use from within MPS, language engineers have to redefine the syntax of such languages using the concepts and editor features of MPS, which is a tedious and error-prone endeavor.

In this chapter, we detail an approach to take an existing context-free grammar (e.g., from a parser generator tool) of a textual language and convert it automatically to MPS concept definitions. As a result, such languages can be imported into MPS without having to write abstract syntax definitions by hand. Furthermore, the approach supports loading parse trees of existing programs into automatically generated MPS editors, so that they become available for reuse immediately.

Companies in the Eindhoven (The Netherlands) region (e.g., Canon Production Printing and ASML) have been using DSLs for several years [5]. Some of these companies use textual LWBs, projectional LWBs, or both, such as Canon Production Printing. When companies are using both types of LWBs, it is often desired to reuse existing textual languages within a projectional LWB and vice versa. If such a reuse facility exists, companies will avoid the costs of reimplementing features and maintaining the same functionality in different platforms. Likewise, developers can be more productive from the engineering point of view and invest more time in developing new features or improving existing ones. Finally, the reuse strategy could reduce time to market for new products.

In this chapter, we present an approach toward bridging the gap between textual and projectional LWBs, which has been implemented in the context of the Rascal (textual) and MPS (projectional) language workbenches. Our Rascal2MPS [6] takes a Rascal grammar and converts it to equivalent concept hierarchies and editor definitions in MPS.

The contributions of this chapter can be summarized as follows:

- A generic bridge between textual and projectional LWBs. Employing this bridge, developers can obtain a projectional language in JetBrains MPS from a context-free grammar written in Rascal.
- A mechanism to generate projectional editors from a context-free grammar. This mechanism uses a set of pretty-printing heuristics that takes into account the production rules' structure.
- A tool to import existing programs written in a textual language as projectional models of the generated language.

The structure of this chapter is as follows: in Sect. 2, we describe the motivation that supports this work and the problem statement. Then, in Sect. 3, background information about software language engineering is presented. In Sect. 4, we present our solution and its architecture. Then, we evaluate the current approach by comparing an ad hoc implementation of JavaScript against a generated version (Sect. 5). In Sect. 6, we discuss the limitations of the current approach. We conclude this chapter with related work and future research directions (Sects. 7 and 8).

2 Motivation

A DSL offers programming abstractions that are closer to domain requirements than general programming languages [7]. Likewise, DSLs offer syntax closer to the domain expert's knowledge. DSLs have been around for a few decades, but they have not been widely adopted in the industry yet [8, 9]. The limited adoption of DSLs in the industry is partly due to the lack of mature tools [10, 11].

Nowadays, language engineers have different tools and metalanguages to choose from when implementing a new language. The right selection of such tools is essential for the language's success. Likewise, this means that companies end up with diverse ecosystems of languages and tools. These tools are continuously changing to support diverse business requirements, depending on what they want to achieve or the organization's needs. Communication between tools and languages is often required to share functionalities among different components. When there is no communication between platforms, developers could reimplement these features. However, reimplementing these functionalities is a cumbersome activity, and it does not fix the problem in the long term because, at some point, it might be required to reimplement those features again.

For instance, there are several textual languages at Canon Production Printing that they have been developing and maintaining over the years. However, they have more recent languages that were developed using a projectional LWB. They have recently found that they require to interoperate languages, which means reusing language concepts across LWBs. This interoperation allows them to address new business needs and reduce the time to market. Therefore, they demand a bridge that supports the reuse and translation of existing languages across heterogeneous LWBs.

3 Background

In this section, we present some of the basic concepts used in this chapter. The concepts described below are mostly about Software Language Engineering (SLE). Mainly, we focus on discussing the language's syntax and its definition in both textual and projectional LWBs.

3.1 Software Language Engineering

Software Languages A software language is a means of communication between programmers or end users and machines to develop software. Languages are often divided into three main components, namely, syntax, semantics, and pragmatics [2, 12]. A language's syntax is a set of rules that define valid language constructs, such as defining a group of rules that captures expressions or statements. The language's syntax can be expressed in a concrete and abstract way. The concrete syntax is designed as the user interface for end users to read and write programs, whereas the abstract syntax is the interface to the language implementation. The semantics of a language is a mapping between syntactic elements and their meaning. Such mapping can be defined in different manners, such as operational semantics or model-to-model transformations [2]. Language pragmatics describes the purpose of the language constructs, and it is defined informally often in natural language through narrative and examples.

Language-Oriented Programming (LOP) LOP is an approach to software development where the main activity in development consists of defining and applying multiple DSLs [3, 13]. Programmers define custom languages to capture aspects of a software system in a structured way. The idea is that each language captures the essential knowledge or aspects of a domain problem so that the productivity increases and domain knowledge is decoupled from implementation concerns. In other words, a DSL captures the *"what"* of the domain, whereas compilers, code generators, and interpreters define the *"how."*

Language Workbench To help language engineers develop software languages, they rely on metaprogramming tools called LWBs. These tools simplify and decrease the development cost of software languages and their tooling [3]. A LWB offers two main features: a specialized set of metalanguages for defining the syntax and semantics of DSLs and affordances to define various IDE services such as syntax highlighting, error marking, and auto-completion. In this chapter, we are going to focus on the former. There are two types of LWBs, namely, textual (also called syntax-directed) and projectional (also called structural) [1, 2, 14]. The main difference between these types is how languages are described and how programs are edited. A textual LWB employs plain text and parsing to map concrete syntax to the internal structures of the LWB. For instance, Rascal uses context-free grammars as formalism [15] for defining the language's syntax. A projectional LWB allows a program's AST to be edited directly [16]. For instance, MPS uses an AST Concept Hierarchy [14] to define the language's structure, and MPS implements a projectional editor for manipulating programs. A *projectional editor* is a user interface (UI) for creating, editing, and manipulating ASTs.

3.2 Syntax of Textual and Projectional Languages

As mentioned before, a software language's syntax is a set of rules that describe valid programs [2]. Usually, it is divided into two, namely, concrete syntax and abstract syntax. In this subsection, we describe how different LWBs represent both types of syntaxes.

In textual LWBs, a language's concrete syntax is usually specified using Context-Free Grammars (CFGs), while in projectional LWBs, the concrete syntax is expressed as AST projections. Below we explain both approaches and highlight their main differences. To clarify the differences between textual and projectional LWBs, we will use Rascal and MPS. Table 1 shows a comparison of the notations used by these two platforms to define language's syntax.

Context-Free Grammars A CFG is a formalism for describing languages using recursive definitions of string categories. A CFG C is a quadruple:

$$C \rightarrow (S, NT, T, P)$$

in which S is the start symbol ($S \in NT$), NT is a set of syntactic categories also known as nonterminals, T is a set of terminal symbols, and P are production rules that transform expressions of the form $V \rightarrow w$. V is a nonterminal ($V \in NT$), and w could be zero or more nonterminal or terminal symbols ($w \in (T \cup NT)$).

For example, a CFG that describes the addition of natural numbers N is shown below:

$$G = (Exp, \{Exp, Number\}, \{+\} \cup N, P)$$

Table 1 Comparison between notations used for describing languages in textual and projectional LWBs

Language	Rascal	MPS
Concrete syntax	Context-free grammar	Projectional editor definition
Abstract syntax	Algebraic data rype	AST concept hierarchy

The production rules P are defined as follows:

$$start \rightarrow Exp \tag{1}$$

$$Exp \rightarrow Number \tag{2}$$

$$Exp \rightarrow Exp + Exp \tag{3}$$

$$Number \rightarrow i\,(i \in N) \tag{4}$$

By applying the previous production rules, we can write the arithmetic expression $a + b$ (where $a, b \in N$) as:

$$start \rightarrow Exp$$
$$Exp \rightarrow Exp + Exp$$
$$Exp + Exp \rightarrow a + Exp$$
$$a + Exp \rightarrow a + b$$
$$a + b$$

Once there are no more nonterminals (NT), we cannot rewrite the expression $a + b$ because there are no production rules that can be applied. We say that a program is syntactically valid if there is a derivation tree from the start symbol to the string that represents the program.

For instance, the concrete and the abstract syntax of the language described above can be implemented in Rascal, as shown in Listings 1 and 3, respectively. The first one defines two nonterminals, namely, *Exp* and *Nat*. The *Exp* rule contains two productions, for literal numbers and addition. The *Nat* nonterminal defines natural numbers. AST Listing 3 defines an Algebraic Data Type (ADT) that captures the structure of the language with two constructors: *nat(...)* and *add(...)*. The terminals of the expression grammar (i.e., Nat) are represented using built-in primitive types of Rascal (i.e., int).

Syntax in Projectional LWBs In a projectional LWB, the syntax is also divided into its concrete and abstract representation. The concrete syntax corresponds to an editor definition, whereas the abstract syntax is defined in a concept hierarchy.

Projectional editors do not share a standard formalism for defining abstract syntax; therefore, each platform provides its own formalism. MPS uses a node

Listing 1 Concrete syntax of addition and numbers in Rascal

```
start syntax Exp = number: Nat nat | addition: Exp lhs "+" Exp rhs;

lexical Nat = digits: Natural;
```

Listing 2 Lexical library

```
lexical BasicString = [a-z]*[a-z];
lexical Natural = [0-9]+;
lexical String = "\"" ![\"]* "\"";
```

Listing 3 Abstract syntax of addition and numbers in Rascal

```
data Exp = adddition(Exp lhs, Exp rhs) | number(int n);
```

```
concept Addition extends    BaseConcept
                 implements Expression

  instance can be root: true
  alias: <no alias>
  short description: <no short description>

  properties:
  << ... >>

  children:
  left  : Expression[1]
  right : Expression[1]

  references:
  << ... >>
```

```
concept Number extends    BaseConcept
               implements Expression

  instance can be root: false
  alias: <no alias>
  short description: <no short description>

  properties:
  value : integer

  children:
  << ... >>

  references:
  << ... >>
```

Fig. 1 Concept definition of addition (left) and numbers (right)

concept hierarchy [14]. For instance, the AST representing a language for describing the addition of natural numbers is shown in Fig. 1. The MPS implementation uses an *Expression* interface and two concepts, namely, *Addition* and *Number*. To represent integer numbers, we use the built-in *integer* data type.

How the users will edit expressions of this kind is defined by an editor definition. However, MPS also offers a generic *reflective editor*, so that every concept in MPS comes with a default editor. A reflective editor is a projectional representation of an AST that developers can use out of the box. An example of an arithmetic expression program using the reflective editor is shown in Fig. 2.

4 Approach: Projecting Textual Languages

This section presents a mechanism for enabling textual languages usage in a projectional editor by generating a projectional language from a grammar. In other words, the current approach translates existing textual languages into equivalent projectional languages, including both structure and editor aspects. Then the translation of existing textual programs into equivalent models of a generated projectional language is discussed. We first show a general overview of the approach. Then,

Fig. 2 Reflective editor for
the operation a + b, where
$a = 1$ and $b = 6$

```
addition {

    left :
        number {
            value : 1

        }
    right :
        number {
            value : 6

        }
}
```

we explain a generic mapping between CFGs and the structure of a projectional
language. Afterward, we describe the derivation of a projectional editor from a
grammar; we show how to derive the editor aspect for each generated concept in
the language structure. Finally, we explain the translation of textual programs to
projectional models that conform to a generated projectional language. Although
the current approach is implemented using Rascal and MPS, its principles can be
adopted in the context of other LWBs.

4.1 Mapping Grammars to Concept Hierarchies

This section contains the description of the mapping between a grammar and the
structure of a projectional editor. The current approach analyzes a CFG, namely,
production rules, nonterminal, terminal, and lexical symbols. To illustrate each of
the concepts of the mapping, we use the grammar for the *Addition language* shown
in Listing 1.

Nonterminal Symbols The counterpart of a nonterminal symbol in MPS is an
interface.

An interface is a programming concept that may define the public, shared
structure of a set of objects (typically described by classes). In MPS, interfaces
are represented as concepts, and their instances are called nodes. In the same way
that interfaces may have multiple implementations (the classes), a nonterminal is
"realized" by one or more productions. For instance, in Listing 1, there are two
nonterminals, namely, Exp and Number. Thus, these two nonterminals map to two
interfaces with the same name in the generated projectional language. The definition
of the Exp interface in MPS is shown in Listing 4.

Listing 4 Definition of the Exp interface in MPS

```
interface concept Exp extends <none>

  properties:
  << ... >>

  children:
  << ... >>

  references:
  << ... >>
```

Listing 5 Mapping a CFG start symbol into a MPS concept

```
concept prog extends <default> implements Program

  instance can be root: true
  alias: <no alias>
  short description: Exp

  children:
  expression :Exp[1]
```

Furthermore, one additional nonterminal that we have not mentioned is the start symbol. Structure concepts in MPS have a property named *instance can be root*. This attribute indicates whether the concept can be used to create an AST root node [14]. In our mapping, we take the start symbol of the grammar, and create a concept in MPS. This concept will have the property *instance can be root* set to true. For instance, in Listing 5, we show an example using the expression language, assuming we have a start symbol Program with a single production, prog.

Productions A nonterminal rule has one or more productions. As we mentioned before, a nonterminal in a CFG is mapped to an interface concept in MPS. Therefore, to keep the relationship between a nonterminal and their productions, we map each production as an MPS *concept*. Each *concept* must implement the interface of the nonterminal. Moreover, the AST symbols in the production rule are mapped to either the *children* or the *properties* field. When the symbol is a nonterminal, it is defined in the *children* field, and when the symbol is terminal or a lexical, it is mapped in the *properties* field. Note that symbols that are only relevant to concrete syntax, such as keywords and operator symbols, are not mapped here, since they are not part of the abstract syntax; they will be used to define the editor aspects (see below).

For instance, addition (Listing 1) is a production rule of the nonterminal Exp. This production rule is mapped into an MPS concept that implements the Exp interface. The resulting concept in MPS is shown in Listing 6.

Listing 6 Result of mapping a production rule to a concept in MPS

```
concept addition extends <default> implements Exp

  instance can be root: false
  alias: +
  short description: Exp + Exp

  children:
  lhs :Exp[1]
  rhs :Exp[1]
```

Listing 7 Lexical mapping

```
concept digits extends <default> implements <none>

  instance can be root: false
  alias: <no alias>
  short description: <no short description>

  properties:
  nat: Natural

  children:
  << ... >>

  references:
  << ... >>
```

Lexicals Lexicals define the terminals of a language and are typically defined by regular expressions. Rascal allows full context-free lexicals, but here, we assume that all lexicals fall in the category of regular languages that can be defined by regular expressions.

To ease the mapping between Rascal lexicals and MPS concepts, we define a Rascal module that contains a set of default lexicals. These lexicals define the syntax of identifiers, string literals, and integer numbers. Developers can use these lexicals in their Rascal grammars, but it is also possible for users to include their lexicals. In this case, developers must describe the mapping to MPS manually.

Each lexical is mapped to a concept, like any other nonterminal, and a *constrained data type*. To illustrate this, Listing 1 contains Nat's definition, which consists of a single production, called `digits`. This production rule references Natural, which is one of the predefined lexicals (Listing 2). As a result, the lexical Nat is translated into a concept, called `digits` (Listing 7), and a *constrained data type*, called Natural (Listing 8). The `digits` concept has a single property of type Natural, a *constrained data type* capable of capturing natural numbers using the regular expressions engine of MPS.

Listing 8 Result of mapping a Rascal lexical to an MPS constrained data type

```
constrained string datatype: Natural

  matching regexp: [0-9]+
```

Listing 9 Concept mapping for a list of symbols

```
concept groupExp extends <default> implements Exp

  instance can be root: true
  alias: <no alias>
  short description: Exp

  properties:
  << ... >>

  children:
  exps :Exp[0..n]

  references:
  << ... >>
```

List of Symbols In CFG, it is possible to define a group of symbols of the same type, often expressed using Kleene's star (*) and plus (+). Kleene's operators (star and plus) are unary operators for concatenating several symbols of the same type. The first one denotes zero or more elements, and the second one denotes one or more elements in the list. The current approach detects both operators (Kleene's star and plus) in productions. The operators are represented in MPS as children of a concept with cardinality zero-to-many (0..*) and one-to-many (1..*), respectively. For instance, let us add to the language shown in Listing 1 the following production:

start syntax Exp = ... | groupExp: Exp* exps;

This production defines zero or more expressions (Exp). The resulting mapping of the production groupExp is shown in Listing 9.

4.2 Mapping Grammars to Editor Aspects

This section presents the mapping between a grammar and the editor aspect in MPS. For creating the editor aspect of the language, we use the language's layout symbols, namely, literal and reference symbols. In this context, a reference symbol is a pointer to a nonterminal symbol (which can be lexical or context-free). come with the language.

Listing 10 Generated editor for addition

```
<default> editor for concept addition
  node cell layout:
    [- % lhs /empty cell: % + % rhs /empty cell: % -]

  inspected cell layout:
    <choose cell model>
```

Literals Literal symbols may be part of productions to improve the readability of code or disambiguate. They form an essential aspect of the concrete syntax and can be leveraged to obtain projectional editors.

To create an editor, we first take each production rule; we look at each symbol and keep track of its order. It is essential to keep track of the order because it affects how the editor displays the elements. In this process, we consider two types of symbols, namely, *literals* and *references*. If the symbol is a literal, it is added to the *node cell layout* as a placeholder text. Moreover, this is used to define the syntax highlighting of the resulting editor. The literals are displayed with a different color to show the users that they are reserved words of the language. As a result, the current approach offers a binary coloring scheme: keywords are blue and the remaining symbols in black. Instead, if it is a nonterminal symbol, we create a *reference*.

For example, the production rule that defines the addition between natural numbers has three symbols: *lhs*, +, and *rhs*. Following the approach, we first take the *lhs* symbol and create a reference to its type Exp; then, we take the literal, +, and copy it to the editor, and finally, we create a reference to the *rhs* symbol, which is also of type Exp. Listing 10 shows the generated editor for addition. This editor has two references, namely, *lhs* and *rhs*. Editors use references to access concept properties. For instance, in the editor, the reference lhs creates a link to the lhs children in the addition concept. Moreover, the editor, for *addition*, has a literal (+) in between the two references. The literal is shown as a placeholder text for users to write expressions like 5 + 6.

List of Symbols The editor aspect for a list of symbols (zero-to-many and one-to-many) is based on creating a collection of cells. More concretely, each list of symbols is translated into an *indent cell* collection. Listing 11 shows the generated editor aspect for the groupExp production.

4.3 Editor Improvement: AST Pruning

Having defined a mapping from CFGs to the editor aspect in projectional languages, we will improve the generated projectional editor. The editor can be improved by pruning the grammar to enhance IDE services (e.g., auto-completion). To prune the

Listing 11 Editor mapping for a list of symbols

```
<default> editor for concept groupExp
  node cell layout:
    [-
     (- % exps % /empty cell: -)
    -]

  inspected cell layout:
    <choose cell model>
```

grammar, we eliminate chain rules (also known as unary rules) from the productions. To eliminate the chain rules, we first collect all the productions with a single parent and are referenced once in the grammar. Then, we merge the single reference with its parent.

To illustrate this process, let's consider the following production:

$$A \rightarrow A|b|c|d$$

Long production rules are often split into smaller production rules for readability. For example, a language engineer can also write the previous production as:

$$A \rightarrow A|B$$

$$B \rightarrow b|c|d$$

The second alternative impacts the language's structure because it introduces a new nonterminal B. This new nonterminal is translated in the AST as an extra node. To illustrate the difference between both versions, Fig. 3 shows a tree view of the ASTs. From the right-most AST in Fig. 3, we observe that node B is referenced once in the language. Thus, production $A \rightarrow B$ represents a chain rule. This chain rule is translated to the end users as an extra keystroke to access the leaf nodes b, c, d via B. If we remove the chain rule, we avoid creating an extra node (B) before accessing the terminals (b, c, d) in the projectional editor.

For example, if users want to create a node b, they can call auto-complete, and they will obtain two options, A or B. Based on the AST shown in Fig. 3, they select to create a node B. However, they have not reached b yet. Thus, they must press tab completion again, and then they get all the options of B: b, c, and d. In contrast, if we prune the chain rule, meaning we remove concept B, we can omit the second tab completion because all the options will be visible from the first tab completion. Removing chain rules from a grammar impacts both the structure and the editor of a projectional language since removing a concept means the editor of such concept is no longer needed. As a result, we enhance the user's interaction with the projectional editor by removing the chain rules.

Fig. 3 Tree-based view
comparison

4.4 Translating Textual Programs into Projectional Models

We extend the approach to translating existing textual programs into projectional models. This extension's motivation is that we want to offer a mechanism for importing existing textual programs into the generated projectional language. We did not consider a manual translation because it is cumbersome, and tools can automate it.

To this aim, we applied the same approach proposed for generating languages. However, instead of only using a grammar as input, it takes both the program and the grammar. We use the grammar for creating a parser; then, the parser creates a parse tree of the program. Both Rascal and MPS offer support to write and read XML files, so we define an XML schema to serialize and deserialize parse trees as XML files. The former acts as an intermediate representation that supports the communication between platforms. The current approach is implemented in Rascal and MPS. However, it is possible to support other platforms by implementing the XML schema (Listing 12). In the textual world, the schema serializes the parse tree, while in the projectional world, the projectional LWB deserializes the XML and uses it to create the projectional model.

The current approach uses the XML file as the input of an MPS plug-in. The plug-in traverses the XML tree and creates a model that conforms with the generated language. If the translation is correct, the generated model should be a valid instance of the generated projectional language.

4.5 Architecture

The approach to bridge textual and projectional LWBs contains five components: Rascal2XML, XML2MPS, *XMLImporter*, *ImportLanguage*, and *ImportProgram*. The solution has been implemented using Rascal MPL and Jetbrains MPS. We consider two different architectures for the implementation of the current approach. The first one was based on integrating Rascal directly into MPS, including Rascal as a Java library in MPS. This architecture allows us to call Rascal parsers directly from MPS. However, this approach does not allow reusability, and this integration should be repeated for any textual LWB. Instead, the second architecture uses an intermediate format to communicate between a textual LWB and MPS. In the

Listing 12 Simplified XML schema for exchanging information between LWBs

```xml
<xs:schema attributeFormDefault="unqualified" elementFormDefault="qualified"
  xmlns:xs="http://www.w3.org/2001/XMLSchema">
  <xs:element name="root">
   <xs:element name="nonterminal">
     <xs:element type="xs:string" name="name"/>
     <xs:element name="production" maxOccurs="unbounded" minOccurs="0">
      <xs:element type="xs:string" name="name"/>
      <xs:element name="arg" maxOccurs="unbounded" minOccurs="0">
        <xs:element type="xs:string" name="name"/>
        <xs:element type="xs:string" name="type"/>
        <xs:element type="xs:string" name="cardinality"/>
      </xs:element>
      <xs:element name="layout">
        <xs:choice maxOccurs="unbounded" minOccurs="0">
          <xs:element name="ref">
           <xs:element type="xs:string" name="name"/>
           <xs:element type="xs:string" name="type"/>
          </xs:element>
          <xs:element name="lit">
           <xs:complexType mixed="true">
             <xs:element type="xs:string" name="name" minOccurs="0"/>
             <xs:element type="xs:string" name="type" minOccurs="0"/>
           </xs:complexType>
          </xs:element>
        </xs:choice>
      </xs:element>
     </xs:element>
   </xs:element>
   <xs:element name="keywords">
     <xs:element type="xs:byte" name="keyword"/>
   </xs:element>
   <xs:element name="lexical">
     <xs:element type="xs:string" name="name"/>
     <xs:element name="arg">
      <xs:element type="xs:string" name="name"/>
      <xs:element type="xs:string" name="type"/>
     </xs:element>
   </xs:element>
   <xs:element type="xs:string" name="startSymbol"/>
  </xs:element>
</xs:schema>
```

following paragraphs, we describe each of the components of this architecture and how they interact with each other. All the code is available on a GitHub repository.[1]

Rascal2XML This module is written in Rascal, and it is responsible for generating an XML representation of Rascal grammars and existing textual programs. This module produces an XML file that is used as input for the module XML2MPS.

XML2MPS This MPS project holds the logic for generating MPS language definitions and model instances. It is responsible for creating MPS concepts and interfaces from an XML file. Both ImportLanguage and ImportProgram use this library.

---

[1]https://github.com/cwi-swat/rascal-mps.

ImportLanguage This is an MPS plug-in that enables the import of languages. It creates the user interface (GUI) for importing a textual language. The GUI displays a pop-up that takes the grammar (in XML format) as input, calls the *XMLImporter*, and produces a projectional language.

ImportProgram This is an MPS plug-in that enables the import of programs. This plug-in takes as input an XML file that contains a program, and it produces a projectional model. To create the projectional model, this plug-in relies on the XML importer to read the XMLFile and in XML2MPS to create the MPS nodes.

XMLImporter This is a Java library for traversing the tree-like content of the XML files. This is used to map textual languages to projectional languages and translate textual programs as projectional models.

5 Case Study

In this section, we present a case study to evaluate our approach. The language we have chosen for this purpose is JavaScript (ECMAScript 5) because there is an existing implementation of it for MPS, and it allows a proper validation of Rascal2MPS. First, we explain the definition of the language. Then, we show how we create a mapping between the textual language and the generated projectional language. Afterward, we generate a projectional editor based on the language's concrete syntax. Finally, we import existing textual programs as valid MPS models that conform to the generated projectional language. This section concludes with a brief discussion based on results.

5.1 Language Description

So far, we have presented a way of applying the approach to a toy language of expressions. Now we will apply it to a well-known and widely used language. To show the applicability of the approach to a real-world language, we reused the existing grammar definition for JavaScript, included in Rascal's standard library. This grammar can be found in GitHub.[2] This evaluation aims to use a Rascal implementation of the JavaScript grammar and obtain the equivalent language in MPS.

First, we must sanitize the existing grammar to meet our solution's constraints, as described in (Sect. 6). It is essential to mention that this sanitization process is entirely manual. In this grammar, the sanitization process consists of adding labels

---

[2]https://github.com/usethesource/rascal/blob/master/src/org/rascalmpl/library/lang/javascript/
saner/Syntax.rsc.

to all the production rules and variable names to all symbols and changing lexicals to use either one of our predefined lexical types or a user-defined construct. The resulting sanitized grammar can be found on GitHub.[3]

We then used this grammar as input to generate the XML that encodes the grammar definition into the intermediate format. This XML representation is also available on GitHub.[4] The XML file can then be imported into MPS. In MPS, we use the plug-in that we built, and we use the XML file as an input to successfully generate the projectional version of JavaScript.

To evaluate our generated version of JavaScript, we decided to compare it against an ad hoc MPS implementation of such a language called *EcmaScript4MPS*.[5] *EcmaScript4MPS* is a fine-tuned implementation of JavaScript for MPS. In other words, the implementation considers how developers use JavaScript editors and the features offered for JavaScript in IDEs. To compare both implementations, we show several examples of language elements and programs of both implementations. For the rest of this section, we will refer to the generated version as JsFromRascal and the MPS ad hoc implementation as JsManual.

5.2 Editor Aspect

To compare the editor of both languages, we present how a program looks like in both editors. The JsFromRascal program was created using the approach described in Sect. 4.4. This approach takes a textual program as input, and the tool parses it and produces an XML file with the resulting parse tree. It is important to mention that we did not tweak the resulting program; we used the generated version as is. Figure 4 shows the resulting program using the JsFromRascal editor.

In contrast, the program for JsManual was written by hand because we did not have a mechanism, like the one described before, for arbitrary textual programs. However, the handwritten program is the same as the one used for JsFromRascal. The resulting program in the JsManual editor is shown in Fig. 5.

As can be seen from Figs. 4 and 5, the program in the JsFromRascal editor takes up more lines of code than its counterpart in JsManual. According to the JavaScript standards, the JsManual editor makes the program look more readable due to the ad hoc implementation of the editor, which places break lines and whitespaces in the right place. The JsFromRascal editor splits up statements and expressions into several lines based on the implemented heuristics. Instead, the JsManual editor does not break these language constructs into several lines. However, it forces users

---

[3] https://github.com/cwi-swat/rascal-mps/blob/master/Rascal2XML/src/Grammars/JS/JSGrammar2.rsc.

[4] https://github.com/cwi-swat/rascal-mps/blob/master/Examples/JS_Grammar.xml.

[5] https://github.com/mar9000/ecmascript4mps.

```
function
  substrings
(
  str1
)
{ var
    array1 = []
  ;
  for
  ( var
    x = 0
    y = 1
  ;
    x < str1 . length
  ;
    x ++
    y ++
  )
    { array1 [ x ]
      = str1 . substring ( x
        y
      )
      ;
    }
  var
    combi = []
  ;
  var
    temp = ""
  ;
  var
    slent = Math . pow ( 2
      array1 . length
    )
  ;

  for
  ( var
    i = 0
  ;
    i < slent
  ;
    i ++
  )
    { temp = "" ;
      for
      ( var
        j = 0
      ;
        j < array1 . length
      ;
        j ++
      )
        { if
          ( ( i & Math . pow(2,j)
            )
          )
            { temp += array1 [ j ]
              ;
            }
        }
      if
      ( temp !== ""
      )
        { combi . push ( temp
          )
          ;
        }
    }
  console . log ( combi . join("\n")
  )
  ;
}
```

Fig. 4 The substring JavaScript program displayed using the JsFromRascal editor

to define variables outside *for* statements due to the language's name resolution implementation.

Another difference between the editors is the usage of the dot operator (.). This operator is often used in programming languages to access fields or methods. For instance, JsFromRascal identifies it as a binary operator (e.g., "+," "−"), and therefore the editor introduces whitespaces before and after the dot operator. This is an example of the limitations introduced by the heuristics; they are rigid. A

```
program substring
-----------------------------------------------------
function substring(str1) {
  var array1 = [],
      x = 0,
      y = 1;
  for (; x < str1.length; x++) {
    array1[x] = str1.substring(x, y);
  }
  var combi = [];
  var temp = '';
  var slent = 'Math.pow(2, array1.length)';
  var i = 0;
  for (; i < slent; i++) {
    var temp = '',
        j = 0;
    for (; j < array1.length; j++) {
      if (i & 'Math.pow(2,j)')
        {
            temp += array1[j];
        }
    }
    if (temp !== '')
      {
          combi.push(temp);
      }
  }
  'console.log(combi.join("\n"))';

}
```

Fig. 5 The substring JavaScript program displayed using the JsManual editor

customization mechanism might be needed to make such heuristics more flexible; thus, they can be adapted to different languages and scenarios.

In sum, the JsManual editor is more appealing, and visually, it looks more like a textual program written using a plain text editor than the one generated using JsFromRascal. This kind of difference was expected because the JsManual editor is implemented in an ad hoc way to offer the best experience for this language, while the JsFromRascal editor is obtained through a generic tool that works for various languages. However, the JsFromRascal editor can be manually fine-tuned to achieve the desired editing experience. The knowledge of the JsFromRascal editor depends entirely on two core elements, the information contained in the grammar and the set of heuristics applied to such grammar. On the one hand, the creation of ad hoc editors from scratch, such as the one made for JsManual, is a cumbersome activity. On the other hand, a generated editor speeds up editors' development process because they use generic abstractions that can be applied to several languages, so that developers can focus on fine-tuning the generated editors on edge cases based on platform-specific features and the language's coding styles.

5.3 Program's Usability

Now we are going to discuss the usability aspects of both editors. Here we only focus on the ease of creating and editing programs with the editors mentioned above. First, we investigate the tab-completion menu, which is one of the critical aspects of a projectional editor since it allows users to navigate through the language's structure (AST). In Fig. 6, we present a code completion menu for a *for* statement in JsFromRascal, and in Fig. 7, we present the equivalent using JsManual. Both editors show similar information: the concept's name and a brief description. However, the JsFromRascal editor also displays the structure of the child nodes of such a concept, which might help developers understand how to use concepts or remember the concept's syntax.

5.4 Discussion

Projecting Grammars as Language Structures The first goal and building block for this project is to recreate the structure of a language in two different LWBs. This goal was previously achieved and explained by Ingrid [17]. We wanted to try a different solution in which we do not directly integrate both platforms, but instead, we define an intermediate format to make the solution more general. Section 4.1 describes the process for mapping a textual language definition into a projectional language definition. As shown in Sect. 5.1, the current approach works, yet some considerations must be taken into account to generate a proper language. We understand that the way we treat lexicals might be cumbersome since the complex structure's mapping must be manually defined. We also think this could be solved by defining some pre-processing strategies to capture lexicals and generate them into the second platform.

Editor Aspect: Language Usability The editor aspect of a language is essential because it is the user interface to the language. Nevertheless, implementing a good editor is cumbersome. As shown in Sect. 5.2, usability is one of the main differences between ad hoc and generated implementations. In the generated version, we applied heuristics from the literature (e.g., well-known formatting and pretty-

```
program substring
--------------------------------------------------
function substring(str1) {
  var array1 = [],
      x = 0,
      y = 1;
  for (; x < str1.length; x++) {
    array1[x] = str1.substring(x, y);
  }
  var combi = [];
  var temp = '';
  var slent = 'Math.pow(2, array1.length)';
  var i = 0;
  for (; i < slent; i++) {
    var temp = '',
        j = 0;
    for (; j < array1.length; j++) {
      if (i & 'Math.pow(2,j)')
        {
          temp += array1[j];
        }
    }
    if (temp !== '')
      {
        combi.push(temp);
      }
  }
  'console.log(combi.join("\n"))';

}
```

Fig. 6 JsFromRascal editor tab-completion menu of a *for* loop

```
for
 N for                    for ( Expression ; Expression ; Expression ) Statement
 N for   for ( var VariableDeclarationNoIn ; Expression ; Expression ) Statement
 N for                                  for ( Expression in Expression ) Statement
 N for                                      for ( var in Expression ) Statement
```

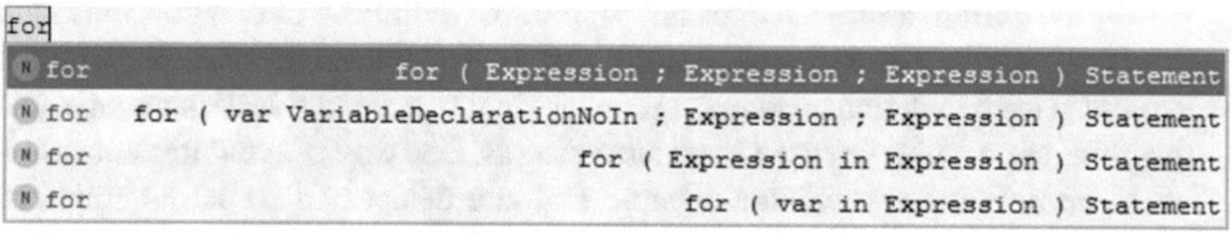

Fig. 7 JsManual editor tab-completion menu of a *for* loop

printing approaches) to try to identify production rule patterns generically. However, these heuristics have limited power, and of course, they might not fit every language, especially if we compare them against custom implementations. Nonetheless, with the current approach, we show that it is possible to apply existing heuristics to create projectional editors based solely on the language's grammar. Besides, the current approach considers the language's structure to generate a projectional editor that, in some cases, might be more appealing than the reflective MPS editor.

To improve the current approach, we could have implemented more heuristics or define a mechanism for customizing them. We might also require additional information other than the information contained in the grammar. Also, languages' coding style and user feedback are fundamental to improve the quality of generated editors. In other words, we need more information to implement the heuristics in a less rigid fashion and therefore improve the editor generation.

6   Limitations

This section discusses the limitations of the approach, the rationale behind them, and possible solutions to overcome them. These limitations are based on assumptions and constraints in the grammar. Besides, there is also a technical limitation related to how the mapping is implemented.

Summary: Grammar Preconditions

- Nonterminal symbol name and production rule labels within a grammar must be unique.
- Symbol labels within a production rule must be unique.
- Lexicals can be either one of the MPS predefined data types or the lexical must be defined by hand using the lexical library.
- Each production rule and each symbol within a production rule must be labeled.

1. The names of the nonterminal symbols in a grammar must be unique. In other words, the current approach does not support the definition of two concepts with the same name. The rationale behind this is that the name of a nonterminal symbol is used to define an interface concept in the generated MPS language, and the production labels are used to create concepts. One way to avoid this constraint could be defining a renaming scheme that can detect and fix name conflicts. However, this solution might introduce a side effect on the language's usability; projectional editors use these names for IDE services such as tab completion, so they must be descriptive enough for end users. Also, other language components

must be refactored according to the renaming mechanism. Therefore, we did not implement an automatic renaming scheme, and we preferred to include it as a limitation of the current approach.

2. In the mapping between a Rascal grammar and an MPS language, symbol labels are used as variable names, either for `children` or `references` in MPS concepts. These names should be unique within the same concept, yet not for the whole language. For instance, if we define concepts A and B, both can contain a reference of a child named *name*; however, A cannot have more than one child or reference called *name*. In other words, symbol labels can be reused across concepts but not within the same concept.

3. Lexicals are a challenging concept to deal with because there is no standard way of defining them. However, it is possible to make some assumptions on regularity and define a set of constraints to translate lexical between platforms in an automatic way, but this requires considerable effort. As a result, we did not want to restrict regular expressions, so we included lexicals that represent MPS built-in types (e.g., string, int) to the lexical library. The current approach does not limit users from defining custom lexicals. However, users must manually define a mapping between the custom lexical defined in Rascal and the right translation for MPS. Section 4.1 describes the details on how to support custom-defined lexicals.

4. It is required to label all the production rules and symbols within a production rule because the approach uses the labels for naming concepts or children reference fields. A solution could be to generate placeholder names, yet this introduces other issues such as nondescriptive names and name matching issues when importing existing textual programs.

5. The current approach does not take advantage of name resolution, especially for code completion, which is a keystone for projectional LWBs. For instance, in MPS, concept hierarchies do not rely on trees' definition; instead, they use graphs.

6. The current implementation supports the mapping of lists and separated lists of symbols into MPS language concepts (editor and structure aspects). However, the mapping for separated lists is partially implemented. The current approach treats separated lists just as a list. As a result, the separator symbol is ignored for the generation of the editor.

The current approach does not support language nor program evolution. In other words, the current approach considers languages as stand-alone units. It does not consider that changes might happen to the language. For example, if a developer uses a textual language A and generates a projectional language A* inside MPS, the current approach only accepts valid programs according to A. If there are changes to the original language A, those changes cannot be patched in the generated versions. This forces to regenerate the whole language from scratch or make changes by hand. Some changes do not break the importing of programs:

- Addition of language constructs to the grammar and then using them in a program. This means that the plug-in for importing programs, *ImportProgram* (Sect. 4.5), will not find such elements. As a result, the plug-in notifies the user.
- Modification of existing language constructs (e.g., adding or removing parameters). As expected, this type of change often ends up in a failure.

In sum, language engineers and users, in general, should be aware of the language's version and the version used to define programs. We see this problem as an opportunity for future extensions of the current approach to supporting languages and programs' evolution.

7   Related Work

Projectional LWBs allow users to manipulate the programs' AST directly; therefore, parsing technology is no longer needed. In contrast, textual LWB parsing is essential. This section presents the state of the art in grammar to model transformation and editor generation.

7.1   *Grammar to Model*

The generation of models from grammars is essential for the current approach. Thus, we identified the following related work in this direction.

Ingrid [17] is a project that attempts to bridge the gap between textual and projectional LWBs. Their approach uses ANTLRv4 [18] as textual LWB and JetBrains MPS as projectional editor. Ingrid is implemented as a hybrid solution in Java/MPS project. Ingrid bridges textual and projectional LWBs in three steps: firstly, the grammar must be parsed, and relevant information about the structure and other required language elements is stored as linked Java objects. Secondly, the stored structure is traversed, and equivalent MPS model nodes and interfaces are constructed. Finally, an editor is generated for each MPS Language Concept Node. There are some high-level similarities between Ingrid and Rascal2MPS. Both projects perform the steps taken for parsing, gathering information about the language, generating an intermediate structure to represent the language, and finally generating a model from the said intermediate structure. The main differences are in the architecture, design, and implementation choices of both projects, which have various consequences for using the respective tools. The main architectural difference is in the choice of the intermediate structure. Whereas we chose an external file-based format (see Sect. 4.5), Ingrid uses an internal representation of linked Java objects. This decision enables them to use the ANTLRv4 parser implemented in Java and the ability of MPS to call into Java executables directly. Thus, the Ingrid MPS plug-in can call the parser and start the data extraction process internally. In contrast, Rascal2MPS keeps both LWBs separate; they can communicate only through an external intermediate format. Some of the advantages of not using an intermediate format are:

- The solution becomes a one-step process, making it more efficient for the language engineer.
- All implementation is done on one side of the bridge (projectional LWB), simplifying the development.
- The language engineer does not need to maintain both the textual and projectional LWB.

However, this approach has a significant downside: the projectional LWB must call the grammar parser directly. Thus, there is a strong coupling between the projectional LWB and the specific grammar parser. In the case of Ingrid, the MPS plug-in calls into the Java ANTLR parser. However, the ANTLR parser is not the only one. If we wished to extend Ingrid to support Rascal, we would need to replace ANTLR parser calls with Rascal parser calls. This can lead to several problems: (i) The architecture must allow this replacement. This can be partially solved using interfaces and abstractions over the parser, but the problem of potentially different APIs remains. A complete mapping from ANTLR parser function calls to Rascal parser function calls would have to be made in the worst case. (ii) The parser needs to be implemented in Java. ANTLRv4 already has a Java-based parser and is a prime candidate for integration with the Java-based MPS. However, this is not necessarily true for any given textual LWB. If one is not available, the language engineer would either have to implement the parser in Java or find some way to expose the parsing features to a Java environment.

Rascal2MPS addresses the problem of bridging the gap between the textual and projectional worlds in a generic fashion. In other words, neither side of the solution is aware of the other; they communicate only through the intermediate file-based format. This format serves as a contract between the different parts of the solution. If the intermediary file is generated from an ANTLR-, Rascal- or Xtext-based grammar is irrelevant to the implementation on the side of the projectional LWB.

Another difference between Ingrid and Rascal2MPS lies in the editor generation. While Ingrid does identify the problem of usability of the reflective editor and discusses several solutions, such as heuristics or prompts during the import process, they have not been implemented. Ingrid only generates an editor containing the node's structural elements, i.e., the literals and references to other nodes. It is then left up to the language engineer to apply whitespace to the editor manually. Rascal2MPS goes further and applies heuristics to apply whitespace during the import process automatically. While this does not eliminate the need to edit the editor definitions manually (Sect. 5), it can save time given the right set of heuristics. Finally, Ingrid does not address the problem of language artifacts, i.e., programs created within the textual world. Thus, even after a language has been imported, programs are written using the said language in the textual LWB that needs to be manually recreated as MPS models of the imported language. Rascal2MPS does implement the ability to construct MPS program models using textual source code.

Wimmer et al. [19] describe a generic semiautomatic approach for bridging the technological space between the extended Backus-Naur form (EBNF), a popular grammar formalism, and Meta-Object Facility (MOF), a standard for model-driven engineering. In this approach, an attribute grammar describes the EBNF structure and the mapping between EBNF and MOF. Then, it is used to generate a Grammar Parser (GP). This GP can then be used to generate MOF meta-models from grammars. However, this approach fixates on MOF as the target meta-model directly. In the case of going between LWBs in separate worlds, we do not want to be specific in the target. Instead, Rascal2MPS uses an intermediate format and makes the source and target formalism up to the implementation. Another downside of the given approach is that it requires grammar annotations and additional manual improvements of the generated model to refine the generated model. We seek to limit the actions of the language engineer, especially concerning the source grammar. The Gra2Mol [20] is another project which seeks to bridge the gap between the textual grammar and model worlds. The authors define a domain-specific model transformation language that can be applied to a program that conforms to a grammar and generates a model that conforms to a target meta-model. This language can be used to write a transformation definition consisting of transformation rules. In this way, the presented approach abstracts over the generated meta-model, which would be quite useful in our use case, as we would be able to give the meta-model of the target LWB as input with the transformation definition. In practice, however, this runs into problems when the desired target model is specific rather than generic. For example, the standard storage format for JetBrains MPS is a custom XML format. The models contain much information tied specifically to MPS, such as node IDs and layout structures. Generating these from outside of MPS would be quite tedious and would introduce a dependency on the MPS model format, which may change. Thus, it is best to interact with the MPS model from within MPS itself, where MPS can do the heavy lifting of generating the models.

7.2 Editor Generation

Editor generation is an essential step in bridging the gap between textual and projectional LWBs. It is closely related to the well-known pretty printing problem in the grammar world. Grammar cells [21] is an extension of MPS that offers a declarative specification for defining textual notations and interactions in a projectional editor. Implementing editors with this extension makes it easier to offer a text-like editing experience; thus, it is widely adopted by the MPS community. Our current implementation does not use grammar cells because we restricted our approach on a plain MPS installation. However, this extension's adoption is part of the roadmap for the next iteration of the current implementation.

Van de Vanter et al. [22] identify part of the core problem between the textual and model-based approach. From a system's perspective, a model-based editor allows for easier tool integration and additional functionality. However, language users are often more familiar and comfortable with text-based editing. In this paper, the authors propose a compromise based on lexical tokens and fuzzy parsing. This is not unlike what is offered by MPS. MPS editors are highly customizable and can be made to resemble the text-based editing experience closely.

As introduced by van den Brand et al. [23], the BOX language for formatting text is closely related, as the heuristics for generation white space between language elements is reused in this project. The BOX language is further used in other work on pretty-printing generic programming languages, such as GPP (Generic Pretty Printer) [24], which constructs tree structures of a language element's layout that can be used by an arbitrary consumer.

Syntax-directed pretty printing [25] also identifies several structures for creating language-independent pretty printers. In this approach, a grammar extended with special pretty-printer commands is used as input to generate a pretty printer for such a language. The generated pretty printer can then be reused for any program written in the language the pretty printer was generated for. The annotated grammar approach does limit the form the final pretty printer can have due to the lack of options. Also, annotating an entire grammar can be tedious work. We attempt to limit the required user interaction with the source grammar in our approach, although we did not eliminate it.

Following this research line, Terrence et al. [26] propose *Codebuff*, which is a tool for the automatic derivation of code formatters. *Codebuff* is a generic formatter that uses machine learning algorithms to extract formatting rules from a corpus. This is a neat approach because, as we mentioned before, source code formatting is subjective, it depends on each programmer's style, and it changes across languages. For example, in Sect. 5.2, we showed that applying the same heuristics for any language does not always produce a good editor. Therefore, we consider tools like *Codebuff* as inspiration for future work. We could benefit from their techniques and knowledge to generate editors in a flexible and highly configurable way and perhaps learn from existing source code examples.

8   Conclusions and Future Work

In this chapter, we presented an approach to bridge the gap between textual and projectional LWB. We defined a mapping between textual grammars and projectional meta models; this mapping (Sect. 4) produces the structure and editor aspects of a projectional language. Moreover, our approach allows users to reuse textual programs by means of translating them to equivalent MPS models (Sect. 4.4). To validate our solution, we used as a case study a Rascal grammar of JavaScript (Sect. 5). Based on the grammar definition, we generated a projectional version of JavaScript. To verify the correct mapping of the generated language, we successfully imported existing valid textual JavaScript programs into MPS. In Sect. 6, we discussed some of the limitations of the current approach.

Language evolution is a crucial aspect to look at in the future. Since the current approach assumes that the generation is done only once, we ignore the fact that the textual language and the projectional generated version might change. Then we consider that keeping track of these changes and transferring/applying these changes to the other is essential. If there are changes in the grammar after the projectional language generation, developers must regenerate the whole language, which may lead to losing information (if changes were made on the generated language).

Similarly, this applies to programs written in such languages. We consider that a mechanism for maintaining both versions is worth investigating as future work to keep a bidirectional mapping. Language engineers can switch from one platform to another without losing information. Our approach offers support for a unidirectional mapping from textual to projectional. We believe that a bidirectional communication is required. Because depending on the language, one may benefit more from having a textual or a projectional version of the language. Therefore, to support both sides' changes, we require a bridge to create a textual language from a projectional language. Moreover, to complete the circle, a way of keeping track and propagating changes in both worlds will be required. To avoid losing or reimplementing existing features.

As we described in Sect. 5.4, the usability of generated editors is one of the critical aspects that should be addressed in future research. We found that we can generate editors with limited capabilities (that do not consider domain knowledge or existing formatters). Therefore, we consider as future work exploring artificial intelligence techniques (e.g., machine learning or programming by example) to improve the existing editor (in the style of [26]), maybe by identifying patterns in existing programs or commonalities in the grammar's structure to guide or to customize the generation of the editor aspect.

References

1. Erdweg, S., van der Storm, T., Volter, M., Tratt, L., Bosman, R., Cook, W.R., Gerritsen, A., Hulshout, A., Kelly, S., Loh, A., Konat, G., Molina, P.J., Palatnik, M., Pohjonen, R., Schindler, E., Schindler, K., Solmi, R., Vergu, V., Visser, E., van der Vlist, K., Wachsmuth, G., van der Woning, J.: Evaluating and comparing language workbenches: Existing results and benchmarks for the future. Comput. Lang. Syst. Struct. **44**, 24–47 (2015)
2. Lämmel, R.: The Notion of a Software Language, pp. 1–49. Springer International Publishing, Cham (2018)
3. Fowler, M.: Language workbenches: The killer-app for domain specific languages? (2015)
4. Mernik, M., Heering, J., Sloane, A.M.: When and how to develop domain-specific languages. ACM Comput. Surv. (CSUR) **37**(4), 316–344 (2005)
5. Mengerink, J.G.M., van der Sanden, B., Cappers, B.C.M., Serebrenik, A., Schiffelers, R.R.H., van den Brand, M.G.J.: Exploring DSL evolutionary patterns in practice - a study of dsl evolution in a large-scale industrial DSL repository. In: Proceedings of the 6th International

Conference on Model-Driven Engineering and Software Development - Volume 1: MODEL-SWARD, pp. 446–453. INSTICC, SciTePress (2018)

6. Bartels, J.: Bridging the worlds of textual and projectional language workbenches. Master's thesis, Eindhoven University of Technology, 1 2020

7. Mooij, A.J., Hooman, J., Albers, R.: Gaining industrial confidence for the introduction of domain-specific languages. In: 2013 IEEE 37th Annual Computer Software and Applications Conference Workshops, pp. 662–667 (2013)

8. van Deursen, A., Klint, P., Visser, J.: Domain-specific languages: An annotated bibliography. SIGPLAN Not. 35(6), 26–36 (2000)

9. Krueger, C.W.: Software reuse. ACM Comput. Surv. 24(2), 131–183 (1992)

10. Nagy, I., Cleophas, L., van den Brand, M., Engelen, L., Raulea, L., Xavier Lobo Mithun, E.: Vpdsl: A DSL for software in the loop simulations covering material flow. In: Proceedings of the 2012 IEEE 17th International Conference on Engineering of Complex Computer Systems, ICECCS '12, pp. 318–327. IEEE Computer Society, USA (2012)

11. Verriet, J., Liang, H.L., Hamberg, R., van Wijngaarden, B.: Model-driven development of logistic systems using domain-specific tooling. In: Aiguier, M., Caseau, Y., Krob, D., Rauzy, A. (eds.), Complex Systems Design & Management, pp. 165–176. Springer, Berlin, Heidelberg (2013)

12. Gabbrielli, M., Martini, S.: How to Describe a Programming Language, pp. 27–55. Springer London, London (2010)

13. Dmitriev, S.: Language Oriented Programming: The Next Programming Paradigm. Technical report, Jetbrains, 2004

14. Campagne, F., Campagne, F.: The MPS Language Workbench, Vol. 1, 1st edn. CreateSpace Independent Publishing Platform, North Charleston, SC, USA (2014)

15. CWI-SWAT.: Syntax definition (2020)

16. Donzeau-Gouge, V., Huet, G., Lang, B., Kahn, G.: Programming environments based on structured editors: the mentor experience. Interact Program Environ (1984)

17. Vysoký, P., Parízek, P., Pech, V.: Ingrid: Creating languages in MPS from ANTLR grammars (2018)

18. ANTLR.: https://www.antlr.org/

19. Wimmer, M., Kramler, G.: Bridging grammarware and modelware. In: International Conference on Model Driven Engineering Languages and Systems, pp. 159–168. Springer (2005)

20. Luis Cánovas Izquierdo, J., Cuadrado, J.S., Molina, J.G.: Gra2mol: A domain specific transformation language for bridging grammarware to modelware in software modernization. In: Workshop on Model-Driven Software Evolution, pp. 1–8 (2008)

21. Voelter, M., Szabó, T., Lisson, S., Kolb, B., Erdweg, S., Berger, T.: Efficient development of consistent projectional editors using grammar cells. In: Proceedings of the 2016 ACM SIGPLAN International Conference on Software Language Engineering, SLE 2016, pp. 28–40. Association for Computing Machinery, New York, NY, USA (2016)

22. Van de Vanter, M.L., Boshernitsan, M., Avenue, S.A.: Displaying and editing source code in software engineering environments (2000)

23. van den Brand, M., Visser, E.: Generation of formatters for context-free languages. ACM Trans. Software Eng. Methodol. (TOSEM) 5(1), 1–41 (1996)

24. De Jonge, M.: Pretty-printing for software reengineering. In: International Conference on Software Maintenance, 2002. Proceedings, pp. 550–559. IEEE (2002)

25. Rubin, L.F.: Syntax-directed pretty printing—a first step towards a syntax-directed editor. IEEE Trans. Software Eng. (2), 119–127 (1983)

26. Parr, T., Vinju, J.: Towards a universal code formatter through machine learning. In: Proceedings of the 2016 ACM SIGPLAN International Conference on Software Language Engineering, SLE 2016, pp. 137–151. Association for Computing Machinery, New York, NY, USA (2016)

Engineering Gameful Applications with MPS

Antonio Bucchiarone, Antonio Cicchetti, and Annapaola Marconi

Abstract Gamification refers to approaches that apply gaming elements and mechanics into contexts where gaming is not the main business purpose. Gamification principles have proven to be very effective in motivating target users in keeping their engagement within everyday challenges, including dedication to education, use of public transportation, adoption of healthy habits, and so forth. The spread of gameful applications and the consequent growth of the user base are making their design and development complexity to increase, e.g., due to the need of more and more customized solutions. In this respect, current state-of-the-art development approaches are either too close to programming or completely prepackaged. In the former case, domain and gamification experts are confronted with the abstraction gap between the concepts they would like to use and the corresponding implementation through coding. In the latter situation, customization opportunities are remarkably limited or require again hand-tuning through coding. In both scenarios, programmer tasks are tedious and error-prone, given the intrinsic characteristics of gamified applications, which are sets of rules to be triggered as a consequence of specific events.

This chapter illustrates the language engineering endeavor devoted to the creation of the Gamification Design Framework (GDF) through MPS. GDF is conceived by pursuing two main principles: correctness-by-construction and automation. The former aims at providing a language infrastructure conveying consistency between the different aspects of a gameful application in an intrinsic way. The latter aspires to maximize generative features in order to reduce coding needs. As a result, GDF is implemented by means of MPS as a set of three-layered domain-specific languages, where a lower-level language instantiates and extends the concepts defined from the language(s) above. Moreover, GDF is equipped with generators to automatically

A. Bucchiarone (✉) · A. Marconi
Fondazione Bruno Kessler (FBK) - MoDiS, Trento, Italy
e-mail: bucchiarone@fbk.eu; marconi@fbk.eu

A. Cicchetti
School of Innovation, Design and Engineering (IDT), Västerås, Sweden
e-mail: antonio.cicchetti@mdh.se

create gameful application structural components, behaviors, and deployment into a selected gamification engine.

1 Introduction

Playing is an activity humans do since their birth for (self-)learning, to meet others, to be part of communities, to relax, and so forth. Indeed, we are so used to it that we spend a growing amount of our free time with some form of gaming even in adulthood, and people made a profession out of it [1]. Interestingly, psychologists also observed that by introducing gaming elements and mechanics into "normal"— non-gaming—tasks, it can be possible to promote engagement and even motivate people to achieve certain objectives. As a matter of fact, an increasing number of activities include gamification elements, very often supported by software applications: Internet banking, sport/activity trackers, and shopping/traveling fidelity cards are all (few) examples of application domains targeted by gamification [2].

A fundamental concern of gameful applications[1] is their tailoring to the target domain and users: if a game is detached from the domain interests, the risk is to promote counterproductive/undesired behaviors; similarly, too easy or too complex games could fail engagement objectives due to loss of interest or discouragement, respectively [3]. A direct consequence of the mentioned tailoring needs is the critical contribution and cooperation of application domain and gamification experts: the former ones provide inputs about the engagement issues and desired outcomes, while the latter ones propose corresponding gamification strategies. Such a cooperation conveys gameful application specifications to be implemented in an appropriate target platform.

In the current state of practice, one available implementation option is to pick up a prepackaged gamification application from a repository [4]. The advantage would be to have a quick development phase limited to configuration purposes, at the price of very limited customization possibilities, unless manually tuning the existing implementation. Diametrically opposite, a completely new gamified application can be developed from scratch: this solution necessarily entails longer time to market, with the advantage of realizing a fully customized implementation. Regardless of the choice, the realization and deployment phases introduce an abstraction gap between gamification stakeholders, namely, domain and gamification experts, and the gameful application itself. In fact, the target application is typically implemented as a collection of rules matching incoming event notifications with corresponding game status updates. Therefore, developers need to translate game mechanics and other elements into corresponding rules, while the other stakeholders are required to backtrack state changes into corresponding gaming events.

---

[1] In the remainder of this chapter, we will always refer to software supported gamification, unless explicitly mentioned.

With the growing adoption of gamification in disparate application domains and its spread to a wider range of users, the complexity of gameful software is unavoidably increasing. In this respect, the abstraction gap between design and realization becomes a critical issue: the implementation phase is more tedious and error-prone, due to the number of rules and the customization needs. Moreover, maintenance and evolution activities are harder to manage, due to the disconnection between design and realization.

In order to close the gap between design and implementation of gameful applications, we proposed the Gamification Design Framework (GDF) [5, 6]. GDF is a collection of domain-specific languages (DSLs) devoted to the specification, implementation, and deployment of gameful applications. The framework has been developed by the following three key principles:

Separation-of-concerns : a gamification approach can be described by means of several perspectives. When the complexity grows, an effective way to alleviate it is to manage different perspectives as separate points of view that are later on fused into a complete solution;

Correctness-by-construction : given the growth of gamification employment and range of its potential users, the specification of gameful applications becomes increasingly intricate. In this respect, game rules shall be consistent with mechanisms and elements intended for the target application;

Automation : in order to close the gap between design and implementation, the amount of manually written code shall be reduced as much as possible. Or in the other way around, the degree of automation provided by the framework shall be maximized.

GDF actualizes the mentioned key principles by means of three DSLs that correspond to three abstraction layers any gamified application can be viewed through: (i) the topmost layer defines general mechanics and elements a solution could include, e.g., the concept of point, bonus, challenge, etc.; (ii) the second layer instantiates a subset of the abstract concepts defined on the level above due to the specification of the gameful application under development, for example, number of steps, walker of the week, hundred thousand steps week, respectively; (iii) the third and bottom layer describes the implementation of the concepts above together with their deployment on a gamification engine. Here, configuration parameters can be set, like thresholds to gain points, bonuses, and awards, the timing of challenges activation, and the assignment of players and teams to the defined tasks. Moreover, the layers convey generators enabling the automated derivation of implementation code for the gamified application.

GDF is practically realized by means of Jetbrains MPS and is the result of a challenging language engineering process. In particular, the DSLs included in GDF required a language workbench enabling meta-modeling, semantics specification through generators, and multi-view-based modeling support to ensure the consistency between the different points of view. During the language engineering process, we soon faced the problem of modeling a system of constraints (as it is a gameful application), which tended to be intractable by adopting diagrammatic approaches.

Moreover, we needed a mechanism enabling the introduction and refinement of high-level gamification solutions and concepts without requiring domain experts to modify the language specification, e.g., by adding new consistency checks. As a consequence, the DSLs included in GDF convey a text-based concrete syntax that eases the definition of game rules. Moreover, they exploit the language extension mechanisms provided by MPS to define the interconnections between the different abstraction layers, which implicitly ensures consistency through inheritance relationships.

The remainder of the chapter is structured as follows: Sect. 2 discusses in detail the motivation and contributions of our work. Then, Sect. 3 introduces the case study used to validate GDF. Section 4 illustrates the main components and features of GDF and the included DSLs. Eventually, Sect. 5 discusses advantages, drawbacks, and open challenges in the use of MPS for implementing GDF, including possible future investigation directions, while Sect. 6 draws conclusions about the chapter.

2 Motivations and Contribution

Gamification is a relatively recent field of research consisting of developing game characteristics in non-game contexts [2, 7]. It is a method that focuses on triggering elements of human behavior and psychology in order to provide rewarding, engaging, and exciting experiences for the users. While most of the elements that gamification uses are borrowed from the games (points, badges, leaderboards, etc.), it is specifically intended to help boost engagement and make products more appealing to the user. Gamification concepts and their usage have been reviewed in several research works with positive feedback, yet some doubts persist about its effectiveness. Nevertheless, over the last years, various research studies focused on introducing gamification in software engineering environments [8].

Gamification has shown a wide range of possible uses, varying from gaming in education [9] to online marketing and software apps [10, 11]. Bartel and Hagel presented a learning concept based on a gamification approach to promote students' motivation and engagement in their university education [12]. Moreover, Toda et al. developed an approach for planning and deploying gamification concepts by means of social networks within educational contexts [13].

While many studies have theorized about game design, the two most cited frameworks are **MDA (Mechanics, Dynamics, and Aesthetics)** by Hunicke et al. [14] and the **Elemental Tetrad** by Schell [15]. Rodrigues et al. [16] have conducted a review study that analyzed the literature covering 50 papers published over the time period of 2011 to 2016 using Leximancer software. The study determined and shaped the main concepts proposed in gamification researches. Thirty concepts have been identified related to the gamification main domains. These concepts can be classified by level of relevancy and fit under the fundamental components of gamification frameworks.

Figure 1 includes the two most adopted gamification frameworks, being MDA and Element Tetrad, detailing their concepts and the elements that are included in each concept as reported in the following sections. The figure shows the connectivity between these two frameworks and demonstrates that although they are two different frameworks, they are built on many common basics and pillars.

2.1 MDA

Mechanics, Dynamics, and Aesthetics framework or simply known as MDA facilitates a deliberation of differences between designer and player perspectives. In other words, from the designer's perspective, mechanics produce dynamics, which then produces aesthetics, while, according to a user's perspective, MDA converts into rules, system, and fun. MDA provides one approach of understanding games and how gamification works [17–19].

The elements of MDA are defined as follows:

- **Mechanics.** The concept of mechanics describes the particular components of the game, at the level of data representation and algorithms [14]. Game mechanics involve the distinct set of rules that dictate the outcome of interactions within the system. Points, badges, leaderboards, statuses, levels, quests, countdowns, tasks/quest/missions, and other particular rules and rewards all fall under the category of game mechanics [18]. Moreover, these elements fall under three groups which are the components, the controls, and the courses. Three different types of mechanics are extremely important in games and in gamified experiences: setup mechanics, rule mechanics, and progression mechanics[19].
- **Dynamics.** Hunicke describes dynamics as the runtime behavior of the mechanics acting on the players' inputs to the game and the results of this player interaction in the game over time [14]. Game dynamics refer to the principles that create and support aesthetic experience. Unlike the game mechanics set by the designer, game dynamics describe in-game behaviors and strategic actions and interactions that emerge during play [20], such as context, behavior, consequences, and achievements. Examples of game dynamics contain a sequence of chance, constraints, behaviors, consequence, and finally the achievement.
- **Aesthetic.** It describes the desirable emotional responses evoked in the players, when they interact with the game system [14], in other words, how the game does look, feel, and sound. Aesthetics encompass the various emotional goals of the game: sensation, fantasy, narrative, challenge, fellowship, discovery, expression, and submission [18]. Therefore, aesthetics are the result of how players follow the mechanics and then generate the dynamics. Aesthetics is what gives appeal and fun to the users. Assuming that players will stop playing a game if they do not enjoy themselves, then creating player enjoyment should be the main goal [19].

2.2 Elemental Tetrad

Tetrad proposes that a gamification comprises four concepts being aesthetics, mechanics, story, and technology [15]. None of the four elements have higher importance than the other. However, technology tends to be the least visible to the user, while the aesthetic is the most visible. The concepts of this framework are as follows:

- **Technology.** Technology refers to the tools and systems used to implement or deliver the gameplay. Everything including coding, software, and the devices the user has in their hands falls under technology. Any input or output or choice of technological has an impact on the design of the game.
- **Mechanics.** Schell defines mechanics as the procedures and rules of a game and discusses six mechanics—space, objects, actions, rules, skill, and chance. Space is where the users engage with the game (both virtual worlds and physical space). Objects are tools used by the player to advance in the game. Actions are how the player interacts with objects. Rules govern the game environment. Skills are physical, mental, and social abilities used by a player to progress. Chance refers to the randomness and uncertainty that exist in games [15]. Some inconsistency is shown here as space, objects, actions, skill, and chance are not procedures and rules.
- **Aesthetics.** In most of the concepts that employ it, describes how the game looks, sounds, smells, tastes, and feels. Aesthetic is what the players are most familiar with as it represents everything they see, hear, feel, and perhaps in certain situations even taste and smell during the experience of the game. This is where the game connects to the players' senses. Every piece of art and sound is part of this element.
- **Story.** This element contains the journey, the incredible worlds players find themselves in during gameplay, and the personal relationships between all of the characters in a game. Besides that it can also contain educational or other content that needs to find its way into the game. A way to describe story and differentiate the perspectives of end users and designers is through narratives which can be sorted in three types:
  - *Embedded narrative.* It represents the view of the game designer in terms of structured components and event sequences intentionally embedded in a system by the designers. Hence, embedded narratives align conceptually with game mechanics.
  - *Emergent narrative.* It is created by players during their interaction with the gamification application in a dynamic fashion as they perform different activities. In this way, emergent narratives correspond conceptually to *game dynamics*.

- *Interpreted narratives.* It characterizes the end user's ascribed meaningfulness of experiences with the gamification activities. Given that these narratives are mental representations of the players, they are logically aligned with the concept of game aesthetics.

2.3 Open Issues and Contribution

Although the Mechanics, Dynamics, and Aesthetics (MDA) framework is probably the most widely accepted and practically employed approach to game design, MDA framework has recently been criticized for several weaknesses [2] Other frameworks have been proposed to overcome those limitations, but none has generated sufficient support to replace MDA.

Few studies utilized a more nuanced conceptualization of game narratives and suggested a combination of MDA and the Elemental Tetrad. Ralf and Monu[3] referred to their concept as the Mechanics, Technology, Dynamics, Aesthetics plus Narratives Framework (MTDA+N). This framework, despite its limitations, can serve as a useful theorized concept for teaching fundamentals of game design and clarifying some core concepts especially the game narratives.

Walk et al. [21] aimed to overcome the weaknesses of the well-established MDA framework by placing it on new pillars. They presented the Design, Dynamics, Experience (DDE) framework for the design of computer and video games. Their framework is based on what they determined to be what needs to be produced during the design and development of the game. In addition, they highlight the role of this asset in its contribution to the game experience [21].

A useful and communicable theory of game design is needed to help game designers and academics speak a common language, to legitimize the study of game design among other social sciences, and to educate the next generation of game designers. While game design is a discipline with its own rules, gamification is more of a method that facilitates engagement and entertainment. When working on game design and/or integrating gamification into a product, it is important to keep in mind the users' motivations, feelings, and contexts. The application of **model-driven engineering for gamification** has been studied over the past years and showed promises. However, the drawback is that the applications have been particular to specific cases which limits the interest as the approach of each meta-model would vary from case to case.

---

[2]https://gamedesignadvance.com/?p=2995.

[3]http://www.firstpersonscholar.com/a-working-theory-of-game-design/.

One important issue hindering the adoption of gamified solutions is that currently they are conceived as separate mechanisms to be designed and developed as side applications. This means that, for example, a teacher willing to introduce gaming aspects to her course is required to create her own gameful application, possibly customized for course content and learning objectives, or alternatively enrich an existing learning platform with gamification elements. Even more, in both cases, the specification of the target application would require expertise in game development and programming skills since there exists a gap between the definition of games and their concrete implementation and deployment. In this respect, we envisioned the definition of **a software engineering approach for gameful applications** such that the *game* part should be designed in its main ingredients and deployed on an appropriate *gamification engine* [22]. Based on this, gameful concepts and elements would be handled as specific concerns of software applications. Therefore, the gaming aspects would be kept separate and plugged in existing applications instead of requiring ad hoc extensions of the applications themselves. The main advantages of this vision are increased scalability and maintainability of the gameful mechanisms, which would not get intertwined with irrelevant aspects from a gamification point of view. Moreover, it would make it easier to integrate gamification elements into existing applications.

As a step forward the realization of our vision, we proposed a **Gamification Design Framework (GDF)** [5, 6]. GDF is a solution for the design and deployment of gamified applications through model-driven engineering mechanisms. In particular, it is based on a set of well-defined modeling layers that start from the definition of the main gamification elements, followed by the specification on how those elements are composed to design games, and then progressively refined to reach concrete game implementation and execution. The layers are interconnected through specialization/generalization relationships such that a multilevel modeling approach is realized [6]. The choice of a multilevel modeling approach came out directly from the nature of gamification applications: gamification principles, instantiated in terms of game elements, in turn materialized as game element instances [23].

To characterize GDF and to make it conform to the frameworks already introduced, such as those presented in Fig. 1, we tried to define it incrementally covering for now some of the concepts and the elements already introduced in the literature. Our goal is not to introduce a new conceptual framework for gamification but a modular, extensible, and useful environment to program gamified applications in different contexts and with different objectives. Figure 2 shows in green the concepts and the elements supported now by GDF and presented in this chapter.

The language engineering process toward the concrete implementation of GDF required a relevant effort due to the intrinsic characteristics of the problem domain (i.e., gamification), the need for allowing all the stakeholders to participate to game specifications, and the availability of adequate language workbenches (see a deeper discussion in Sect. 5). By going into more details, gamified applications are mainly

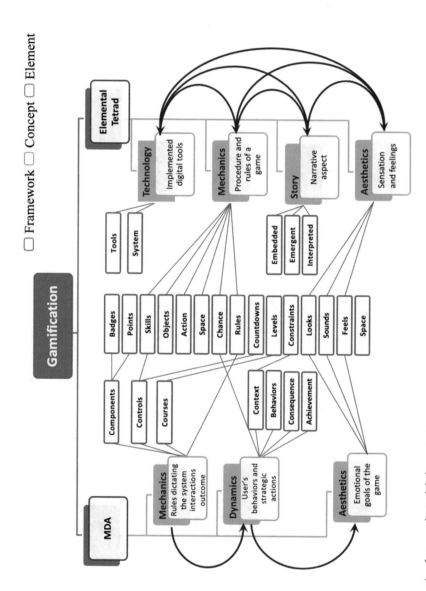

Fig. 1 Gamification frameworks and their concepts

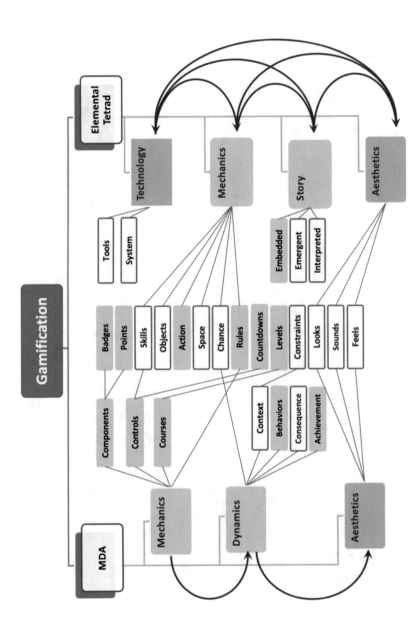

Fig. 2 Gamification concepts and elements supported by GDF

collections of rules orchestrating challenges, players'/teams' actions, points and bonuses gains, and so forth. In this respect, we need a solution able (1) to be easily used by those defining new gamified applications and (2) to be easily extended when switching from one application domain to another. As a consequence, we needed a language workbench enabling easy maintenance/extension of the DSLs and also relieving the users of consistency management.

After several attempts and failures with different alternatives, we opted for MPS workbench. The details of GDF realization by means of MPS are carefully described in Sect. 4 where we present how we have exploited the main features offered by this workbench, notably the projectional editors, the language extension mechanisms, and the support for code generators.

3   Case Study: PapyGame Design with GDF

We have used and validated GDF in diverse application domains, like smart mobility and education [5]. In this section, we report further details about another recent usage scenario, that is, how we have used GDF as core component of a specific gamified software modeling environment called **PapyGame**[4] The choice of this case is due to its consistency with our vision of future software engineering of gamified applications (see Sect. 2.3) and the required contribution of multiple stakeholders. In particular, in PapyGame, the Papyrus[5] modeling tool has been extended with gamification features. The objective of the gamification is to help master degree students in Computer Science in learning specific modeling aspects using Papyrus for UML [24].

Each *student assignment* in PapyGame is composed of a set of *levels* (grouped in series) that each student should deal with. For each level, an exercise is assigned, and each passed level unlocks the next exercise of the next level. To start a PapyGame session, the player must first enter their login and password. Once connected, PapyGame displays a dashboard (see Fig. 3) representing the series of the player. Each completed (successfully) level is displayed in green with the corresponding number of gold coins (GC) and the experience points (XP) rewarded. Remaining levels are colored in gray with a lock except for the first one which is the next level to be played (unlocked).

Each exercise is associated with a specific game type: the *Hangman, when a new part of the man drawing is added with every wrong answer*, and the *On Your Own (OYO), when the student executes the exercise with no help*. At the same time, each

---

[4]https://www.papygame.com.

[5]https://www.eclipse.org/papyrus/.

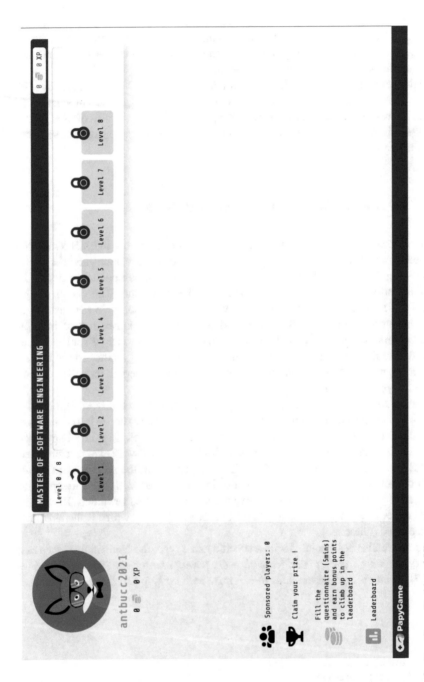

Fig. 3 PapyGame Dashboard UI

Level 1
Type: OYO
Goal: Learn to build Classes
Description: Let's imagine we want to design a database to catalogue all our books.
To begin with, we want to represent the concepts of book but also its authors and publishing
company. Please create following *UML Classes*.
For *class names*, use the *Java class naming convention* (Word1Word2Word3).

Rewards

Errors	Time	XP	GC
0	--	50	2
1	--	30	1
2	--	20	0
3+	--	10	0
Time Rewards			
XP+=	50 − time/2		
GC+=	1 if time < 60		

Correct diagram

Fig. 4 PapyGame: On Your Own (OYO) example

exercise has an associated set of point concepts (experience points, gold coins, etc.)
and rules. All these aspects are defined by the teacher using GDF. In particular,
the teachers execute the following steps in defining each level: (1) choose a game
type among the available games in the system (i.e., Hangman, OYO), (2) define
the goal and the description of the level, (3) create the expected (correct) diagram
in Papyrus according to the level objective, and (4) create the reward rules about
points and eventual bonuses. Figures 4 and 5 show two examples of PapyGame
levels expressed in natural language format in a teacher document.

GDF is used to make this design task of the teacher automatically saved and
deployed in the PapyGame backend. This provides a way to define all the game
elements that regulate the game behavior through specific modeling editors. In
particular this is possible exploiting the editors provided by GDF and its related
generators (see details in Sect. 4). Once the *student assignments* are designed
and deployed, the students can select the respective levels and start to play and

Level 2

Type: Hangman

Goal: Learn to build Properties with primitive Types

Description: Papyrus imports in each UML model a *PrimitiveTypes package* that contains the String, Integer or Boolean types. Use these types to define *attributes in the classes* of the previous level. A book is characterized by a title (text), an edition year (integer) and a format (text). An author is characterized by a last name (text) and a first name (text). A production company has a name (text) and a (text). Please use the *Java naming convention*, but for attributes this time (word1Word2Word3). For *class names*, use the Java class naming convention (Word1Word2Word3).

Rewards

Errors	Time	XP	GC
0	--	70	1
1	--	55	0
2	--	40	0
3+	--	25	0
Time Rewards			
XP+=	70 − time		
GC+=	1 if time < 30		

Correct diagram

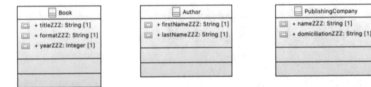

Fig. 5 PapyGame: Hangman example

accumulate points. Figure 6 shows an example. It presents the associated UML diagram containing a set of classes connected with the generalization relationship. The goal of this level is to help players/students associate the right attributes and operations to the right class in the hierarchy. This is done using a drag-n-drop facility. An incorrect user selection (moving an operation into a class that is not the one that should contain it) adds a part of the hangman's body (lower part of Fig. 6). If the players manage to place all operations correctly without the body of the hanged person being completely displayed, they win. The number of gold coins and XP is calculated according to the number of errors (bad drag-n-drops). If the hangman's body is completely displayed, the player loses, and the next level stays unlocked. As a consequence, they will have to play this level again. Whether they won or lost, after the completion of the game, PapyGame players are returned to the Dashboard view.

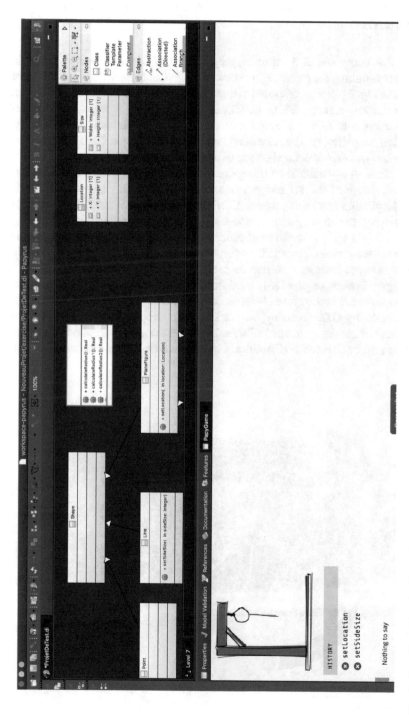

Fig. 6 PapyGame Exercise Example

4 Engineering the Gamification Design Framework (GDF) with MPS

The GDF is composed of a set of languages, each of which defined to cover the artifacts constituting the gamification stack. A graphical representation of this stack is shown in Fig. 7 [6]: it is composed of a set of layers that will be referred to as game modeling layers, namely, GML, GaML, and GiML. They represent incremental refinements/specializations of gamification concepts, from higher to lower levels of abstraction, respectively. The remaining layers, i.e., GsML and GadML, are called *utility layers* and can be defined on top of any of the game modeling ones.

GDF conveys a gamification design process that reflects widely adopted practices in the state of the art and practice of the field [2, 25] (see also Sect. 2). Taking inspiration from this process, GDF provides different modeling languages for specifying the main game components, i.e., game elements, and how they interact to build up a gameful application, that is, mechanics. Such components are progressively refined to reach implementation code for a target gamification engine that copes with game instances execution. For this purpose, we selected a specific gamification engine [26] based on DROOLS rule engine.[6] It is an open-source component and exposes its main functionalities as services (Open APIs) that are used by GDF. Notably, services include supporting the definition and deployment of games, accessing information about the game and player state, and supporting the configuration of notifications for communicating game results to the players.

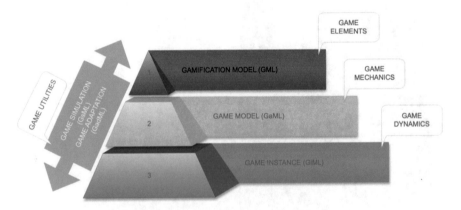

Fig. 7 Languages of the Gamification Design Framework

---

[6]https://www.drools.org/.

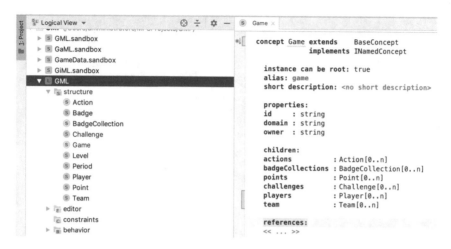

Fig. 8 The Gamification Model Language (GML)

The *Gamification Modeling Language (GML)* is used to represent the set of core elements essential to describe a gameful system (i.e., Point, Badge, Action, etc. introduced in Fig. 2). Figure 8 shows an excerpt of the main GML concepts: a Game concept is composed of a set of properties (i.e., id, domain, and owner) that characterize a specific gameful solution, and a set of *children* concepts that allow to specify the main game elements, that is, the fundamental ingredients of a gamified application. GML conforms to the MPS base language and provides the basic gamification building blocks. Other languages (GaML, GiML, etc.) are derived as lower abstraction levels.

In this respect, a *game designer* should extend/refine GML concepts every time there is a need to introduce new game elements or mechanics.

The *Game Model Language (GaML)* extends GML with concepts used to define concrete game descriptions. As shown in Fig. 9, through GaML, the designer can specify how the game components are assembled to create an application into a GameDefinition. Notably, the concept of Point in GML is specialized in skillPoint and experiencePoint, to distinguish between points gained by means of specific activity goals and points gained due to the progression through the game, respectively. Moreover, dataDrivenAction and evenDrivenAction are exploited to recognize activities based on data (i.e., modeling task completed.) or on events (i.e., surveys filled). In a similar manner, the Challenge concept coming from GML is refined through, e.g., PlayerChallenge and TeamChallenge, to distinguish between challenges intended to be completed individually and the ones to be accomplished as groups of players, respectively.

GaML is generic enough to enable the reuse of the defined gamification concepts into multiple development scenarios (e.g., the distinction between the types of actions and points).

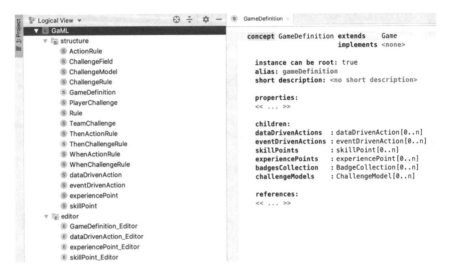

Fig. 9 GameDefinition concept of the GaML

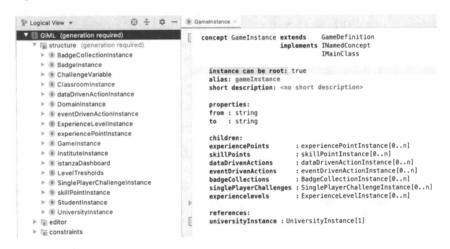

Fig. 10 GameInstance concept of the GiML

A game instance is a `GameDefinition`, as prescribed in GaML, opportunely instantiated to be run by the gamification engine. In general, an instantiation consists of the specification of the players/teams involved in the game; hence, one or more instances of multiple games may run concurrently by means of the same engine. The *Game Instance Model Language (GiML)* binds game definitions coming from GaML with instantiation details, as depicted in Fig. 10. In particular, the `universityInstance` defines *teams* and *players* that play in a certain instance of a game. GiML also supports for single-player *challenges*.

```
concept GameSimulation extends    BaseConcept
                        implements INamedConcept

   instance can be root: false
   alias: <no alias>
   short description: <no short description>

   properties:
   << ... >>

   children:
   listOfExecutions : SingleGameExecution[1..n]

   references:
   game : GameDefinition[1]
```

Fig. 11 GameSimulation concept of the GsML

singlePlayerChallenges demand to players the fulfillment of a specific goal, whose attainment requires a prolonged individual commitment, typically within a limited period. In order to confer a feeling of progress and mastery, GDF supports the definition of *Levels*. Levels are always defined in association with a specific *Point Concept*. For this in GiML, we have identified two types of levels: skillLevels and experiencelevels. The first are related to skillPoints, while the second to the experiencePoints point concepts. GiML instantiates also the badgeCollections. They are used in order to further reward, through a collectible visual representation, the results of a player in terms of specific achievements.

Apart from game modeling languages, GDF provides so-called utility languages. One of them is the Game Simulation Language (GsML), which allows to simulate game scenarios. In particular, a GameSimulation is composed of a GameDefinition and a set of SingleGameExecution elements, as depicted in Fig. 11. In turn, each game execution is made up of a Team and/or a Player that can execute an actionInstance or a challengeInstance (see Fig. 12). In this way, the designer can specify specific game situations and check what state changes are triggered. In this respect, it is important to mention that the target gamification engine[7] provides the necessary features to track the gamification rules triggered during the execution together with the corresponding state changes.

Another utility feature provided by GDF is *adaptation*. This feature leverages specific capabilities of the target gamification engine and, in particular, a recommendation system for generating players' tailored challenges based on game historical data and current status, a mechanism to "inject" new game contents on the fly. With this premise, GadML allows to model those scenarios when a new game content (i.e., a new challenge recommended by the engine) has to be assigned to a specific

---

[7]https://github.com/smartcommunitylab/smartcampus.gamification.

```
concept SingleGameExecution extends     BaseConcept
                               implements <none>

    instance can be root: false
    alias: singleGameExecution
    short description: <no short description>

    properties:
    << ... >>

    children:
    << ... >>

    references:
    team                : Team[1]
    player              : Player[0..1]
    actionInstance      : ActionInstance[0..1]
    challengeInstance : ChallengeInstance[0..1]
```

Fig. 12 Single execution of a game simulation

```
concept newChallenge extends     GameAdaptation
                        implements <none>

    instance can be root: true
    alias: newChallenge
    short description: <no short description>

    properties:
    << ... >>

    children:
    challengeModel : ChallengeModel[1]
    challengeData   : ChallengeData[1]
    challengeDate   : ChallendeDate[1]

    references:
    << ... >>
```

Fig. 13 newChallenge concept of the GadML

player on the fly. In particular, the GameAdaptation concept includes gameId and playerId parameters for a game adaptation, plus a set of children to specify the new challenge to be injected. As Fig. 13 shows, a newChallenge refines a simple game adaptation by defining a ChallengeModel, ChallengeData (i.e., *bonusScore*, *virtualPrize*, etc.), and ChallengeDate (i.e., validity period of time for the challenge).

4.1 MPS Projectional Editors

MPS features "projectional" editing, that is, developers are not editing simple text while providing inputs in MPS; on the contrary, their editing is bound to the abstract syntax tree (AST) inferred by the language definition. In other words, the DSL concepts defined through MPS and used as inputs "activate" specific branches of the AST, and consequently, the editing proceeds by following the available alternatives as per language definition. In this way, the code is always represented as an AST, conforming to the language by construction.

Programs in MPS are represented as instances of concepts, called nodes [27]. In this respect, it is possible to define how the different concepts of a language are visualized to the end user, and each projectional editor provides a representation of the AST with which the user interacts. For each set of concepts in GDF, we have defined editors by means of specific projection rules used to define the desired concrete syntax. These editors can be used by the *game designer* to define the gamification elements, mechanics, and dynamics. At the same time, we added extra editors to define specific game simulations and adaptations.

Figure 14 shows the editor definition for the GameDeclaration concept. At the top level, it consists of a collection cell [− . . . −] which aligns a sequence of

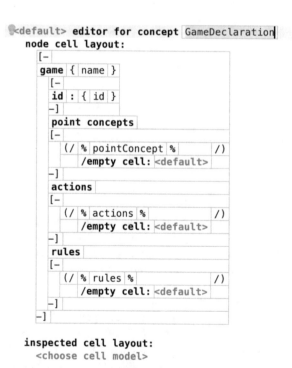

Fig. 14 Editor definition for the GameDeclaration concept

```
<default> editor for concept  ActionDeclaration
   node cell layout:
     [-
     action   { name } {
        [-
        properties :
           (- % property % /empty cell: <default> -)
        -]
     }
     -]

   inspected cell layout:
     <choose cell model>
```

Fig. 15 Editor definition for the `Action` concept

```
<default> editor for concept  DroolsRule
   node cell layout:
     [/
          [> rule { name } <]
          [> ----> when <]
          [> ----->----> (/ % inputs %              /) <]
                            /empty cell: <default>
          [> ----> then <]
          [> ----->----> (/ % statements %          /) <]
                            /empty cell: <default>
          end
          <constant>
     /]
```

Fig. 16 Editor definition for the `Rule` concept

additional cells. The sequence starts with the game `name` and its related `id`. It continues with the sequence of core elements as `point` concepts, `actions`, and `rules`. All these concepts are the key elements to define the points that each player can receive, the actions that lead to the accumulation of points, and the rules that define the overall game behavior.

Actions (and Points) of a game can be defined at design time by a game designer using specific editors as the one illustrated in Fig. 15.

An action of a game, as the point, is defined by a name and by a set or properties that characterize them. For example, an action can represent the interaction that a player does with the application together with information about the instance when it is executed, while a point represents a counter that is updated with a certain value every time a specific action is executed.

As mentioned before, to execute the game actions done by the player, GDF leverages an open-source Gamification Engine component. This component embeds DROOLS, a state-of-the-art rule engine technology based on reactive computing models [28]. For this reason, GDF expresses the rules of a game using the `DroolsRule` concept that regulates the game behavior. A game designer can use the editor depicted in Fig. 16 to specify when a certain rule is triggered and how the different points are accumulated (with the `then` part declaration).

4.2 MPS Generators

The goal of the *generators* in MPS is to go from the business domain (i.e., gamification) to the specific implementation domain (i.e., gamification engine). Each generator is focusing on changing the AST of the specific domain into another AST that is closer to the implementation domain.

In GDF, for each layer introduced in Fig. 7, we have realized a generator as depicted in Fig. 17. This figure represents the internal logic of the GDF as composed of four constituents: (a) Game Model, (b) Game Instance, (c) Game Simulation, and (d) Game Adaptation. Each component is made up of two layers, the former is implemented in MPS, while the latter exploits the gamification engine.[8]

By means of the `Game Model` component, the game designer can specify the core elements of a new game (i.e., points, actions, rules) using the editor depicted in Fig. 14. The GaML generator is used to transform a new game model into the specific elements used by the gamification engine to execute the game. The effect of this transformation is depicted in Fig. 18 where the core elements of a new game are deployed in the gamification engine.

At this point, a gamification designer can instantiate a new game using the `Game Instance` component that exploits the core elements of the game defined in the `Game Model` component and deploys the needed elements in the gamification engine. The `Game Instance` component has been introduced to instantiate the different games starting from the same Game Model. Once the designer have specified the new game, she/he can proceed with the game deployment in the gamification engine. The deployment step is done using the GiML generator able to generate Java code that, when executed, results in the creation of corresponding game instance in the gamification engine.

For example, in the specific case of the teaching modeling domain (described with details in Sect. 3) that we have experimented, the game designer can define the university involved, the set of `SkillPoint` and `ExperiencePoint`, the set of `Actions`, and other information related to the specific game instance (i.e., name, duration, and its description), as depicted in Fig. 19. Starting from a *Game Instance* model, as the one in Fig. 19, and using the generator introduced in Fig. 20, this component is able to deploy the game instance in the target gamification engine calling specific REST APIs[9] supplied by the latter.

GDF also provides support for the simulation of the behavior of a running game and the definition of new game contents and their assignment to a specific player on the fly (i.e., game adaptation). To simulate the defined games, GDF uses the GsML component. A game simulation is defined by a *Player* that should execute

---

[8]The engine is available in GitHub under the Apache License Version 2.0 https://github.com/smartcommunitylab/smartcampus.gamification and is available as a stand-alone application as well as software as a service (SaaS).

[9]https://dev.smartcommunitylab.it/gamification-v3/swagger-ui.html.

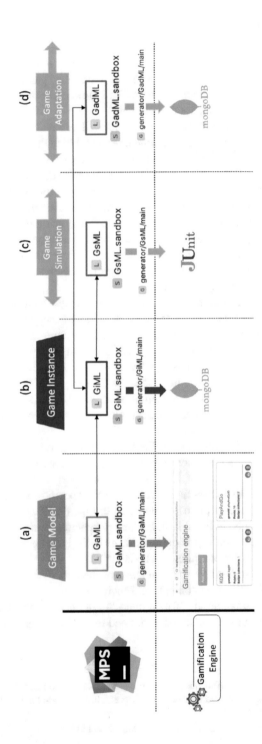

Fig. 17 The GDF internal logic

Fig. 18 Game Model in the gamification engine

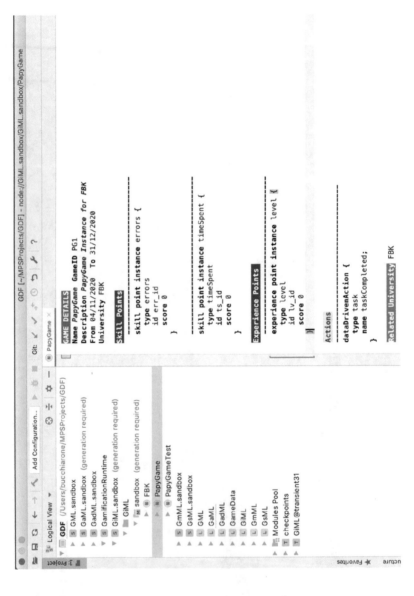

Fig. 19 Game Instance Model for the PapyGame scenario (see Sect. 3)

```
┌ root template   ┐
│ input GameInstance │
└                 ┘

public class map_gameInstance extends GameTest {

    private PlayerService playerSrv;
    private static final String GAME_ID = "$[gameID]";


    @Override
    public void initEnv() {
        // add all the Teams defined for this game instance

        $LOOP$ {
            TeamState team = new TeamState(GAME_ID, "$[teamName]");
            List<string> members = new ArrayList<String>();
            $LOOP$ [members.add("$[playerName]"); ]
            playerSrv.add(team);
        }

    }
    @Override
    public void defineGame() {
        // add all the GameDefinition elements
        List<String> actions = new ArrayList<String>();

        // Add Game DataDriven Actions
        $LOOP$ [actions.add("$[actionName]"); ]
        // ......
```

Fig. 20   Game instance generator

```
┌ root template    ┐
│ input GameSimulation │
└                  ┘
public class map_GameSimulation extends GameTest {
    private static final String GAME_ID = "$[gameID]";
    @Override
    public void defineExecData(List<GameTest.ExecData> execList) {

        $LOOP$ {
            Map<String, Object> payload = payload = new HashMap<String, Object>();
            $LOOP$ [payload.add("$[dataType]", "$[dataValue]"); ]
            GameTest.ExecData input = new GameTest.ExecData(GAME_ID, "$[actionType]", payload);
            // select a player randomly to assign a specific simulation action
            input.setPlayerId("$[playerId]");
            execList.add(input);
        }
    }
}
```

Fig. 21   Game simulation generator

an *actionInstance* or a *challengeInstance*. Starting from a *GameSimulation* model specified using GsML and containing the elements we mentioned earlier, we used the generator introduced in Fig. 21 to derive the corresponding Java code.

In this case, a jUnit test, as the one depicted in Fig. 22, is generated. In the specific case, it represents a game simulation where a specific player (i.e., Alice) executes the taskCompleted action with 1 errors and 20 timeSpent.

Finally, whenever a game adaptation (i.e., new challenge) must be executed for a specific player of a team, GDF provides the Game Adaptation component. It

```java
@Override
public void defineGame() {
    mongo.getDb().drop();
    List<GameConcept> concepts = new ArrayList<~>();
    concepts.add(new PointConcept( name: "moves"));
    concepts.add(new PointConcept( name: "errors"));
    concepts.add(new PointConcept( name: "points"));
    concepts.add(new PointConcept( name: "gold coins"));
    concepts.add(new PointConcept( name: "timeSpent"));
    List<String> actions = Arrays.asList("taskCompleted", "surveyDone", "playerInvited");
    defineGameHelper(DOMAIN, GAME, actions, concepts);
    try {
        loadClasspathRules(GAME,  classpathFolder: "rules/"+GAME);
    } catch (IOException e) {
        // TODO Auto-generated catch block
        e.printStackTrace();
    }
}
@Override
public void defineExecData(List<ExecData> execList) {
    Map<String, Object> d = new HashMap<~>();

    d.put("errors", 1.0);
    d.put("timeSpent", 20.0);
    ExecData data = new ExecData(GAME,  actionId: "taskCompleted",  playerId: "alice", d);
    execList.add(data);|
}
@Override
public void analyzeResult() {
    assertionPoint(GAME,  score: 1.0 + 1.0,  playerId: "alice",  conceptName: "gold coins");
    assertionPoint(GAME,  score: 30.0 + 40.0,  playerId: "alice",  conceptName: "points");

}
```

Fig. 22 Excerpt of the jUnit test for the game simulation

is supported by a generator to generate a Java code that leads to the adaptation of a database (as depicted in Fig. 17d) that the gamification engine uses to update the specific game instance.

5   Lessons Learned and Future Investigations

As mentioned in Sect. 2.3, the language engineering process devoted to the creation of GDF constituted an endeavor due to diverse challenges, summarized as follows and discussed in detail after:

- scalability of modeling techniques, and in particular of diagrammatic forms, in the case of systems of logical constraints;
- multiple levels of concepts definitions and corresponding instantiations;
- usability of available multilevel modeling workbenches.

The first problem can be regarded as general and not due to the specific application domain and the language workbench taken into account. Indeed, using diagrammatic representations for complex systems of logical constraints tends to become quickly intractable: modeling sequences of events together with their preconditions and constraints, possibly also including negative statements, makes the size of the specifications to exponentially grow with the number of handled variables/events. We already gained large experience in modeling smart mobility applications and incurred in the same scalability problem we faced for gamification [29]. As a consequence, after some preliminary attempts and the necessary investigation of the state of the art, we decided to opt for a text-based modeling solution. Admittedly, at this point, we could have chosen a different language workbench, notably XText,[10] for trying to implement GDF. However, the language import feature embedded in MPS caught our attention, and we decided to give it a try, without a thorough comparison with possible text-based alternatives.

The second among the listed challenges can be reduced to a separation-of-concerns need [30]: in order to cope with the growing complexity of gameful applications, it is desired to partition their design and development into smaller, typically simpler, sub-problems. More precisely, sub-problems would be (i) the definition of gaming elements and mechanics in general; (ii) the specification of selected elements and mechanics for a certain game; and (iii) the deployment of game elements and mechanics of a specific gamification engine, including the configuration of players and teams. It is worth noting that in order to make this separation effective, consistency support shall also be provided, such that, e.g., it would not be possible to use a game element when not permitted by the mechanics used in the game itself. In this context, the language import feature provided by MPS reveals its criticality: since MPS is based on projectional editing, it is simply not possible to produce ill-formed models. As a direct consequence, since, e.g., models in (ii) originate from the definitions in (i), a mechanism or element defined in (i) can only be used in (ii) as conforming to the language definition. In the same way, a deployment specification in (iii) can be only done as conforming to the definition of the game provided in (ii).

In the MDE literature, separation-of-concerns and consistency management have been widely investigated, and in fact, there exist solutions like multilevel modeling and megamodeling that would suit for GDF purposes. Nonetheless, while from a theoretical perspective those approaches are valid, the same cannot be said about availability of tools. As a matter of fact, in our experience, MPS has been the first workbench delivering language engineering support with a tractable level of complexity, even for persons not necessarily MDE experts. Here it is important to remind that GDF is intended to be extensible to new game elements, mechanics, etc., and to be used by all gamification stakeholders. Therefore, the usability of the language workbench is of critical importance. As mentioned before, the language extension mechanisms provided by MPS allow to import existing languages and extend them

---

[10]https://www.eclipse.org/Xtext/.

by operating limited refinements, both for new concepts, new constraints, and so forth. At the same time, consistency management is implicitly built by means of inheritance relationships.

As expected, also MPS requires a training period, and the learning curve might be steep. In our experiences, people with programming backgrounds might have some advantage in the learning phase, while MDE experts might find some of the features as unexpected and/or counterintuitive. Indeed, MPS exploits a precise set of tools that need to be carefully understood in order to be able to use the workbench effectively. In other words, while MPS demonstrates to be fairly simple to use for entry levels, when users require advanced features, the workbench exposes a rather complex and extensive set of details that need to be taken care of. In this respect, the vast availability of tutorials and examples falls short, because a more conceptual description about how different portions of the workbench are kept together would be required. Moreover, the need for a language debugger increases with the size of the project; in fact, in most cases, a language engineer understands that a specification is wrong due to some unexpected behavior of the resulting artefacts, while the reason of the malfunctions remains completely hidden.

For the current version of GDF, we expect gamification stakeholders to optionally define new game elements and mechanics, while the typical use would be to instantiate existing mechanics and elements in corresponding game definitions. In turn, game definitions would be exploited to define gameful application deployments on a selected gamification engine. Moreover, GDF provides languages to define game monitoring and adaptations at runtime. While in most cases it is enough to define game elements and state change rules, the specifications might grow in their complexity and require fine-tuning for which stakeholders would require MPS experts' help. In this respect, we are planning future refinements/extensions of GDF to make the specification of gameful applications simpler. Notably, we would abstract from the MPS workbench itself by means of, e.g., a web interface for game definitions; moreover, we would like to investigate easier ways of specifying detailed game behaviors, especially to relieve stakeholders of the burden due to hand-tuning the generators embedded in GDF.

6   Conclusions

Gamification is increasingly gaining popularity as a tool to promote engagement in target human activities. In this respect, gameful applications development is facing growing complexity that requires adequate design and deployment support. In this chapter, we presented GDF, a framework for the design and deployment of gameful applications. In particular, GDF is made up of domain-specific languages allowing for stepwise refinement of application definitions, from higher levels of abstraction to implementation code to be run on a gamification engine.

GDF has been engineered by using MPS due to three main reasons: the need to provide text-based DSLs, the availability of language extension mechanisms conveying consistency management between abstraction layers, and the provision of generators to automatically derive implementation code.

GDF has also been validated against multiple case studies in diverse domains, notably education, smart mobility, and training in modelling. In this respect, MPS demonstrated powerful capabilities but also a steep learning curve that could be unacceptable for non-software engineers. In this respect, one of the main future research directions we are pursuing is the integration of simplified user interfaces, e.g., dashboards, to alleviate the complexity of game definitions for GDF users.

References

1. Seaborn, K., Fels, D.I.: Gamification in theory and action: a survey. Int. J. Hum.-Comput. Stud. **74**, 14–31 (2015)
2. Deterding, S., Dixon, D., Khaled, R., Nacke, L.E.: From game design elements to gamefulness: defining "gamification". In: Lugmayr, A., Franssila, H., Safran, C., Hammouda, I. (eds.), *Proceedings of the 15th International Academic MindTrek Conference: Envisioning Future Media Environments, MindTrek 2011, Tampere, September 28–30, 2011*, pp. 9–15. ACM, New York (2011)
3. Hanus, M.D., Fox, J.: Assessing the effects of gamification in the classroom: a longitudinal study on intrinsic motivation, social comparison, satisfaction, effort, and academic performance. Comput. Educ. **80**, 152–161 (2015)
4. TechnologyAdvice.com. Compare 120+ gamification platforms. https://technologyadvice.com/gamification/ (2019)
5. Bucchiarone, A., Cicchetti, A., Marconi, A.: GDF: a gamification design framework powered by model-driven engineering. In: Burgueño, L., Pretschner, A., Voss, S., Chaudron, M., Kienzle, J., Völter, M., Gérard, S., Zahedi, M., Bousse, E., Rensink, A., Polack, F., Engels, G., Kappel, G. (eds.) 22nd ACM/IEEE International Conference on Model Driven Engineering Languages and Systems Companion, MODELS Companion 2019, Munich, September 15–20, 2019, pp. 753–758. IEEE, New York (2019)
6. Bucchiarone, A., Cicchetti, A., Marconi, A.: Exploiting multi-level modelling for designing and deploying gameful systems. In: Kessentini, M., Yue, T., Pretschner, A., Voss, S., Burgueño, L. (eds.) 22nd ACM/IEEE International Conference on Model Driven Engineering Languages and Systems, MODELS 2019, Munich, September 15–20, 2019, pp. 34–44. IEEE, New York (2019)
7. S. Deterding, M. Sicart, L.E. Nacke, K. O'Hara, D. Dixon, Gamification: using game-design elements in non-gaming contexts. In: Tan, D.S., Amershi, S., Begole, B., Kellogg, W.A., Tungare, M. (eds.) Proceedings of the International Conference on Human Factors in Computing Systems, CHI 2011, Extended Abstracts Volume, Vancouver, BC, May 7–12, 2011, pp. 2425–2428. ACM, New York (2011)
8. García, F., Pedreira, O., Piattini, M., Cerdeira-Pena, A., Penabad, M.R.: A framework for gamification in software engineering. J. Syst. Softw. **132**, 21–40 (2017)
9. Lee, J.J., Hammer, J.: Gamification in education: what, how, why bother? Acad. Exchange Quart. **15**(2), 2 (2011)
10. Zichermann, G., Cunningham, C.: Gamification by Design: Implementing Game Mechanics in Web and Mobile Apps, 1st edn. O'Reilly Media, Inc., Sebastopol (2011)
11. Hugos, M.: Enterprise Games: Using Game Mechanics to Build a Better Business. O'Reilly Media, Inc., Sebastopol (2012)
12. Bartel, A., Hagel, G.: Engaging students with a mobile game-based learning system in university education. In: 2014 IEEE Global Engineering Education Conference (EDUCON), pp. 957–960 (2014)

13. Toda, A.M., do Carmo, R.M.C., da Silva, A.P., Bittencourt, I.I., Isotani, S.: An approach for planning and deploying gamification concepts with social networks within educational contexts. Int. J. Inf. Manage. **46**, 294–303 (2019)
14. Hunicke, R., Leblanc, M., Zubek, R.: MDA: a formal approach to game design and game research. In: Proceedings of the Challenges in Games AI Workshop, Nineteenth National Conference of Artificial Intelligence, pp. 1–5. AAAI Press, Menlo Park (2004)
15. Schell, J.: The Art of Game Design: A Book of Lenses. Morgan Kaufmann Publishers Inc., San Francisco, CA (2008)
16. Rodrigues, L.F., Oliveira, A., Rodrigues, H.: Main gamification concepts: a systematic mapping study. Heliyon **5**(7), e01993 (2019)
17. Elverdam, C., Aarseth, E.: Game classification and game design: Construction through critical analysis. Games Culture **2**(1), 3–22 (2007)
18. Kim, B.: Designing gamification in the right way. Libr. Technol. Rep. **51**, 29–35 (2015)
19. Robson, K., Plangger, K., Kietzmann, J.H., McCarthy, I., Pitt, L.: Is it all a game? understanding the principles of gamification. Bus. Horiz. **58**(4), 411–420 (2015)
20. Camerer, C.F.: Behavioral Game Theory: Experiments in Strategic Interaction. Russell Sage Foundation, New York, NY (2003)
21. Walk, W., Görlich, D., Barrett, M.: Design, Dynamics, Experience (DDE): An Advancement of the MDA Framework for Game Design, pp. 27–45. Springer International Publishing, Cham (2017)
22. Bucchiarone, A., Cicchetti, A., Marconi, A.: Towards engineering future gameful applications. In: Proceedings of the ACM/IEEE 42nd International Conference on Software Engineering: New Ideas and Emerging Results, ICSE-NIER '20, pp. 105–108. Association for Computing Machinery, New York, NY (2020)
23. Atkinson, C., Kühne, T.: Model-driven development: a metamodeling foundation. IEEE Softw. **20**(5), 36–41 (2003)
24. Bucchiarone, A., Savary-Leblanc, M., Pallec, X.L., Bruel, J.-M., Cicchetti, A., Cabot, J., Gerard, S., Aslam, H., Marconi, A., Perillo, M.: Papyrus for gamers, let's play modeling. In: Guerra, E., Iovino, L. (eds.) MODELS '20: ACM/IEEE 23rd International Conference on Model Driven Engineering Languages and Systems, Virtual Event, Canada, 18–23 October, 2020, Companion Proceedings, pp. 5:1–5:5. ACM, New York (2020)
25. Salen, K., Zimmerman, E.: Rules of Play: Game Design Fundamentals. MIT Press, Cambridge, MA (2004)
26. Kazhamiakin, R., Marconi, A., Martinelli, A., Pistore, M., Valetto, G.: A gamification framework for the long-term engagement of smart citizens. In: IEEE International Smart Cities Conference, ISC2 2016 (2016), pp. 1–7
27. Voelter, M., Lisson, S.: Supporting diverse notations in mps' projectional editor. In: Combemale, B., DeAntoni, J., France, R.B. (eds.) Proceedings of the 2nd International Workshop on the Globalization of Modeling Languages co-located with ACM/IEEE 17th International Conference on Model Driven Engineering Languages and Systems, GEMOC@Models 2014, Valencia, September 28, 2014. CEUR Workshop Proceedings, vol. 1236, pp. 7–16. CEUR-WS.org, 2014
28. Herzig, P., Wolf, B., Brunstein, S., Schill, A.: Efficient persistency management in complex event processing: a hybrid approach for gamification systems. In: Theory, Practice, and Applications of Rules on the Web—7th Int. Symp., RuleML 2013, July 11–13, 2013. Proceedings. LNCS, vol. 8035, pp. 129–143. Springer, New York (2013)
29. Bucchiarone, A., Cicchetti, A.: A model-driven solution to support smart mobility planning. In: Proceedings of the 21th ACM/IEEE International Conference on Model Driven Engineering Languages and Systems, MODELS '18, pp. 123–132. Association for Computing Machinery, New York, NY (2018)
30. De Lara, J., Guerra, E., Cuadrado, J.S.: When and how to use multilevel modelling. ACM Trans. Softw. Eng. Methodol. **24**(2), 12:1–12:46 (2014)

Learning Data Analysis with MetaR

Manuele Simi

Abstract The analysis of biological data is an important part of modern biological and medical research. Many statistical and computational tools are available for statisticians and data scientists, providing them with both computational power and flexibility. However, these tools are often not suitable for biomedical researchers performing data processing and simple analyses. Learning to code is indeed challenging and quite difficult when coming from a non-technical background. This chapter introduces MetaR, a tool designed to help biologists and clinicians to learn, and perform, the basis of data analysis. Originally created as an educational software, it eventually evolved into a mature and stable Domain Specific Language (DSL) used to support various aspects of a research project up to the creation of figures suitable for scientific publications. MetaR generates to R code, but users do not even see it. By providing high-level abstractions, MetaR hides most of the details of each step in the data analysis process. Because of its capability to blend scripting and graphical elements, it provides a novel approach to the practice of analyzing data. Simplified executions and syntax-completion are additional features that make MetaR easy to use for beginners. Language composition is available for advanced users that wish to contribute and extend the project. In our data-rich age, there is a great divide between biomedical researchers and data analysts. MetaR has proved to be an educational bridge between these two worlds.

1 Introduction

Bioinformatics is an interdisciplinary field of study that combines biology with computer science to understand biological data. The analysis of these data is

M. Simi (✉)
Englander Institute for Precision Medicine, Weill Cornell Medicine, New York, NY, USA

Institute for Computational Biomedicine, Weill Cornell Medicine, New York, NY, USA

Department of Physiology and Biophysics, Weill Cornell Medicine, New York, NY, USA
e-mail: mas2182@med.cornell.edu

an important part of most modern clinical and genomic studies. However, while statistical and computational tools are available for statisticians and data scientists, providing them with both computational power and flexibility, they are often not suitable for biomedical researchers looking to perform data processing and simple analyses.

Following a long track record of success in providing tools and services to support the conduct, management, and evaluation of research, the Informatics Core at the Clinical & Translational Science Center (CTSC)[1] at Weill Cornell Medicine (WCM) has put effort and funds to create new computational methods to facilitate data analysis.

For this purpose, the CTSC has developed MetaR [1, 2], a new kind of interactive tool providing high-level data abstraction, manipulation, and visualization. MetaR is composed of a set of data analysis languages built with the Language Workbench Technology [3] offered by JetBrains Meta Programming System (MPS) [4] to make data analysis easier for biologists and clinicians with minimal computational skills.

The goal of the MetaR project is to provide a tool for educating biomedical researchers in data analysis by keeping the learning curve as smooth and simple as possible.

---

2   Domain

2.1   *What Is Data Analysis?*

Data analysis commonly refers to a set of methods for inspecting, cleaning, transforming, modeling, interpreting, and visualizing data to discover useful information for downstream decision-making activities. However, data analysis is much more than a set of formal technical procedures: it involves goals, relationships, and ideas, in addition to working with the actual data itself. Simply put, data analysis includes ways of working with information (data) to support the goals and plans of a business or research project.

To be effective, the data analysis process must be based upon the domain and mission of the organization, as well as the skills of the team in charge of working with the data. Bioinformatics [5] is the field that creates and applies data analysis techniques to biological data. Such techniques mainly include the development of computational methods to analyze small and large collections of data to make new interpretations or predictions, come up with biological insights, and, ultimately, help advance biomedical research.

---

[1] https://ctscweb.weill.cornell.edu/.

In bioinformatics, there are several types of analysis techniques depending on the nature of the data to analyze, the domain, and the technology. The branch of data analysis in the scope of this chapter is called *Statistical Data Analysis*. In particular, MetaR focuses on procedures of performing various statistical operations over biological datasets (see Sect. 6).

2.2 Which Data?

The initial focus of MetaR was on analysis of RNA-Seq data [6] and the creation of heatmaps (a type of plot we encounter later in the chapter) for educational purposes. Next-generation sequencing is without doubt one of the most important technological advances in molecular biology of the past 15 years. Data coming from RNA sequencing experiments determine the identity and abundance of RNA molecules in biological samples, providing the investigator with a snapshot of the activity in cells. The analysis of these data produces new knowledge and insights from basic science, to drug discovery, to medical treatments.

Nevertheless, since the beginning, MetaR has been conceived to be readily extended to support a broad range of data.

2.3 The R Statistical Language

The most popular tool for statistical data analysis is probably R [7], a language and environment for statistical computing. Especially in academia, many researchers and scholars write programs in R for processing and manipulating data, analyzing the relationships and correlations among datasets, visualizing results, and more. R also helps to identify patterns and trends for interpretation of the data.

R provides many features, notably:

- Data cleaning and reduction
- Data visualization
- Statistical hypothesis testing
- Statistical modeling
- Data analysis report output (with R markdown)

Due to its expressive syntax and a great number of packages (see Sect. 2.5.2) that extend its capabilities, R has grown in popularity in recent years. However, even for an experienced programmer, learning R can be a frustrating challenge. It is frequently stated that R is a programming language built by data scientists for data scientists and this results in a mixed approach to the language. There is a lot of unusual coding syntax and daily practice problems to work through before a programmer can be productive with R. Plus, R is a command-line program, which means that the R command console interprets each line of code as it is entered and, if it is valid, executes it and returns the result in the console. This sets R apart from other more friendly and visual languages and, because of this, biomedical researchers have even fewer chances to approach data analysis with R. It is not surprising that many beginners give up or drop off at points along their climb up this "learning hill."

With the MetaR DSL, we tried to eliminate (or reduce) the so-called cliff of boring (the lapse of time between starting to learn and seeing the results). In MetaR, most of the details of the R language are hidden or made optional; familiar keywords based on the domain help users to identify what to expect as input and output from each command. A shift in the programming paradigm (see Sect. 2.5.1) also simplifies the understanding of the program's logic.

2.4 MetaR Languages

The MetaR Languages[2] (we refer to them also as MetaR software or simply MetaR) have been under active development since late 2014. Initially, the CTSC created MetaR as an educational tool to introduce biologists and clinicians to data analysis. Despite retaining this original purpose, over the years, it has eventually evolved into a mature and stable Domain Specific Language (DSL) used to support various aspects of a research project up to the creation of figures suitable for scientific publications.

> DSLs are smaller and easier to understand, they allow nonprogrammers to see the code that drives important parts of their business. By exposing the real code to the people who understand the domain, you enable a much richer communication channel between programmers and their customers.

Martin Fowler [8]

Learning to code is indeed a challenging endeavor and quite difficult when coming from a non-technical background. MetaR fills this gap within health care research projects by bringing biomedical researchers closer to data scientists so they can establish a more fruitful collaboration.

---

[2]https://metar-languages.github.io/.

2.5   Relation with R

MetaR generates R code in the form of R scripts.

R scripts are text files with lists of R instructions to execute from the command line. Later in this chapter, we will learn that the main concept in MetaR is called `Analysis` (Sect. 4.2.3) and is composed of `Statements` (Sect. 4.2.2). Each instance of the `Analysis` concept is transformed into an executable R script, while each instance of `Statement` generates a piece of R code fitting in the script.

2.5.1   Programming Paradigm

Even if it is largely classified as a functional language, R can be considered a multi-paradigm language. It mostly relies on functions, but also has statements, objects, states, and other elements belonging to other paradigms. Such versatility is one of the reasons why many programmers have difficulties with their approach to R.

The way MetaR composes analyses makes a big shift in the programming paradigm from R: *MetaR is a DSL that follows the imperative paradigm.* Each statement is executed and generates results available for the next statements. We found that this step-after-step method of proceeding, with a sequence of statements, is easier to understand and follow for our users.

2.5.2   External Packages

Many of the R capabilities come from packages, the fundamental units of which are created by the R community to share reusable R code. Recently, the official repository (CRAN[3]) has reached 10,000 packages published, and many more are publicly available online. Each package must be independently installed in the local system before being used by R commands.

The R code generated by a `Statement` typically relies on one or more packages. Each `Statement` is configured (by the language designer) with the list of packages it will require at runtime. R commands to install these packages are automatically generated when the `Analysis` is built. In addition, several packages used by MetaR for the analysis and comprehension of biological data are released by the Bioconductor project [9].[4] These packages require a sort of "non-standard" installation, also transparently handled by MetaR.

---

[3] https://cran.r-project.org/.

[4] https://www.bioconductor.org/.

3 Development and User Community

3.1 Development

Two senior language engineers designed and developed the core languages of
MetaR. At different times, rotating students and summer interns joined the team
to work on selected parts of the software.

3.2 Target Audience

MetaR's data analysis languages are tailored for users with a diverse range of
experience. They can be used by:

- Biologists, clinicians, and other biomedical researchers with limited computational experience, who wish to understand how data analysis works. No
  programming skills are required to start analyzing data for these users. They
  represent the majority of users.
- Students, looking for a relaxed entry point to the field.
- Bioinformaticians, who need to perform repetitive analyses and find it beneficial
  to design and use specialized analyses micro-languages [10] to increase productivity and consistency of data analysis.
- Analysis experts, who wish to create and package state-of-the-art analysis
  methods into user-friendly MetaR languages.

MetaR is obviously not a replacement for R. It is much less flexible and, mainly,
it covers a very small subset of what can be done with R. As stated, its goal is to
provide an alternative and gentle introduction to the topics of data analysis. We do
not expect that R programmers drop R and start using MetaR. However, they can
package their reusable code as MetaR statements, as an additional way to distribute
their work to a different audience.

3.3 User Community

Since January 2015, the CTSC has been offering periodical training sessions to
introduce data analysis with MetaR to technicians, students, postdoctoral fellows,
and faculty who hold an appointment in one of the CTSC institutions. Occasionally,
sessions also include participants from other institutions in NYC or visiting fellows.
Detailed training material has been developed to support these sessions.

We offer two different types of sessions:

- Hands-on sessions, where participants bring their laptop with MetaR installed to
  get a hands-on experience during the 2 h of the session

- Demo sessions, where the instructor demonstrates in 1 h how to use MetaR and participants try to determine whether MetaR can help with their projects

As of Summer 2020, more than 40 training events have been held, with a total participation of approximately 300 trainees. Many of them followed up with questions or requests of support and concretely tried to use the tool to analyze their data. These sessions have been (and still are) mutually beneficial: while participants learn about MetaR and get a gentle introduction to data analysis, instructors collect feedback and new requirements. In fact, many features added to MetaR over the years emerged from discussions that occurred during the training events.

4   Requirements, Design, and Architecture

It is easy to lose sight of a program when looking at all its functions and classes.

Bjarne Stroustrup [11]

Omitting non-essential elements is especially important when the user is a computational beginner. In MetaR, design and implementation choices described in this and the next sections were taken with the principle of keeping the attention of the user on the data analysis.

Examples of application of this principle are found:

- In keeping what the user needs visible within the analysis and taking out details that can be optionally included in other concepts and then imported, as with styles (see Sect. 6.3)
- In the static typing of data sources, in which the structure is anticipated with respect to the execution (see Sect. 4.2) and cannot be changed
- In creating a simplified and monitored execution of the analysis (see Sects. 7.3.1 and 7.3.2)
- In the virtualization of the execution environment, where, once the initial settings are activated, MetaR automatically executes all the analyses in the selected target environment (see Sect. 7.3.3)

4.1   Requirements of the Project

MetaR has been created with the intention of making available to biomedical researchers a *new instrument to learn and perform data analysis through high-level abstractions*. Such abstractions revolved around many stages of the data analysis process, particularly:

- Data sources, in which we model the data and their structure
- Data inspection, in which we check and validate the data

- Data manipulation, in which we change the structure of the data
- Handling of results, in which we hold and maintain the results
- Plotting, in which we generate graphical representations of the data
- Execution, in which we build and execute the analysis
- Virtualization, in which we virtualize the execution environment

Another strong requirement of the project was the creation of a tool blending the boundary between programming/scripting languages and graphical user interfaces. This was deemed critical to support the educational goals of MetaR.

4.2   DSL Design

At its highest level, the design focused on the following aspects of the *problem domain*:

- The input data
- What operates on the input data and how to support new methods
- What is executed
- Execution of the generated code

This section presents the solutions adopted to address these aspects. Each of these solutions was pondered keeping in mind the goal of smoothing the learning curve for beginners. Occasionally, this required favoring simplicity over flexibility.

Section 6 reports use cases that demonstrate how these abstractions work in practice, while Sect. 7.3 covers the execution environment.

4.2.1   Surrogating Data Sources

The data to analyze can be really big and we obviously do not want to represent their entire content in memory. MetaR introduced the term *Data Object Surrogate* (DOS) to describe the way it refers data sources.

A Data Object Surrogate is an object that models a source of data, such as a table or an image.

When a DOS is created, it contains only limited information from the original data source, just enough to facilitate referring the source for the purpose of data analysis.

Since working with RNA-Seq data often requires using tables of data as inputs, the most important DOS is the Table concept defined in the metar.tables language (Fig. 1).

```
Table MyTableWithData.tsv [...]
File Path
   /Users/manuelesimi/MPSProjects/MetaRPaper/Figure1/MyTableWithData.tsv
Columns
   gene_name: string
   gene: string
   SAMPLE1: numeric
   SAMPLE2: numeric
   SAMPLE3: numeric
   SAMPLE4: numeric
   SAMPLE5: numeric
   SAMPLE6: numeric
   SAMPLE7: numeric
   SAMPLE8: numeric
```

Fig. 1 An instance of the `Table` concept as shown in the projectional editor. The user selects the file (a TSV in this case) containing the data by browsing the local file system. Following up the selection, MetaR creates a DOS for the table

Each `Table` instance holds the information to refer and use the table within a MetaR program: location, columns along with the type of their data, and name of the table. In Sect. 6, we will see how to enrich a `Table` with further information that helps analyze the data.

By design, DOSs are *immutable objects*. This means that the information of these objects cannot be changed after the object is created. When changes are required, a new DOS is created. While this does not allow the flexibility of other environments, it makes MetaR analyses easier to understand for unexperienced users.

4.2.2 Operating on the Data

Once we had the data modeled in MetaR, the design focused on the way the user interacts with the data coming from the data sources. We needed an abstraction for the building blocks of the data analysis process, something that takes some inputs (often including one or more DOSs) and generates a result to use in the downstream steps.

These were the premises upon which the abstract `Statement` concept and some supporting interfaces were created. The goal of `Statement` is to model how an inheriting concept delivers a specific functionality and how it will integrate with other statements.

A statement is an abstraction over one or more steps in the data analysis process.

When a user adds a node based on `Statement`, the projectional editor creates the syntax for the statement. To be consistent, we enforced having (most of) the

statement input language elements ... → results [dos|plot]

Fig. 2 Template for syntax of a `Statement` in the projectional editor

```
subset rows MyTableWithData.tsv when true: $(gene_name) != " " -> subsetTable
```

Fig. 3 A sample statement. This instance of the `subset rows` statement takes as input a reference to a `Table` instance and a Boolean condition. It thus creates an output DOS named `subsetTable` containing only the rows matching the condition (gene name not empty, in this example)

`Statements` following the same syntax's template. A typical syntax is shown in Fig. 2.

The keywords in the statement are expressed using a domain language as close as possible to a natural language. For those statements expected to generate an output, an arrow points to what will be the result(s) of the statement after the execution. Of course, the type and cardinality of the inputs/results vary from one statement to another, depending on what the statement does. This mirrors commands executed from the command line in any operating system.

MetaR also has expressions, but they are not first-level concepts. Rather, they can be created as language elements to input to statements wherever they are accepted. Figure 3 shows an instance of the `subset rows` statement operating on the table in Fig. 1 that makes use of the `Expression` concept.

Eventually, a `Statement` node generates a snippet of R code that, once executed, creates the expected results and makes them available to other statements' R code.

4.2.3 Analyses

The next step in the design was to decide how to hold together the `Statements` nodes in a cohesive way to then generate the R script to execute. This choice had the greatest impact because it would be the entity that a user would interact the most with, ultimately determining the level of interactivity and productivity of MetaR.

MetaR offers the `Analysis` concept as a means of collecting a set of `Statement` nodes that together express how data is to be analyzed. An instance of `Analysis` takes care of creating a consistent environment to build the data analysis steps and to control the subsequent code generation and execution phases.

An analysis often imports one or more DOSs, performs data transformations, and outputs some generated DOSs as tables or plots.

```
Analysis MakeUpperCase
{
   import table MyTableWithData.tsv
   transform table MyTableWithData.tsv -> upperCaseGenes {
      make uppercase values gene_name
   }
   write upperCaseGenes to "UpperCaseGenes.tsv " [...]
}
```

Fig. 4 An Analysis instance as shown in the projectional editor. The editor of an Analysis node offers an interface similar to that of a script in a traditional editor, but provides a more interactive and intelligent user interface. This analysis works with the table of data presented in Fig. 1

Figure 4 shows an Analysis instance with three Statements nodes:

- import table, which adds a table to the analysis and makes it available for the next statements
- transform table, which applies a small change to the values in a column of the table and outputs a new table
- write, which serializes the transformed table on the file system

The Analysis interface can also display buttons, images, and other visual objects directly as part of the language. This feature takes advantage of the ability of JetBrains MPS to embed arbitrary graphical elements in the projectional editor. Figure 4 shows one of these elements: the button next to the write statement allowing for selection of the destination folder to save the serialized table. More of these elements are described in Sect. 7.1.

4.3 Other Relevant Design Aspects

As mentioned, MetaR puts great emphasis on the impact of the design choices on the user experience. In this regard, DOSs and statements have been designed with extra features to further simplify the writing of the analysis. These features are often supported by MPS built-in mechanisms.

4.3.1 Auto-completion and Scope

Auto-completion plays a crucial role in MetaR and is deeply exploited at several levels to improve the user experience. It is through auto-completion that MetaR achieves many of its educational and learning purposes, as it avoids almost any knowledge of the DSL syntax prior to its usage.

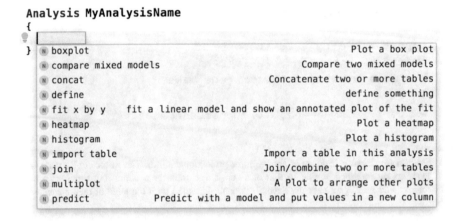

Analysis MyAnalysisName

Fig. 5 Auto-completion inside the `Analysis` node. The figure shows what happens when auto-completion is triggered on an empty line, suggesting `Statement` elements that can be inserted at the cursor point

Auto-completion is strictly connected with the notion of *scope*, the list of language elements that can be referred in each statement of the analysis. This list depends on the *lexical environment* that coincides with the previous statements, the languages imported in the model, and the constraints defined for the reference.

For instance, a table may be suggested as input in a particular point if the table has been made available by a previous statement. In Fig. 4, the `preview table` statement can take the table `MyTableWithData.tsv` as input because `import table` adds the table to the lexical scope.

In a freshly (and empty) created instance of `Analysis`, auto-completion proposes the list of available `Statements` (Fig. 5).

Users can change the default lexical environment with custom-defined regions (or *blocks*) of `Statement` nodes. These regions are nested inside the main `Analysis` block and are especially useful in case of analyses with long sequences of statements or many DOSs. A block inherits the lexical environment of the parent block and its language elements are not visible outside the block itself.

This feature enables less experienced users to work with a smaller set of references. We found this option particularly useful during our training sessions (see Sect. 3) (Fig. 6).

4.3.2 Future DOSs

One of the advantages of MetaR compared to R is its capability to "predict" the structure of a DOS resulting from a statement *before* actually executing the statement (hence the entire analysis). This type of DOS is called *future* DOS. It allows for the tracing of all its possible transformations in advance and thus enables

(a)

```
{
  import table MyTableWithData.tsv
  import table DataInsideScope.tsv

  subset rows DataInsideScope.tsv when true: $(gene) != " " -> subset

}
```

(b)

```
{
  import table MyTableWithData.tsv
  // define a nested lexical scope
  {
    import table DataInsideScope.tsv
  }
  // end of the scope

  subset rows DataInsideScope.tsv when true: $(<no name>) != " " -> subset

}
```

Fig. 6 Lexical scope. The figure shows how a custom-defined scope impacts on visibility. In the two analyses, we import the same two tables. In the first analysis (**a**), the subset rows statement can reference both tables because they are both part of its lexical environment. In the second analysis (**b**), the second table is imported in a custom defined scope; outside of the nested block, this table is not visible and therefore cannot be used by statements

the creation of the entire data analysis at once. There is no need to write a statement, build, run, check the results, and then go back to the editor to write the next statement. Statements are simply created and added to the analysis one after the other. This results in saving a lot of time and, mainly, keeping users focused on the data analysis' logic with fewer distractions (Fig. 7).

4.4 Structure of the Project

From the implementation point of view, MetaR is a vast project composed of several modules that in turn relies on an ecosystem of plugins.

Table 1 shows how the modules of the project are classified.

The complexity of the languages fluctuates from one to another. Core languages, such as metar.tables, can have hundreds of concepts and several supporting interfaces. Others have a few concepts that provide a specific extension or feature to reuse in the core DSL. Solution modules usually collect Java code invoked from the *behavior, constraints, typesystem,* and *generator* aspects of concepts.

```
Analysis PredictDOSs
{
  import table MyTableWithData.tsv
  transform table MyTableWithData.tsv -> transformedTable {
      drop column SAMPLE1
  }
  subset rows transformedTable when true: $(                ) -> subset
}
```

SAMPLE2 in transformedTable	columns (Figures.PredictDOSs)
SAMPLE3 in transformedTable	columns (Figures.PredictDOSs)
SAMPLE4 in transformedTable	columns (Figures.PredictDOSs)
SAMPLE5 in transformedTable	columns (Figures.PredictDOSs)
SAMPLE6 in transformedTable	columns (Figures.PredictDOSs)
SAMPLE7 in transformedTable	columns (Figures.PredictDOSs)
SAMPLE8 in transformedTable	columns (Figures.PredictDOSs)
gene in transformedTable	columns (Figures.PredictDOSs)
gene_name in transformedTable	columns (Figures.PredictDOSs)

Fig. 7 Predicting the output of a statement. In this analysis, the original imported table is transformed and one of its columns is removed from the table with the transform table statement. The output table is then used by the subset rows statement. Here, when auto-completion is triggered to list the columns of the table, the dropped column (*SAMPLE1*) is not suggested. This is a consequence of the output prediction applied to the transform table statement

Table 1 MetaR modules

Module type	# of modules
Language	31
Solution	3
Plugin Solution	4
Build Solution	1
DevKit	1

The Plugin Solutions extend the IDE to improve the user experience. These are discussed in Sect. 7.

Finally, the remaining two modules are dedicated to the tool distribution. The Build Solution uses the DSL defined in the MPS Build Language[5] to automate the building and packaging of the MetaR plugin and make it compatible with the specifications of the JetBrains Plugins Repository (see Sect. 8). The DevKit module is a convenient way to group modules used during the training events (see Sect. 3).

5 Language Composition

MetaR has been developed in a research community, where collaboration prevails (or should) over competition. For this reason, MetaR offers a means to contribute to the project with new features that can be plugged in the DSL with minimal effort by advanced users. This is possible thanks to the very particular way JetBrains MPS maintains and manipulates the language definition.

---

[5]https://www.jetbrains.com/help/mps/build-language.html.

Differently from other language workbenches and development environments, MPS maintains the language definition in an Abstract Syntax Tree (AST) [12]. Working directly with the AST has the advantage of facilitating the creation of *composable languages* and making them seamlessly integrate.

Language composition has been a pillar of MetaR since its inception. Two languages compose when elements of language B can be used or referred by elements of language A. Since MPS works with ASTs, this translates to attaching nodes defined in B as children of a node defined in A. Favoring composition makes it possible to create micro-languages [10] that integrate directly with the core DSL.

The design of the elements to compose in MetaR builds on top of a previous work [13] where we experimented and assembled our experience with language composition and MPS.

Inheritance (or generalization) relationships across concepts of two languages are the primary mechanism used to compose these languages.

The structure of a language in MPS is defined by a set of concepts. Mirroring what is available in object-oriented programming, a concept can extend another concept and implement multiple concept interfaces. On the other hand, interfaces can extend several other interfaces. All these relations permit the modeling of complex contracts among concepts, achieving language composition.

What can be primarily composed in MetaR are statements inside the analysis. Or at least this is the type of composition most visible to the end user. Several concepts and interfaces in the `metar.tables` language define the rules for code editing and rendering of new statements. These rules mainly affect how statements are expected to behave, take their inputs, expose their outputs, and generate the R code to ultimately execute the analysis of the data.

Defining a new `Statement` concept compliant with these rules makes it immediately available to be used inside an analysis, no matter in which language it is defined: it just needs to be part of the lexical environment. New statements simply and seamlessly compose with MetaR through language composition without any intervention in the host language(s).

With these techniques, several *micro-languages* have been created and incorporated in MetaR. We call a language a micro-language when it has a very small structure (sometimes even just one concept) offering extensions to MetaR core DSL. Each of them provides abstractions designed for a specific purpose (typically, new statements). When combined through language composition, micro-languages provide complementary features and make it possible to write richer MetaR analyses.

One of the most prominent examples of a micro-language is the BioMart language (see Sect. 6.4).

6   Working with MetaR Languages

In this section, we walk through a selection of cases to demonstrate some usage scenarios for MetaR. Most of them use tables with the following structure as input DOSs:

1) Most of the columns represent biological samples.
2) One of the columns is the gene name or identifier (or both).
3) Each row includes information about a single gene.
4) Each value in the matrix is the number of reads mapped to each gene for the sample.

Tables with this type of information are called *tables of counts*.

6.1   Data Annotation and Manipulation

Managing the various input objects used in data analysis can be challenging. Each step of the process might need to refer to these objects and their structure several times. Occasionally, different steps access the data in completely different ways. Section 4.2.1 introduced Data Object Surrogates as a means of creating a uniform model for input data sources.

As a further step toward harmonizing the access to data, MetaR offers a mechanism to hand in data to statements in a simplified way. The mechanism is called *data annotation* and, as its name suggests, allows metadata to be added to a data source. There are two types of metadata:

- labels: assigned to columns and used to replace list of columns' names
- usages: assigned to labels to group them for special purposes

Labels are especially beneficial for those statements that manipulate the structure of data sources and require referring multiple columns. These statements change the structure of Data Object Surrogates to enable a more convenient consumption and further data analysis with other statements. To a certain extent, each data manipulation statement can be viewed as an implementation of the Adapter Pattern [14].

Usages are required by some statements to select labels. For instance, the heatmap statement (see **UC5**) requires the usage *heatmap* to be associated with the groups of samples to compare.

In this first set of cases, we demonstrate how annotations are exploited by some statements performing data manipulation on tables.

The main advantage of data annotation is accessing the data through metadata instead of the actual structure of the data source.

Fig. 8 Defining labels for a table. This instance of `ColumnLabelContainer` defines a single label named *ToDelete*

```
Column Labels and Usages

Define Usages:
   << ... >>

Define Labels:
   ToDelete used for << ... >>
```

Table `MyTableWithData.tsv` [...]
File Path
   /Users/manuelesimi/MPSProjects/MetaRPaper/Figure1/MyTableWithData.tsv
Columns
   gene_name: *string*
   gene: *string*
   SAMPLE1: *numeric*
   SAMPLE2: *numeric*
   SAMPLE3: *numeric*
   SAMPLE4: *numeric* **[ToDelete]**
   SAMPLE5: *numeric*
   SAMPLE6: *numeric*
   SAMPLE7: *numeric*
   SAMPLE8: *numeric* **[ToDelete]**

Fig. 9 Using labels to annotate a table. In this `Table` instance, two columns are labeled with *ToDelete*. Multiple labels can be associated with each column and auto-completion is available to insert labels next to the column's type

```
import table MyTableWithData.tsv
transform table MyTableWithData.tsv -> transformedTable {
    drop columns which have label ToDelete
}
```

Fig. 10 Transforming a table using labels. The `transform table` statement deletes two columns (SAMPLE4 and SAMPLE8) which have been labeled with *ToDelete* without using their name

UC1

Starting from the table in Fig. 1, we are going to enrich it with metadata and show how statements benefit from them. The `ColumnLabelContainer` concept in MetaR allows for the definition of labels in the model and, optionally, groups of labels for a specific purpose with `Usages`. Figure 8 shows an instance of the concept.

In Fig. 9, we again present the table from Fig. 1, this time annotated with the label defined in Fig. 8.

We are now going to demonstrate how to drop the columns from the table using the label *ToDelete*. The snippet in Fig. 10 shows an instance of the `transform table` statement that refers the columns to drop via the selected label instead of listing them one by one with their name.

```
Table MySecondTableWithData.tsv  [...]
File Path
  /Users/manuelesimi/MPSProjects/MetaRPaper/Tables/MySecondTableWithData.tsv
Columns
  gene_name: string
  gene_id: string [ ID ]
  SAMPLE9: numeric
  SAMPLE10: numeric
  SAMPLE11: numeric
  SAMPLE12: numeric
  SAMPLE13: numeric
  SAMPLE14: numeric
```

Fig. 11 A table with one label. This table has five columns with samples and one column (*gene_id*) with a single annotation

```
import table MyTableWithData.tsv
import table MySecondTableWithData.tsv
join ( MyTableWithData.tsv , MySecondTableWithData.tsv ) by label ID -> joinedTable
```

Fig. 12 Joining tables by label. The two imported tables have common information in columns with different names. The *ID* label assigned to both columns is used by the join statement to merge the two tables

In this example, we have only two columns to drop, and listing them by name would not be difficult. However, tables may have tens or hundreds of columns. Avoiding listing all their names and replacing such long lists with just a single label drastically reduces the time needed to write the analysis and greatly improves its readability.

UC2

We show another way to exploit data annotation, this time across tables. Given two tables with a different structure, we want to merge them. For this case, the first table is the one in Fig. 9, with an additional *ID* label on the *gene* column, while the second table is presented in Fig. 11.

Comparing this table with the one in Fig. 9, we notice that the columns with the gene identifiers are named differently in the two tables (*gene* vs *gene_id*). This is a very common situation where tables with experimental results come from different sources. With data annotation, MetaR can easily work around this inconsistency by assigning the same label to these columns. Figure 12 illustrates a statement joining the tables in Figs. 9 and 11 through the label *ID*.

UC3

In this last data manipulation use case, we demonstrate how to alter the order of the columns in a table. In Fig. 13, we have a table with two groups of columns, each of three samples, identified by labels.

Figure 14 shows an instance of the reorder columns statement changing the order of the columns in the table by moving them up or down.

```
Table MyCleanedTableWithData.txt [..]
File Path
  /Users/manuelesimi/MPSProjects/MetaRPaper/Tables/MyCleanedTableWithData.txt
Columns
  gene_name: string
  gene: string [ ID ]
  SAMPLE1: numeric [ Sample1-3 ]
  SAMPLE2: numeric [ Sample1-3 ]
  SAMPLE3: numeric [ Sample1-3 ]
  SAMPLE5: numeric [ Sample5-7 ]
  SAMPLE6: numeric [ Sample5-7 ]
  SAMPLE7: numeric [ Sample5-7 ]
```

Fig. 13 Table with two groups of columns identified by labels

```
{
    import table MyCleanedTableWithData.txt

    reorder columns in table MyCleanedTableWithData.txt
```

UP	DOWN	label Sample5-7
UP	DOWN	label Sample1-3
UP	DOWN	label ID
UP	DOWN	label NoLabel

```
    -> reorderedTable

}
```

Fig. 14 Reordering columns by label. By clicking on the buttons, groups of columns from Fig. 13 matching the labels are moved up or down in the order. The columns in reorderedTable will have the following order: *SAMPLE5, SAMPLE6, SAMPLE7, SAMPLE1, SAMPLE2, SAMPLE3, gene, gene_name*

6.2 Data Processing and Visualization

In this section, we present two usages of MetaR performing some typical steps of data analysis. They both process data from input sources and visualize the results in a graphical form. In data analysis, such visual representations of the data are called *plots* and allow them to be analyzed from angles that are not clear in unstructured data.

UC4

A very frequent task is to intersect multiple sets of identifiers to understand which ones are shared among them. Figure 15 demonstrates how to create an UpSet plot [15] that graphically shows the intersections across three sets.

```
{
  define Set of IDs FirstSet {
    GeneA GeneB GeneC GeneD
  }
  define Set of IDs SecondSet {
    GeneA GeneB GeneC GeneD GeneE GeneF
  }
  define Set of IDs ThirdSet {
    GeneA GeneB GeneE GeneF GeneG GeneH GeneI
  }
  UpSet { set FirstSet  } -> intersection
           set SecondSet
           set ThirdSet
  multiplot -> preview [ 1 cols x 1 rows ]
```

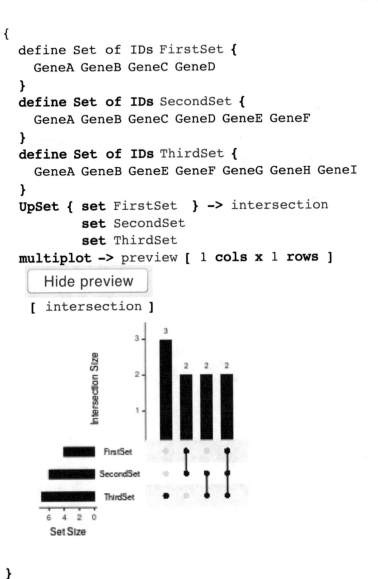

}

Fig. 15 Intersecting sets. Given three sets of identifiers, manually defined with the define set statements, the UpSet statement intersects them and creates a plot showing how many IDs are shared across the sets

Sets of identifiers are usually loaded from DOSs (instead of being manually defined) and they can include up to hundreds of thousands of IDs. UpSet plots do not report which the shared identifiers are, only how many. Other statements (not shown) are available to list and work with them.

Column Labels and Usages

Define Usages:
AllSamples
heatmap

Define Labels:
Sample1-3 **used for** AllSamples heatmap
Sample5-7 **used for** AllSamples heatmap
ToDelete **used for** << ... >>
counts **used for** << ... >>
ID **used for** << ... >>

Fig. 16 Labels and usages for differential expression tests. *Sample1-3* and *Sample5-7* identify the two groups of samples to compare, each composed of three samples. *counts* marks the columns with read counts and *ID* sets the column with the unique identifier for each gene

This use case also introduces a feature appreciated by many MetaR users: the `multiplot` statement. This statement is an example of the capabilities of MetaR to mix graphical elements within the text. `multiplot` creates a preview of one or more plots immediately visible to the user right after the statements that generate the plots. This adds significant assistance to the process of writing the analysis steps.

UC5

A gene is considered differentially expressed if an observed difference or change in read counts or expression levels between two experimental conditions is statistically significant. R has very good packages that implement strategies to calculate when genes are differentially expressed. In this use case, we demonstrate how to perform analysis of gene expression on a table of counts using a method called Limma Voom [16].

Figure 16 shows the labels and usages we need for our analysis.

The analysis operates on the same table and annotations in Fig. 13, with an additional label *counts* on the columns marked with *Sample1-3* and *Sample5-7*.

Figure 17 shows how to invoke Limma Voom to perform a differential expression test on the two groups of samples in our table. An instance of the `limma voom` statement is configured with a model (with one factor: *AllSamples*) to call differences between columns labeled with *Sample1-3* and *Sample5-7*. Limma Voom uses this model to define the mean and variance of the data. It is possible to define complex linear models by typing $+$ followed by the name of a usage attached to the counts table and repeat to add multiple factors to the model.

```
{
  import table MyCleanedTableWithData.txt
  // run a diff expression test
  limma voom counts= MyCleanedTableWithData.txtmodel: ~ 0 + AllSamples
    comparing Sample1-3 - Sample5-7 -> stats: resultsTable normalized: default
  // filter the results according to values in a column
  subset rows resultsTable when true: $(logFC) <= -4.5 | $(logFC) >= 4.5 -> subsetTable
  // join the results with the original table
  join ( subsetTable, MyCleanedTableWithData.txt) by label ID -> joinedTable

  heatmap with joinedTable select data by one or more label Sample1-3, label Sample5-7
    -> heatmap no style [
    show names using group ID
    annotate with these groups:AllSamples
    scale values: scale by row
    cluster columns: false cluster rows: true
  ]

  multiplot -> preview [   1 cols x 1 rows ]    Hide preview

    [ heatmap ]
```

```
  // save the heatmap to an external PDF file
  render heatmap as PDF named "heatmap.pdf" [...] no style
}
```

Fig. 17 Analysis for differentially expressed genes. Given two groups of samples identified with the labels *Sample1-3* and *Sample5-7*, the limma voom statement finds differentially expressed genes by comparing the two groups and then stores the results in resultsTable. The subset row and join statements do some data processing by filtering the results and joining them with the original table of counts. Finally, a heatmap plot is created to visualize the counts of the genes that are differentially expressed; the plot is saved in a PDF format with the render statement

The sequence of statements in Fig. 17 shows a typical pattern in statistical data analysis:

- A statistical method is executed over the data.
- Data are manipulated (first to filter them and then to create more suitable structures for the next steps).
- The results are visualized in a plot.
- The plot is saved on an external file as image, ready to be included in a talk or scientific manuscript.

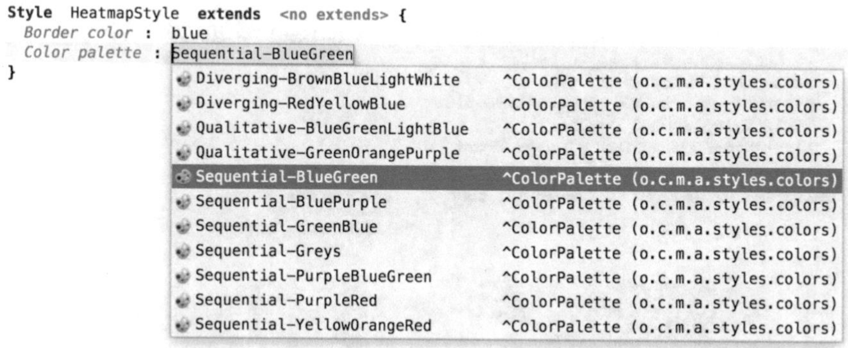

```
Style HeatmapStyle extends <no extends> {
  Border color : blue
  Color palette : Sequential-BlueGreen
}
```

Diverging-BrownBlueLightWhite	^ColorPalette (o.c.m.a.styles.colors)
Diverging-RedYellowBlue	^ColorPalette (o.c.m.a.styles.colors)
Qualitative-BlueGreenLightBlue	^ColorPalette (o.c.m.a.styles.colors)
Qualitative-GreenOrangePurple	^ColorPalette (o.c.m.a.styles.colors)
Sequential-BlueGreen	^ColorPalette (o.c.m.a.styles.colors)
Sequential-BluePurple	^ColorPalette (o.c.m.a.styles.colors)
Sequential-GreenBlue	^ColorPalette (o.c.m.a.styles.colors)
Sequential-Greys	^ColorPalette (o.c.m.a.styles.colors)
Sequential-PurpleBlueGreen	^ColorPalette (o.c.m.a.styles.colors)
Sequential-PurpleRed	^ColorPalette (o.c.m.a.styles.colors)
Sequential-YellowOrangeRed	^ColorPalette (o.c.m.a.styles.colors)

Fig. 18 A style for a heatmap. This `Style` instance defines the color of the border in the plot and the color palette to use

6.3   Styles

There are many aspects of a graphical representation that can be customized. In R, each instruction has its own way (i.e., input parameters) to create such customizations, and this can be very confusing for beginners. MetaR offers the `metar.styles` language to define *styles* to bind to plots. The goal of this language is to shape a uniform way to customize any type of plot.

UC6
The `Style` concept in the `metar.styles` language is the entry point for customizing plots. An instance of this concept can be optionally attached to a statement that outputs a plot and helps to define its visualization.

Figure 18 illustrates an example of a `Style` instance. Many pre-configured graphical settings are distributed with `metar.styles`. Color palettes listed in the auto-completion menu are just an example of these. Nevertheless, users can create their own and/or extend existing styles.

Figure 19 shows what happens when the style selected in Fig. 18 is applied to the heatmap plot created in **UC5**.

6.4   Interactive Statements

By combining the *editor*, *behavior*, and *constraints* aspects of a concept, it is possible to add *interactive statements* to MetaR. Interactive statements improve the user experience by adding a dynamic facet to the analysis. Their goal is to extend auto-completion to what is available in the lexical scope, by searching for language elements even outside it.

```
{
  heatmap with joinedTable select data by one or more label Sample1-3, label Sample5-7
    -> heatmapWithStyle HeatmapStyle [
    show names using group ID
    annotate with these groups:AllSamples
    scale values: scale by row
    cluster columns: false cluster rows: true
  ]
  multiplot -> preview [  2 cols x 1 rows ]   Hide preview

    [ heatmap ]                                  [ heatmapWithStyle ]
```

```
}
```

Fig. 19 Heatmaps with different styles. The style in Fig. 18 is associated to a copy of the heatmap created in Fig. 17. When auto-completion is triggered next to the `heatmapWithStyle` plot, `Style` instances in the lexical scope are prompted for selection. The `multiplot` statement in the figure shows both heatmaps next to each other to appreciate the differences due to their different styles

UC7

BioMart is a web service accessed through the home page of Ensembl.[6] It can be used to query a collection of Ensembl databases for ID mapping and feature extraction. The `metar.biomart` language is dedicated to interfacing the BioMart services.

The language provides the interactive `query biomart` statement to assemble specific queries to retrieve data. As the user auto-completes the information in the projectional editor, the statement sends queries to the remote BioMart services to provide values (wrapped on the fly inside language elements) for the next input according to the selected information.

Each part of the statement auto-completes based on the previous selected inputs. In Fig. 20, the list of datasets in the drop-down menu is retrieved from the database *Ensembl Genes 102* as soon as it is selected in the first part of the statement. In the same way, the next input will propose the list of attributes retrieved for the selected dataset (Fig. 21).

The output of `query biomart` is a DOS (table) with the results of the queries. As for other future DOSs (see Sect. 4.3.2), this is just an anticipation of the structure

---

[6]https://www.ensembl.org/.

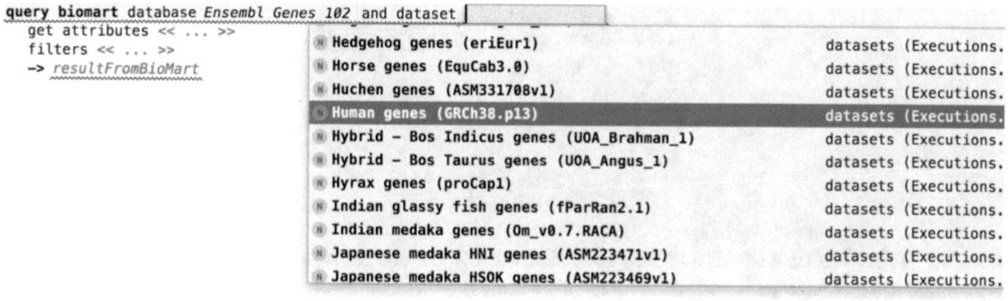

Fig. 20 Querying a remote service. When auto-completion is triggered, the `query biomart` statement interfaces with the remote BioMart services and creates the appropriate language elements to propose for selection

```
// get the gene names from BioMart
query biomart database Ensembl Genes 102 and dataset Human genes (GRCh38.p13)
    get attributes Gene name from feature of types string with column group annotation    ID
    filters << ... >>
    -> resultFromBioMart
```

Fig. 21 A complete `query biomart` instance

of a table with data returned by the remote BioMart services when the analysis is executed.

7 Advanced Exploitation of MPS

JetBrains MPS is not only a language workbench to create DSLs, it also provides a wide range of additional instruments to build a comprehensive working environment around the DSL itself.

MetaR leverages some of these MPS features to make its delivered functionalities and the user experience unique. This section presents some notable capabilities of MetaR that would not have been achieved with any other language workbench than MPS.

7.1 Graphical Elements

In MetaR, graphical elements are mixed with statements in the `Analysis` editor. We have already encountered some of these elements in Sect. 6. These inclusions are possible thanks to the capabilities of MPS to embed Java Swing components inside the editor's cells.

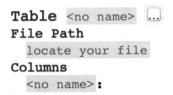

Fig. 22 Table editor with Browse button. The button, placed next the <no name> red label, opens a file selection dialog to locate the file to configure the Table instance

Graphical elements in MetaR have two different functions:

1) Triggering actions—these actions typically support the statement's purpose.
2) Displaying results—the results coming from one statement or multiple statements are shown in between the statements.

On a small scale, the second function can be compared to Jupyter Notebooks[7] where snippets of code generate results inside a notebook's cells.

7.1.1 Buttons

MetaR comes with a language (metar.ui) for adding cells with buttons to the projectional editor and associating actions with them. We have already seen some buttons next to statements to show/hide/move cells in the editor (see Figs. 14, 15, and 17).

The Table (Sect. 4) editor uses buttons differently. In this case, the action associated with the button is to open the File Open Dialog box on the local system and allow for locating and selecting the file with the table (Fig. 22).

7.1.2 HTML Tables

Sometimes it is useful to visualize a snapshot of a table's content directly inside the editor. The preview table statement allows for the creation of a small customized preview by embedding an HTML table inside a cell. Columns and rows of this preview can be resized as desired as shown in Fig. 23.

7.1.3 Auto-refreshable Images

In Figs. 15 and 17, we saw how the multiplot statement displays images inside one or more cells in the editor. The same images are also available as preview in the inspector of the concept.

---

[7]https://jupyter.org/.

```
{
  preview table MyTableWithData.tsv [  5 cols x 6 rows ]
```

Hide preview	DefaultStyle

	gene_name	gene	SAMPLE1	SAMPLE2	SAMPLE3
1	0610012D04Rik	ENSMUSG00000089755	0.00	1.21	0.00
2	1010001N08Rik	ENSMUSG00000097222	1.00	0.00	0.00
3	1200007C13Rik	ENSMUSG00000087684	0.00	1.21	0.00
4	1500015O10Rik	ENSMUSG00000026051	221.96	1253.98	23.77
5	1500035N22Rik	ENSMUSG00000059631	9.95	6.07	5.78
6	1700001K19Rik	ENSMUSG00000056508	0.00	0.00	0.00

```
}
```

Fig. 23 Table with in-line HTML preview. A snapshot of the table's content is visualized by the `preview table` statement inside a Java Swing component

Images in MetaR are auto-refreshable. This means that whenever the image changes, it is automatically reloaded in the cell. To achieve this result, MetaR uses a Project Plugin. This type of MPS plugin provides a way to integrate Java code with the IDE functionalities. They are created with the `jetbrains.mps.lang.plugin.standalone` language and held inside solutions.

The concept in charge of displaying a specific image also registers a listener of the image file in the plugin. The plugin makes sure that the listener subscribes on the file exactly once and is triggered at the right time. When the analysis is executed and a change is detected, the listener invokes the Java code inside another solution and the image is automatically refreshed in all of the cells where it is currently loaded.

7.2 Table Viewer Tool

Tools are extensions of the original MPS IDE. They provide customized views to open with the context menu. The MPS plugin language (`jetbrains.mps.lang.plugin`) supports the creation of plugin solutions that define new Tools.

The MetaR Table Viewer is a Tool associated with the `Table` concept and its descendants. The viewer adds to the MPS interface the capabilities to load the table's content and show it in a graphical context inside a view. Wherever a table

`import table` `MyCleanedTableWithData.txt`

gene_name	gene	SAMPLE1	SAMPLE2	SAMPLE3	SAMPLE5	SAMPLE6	SAMPLE7
0610012D04...	ENSMUSG00...	0	1.213924422	0	4.61675374	3.084946184	3.895876684
1010001N08...	ENSMUSG00...	0.995321867	0	0	2.30837687	6.169892368	1.298625561
1200007C13...	ENSMUSG00...	0	1.213924422	0	3.462565305	10.28315395	11.68763005
1500015O10...	ENSMUSG00...	221.9567764	1253.983928	23.76955865	1037.615403	1553.784561	1045.393577
1500035N22...	ENSMUSG00...	9.953218673	6.069622108	5.781784536	1.154188435	2.056630789	3.895876684
1700001K19Rik	ENSMUSG00...	0	0	0	2.30837687	2.056630789	2.597251123
1700016P03Rik	ENSMUSG00...	311.5357445	267.0633728	123.3447368	49.6301027	37.01935421	29.86838791
2010005H15...	ENSMUSG00...	0	0	0	2.30837687	3.084946184	2.597251123
2200002D01...	ENSMUSG00...	60.7146339	55.8405234	13.49083059	154.6612503	144.9924707	163.6268207
2310003L06...	ENSMUSG00...	3.981287469	3.641773265	0.642420504	24.23795713	21.59462329	33.76426459
2310081O03...	ENSMUSG00...	0.995321867	1.213924422	0.642420504	11.54188435	4.113261579	11.68763005
4833427G06...	ENSMUSG00...	12.93918427	37.63165707	2.569682016	56.55523331	44.21756197	46.75052021
4930430E12...	ENSMUSG00...	0	0	1.284841008	11.54188435	17.48136171	3.895876684
4930486L24...	ENSMUSG00...	42.79884029	24.27848843	22.48471764	109.6479013	110.0297472	99.99416822

Fig. 24 Table Viewer Tool. The tool is immediately available for those tables directly loaded from the file system (e.g., `Table` nodes) and their references (like the `import table` statement in the figure). Other tables (future DOSs; see Sect. 4.3.2) become visible after the analysis has been run and the content of the table has been created. In this latter case, the tool is available after the first execution of the analysis

name appears (in a `Table` or an `Analysis` node), the tool can be opened to see the rows and columns of that table along with their values. Rows are dynamically loaded as the user scrolls down the content (Fig. 24).

7.3   Execution

MPS provides *Run configurations* (`jetbrains.mps.execution.configurations`) to define how to execute processes starting from selected nodes in the language. MetaR uses these configurations to run the R scripts that it generates from the `Analysis` node.

7.3.1   RunR Configuration

The RunR configuration is a plugin solution in MetaR for the execution of analyses. By right-clicking on any descendant node of the `Analysis` node, it is possible to trigger the RunR configuration from the context menu. A setting editor dialog for the configuration is opened to customize the execution.

When the configuration is started, it first builds the current model and then runs the generated R script for the analysis. The configuration includes *Commands* (defined with the `jetbrains.mps.execution.commands` language) to invoke the R runtime installed on the local system with the proper parameters (including, of course, the location of the R script).

```
Analysis DiffExp2
{
    import table MyCleanedTableWithData.txt
    // run a diff expression test
    limma voom counts= MyCleanedTableWithData.txt model: ~ 0 + AllSamples
        comparing Sample1-3 - Sample5-7 -> stats: resultsTable normalized: default
    // filter the results according to values in a column
    subset rows resultsTable when true: $(logFC) <= -4.5 | $(logFC) >= 4.5 -> subsetTable
    // join the results with the original table
    join ( subsetTable, MyCleanedTableWithData.txt ) by label ID -> joinedTable

}
```

Run: R Script R DiffExp2 ×

```
/usr/local/bin/docker run -v /Users/manuelesimi/MPSProjects/MetaRPaper/Tables:/Users/mar
Loading required package: limma
Loading required package: edgeR
Loading required package: plyr
Loading required package: Cairo
Loading required package: data.table
STATEMENT_EXECUTED/LAVHBJJHSI/
STATEMENT_EXECUTED/LDDJDSDHJD/
STATEMENT_EXECUTED/LDDJDSDHJD/
STATEMENT_EXECUTED/TSOSTJMRMY/
STATEMENT_EXECUTED/JHJGJIREWC/

Process finished with exit code 0
```

Fig. 25 Monitoring the Execution. Users can follow the execution as statement IDs are printed and linked to statements in the Run view. When the user clicks on the link, the target statement is highlighted in the editor

7.3.2 Monitored Execution

MetaR users are not experts at debugging problems in a program, however, and in any execution things can fail for several reasons. Since the R script is not directly visible, MetaR offers a way to monitor the progress of the execution and understand which statement generates an error, if one occurs.

Each statement has an ID assigned, which is basically the identifier of the node. As the execution advances, the statement IDs are sent to the Run view (see Fig. 25) and printed. Inside the view, the text is properly linked to the node in the AST with the same ID. Whenever an error occurs (also printed in the Run view), the user can click on the link and get to the root of the problem (the statement that generates the error messages).

This is obviously not a debugging tool, yet it gives users an idea of where to investigate an execution problem.

7.3.3 Integration with Container Technology

Reproducibility of results is a key point in research. The scientific community does not accept or consider valid results that cannot be reproduced. This also applies to data analysis: if the same analysis is executed with the same inputs several times, it must yield exactly the same results.

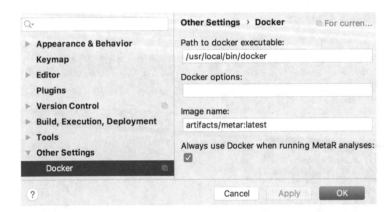

Fig. 26 MPS preferences with Docker. In the preferences window of MPS, it is possible to set in which Docker image MetaR analyses are executed

Any software application (including MetaR) needs some sort of runtime support from other software. This is critical in terms of reproducibility, because these external dependencies introduce a level of uncertainty that is difficult to control.

Several years ago, container technology was introduced to provide fully capable execution environments on any computer supporting the technology. There is no need for the user to deal with installation of libraries and dependencies, downloading packages, messing with configuration files, etc.; everything is made available in a single package called *image*. MetaR integrates with Docker [17], the most popular container technology. Extensions to default MPS configuration settings have been created in MetaR to set the required information.

When options in Fig. 26 are set, each MetaR analysis becomes a *containerized application*; it is automatically executed inside the virtual environment created starting from the selected Docker image. This small and lightweight environment, called *container*, guarantees that whenever and wherever the analysis runs, it will always use the same software packaged in the image. Typically, the R runtime and common R packages are deployed in the image. From the user point of view, once the checkbox in Fig. 26 is checked, it is handled transparently and seamlessly by MetaR.

8   Distribution

MetaR is an open source software distributed under the terms of the Apache License, Version 2.0, and available on GitHub.[8] Its installation is straightforward since

---

[8]https://github.com/MetaR-Languages/MetaR.

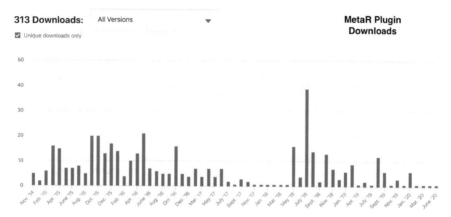

Fig. 27 MetaR Plugin Unique Downloads. The figure shows the total unique downloads of the MetaR plugin since its first release as recorded by the JetBrains Plugins Repository. Unique downloads do not include multiple downloads from the same user or host

MetaR is distributed as a plugin available in the JetBrains Plugins Repository.[9] All of its dependencies are automatically resolved and installed with the MetaR plugin.

Figure 27 shows the statistics of unique downloads of MetaR over the years. These statistics do not include the installations performed during our training events.

9   Conclusions

MetaR exploited JetBrains MPS in many ways. The generation of code in a target language (the R language) simplified the implementation by removing the need to develop our own language runtime system for the DSL. The possibility to extend the IDE with custom tools/plugins served the requirements of the project very well. The Build Language provided a convenient way to package the software as MPS plugin and to manage its dependencies. The MPS Plugins Repository, along with its automatic dependency resolution among plugins, saved us from creating our own distribution website and spared our users from numerous tedious installation instructions. Above all, by coordinating and putting together the features offered by each aspect of the language definition, we achieved a homogeneous approach for many steps of the data analysis process.

Graphical elements with scripting, auto-completion, high-level abstractions over data and instructions, language composition, automatic installation of dependencies for each individual statement, extensions to the environment, seamless integration with external technologies, and solutions to package and distribute the software all

---

[9]https://plugins.jetbrains.com/plugin/7621-org-campagnelab-metar.

smoothly combined in MetaR to serve the purpose of the project. We were able to achieve everything we planned and beyond, and to create languages with a runtime support somehow unique in the DSL landscape.

The main lesson learned from this experience is that biologists and clinicians can use the tools of bioinformatics and get closer to data scientists. And when different profiles can speak (almost) the same computational language, misunderstanding is reduced and the speed of a research project is greatly enhanced. In our data-rich age, MetaR has proved to be an educational bridge between these two worlds.

Acknowledgments Work reported in this chapter was supported by the National Center for Advancing Translational Science of the National Institute of Health under awards number UL1RR024996 and UL1TR002384. Additional support was provided by the National Institute of Health NIAID award number 5R01AI107762-02 to Fabien Campagne.

References

1. Campagne, F., Digan, W.E.R., Simi, M.: MetaR: simple, high-level languages for data analysis with the R ecosystem. (2015). [Online]. https://doi.org/10.1101/030254
2. Simi, M.: MetaR Case Study. (2020). [Online]. https://resources.jetbrains.com/storage/products/mps/docs/MPS_MetaR_Case_Study.pdf
3. Erdweg, S., van der Storm, T., Völter, M., et al.: The state of the art in language workbenches. In: Lecture Notes in Computer Science. (2013).
4. Dmitriev, S.: LOP – Language Oriented Programming: the next programming paradigm. (2004). [Online]. https://resources.jetbrains.com/storage/products/mps/docs/Language_Oriented_Programming.pdf
5. Di Gesù, V.: Data analysis and bioinformatics. In: Pattern Recognition and Machine Intelligence. PReMI 2007. Lecture Notes in Computer Science, vol. 4815. (2007).
6. Chu, Y., Corey, R.D.: RNA sequencing: platform selection, experimental design, and data interpretation. Nucleic Acid Therap. **22**(4), 271–274 (2012)
7. Ihaka, R., Gentleman, R.: R: a language for data analysis and graphics. J Comput Graphical Stat. **5**(3), 299–314 (1996)
8. Fowler, M.: Domain-specific languages. Addison-Wesley (2010)
9. Gentleman, R., Carey, V., Huber, W., Irizarry, R., Dudoit, S.: Bioinformatics and computational biology solutions using R and Bioconductor. Springer, Berlin (2005)
10. Bentley, J.: Programming pearls: little languages. Commun ACM. **29**(8), 711–721 (1986)
11. Stroustrup, B.: Programming: principles and practice using C++, 2nd edn. Addison-Wesley Professional (2014)
12. Aho, V.A., Lam, S.M., Sethi, R., Ullman, D.J.: Compilers: principles, techniques, and tools, 2nd edn. Addison-Wesley Longman, Boston, MA (2006)
13. Simi, M., Campagne, F.: Composable languages for bioinformatics: the NYoSh experiment. PeerJ. **2**(562), e241 (2014)
14. Gamma, E., Helm, R., Johnson, R., Vlissides, J.: Design patterns: elements of reusable object-oriented software, pp. 139–142. Addison Wesley (1994)
15. Conway, R.J., Lex, A., Gehlenborg, N.: UpSetR: an R package for the visualization of intersecting sets and their properties. Bioinformatics. **33**(18), 2938–2940 (2017)
16. Ritchie, E.M., Phipson, B., Wu, W.D., Hu, Y., Law, W.C., Shi, W., Smyth, K.G.: Limma powers differential expression analyses for RNA-sequencing and microarray studies. Nucleic Acids Res. **43**(7), e47 (2015)
17. Merkel, D.: Docker: lightweight linux containers for consistent development and deployment. Linux J. **2014**(239), 2 (2014)

Part III
Teaching and Learning with JetBrains MPS

Teaching MPS: Experiences from Industry and Academia

Mikhail Barash and Václav Pech

Abstract In this chapter, we present our experience on teaching MPS to industry professionals and university students. JetBrains has run its commercial courses on MPS both online and on-site for 19 different customers coming from 12 countries over the past 5 years, for some repetitively. The participants typically started the courses with no or little language engineering background and no experience with MPS. Although language design with MPS was the main objective of the courses, some general language engineering topics were also covered, and motivation into the domain was provided. We also report our teaching experience of a course on the implementation of domain-specific languages (DSL), given at universities in Finland, Norway, and Canada. The course, aimed at a broad audience of computer science students, covers DSL design principles and implementation techniques using three text-based language workbenches (Eclipse Xtext, Spoofax, Rascal MPL), prior to introducing MPS. By the time MPS is discussed, students have an understanding of what language implementation comprises of and are somewhat fluent in language engineering terminology. This enabled us to focus on language implementation techniques that are distinctive in MPS. We discuss in this chapter the experience we gained during these courses and the evolution of the educational approach.

M. Barash (✉)
Bergen Language Design Laboratory, University of Bergen, Bergen, Norway
e-mail: mikhail.barash@uib.no

V. Pech
JetBrains s.r.o., Praha, Czech Republic
e-mail: vaclav.pech@jetbrains.com

293

1   Teaching MPS in Industry: Experience of JetBrains

1.1   History and Motivation

JetBrains has been offering courses for industry professionals since 2015 [32]. Initially, these courses were made on an ad hoc basis as clients approached JetBrains and asked for training individually. The content and structure of the courses stabilized as we ran a couple of these early courses, which allowed us to put out an official offer of two courses in 2017—the *Introductory MPS* course and the *Advanced MPS course*. The courses were organized either at the JetBrains office in Prague or at the client premises. More than 130 people have passed these courses during the first 2 years. The two courses followed one after the other, but it was not mandatory that the students must pass the Introductory course before they sign up for the Advanced one. This demanded the lectures of the Advanced course to invest some initial time into bringing everybody up to the same level, until the online version of the Introductory course became available in 2019 and allowed the students to self-study the materials before joining the Advanced course.

1.2   Going Online

On-site courses proved not to be practical for all clients.

- *Individuals*, for example, found it inconvenient to wait for a large enough group of students to form for a course to start.
- The *travel costs* (both time and money), on the other hand, were increasing the expenses incurred by clients outside of Europe.
- *Students and academy workers* sometimes could not afford the price associated with the courses.
- Innovators, who only wanted to test the waters and see if MPS is an answer to their questions, did not want to *invest the time* necessary to organize and pass a traditional course.

This led us to considering online variants of the courses. Both Introductory and Advanced courses have been migrated into the JetBrains online learning platform Stepik (http://stepik.org). The contents of the online courses are identical to the contents of the on-site courses. However, there have been several changes required:

- Each course is split gradually into *modules*, *lessons*, and *steps*. A typical lesson takes about 30 min to complete and contains between 5 and 15 steps.
- The trainer's explanation is replaced with pre-shot screencasts, typically 3–8 min long.
- The theory is then explained again statically using text and images. Step-by-step tutorials guide the students through the practical aspect of the chapter.

- The students can leave comments for the trainer whenever they get stuck or find some information puzzling or incomplete. This proved to be an efficient mechanism to improve the quality of the course over time.
- The instructions of the online tutorials must be more detailed compared to the instructions in printed tutorials, since the cost of a student making a mistake is much higher in the online course. For the same reason, the common traps have to be identified, and fallback instructions should be provided to help students to avoid getting stuck. This is where comments proved to be indispensable.
- Independent exercises provide an example solution in the following steps and rely on the student not to jump ahead.
- Quizzes with test questions are scattered throughout the course to ensure the students understand the topics.
- Live online discussions with the trainer can be organized to give the students an opportunity to ask for additional explanation, get the trainer's opinion on applicability of MPS to their particular problem domain, or discuss MPS beyond the scope of the course.

Elementary Course In parallel to these online courses, the free online educational content has evolved into a course of its own right. This course was named *Elementary*. Although not as in-depth as the Introductory course and lacking the possibility to chat with the teacher, the Elementary course provides a zero-ceremony option at a zero cost. This clearly rings a bell with many MPS fans. To date, this is the most popular online course of these three.

Online courses proved to require smaller organizational ceremony compared to on-site courses. Especially, the number of individual participants has increased, thanks to the online option. During the first 18 months, 350 students have passed any of the online MPS courses.

1.3 The Participants

The students of the courses can be categorized into several groups (listed roughly by the numbers in our courses).

Group 1. Language engineering experts who want to expand their expertise into a new territory. They typically join the courses with ideas of their next language already sketched in their heads and want to discuss them further.

Group 2. Software developers who understand programming well and want to learn more about language engineering and MPS in order to use it on their next project. They frequently join the courses skeptical about introducing a new piece of technology into the project and are to a great level unaware of the possibilities of today's DSLs.

Group 3. Project managers and architects who want to understand the field of DSLs as well as the MPS technology itself in order to assess it and weigh its benefits. Their programming skills are frequently a bit rusty; on the other hand, they do not need to go in depth into all the exercises in order to get the information they need about the technology.

Group 4.   Domain experts who will eventually be using the languages designed in MPS. They typically lack programming skills beyond basic syntax of some scripting languages.

Group 5.   Technically savvy business owners who want to see if the technology fits their idea of a new product.

While the Introductory course is relevant to all five groups, only Groups 1 and 2 should consider the Advanced course.

- Groups 1, 3, and 5 are usually self-motivated and enthusiastically pass the courses, optionally skipping parts that they think are not relevant to their business at the moment. During live interactions, they tend to focus on their problem domain.
- Group 2 needs to be first sold on the idea of DSLs and their relevance to their current activities. Practical examples of integrating MPS into the typical technology stacks should be provided to relieve them of some of their doubts. If this succeeds, they normally make fast progress and successfully pass the courses.
- Group 4 is usually the biggest challenge, especially if they are mixed in a group of people belonging to some of the other four categories. Their lack of solid programming skills slows them, and thus the whole group, down. Additionally, the purpose of using DSLs in their particular case must be explained to them before they gain motivation to go through the exercises. These people rarely sign up for the online courses.

The courses assume no prior knowledge beyond general programming abilities and experience with software development. As MPS is a Java-based system, knowledge of Java programming helps the students make progress faster. A prior knowledge of competing language engineering tools has somewhat ambivalent effect. Since the MPS editor is based on the technology of projectional editing and the language definition uses object-oriented principles instead of grammars and parsers, people versed in parsing must mentally overcome the abstraction gap, which is not always easy, especially when it is combined with an *a priori* skepticism toward the projectional technology. In general, self-motivated students fare much better than students signed up by their employers without first highlighting the relevance of the technology to their job.

1.4   Topics Covered in the Courses

Introductory Course The Introductory course (see Table 1) focuses on the fundamentals of the MPS technology as well as the language engineering domain in general. On top of the general description of the technology and motivational

Table 1 Outline of the Introductory MPS course given by JetBrains. The course is meant for participants with no or minimal knowledge of both MPS and language engineering and is focused on the practical application of MPS, based on two major examples and a few shorter exercises. The duration of the course is 16 h

Language engineering: fundamentals of language design
Examples of existing MPS usages
Understanding the MPS user interface
MPS project structure and dependencies
Commanding the projectional editor
Introduction into the aspects of language definition
Effective navigation around code
Constraints and scoping
Language manipulation API: the SModel language
BaseLanguage and its extensions
Modularizing the editor definition and making the editor fluent
Quotations and antiquotations
Generator templates and macros
Tooling for language engineering

examples, it explores the essential aspects of language definition—STRUCTURE, EDITOR, and GENERATOR. It also touches on some of the other aspects, like CONSTRAINTS and INTENTIONS, to make the exercises more realistic.

The Introductory course aims at making the students aware of the technology and being able to create simple languages with it. It first introduces the students into the user interface of the MPS tool. They need to know where to look for what type of information and how to trigger the basic actions of the IDE. Second, the logical structure of an MPS project is explained. The students learn the basic terminology, such as *node*, *model*, *module*, *language*, *generator*, and *solution*, their mutual relationships, as well as the way to set dependencies between them.

The first practical exercise exposes the students to the projectional editor. They need to learn the basics of manipulating projectional code (code completion, intentions, selection, etc.) while using a relatively simple language (like the Robot Kaja sample), as unfamiliarity with the editor would add complexity to the following, more involved, exercises. Essential debugging facilities, such as the reflective editor, the node explorer, and the hierarchy tree, are explained and used as well.

Language implementation itself is taught on a simple Robot Kaja language extension. The limitations of in-language abstractions are discussed and then a new command is created. The implementation starts with the STRUCTURE and the EDITOR. Then the GENERATOR is implemented to translate this new robot command into a piece of code in plain Robot Kaja language. The generator plan and transient models are explored along the way. A simple example of employing CONSTRAINTS and INTENTIONS follows.

The whole process of language creation is then repeated during the next exercise when a new language is built from scratch. Unless the client demands a customized domain to be used for the example, the students are guided through creating a state chart language that is generated into an XML format. This exercise adds the notions of parent–child relationships and references as well as the corresponding EDITOR and GENERATOR facilities related to them. Concept inheritance is also utilized.

As a wrap-up activity, the students get the task to implement a language from scratch by themselves. This quickly discovers the areas where the students lack the necessary skills and allows the teacher to fix this.

Apart from the possibility to choose a domain for the major exercise, the Advanced course does not allow for customization. This seems not to be of any limitation, since the fundamentals of the technology must be covered in their entirety.

Advanced Course The Advanced course explores some of the topics further and adds a few new ones, as outlined in Table 2. The goal of this course is to make the students competent in language implementation. The Shapes sample language is typically used as a starting point for the students to build nontrivial improvements in. The language should be enhanced with variable declarations and references, which leads to key principles like mapping labels, type system rules, scopes, and name uniqueness constraints. The code should be made more convenient to edit, which leads the students to using transformation menus, substitute menus, action maps, and node factories. Checking rules, quick fixes, intentions, and generator template modularization are also covered in this exercise.

The second part of the course consists of several independent chapters, each dedicated to a particular topic and explained using one of the MPS sample projects. The chapter on language testing, for example, explains how to create node, editor tests, and generator tests and lets the students practice it using the Robot Kaja

Table 2 Outline of the Advanced MPS course, which is a follow-up to the Introductory course and is based on one major example project and several single-purpose projects. The duration of the course is 16 h

Making the editor fluent with substitutions and transformations
Checking rules and quick fixes
Enhancing the structure with attributes
Commenting out code and documentation comments
Advanced structure: specialized links, customized presentation
Leveraging the full power of the SModel language
Concept functions
Dependency analysis
Testing and debugging of languages
The build language
Building MPS and IDEA plugins
Language versioning and migrations

language. The chapter on the build language uses the Calculator language sample to let the students create a language plugin as well as an independent IDE out of it. These chapters do not depend on one another and so can be included, excluded, or rearranged based on the participants' preferences.

The Process In general, the courses avoid spending excessive amounts of time explaining a single aspect of language definition, such as the EDITOR. Instead, they are organized into tasks. These tasks frequently require changes in several aspects of language definition, which ensures that the students iteratively revisit the individual aspects and gain additional details to the knowledge of the aspect that they have acquired in the previous iteration. This process is more engaging as it better balances the theoretical part with practical exercises.

It proved to be beneficial to adjust the exercises with the domain of the client. Not only does it increase motivation but also helps the students to feel more at ease with a tool that is very new to them. The feeling of actually prototyping a system that they will be implementing eventually for real engages the students and encourages concrete questions and discussions even beyond the scope of the exercise at hand.

Initially, the on-site courses took 3 days to complete, but the experience showed us that it is difficult to focus on a subject of this complexity for three subsequent days. Two days per course now seem to be the optimum, which naturally shifted some topics from the Introductory course into the Advanced one and left some topics out of the Advanced course completely.

Online courses tend to take about 25–50% more time to complete than their on-site variants. Despite that, we see a strong preference for online courses among the students.

Customized Courses Occasionally, JetBrains receives requests for highly customized training courses that would cover topics specified by the client and focus on the problem domain of the client. Sometimes this also includes consultancy around the architecture or a specific implementation of a DSL-based solution. These customized courses typically require expertise across several domains of the MPS technology stack, which is difficult to cover by a single lecturer, if the depth of the information given should stay the same in all the areas of the client interest. In order to offer the client the possibility to have each topic covered by an MPS expert on that particular subject, these customized courses are typically organized at the JetBrains premises.

Getting Feedback Collecting feedback from the students proved to be an essential way to improve the quality of the courses. The primary way to collect feedback from the online courses are the comments. These are conveniently located at every step of the material, which makes the context of the comment easy to refer to. Arguably, the feedback obtained immediately as the students go through the course is more accurate than the feedback collected at the end of the course. Collecting feedback during live on-site courses is the sole responsibility of the lecturer. She has to keep notes of the frequent questions and the issues that the students run into and incorporate them into the course materials. The usefulness of the after-course feedback forms that students fill out after they have finished the courses has been decreasing over time as the courses matured. They helped to direct and focus the courses at a coarse-grained level when at the beginning, but the answers to the feedback forms had become predictable as the contents of the course settled, and we have thus abandoned these feedback forms recently.

2 Teaching MPS in an Academic Environment

The first author has given a series of courses on the implementation of domain-specific languages at the University of Turku (Finland), Åbo Akademi University (Finland), the University of Bergen (Norway), and Queen's University (Kingston, Ontario, Canada) to groups of students both with and without a background on model-driven software development and software language engineering. A substantial part of these courses was devoted to language implementation with MPS.

2.1 A Course on Domain-Specific Languages

Position in Curriculum The course "Introduction to Domain-Specific Programming Languages" aims at attracting students to the field of software language engineering and exposing them to a wide range of techniques to implement languages in practice. A motivation to study language design and implementation is drawn from domain-specific languages (DSL), and a part of the course is devoted to DSL design principles.

The course has been lectured as both a short course and a full course, thus giving 3–5 ECTS study points. The course is optional and available to (computer science) students at all levels; several students majoring in economics and information systems have also attended the course. The only requirement to join the course is a background in any object-oriented programming language, though previous knowledge about programming paradigms, formal language theory, or theory of computation is beneficial.

Course Format A full version of the course, with 14 in-class sessions in total, is centered around 5 lectures and 9 hands-on tutorials (see Table 3). There are two 90-minute sessions per week, and 6 h per week are allocated for self-studying. Similarly to other courses related to software language engineering [2], the lectures are a combination of theory and practice, with theory explained on the slides and in discussions and then illustrated by the lecturer by live coding the examples [2]. Live coding is partly interactive, and suggestions from the students can be implemented. Having separate sessions in a computer class, where students could experiment on their own (rather than copying teacher's solutions) could be a better option [2]. Still, tutorial-like lectures do require students to use computers themselves to

Table 3 Outline of the university course

	Topic	Content	Book	Format
1	Zoo of DSLs	Examples, semantic models	[16]	Lecture
2	External DSLs	AST, IDE services	[16, 37]	Lecture
3	Eclipse Xtext	Grammars, EMF, validation, formatting	[7]	Tutorial
4	Eclipse Xtext	Type system, code generation	[7]	Tutorial
5	Spoofax	Typing rules for expressions		Tutorial
6	DSL design concerns	Best and worst practices	[22, 37]	Lecture
7	Metaprogramming	Rascal		Tutorial
8	Projectional editing	Examples, equation editor analogy		Lecture
9	MPS	Structure, editor	[10]	Tutorial
10	MPS	Type system	[10]	Tutorial
11	Code generation	XML, XSLT, MPS TEXTGEN aspect	[10]	Tutorial
12	MPS	GENERATOR aspect	[10, 37]	Tutorial
13	MPS	Extending Java		Tutorial
14	LOP in practice	Language-oriented programming	[37]	Lecture

implement explained techniques and mini-tasks given to students to experiment with implementation.

A short version of the course is structured in a flexible way and is adapted to the interests of students. The course was given twice at Bergen Language Design Laboratory at the University of Bergen in Norway: the first version had a hands-on tutorial on Eclipse Xtext and a demo of MPS, while the second iteration of the course focused on using MPS for extending Java. Students of the School of Computing of Queen's University in Kingston in Canada took a short version of the course with a hands-on tutorial on MPS.

Materials The course is based mainly on five books authored by industry experts, thus exposing students to a practitioner's view on language implementation: M. Fowler's book on domain-specific languages [16] is used for showcasing the theory of internal and external DSLs, the book on DSL engineering by M. Voelter et al. [37] gives material on external DSLs and IDE services, L. Bettini's book [7] is a foundation for tutorial lectures on Eclipse Xtext and Xtend, F. Campagne's book [10] is used to compile the tutorial on MPS, and S. Kelly and J.P. Tolvanen's book [22] is used in discussions on language design practices.

Slides of the course are available online at dsl-course.org.

Similar Courses There are multiple courses on domain-specific languages, software language engineering, and model-driven engineering given at various universities (see, e.g., [1], [2], [9], [12]). To the best of our knowledge, our course covers one of the widest ranges of language implementation techniques.

2.2 Teaching MPS Within the Big Picture of Language Engineering

The course is divided into four principal parts. The *first part* is an extensive zoo of domain-specific languages including formatting languages, graphical rendering languages, data description languages, and business process languages. A wide coverage of domains helps students get an informal idea about what a DSL is. A pseudo-realistic example [4] that explains the need, adoption, and evolution of domain-specific languages and tools is presented.

The *second part* of the course focuses on general properties of domain-specific languages. It starts with a discussion on internal and external DSLs, advantages of using them and possible problems, and design guidelines [20, 21] and continues with an overview of integrated development environments (IDEs). Students are familiarized with technical requirements for standard IDE services such as syntax-aware editing, code formatting and folding, code completion, code navigation and hyperlinking, code outlining, name refactoring, and automatic code corrections. An informal comparison of how these features can be implemented in several language workbenches follows later in the course.

The second part of the course also introduces a simple external language—*Entities Language* [7]—that will be later implemented using several language engineering tools. This choice of (a trivial) Entities Language is dictated by a learning objective of demonstrating different aspects of language implementation (such as the definition of a type system and code generation of object-oriented code) rather than that of exercising language design skills. A code example in Entities Language is given below:

```
entity Person {
    text name
    number YoB
    name = "John"
    YoB = 1900
}
entity Employee extends Person {
    number salary
    name = "Mary" // inherited field
    salary = 30 * (20 + 80)
    print salary
}
```

Each `entity` corresponds to a class in object-oriented programming, and an `entity` can extend another declared `entity`. The language has three primitive data types—number, `toggle`, and `text`—that correspond respectively to the integer, Boolean, and string types in common programming languages. Moreover, each `entity` becomes a data type and fields of that type can be declared. The body of an `entity` is a sequence of fields declarations and statements (assignment and

Table 4 Topics covered in the course when discussing different language workbenches

Tool	Entities definition	Expressions sublanguage	Code generation	Typing rules	Scoping rules
Eclipse Xtext	Yes	No (constant expressions only)	Yes (M→T)	Yes[a]	Yes[a]
Spoofax	Yes	Yes	No	Yes[b] (expressions only)	No
Rascal MPL	Yes	Yes	Yes (evaluation[c])	No	No
MPS	Yes	Yes[d]	Yes (M→T, M→M)	Yes	Yes

[a] imperative Java/Xtend code [7]
[b] declarative NaBL2 code [24]
[c] evaluation defined for both abstract and concrete syntaxes
[d] imported from MPS BaseLanguage
M→T, model-to-text transformation; M→M, model-to-model transformation

print), which can occur in any order. From within the body of an entity that extends another entity, it is possible to access the fields declared in that other entity, following the standard semantics of class inheritance. Entities Language is supposed to be transpiled into an object-oriented language, for example, Java.

The *third part* of the course discusses language workbenches Eclipse Xtext [15] and Spoofax [19, 41] and gives an overview of metaprogramming language Rascal [23]. Our hypothesis is that the students will better perceive techniques of language engineering in MPS when they already are familiarized with language implementation approaches in a text-based language workbench. Instead of choosing a single language workbench for this purpose, a combination of three tools is showcased to the students, with different focus when discussing each of them (see Table 4 for summary).

Eclipse Xtext Implementing Entities Language in Eclipse Xtext starts with a grammar definition. To keep the focus on language implementation issues (such as IDE services) rather than on grammar rules for arithmetical expressions with priority of operations,[1] expressions can only be constants. A point is made that grammar rules correspond to EMF Ecore [17, 33] object model, thus preparing the students to the object-oriented way on defining concepts in MPS.

Type checking and scoping rules are implemented using imperative code in Java and Xtend [8]. Code formatting is implemented in Xtend using an internal DSL that ships with Xtext. This is expected to bring students' attention to the *language-oriented programming* approach used for language definition: this point is again

---

[1] This is not completely trivial because Xtext is based on a recursive descent parser that forbids left recursion in grammar rules; cf. syntactic rules in Spoofax mentioned later.

mentioned later in the course when explaining how language aspects are defined in MPS using DSLs tailored for each aspect [13]. Entities Language is transpiled in a straightforward way into Java. Implementation of code generation uses multiline template expressions of Xtend [7, 17] and is thus a model-to-text transformation.

Spoofax Students are then introduced to a more formal way of defining typing rules for expressions when language workbench Spoofax is discussed.[2] The grammar of the Entities Language is redefined in Syntax Definition Formalism SDF3 [11, 19] that has built-in capabilities for defining priority of arithmetic operations. Since Spoofax uses Generalized LR parsing algorithm [18], context-free rules of arbitrary form can be used. This allows defining rules for expressions in a natural way (e.g., $Expr \rightarrow Expr + Expr$). Typing rules are defined using a declarative language NaBL2 [24] that enables definitions similar to a mathematical notation (along the lines of e_1 : INT, e_2 : INT $\Rightarrow$ $e_1 + e_2$: INT). An informal comparison with the type system implementation in Xtext is made at this point, and students are expected to be able to value the benefits of declarative specifications, where the gap between the formalization and the implementation of a type system is reduced [8, Sect. 7.3]. This is yet another preparatory step for the students before they are familiarized with MPS.

Despite a powerful model transformation mechanism of Spoofax, code generation techniques are not discussed at this point. Doing otherwise would require explaining model transformations twice: both for Spoofax and then later for the case of MPS.[3]

Rascal MPL The course continues with an implementation of Entities Language using metaprogramming language Rascal, with the focus on yet another aspect of expressions sublanguage—that of their evaluation. While discussion of expressions evaluation was possible already in the case of Xtext, this topic is left for Rascal to demonstrate the idea of code quotations: a method with signature `eval((Expr)'<Expr e1> + <Expr e2>')` quotes the concrete syntax of an addition expression and can perform calculations on variables `e1` and `e2`. This

---

[2]In an alternative curriculum, we could have only showcased a single text-based language workbench in the course—Eclipse Xtext—with type system and scoping rules defined using Xsemantics [8] and expressions sublanguage imported from xBase [14]. A decision has been made, however, to expose students to a larger variety of tools.

[3]Though code generation mechanisms in both Spoofax and MPS are similar *conceptually*, there are two important differences. First, in MPS, code to be generated is essentially a quotation, and only valid fragments of code can be emitted, whereas Spoofax allows emitting any strings [28]. Second, in MPS, code to be generated is a *sample output*, whose varying parts are explicitly marked with generation *macros*, the machinery of which is defined in the Inspector window. For example, for the STRUCTURE definition concept `VarDecl{type, name}`, a possible GENERATOR definition is `private $MACRO[int] $MACRO[amount];`. In Spoofax, the output is essentially an interpolated string: `VarDecl(type, name) -> private [type] [name];`. Hence, to avoid possibly confusing the students, a decision has been made to explain code generation only for the case of MPS. In a more extensive course, however, explaining both mechanisms seems to be beneficial.

"light" exposure to the notion of quotation is again preparing the students for the language implementation in MPS.

By this point in the course, students have an understanding of what language implementation comprises of and are expected to be somewhat fluent in the language engineering terminology. The course can then continue with the *fourth part*, which is devoted to the language implementation in MPS.

Explaining Projectional Editing Before starting to implement Entities Language in MPS, a detailed discussion on projectional editing takes place. We find this important since the projectional editor of MPS both is its most distinctive and powerful feature and the one that prevents a wide adoption of MPS due to its perceived clumsiness [29].

The discussion on the projectional editing starts with examples of non-programming environments, which include:

- sound editing software (e.g., Adobe Audition[4]) that supports the graphical editing of sound waves (thus, one projection is audible and the other one is visual);
- rich text editors with support of textual, graphical, and tabular notations;
- file system explorers that have several visual representations of file system elements (e.g., "large icons," "list") and allow for graphical editing of the file system (by dragging and dropping the files and folders onto each other);
- XML-based file formats (e.g., Microsoft PowerPoint), where an animation can be edited both in the tool's visual interface and in code;[5]
- vector graphics editing software (e.g., Inkscape[6]) that allows both the visual editing of an image and a direct manipulation of its SVG representation;
- diagrams editing software (e.g., SmartArt tool of Microsoft Word) that enables the visual and textual editing of the diagram's structure and elements;
- HTML editing tools (in the style of Microsoft FrontPage) that allow both the rich text-based and the code-based editing of HTML code.

The following examples of programming environments that use projectional editing are mentioned in the course:

- office database management systems (e.g., Microsoft Access), where table definition queries are themselves represented as tables, and SQL queries have textual, tabular, and graphical projections;
- computer algebra systems (e.g., PTC Mathcad[7]) that allow visually enhanced control flow instructions with a graphical rendering of mathematical formulae and support diagram notations (such as plots) directly in code;

---

[4]http://adobe.com/products/audition.

[5]https://docs.microsoft.com/en-us/office/open-xml/working-with-animation.

[6]https://inkscape.org.

[7]https://www.mathcad.com.

- rapid application development studios and form builders that allow both visual and text-based editing of GUI forms;
- Scratch-like programming environments [27], where the code is constructed from graphical blocks corresponding to the programming language statements.

Analogy with Equation Editor A more detailed explanation of projectional editing is done using the analogy of Equation Editor in Microsoft Office. To explain how a formula

with three placeholders can be entered by a user of an Equation Editor, the following object model is suggested: a class Sum with three fields lowerBound, upperBound, and expr, each of type Expression. The graphical rendering of this formula is then a *projection* of an instance of this class. A point here is made that the definition of class Sum repeats the structure of a concept for a summation expression that could be defined in MPS.

Continuing with the object-oriented metaphor, the following example of a matrix rendering in the Equation Editor is considered:

$$\begin{bmatrix} \Box/\Box & \sqrt{\Box} \\ \Box & \Box^{\Box} \end{bmatrix} \tag{1}$$

This matrix can be considered as an edited projection of a two-by-two matrix with four "basic" placeholders

$$\begin{bmatrix} \Box & \Box \\ \Box & \Box \end{bmatrix} \tag{2}$$

which is represented as an instance of class Matrix2x2 with four fields pos11, pos12, pos21, and pos22 of type Expression. In the Equation Editor, editing of projection (2) to get the desired projection (1) is done either by using menu commands and palette or by typing a trigger for a specific kind of placeholder. Typing those triggers ("/," "sqrt," "^") instantiates, respectively, classes Division, Radical, and Exponentiation that all extend class Expression. The (now updated) object model of (1) has field pos11 of type Division, field pos12 of type Radical, and field pos22 of type Exponentiation. This example is used as an intuitive introduction to concept inheritance in MPS.

Another example anticipates discussion on aliases of concepts in MPS. Projection of class SineFunction with field expr of type Expression can be entered in the Equation Editor by typing symbols s, i, and n. The editor treats this combination of letters as a trigger (or alias) of concept SineFunction, which is then instantiated and projected as "sin $\Box$."

To anticipate left- and right-side transformations that can be defined for an editor of a language in MPS, yet another example of the Equation Editor is considered. When an integer expression 2 is already entered by the user in the Equation Editor, typing caret symbol "^" will force the editor to transform the projection of integer constant into a projection $2^\square$ of exponentiation expression with one placeholder.

Finally, projectional editor of MPS is explained by giving an example of an imperative programming language construct. An instance of this construct, say, *if statement*, is represented as a table where a cell is assigned to every lexical element (token) present in the example. Three kinds of cells are then distinguished: immutable cells that represent keywords and special symbols, indentation cells, and mutable cells that contain elements of the abstract syntax of the construct.

These examples are expected to give enough background to students so that they can use a projectional editor of MPS or another tool that features a projectional editor.

Entities Language in MPS At this point, Entities Language can be implemented in MPS. Following the analogy of the Equation Editor, each construct of Entities Language is considered as a class in the object model induced by the language. A point is made about resemblance to Xtext, where grammar rules become classes (instances of EMF Ecore `EClass`) and features of rules become fields of those classes. It is important to convey to students that while in Xtext the object model is populated during the parsing, resulting in an abstract syntax tree that can be further manipulated, in MPS the user edits the abstract syntax tree directly. Another point worth making about comparing language implementation in Xtext and in MPS is that Xtext is mainly based on a general-purpose imperative language to implement language aspects, while MPS follows the approach of language-oriented programming [13].

Expressions Unlike implementations of expression sublanguage in other language workbenches studied in the course, we use language composition [37] to import expressions from MPS BaseLanguage. This allows students to focus on what is distinctive for language definition in MPS rather than to meticulously define the inductive structure of expressions. Nonetheless, an interested student can be given a task to implement expressions sublanguage from scratch in order to practice defining editor actions to achieve text-based-like entry of expressions and then to reimplement the editor using grammar cells [39].

Language Aspects While defining the STRUCTURE and EDITORs for concepts of Entities Language is rather straightforward, lecturer's attention should be given to checking whether the students correctly type in code snippets in MPS projectional editor. A home assignment, similar to some of the exercises discussed in [6], can be given to students to practice their typing experience with MPS. To showcase rich rendering capabilities of the projectional editor, in addition to stylesheets and conditional cells, Java Swing components are used; for example, an editor for a Boolean value features a button component that switches the value. Implementing an action listener for this button demonstrates a less trivial use of the *Inspector* window. To nurture a more productive typing of code in MPS, students are asked to use extensively *Intentions* menu when defining STRUCTURE and EDITORS for concepts.

To reiterate the object-oriented nature of concepts, several methods in the BEHAVIOUR aspect are defined. This is followed by creating CONSTRAINTS and TYPESYSTEM rules for concepts. In addition to implementing standard rules for typing expressions, Entities Language is modified to showcase how physical units (e.g., number [kg] x; x = 10 CHF) can be type-checked, with the goal of practicing the SModel language of MPS. A particular attention is given to quotations and antiquotations, which have been already briefly introduced when discussing metaprogramming language Rascal earlier in the course.

Explaining Code Generation Code generation is perceived as one of the most involved parts in the language definition process. Trying to provide a bridge to already perceived ideas of model-to-text transformations with Xtext, the course first explores TEXTGEN aspect of MPS, where the Entities Language is transpiled into Java. A point is made on why generating textual output may be inferior to using GENERATOR aspect, where target language code is guaranteed to be syntactically correct.

To explain model-to-model transformations in MPS, a dive into XML and XSL transformations is made. Students are expected to practice using XSLT for generating both XML documents and textual output (e.g., Java code). An advanced exercise here would be to ask students to design their own XSLT-like transformation language and then to write an XSL transformation that will convert student's custom language into XSLT. Table 5 can be used to initiate discussion on the resemblance between different XML artifacts, language aspects in MPS, and notions of application software. This brings an alternative way of teaching MPS (discussed in Sect. 2.3) that starts with treating languages defined in MPS as user interface specifications [5].

Even after practicing XSL transformations, we find it useful to explain GENERATOR aspect anew on a blackboard without using MPS. We give examples of target language code and show how we could "annotate" it to form an intuition for macros and template fragments.

To let students practice defining language constructs and generators for them "in the wild" and to reiterate the importance of language composition, the course contin-

Table 5 Conceptual resemblance of XML artifacts, aspects of MPS, and application software

XML artifact	MPS aspect	Application software
XML document	STRUCTURE	Data model
XML schema or DTD	TYPESYSTEM, CONSTRAINTS	Data validation
CSS stylesheet	EDITOR	Graphical user interface
XSL transformation (XML to text)	TEXTGEN (M→T)	Data serialization
XSL transformation (XML to XML)	GENERATOR (M→M)	Business logic
Document Object Model	Abstract syntax tree	Data, metadata

ues with extending MPS BaseLanguage. We offer as assignments adding physical units, `nameof` operator [25], unconventionally layout imperative statements, and other constructs to BaseLanguage.

2.3 A Different Curriculum: Teaching MPS as a Programming Tool En Soi

We describe below an outline of an alternative version of the course, where introducing MPS does not require previous knowledge on other language workbenches.

Reflecting the typical patterns for building software languages [35], the course is divided into three parts:

- MPS as a tool for textual user interfaces [5];
- MPS as a modelling tool [34];
- MPS as a tool for extending existing languages [31].

This choice and order of the parts is dictated by a desire to avoid starting the course with language engineering terminology. In the first part of the course, the students' task is to create a textual user interface for an invoice calculator in MPS. Discussing language aspects at this point avoids mentioning projectional editing [29, 38]. ACTIONS aspect is not mentioned until the second part of the course, where it comes naturally in one of the examples. INTENTIONS aspect is discussed, and a point about importance of domain-specific error support [16, 40] is made. Implementation of the invoice calculator in Microsoft Excel could be discussed for comparison.

Code Generation Code generation is covered in several parts of the course. Discussion starts with the TEXTGEN aspect, where an RTF generator for the invoice calculator is defined. It continues with the GENERATOR aspect, where generators for the invoice calculator to XML and Java are given. Java code generation deliberately comes after RTF and XML to address a frequent opinion of the newcomers that MPS only allows generating Java code.

Projectional Editing Projectional editing often alienates beginners by its perceived clumsiness and limitations [29]; that is why it is not formally introduced until this moment of the course. A discussion *pro* projectional editing follows, stating that most of a traditional editor functionality is replicated in MPS [36].

Entities Language In the second part of the course, MPS is used as a modelling tool to implement domain-specific languages. A running example is Entities language; code generators into Java, JavaScript, and Visual Basic for Applications are discussed. This selection of target languages is motivated by the need to communicate to students that MPS can be used to generate web applications as well as legacy code. A metaphor of object-oriented programming counterparts in MPS is revised, and the students are encouraged to focus on notions used in language engineering [26]. Code generation with the GENERATOR aspect is revisited, with discussion on reductions, quotations, and mapping labels. The discussion continues with the TYPESYSTEM and the DATAFLOW analysis for the Entities Language. This part is concluded by discussing language MIGRATION in MPS.

In the third part of the course, MPS is used to extend Java [31] and Entities Language, where ACTIONS, CONSTRAINTS, and GENERATOR aspects are discussed anew.

3   Lessons Learned

We present below a summary of lessons learned based on our experience in teaching language engineering with MPS in industry and academia:

L1.   *Low ceremony free courses* attract the participants who only want to test the waters before fully committing to learning the technology and who would turn the technology down without trying otherwise.

L2.   *Going online* has increased the reach of the courses by an order of magnitude.

L3.   Paying attention to *step-by-step guidance* is crucial even at later stages, since the participants tend to skip unclear steps or forget things, if not repeated several times in different contexts.

L4.   *Teaching MPS in a wide context of other language engineering tools*, such as language workbenches Eclipse Xtext, Spoofax, and Rascal, gives students a fuller picture of this area. Most importantly, by the time when MPS is introduced in the course, students have already seen what language implementation is comprised of and acquired some language engineering terminology. This enables concentrating on implementation techniques that are distinctive in MPS.

L5.   *Explaining projectional editing by discussing analogies* among both non-programming and programming-related environments seems to facilitate perception of MPS projectional editor. An analogy with an equation editor in a word processor enables introducing object-oriented view on language concepts and the notions of concept aliases and side transformations.

L6.   *Explaining code generation with XML-based examples and XSL transformations* allows the students to explore model-to-model transformations. Availability of (online) tools to run XSL transformations, textual representation of XML trees, and powerful mechanisms of XSLT facilitate students' experience.

L7.   *Using MPS to extend an existing general-purpose language* (e.g., MPS BaseLanguage) seems to interest students as they can see an immediate quasi-practical use of the acquired language engineering skills.

L8.   Covering at least the basics of *domain engineering* motivates the participants to learn the practicalities of the concrete tool. It will also help them imagine how the principles and tooling could be applied to their projects and their infrastructure.

L9. *Language design concerns* should be explored as part of the initial discussions over nontrivial example projects. The pros and cons of the alternative approaches should be presented as well as their consequences to other parts of the project.

4 Concluding Remarks

We presented our experiences in teaching MPS in two inherently different environments. Courses and trainings given in an industrial setting are aimed at experienced developers and business experts, are often adjusted for a particular business domain, and are designed around acquiring practical language implementation skills by the participants. The academic setting tends to give a broader yet less detailed overview of several language implementation techniques, with the goal that students grasp fundamental concepts and differences between approaches and tools.

Attracting students to taking any form of training in the MPS technology has constantly been the biggest challenge. Numerous beginner-level questions on the MPS discussion forum indicate that a large number of professionals attempt to climb the steep learning curve on their own, which frequently leads to suboptimal solutions, shallow opinions, and a lot of frustration.

It remains to see whether joint efforts from both industry and academia in teaching MPS would benefit all the stakeholders. Perhaps a first step already taken in this direction is the availability of teaching materials [3, 30] online.

References

1. Acher, M.: Domain-Specific Languages, course materials. Available at: http://mathieuacher. com/teaching/MDE/201516/DSLAndXtext.pdf
2. Bagge, A.H., Lämmel, R., Zaytsev, V.: Reflections on courses for software language engineering. In: MODELS Educators Symposium 2014, pp. 54–63 (2014)
3. Barash, M.: Introductory course on domain-specific programming languages, course materials. 2017–2020. Available at: http://dsl-course.org
4. Barash, M.: A tale about domain-specific languages, blog post (2018). Available at: https://medium.com/@mikhail.barash.mikbar/a-tale-about-domain-specific-languages-bde2ace22f6c
5. Benson, V.M., Campagne, F.: Language workbench user interfaces for data analysis, PeerJ 3:e800 (2015)
6. Berger, T., Voelter, M., Jensen, H.P., Dangprasert, T., Siegmund, J.: Efficiency of projectional editing: a controlled experiment. SIGSOFT FSE 2016, pp. 763–774
7. Bettini, L.: Implementing Domain-Specific Languages with Xtext and Xtend, Packt Publishing (2016)
8. Bettini, L.: Type errors for the IDE with Xtext and Xsemantics. Open Comput. Sci. 9(1), 52–79 (2019)
9. Cabot, J., Tisi, M.: The MDE diploma: first international postgraduate specialization in model-driven software engineering. CS Education 2011

10. Campagne, F.: The MPS Language Workbench, Vol. 1. CreateSpace Independent Publishing Platform (2014)
11. de Souza Amorim, L.E., Visser, E.: Multi-purpose Syntax Definition with SDF3. SEFM 2020, pp. 1–23
12. Dingel, J.: *Beyond Code: An Introduction to Model-Driven Software Development*, course materials. Available at: http://research.cs.queensu.ca/home/dingel/cisc836_W20/index.html
13. Dmitriev, S.: Language Oriented Programming: The Next Programming Paradigm (2004). Available at: https://resources.jetbrains.com/storage/products/mps/docs/Language_Oriented_Programming.pdf
14. Efftinge, S., Eysholdt, M., Köhnlein, J., Zarnekow, S., von Massow, R., Hasselbring, W., Hanus, M.: Xbase: implementing domain-specific languages for Java, GPCE 2012, pp. 112–121
15. Eysholdt, M., Rupprecht, J.: Migrating a large modeling environment from XML/UML to Xtext/GMF. SPLASH/OOPSLA Companion 2010, pp. 97–104
16. Fowler, M.: Domain-Specific Languages. Addison-Wesley, Boston (2010)
17. Gronback, R.C.: Eclipse Modeling Project – A Domain-Specific Language (DSL) Toolkit. Addison-Wesley, Boston (2009)
18. Grune, D., Jacobs, C.J.H.: Parsing Techniques — A Practical Guide, pp. 1–643. Springer, New York (2008)
19. Kats, L.C.L., Visser, E.: The Spoofax language workbench: rules for declarative specification of languages and IDEs, OOPSLA 2010, pp. 444–463
20. Karsai, G., Krahn, H., Pinkernell, C., Rumpe, B., Schindler, M., Völkel, S.: Design guidelines for domain specific languages. In: Proceedings of the 9th OOPSLA Workshop on Domain-Specific Modeling (2009)
21. Kelly, S., Pohjonen, R.: Worst practices for domain-specific modeling. IEEE Softw. **26**(4), 22–29 (2009)
22. Kelly, S., Tolvanen, J.-P.: Domain-Specific Modeling: Enabling Full Code Generation. Wiley, Hoboken (2008)
23. Klint, P., van der Storm, T., Vinju, J.J.: Rascal: a domain specific language for source code analysis and manipulation. In: SCAM 2009, pp. 168–177
24. Konat, G., Kats, L.C.L., Wachsmuth, G., Visser, E.: Declarative Name Binding and Scope Rules SLE 2012, pp. 311–331
25. Kulikov, P., Wagner, B., De George, A., Wenzel, M.: nameof expression. C# Programming Language Reference. Available at: https://docs.microsoft.com/en-us/dotnet/csharp/language-reference/operators/nameof
26. Lämmel, R.: Software Languages: Syntax, Semantics, and Metaprogramming. Springer, New York (2018)
27. Maloney, J., Resnick, M., Rusk, N., Silverman, B., Eastmond, E.: The scratch programming language and environment. ACM Trans. Comput. Educ. **10**(4), 16:1–16:15 (2010)
28. Metaborg, Concrete syntax in stratego transformations. Available at: http://www.metaborg.org/en/latest/source/langdev/meta/lang/stratego/concrete-syntax.html
29. Minör, S.: Interacting with structure-oriented editors. Int. J. Man Mach. Stud. **37**(4), 399–418 (1992)
30. Pech, V.: JetBrains MPS Elementary Course, online course. Available at: https://stepik.org/course/37360/
31. Pech, V., Shatalin, A., Voelter, M.: JetBrains MPS as a Tool for Extending Java, PPPJ 2013, pp. 165–168
32. Ratiu, D., Pech, V., Dummann, K.: Experiences with teaching MPS in industry: towards bringing domain-specific languages closer to practitioners. In: MODELS 2017, pp. 83–92
33. Steinberg, D., Budinsky, F., Paternostro, M., Merks, E.: EMF – Eclipse Modeling Framework. Addison-Wesley, Hoboken (2008)
34. Voelter, M.: Fusing Modeling and Programming into Language-Oriented Programming – Our Experiences with MPS, ISoLA 1, pp. 309–339 (2018)

35. Voelter, M.: High-Level Structure of DSLs: Three Patterns (2017). Available at: https://languageengineering.io/high-level-structure-of-dsls-three-patterns-7375c8baa2d3
36. Voelter, M., Lisson, S.: Supporting Diverse Notations in MPS' Projectional Editor. GEMOC@MoDELS 2014, pp. 7–16
37. Voelter, M., Benz, S., Dietrich, C., Engelmann, B., Helander, M., Kats, L., Visser, E., Wachsmuth, G.: DSL Engineering: Designing, Implementing and Using Domain-Specific Languages (2013)
38. Voelter, M., Siegmund, J., Berger, T., Kolb, B.: Towards User-Friendly Projectional Editors. SLE 2014, pp. 41–61
39. Voelter, M., Szabó, T., Lisson, S., Kolb, B., Erdweg, S., Berger, Th.: Efficient development of consistent projectional editors using grammar cells. SLE 2016, pp. 28–40
40. Voelter, M., Kolb, B., Szabó, T., Ratiu, D., van Deursen, A.: Lessons learned from developing mbeddr: a case study in language engineering with MPS. Softw. Syst. Model. 18(1), 585–630 (2019)
41. Wachsmuth, G., Konat, G.D.P., Visser, E.: Language design with the Spoofax language workbench. IEEE Softw. 31(5), 35–43 (2014)

Teaching Language Engineering Using MPS

Andreas Prinz

Abstract At universities, computer language handling is most often taught with a focus on compiler theory. However, in practical applications, domain-specific languages (DSLs) are much more important. DSLs implement model-driven technology in an understandable way, as models can be expressed easily using DSLs. One interesting domain for DSLs in this context is language handling itself, and many current tools for language handling are model-driven and based on meta-models. This chapter connects compiler theory and meta-modelling within a university course about language handling. The course features the relevant theory and uses MPS as a practical tool. We show how MPS is used in the course and discuss its suitability.

1 Introduction

Model-driven development (MDD) has created high hopes for easier systems development and shorter development cycles [27]. The central idea still holds: If we can lift the level of abstraction, such that we see the relevant information of a problem and its solution, then the design of solutions becomes much easier. Besides, it is possible to discuss the solutions with the experts. In reality, however, the results were not too promising, (1) because the standard modelling language was chosen to be UML [37]; (2) because models were used as illustrations, and not as specifications; and (3) because of missing or immature tool support. Therefore, many programmers abandoned modelling.

Modelling can be connected to the expertise when the language used for the model is understandable for the experts, i.e., the language has to be a domain-specific (modelling) language [10]. It is important to use full languages, not only

A. Prinz (✉)
Department of ICT, University of Agder, Grimstad, Norway
e-mail: Andreas.Prinz@UIA.no

© The Author(s), under exclusive license to Springer Nature Switzerland AG 2021
A. Bucchiarone et al. (eds.), *Domain-Specific Languages in Practice*,
https://doi.org/10.1007/978-3-030-73758-0_11

notations without semantics. This means DSLs need to be executable in order to be useful for modelling, such that they essentially are high-level programs [4, 30, 54].

In this spirit, languages like SDL [23] and executable UML [31] present a high level of abstraction together with executability. There are attempts to add formality and executability to the OMG MDA framework [6]. This book presents examples of such DSLs, and this chapter looks into how DSLs can be included in computer science teaching.

For systems development, modelling is essential. Modelling means to develop high-level descriptions of the problems and the solutions. These descriptions have to translate into running systems that can be used to experiment with the problems and the solutions until a satisfactory result is achieved. This is only possible if the languages used are formal, allowing to express the important information concisely and formally. Out of such descriptions, programs can be derived—either manually or automatically.

In this chapter, we follow an MDD approach that values formality and complete automatic code generation. The idea of changing the generated code afterward has been abandoned for compilers because it did not bring too good results. Nowadays, developers rarely touch the code generated by compilers. The same should be valid for code generated within MDD.

In this view, MDD is closely related to domain-specific languages (DSL), as it is easiest to write concise models using a concise language adapted to a domain [25]. This way, the complexity of the domain is reduced and captured in the concepts of the DSL. A domain-specific language is a textual or graphical language with abstractions optimized for a domain and with well-defined semantics [53]. A DSL may be preprocessed, embedded, or transformed into other languages for execution, instead of being compiled to machine code using a traditional compiler.

Because the development of DSLs uses high-level descriptions, it is based on the same principles: the language handling tools are generated from high-level descriptions; see [3, 8]. This means MDD is used to define these types of languages. An important aspect of this approach is to provide the language designer with support for rapid development and automatic prototyping of language support tools and allow for working on a high level of abstraction. This way, the language designer can focus on the language and use the language definition to generate tools such as editors, validators, and code generators.

A related aspect is the ease of developing DSLs. Ideally, languages should be put together in a plug-and-play fashion using best-practice language patterns. This flexibility is achieved by language modularity and the ability to reuse existing languages, allowing language extension and language reuse [51].

Despite the importance of domain-specific languages and the tooling for them, many universities still teach language handling with the main focus on compiler theory. For example, in Norwegian universities, there is a strong emphasis on compiler theory and little or no focus on meta-modelling in most of the available computer language handling courses [12, 13].

In contrast, we use an approach to teach DSL technology together with MDD technology under a framework of meta-models and generated code, still under the umbrella of computer language handling. This allows for shifting focus from compiler development to meta-model-based language design and definition.

The primary purpose of this article is to share experiences from teaching meta-model-based language description and to discuss how the tool MPS [24] helps in teaching. We will also discuss meta-languages for covering the different aspects of a language definition when teaching computer language handling.

The chapter presents a course run at the University of Agder the last 10 years and the experiences with the tools and the learning. The article will also discuss the course content and design.

The chapter is organized as follows: Sect. 2 describes the course formalities in order to set the scene. After that, Sect. 3 discusses meta-languages and concepts for simple language design. After that, Sect. 4 describes how MPS supports these meta-languages and concepts. Section 5 describes the experiences with the course and the possible improvements to MPS for the course. Finally, Sect. 6 concludes the chapter.

2 Course Requirements and Challenges

As usual at universities, the course description is given at a very high-level stating content and learning outcomes. As usual, the teacher (author) had a lot of influence on the course description. Please note that the course is a general language engineering course, not an MPS course.

2.1 IKT445 Generative Programming

The course "Generative Programming" started as a course on software engineering and compiler construction. After some years, it turned out that compiler construction was too far from the typical work tasks of our students. The relevant area for students would be domain-specific languages. In addition, the area of model-driven development (MDD) had to be taught to them. These two ideas led to a new version of the course covering MDD and DSL. The course IKT445 "Generative Programming"[1] has the following course description.

Level:	MSc
Duration:	1 semester
Prerequisites:	Object-oriented programming, UML modelling
Credits:	7.5 ECTS credits
Literature:	[1] [8]
Exam:	Multiple-choice tests (50%) and project (50%)

---

[1] See also the course home page https://www.uia.no/studieplaner/topic/IKT445-G.

Content: • Model-driven development and meta-models
• Handling of structural, syntactical, and semantic language aspects
• Code generator theory and application
• Handling systems containing generated and manual code
• Grammars, languages, and automata

Learning outcomes:
On successful completion of the course, the student should:

• Know the concepts and terms of language description and use them correctly in arguments
• Be able to apply best practice of language engineering
• Be able to analyze and design high-level language descriptions capturing all language aspects
• Be able to translate between languages, grammars, and automata
• Be able to design code generation from high-level descriptions

2.2 Selecting a Tool for the Course

This course uses a tool to support learning. However, immature or overly complex tools and technologies can demotivate students and, in some cases, even make them avoid meta-model-based projects. Students need stable tools with good documentation and easily understandable meta-languages. The tool has to be conceptually clear in its underlying platform. Finally, it must be usable for novices, as our students are inexperienced developers; they want to copy and paste program text.

Currently, such a tool does not exist, and when the course started, the situation was even worse. Tools are not designed for teaching, and it is very challenging to develop a neat tool with industrial strength at a university. Moreover, at our university, we want to use a public-domain tool.

So we need to compromise and select an existing tool. As MDD is very close to meta-modelling [3], in principle, the choice can be made related to MDD tools as well. The Eclipse infrastructure [9] around xText [5] is the first choice in this area, in particular connected to EMF [50]. We also looked into Microsoft Studio [32] with its DSL package. Another candidate would be Rascal [28] among many university-based tools.

In the evaluation of these tools, university-based tools usually are not stable enough and provide little documentation. Microsoft Studio provided good integration, documentation, and ease of use but had a somewhat limited selection of meta-languages. Therefore, with Microsoft Studio students had to work on a relatively low level of abstraction. Eclipse with xText had good applicability and also a rich set of meta-languages. However, the problem with Eclipse was its general stability and sparsity of documentation. The meta-languages did not fit together;

they changed in short cycles, and consistency between different packages was a nightmare. Changes of plugins during the course were likely.

MPS somewhat combined the advantages of Eclipse and Microsoft Visual Studio, being both integrated and high-level, stable, and user-friendly; see also [15]. All of the other tools failed in being able to handle complete definitions as big languages, for example, SDL in structure, syntax, and semantics as described in [17] and implemented in [43]. MPS can define major languages, as evidenced by the definition of Java [18] (called BaseLanguage) in MPS [39].[2] Moreover, MPS has been extended and used in industrial projects [52].

2.3 Content and Design of the Course

With a tool in place, we could focus on the course design. As meta-modelling and language handling tend to be challenging, the main focus has to be on *learning by doing*. This is achieved with a project that the students work with to get a deeper understanding of the theory; see Sect. 2.4. Also, the course starts with a small project that helps the students to get an overview early in the course. This small project is run as "compiler in a day," where students implement a tiny state chart language with four concepts[3] during one day. This event is usually run remotely by MPS with local support given by the course teachers.

As described in more detail in [13], we have investigated how a course that primarily focused on compiler theory could be updated to include meta-model-based approaches to language definition and a particular focus on determining the optimal abstraction level for each language aspect. Based on this, the course contains seven units that cover meta-model-based and compiler-based approaches to language definition. A small Petri net language with six concepts is used as sample language.

Unit 1   Introduction: Compilers, languages, meta-languages
Unit 2   Structure: MDA, meta-models, abstract syntax
Unit 3   Editors: Graphical and textual editors, connection to the structure
Unit 4   Constraints: Static and dynamic checks, type systems, constraints, lexic
Unit 5   Parsers: Grammars, top-down and bottom-up parsing, errors
Unit 6   Transformations: Code generation, M2M, M2T, templates, generators
Unit 7   Execution: Interpreters, runtime environments

Each of the seven units runs for 2 weeks with the following layout:

1. Short lecture of the main theory
2. Individual study: reading, videos, experiments, and test-RAT
3. RAT: IRAT, TRAT, Feedback
4. Project group work: students work with their project

---

[2]Please note that MPS does not define the semantics of BaseLanguage—it is just translated to Java.
[3]We use the number of concepts as an indication of language size for student projects.

In this layout, the readiness assurance test (RAT) is central. It is a multiple-choice test to ensure that the students have the necessary abilities and knowledge to work on more profound problems, typically in their project.

First, the students solve the individual RAT (IRAT) for themselves. Afterward, the same RAT is solved as a team RAT (TRAT), where students discuss in their team about the RAT and agree on a joint solution. Naturally, team results are much better than the individual results. Finally, students get feedback from the teacher in case there is disagreement or the answer is unclear. In the study period before the RAT, students have access to a test RAT that helps them to prepare for the RAT.

2.4 *Projects*

Students work with their project in the seven units and in the final exam period. The project is done in groups of students and is about implementing a small language or extension of a language. The teacher selects the languages in cooperation with the students. Often, one group of students starts the work on the language, and in the later years, other groups improve the implementation and focus on specific aspects of the language. There is also the chance of contributing to existing real-life languages.

Typically, the project has to be small enough for novices to be managed. Most often, the languages are stored in the local git repository of our university, but some languages have wider visibility. The following languages are worth noting.

ODD   implements the overview, design concepts, and details (ODD) protocol. The protocol has seven thematic sections: (1) purpose; (2) entities, state variables, and scales; (3) process overview and scheduling; (4) design concepts; (5) initialization; (6) input data, and (7) sub-models [19, 20]. Each section contains questions to guide modellers in the provision of related model details. ODD emerged as an effort to make model descriptions more understandable. Although ODD is a big step toward verification, validation, and reproducibility of simulation models, the informal character of the answers allows ambiguities in the model description. Our version of ODD[4] with 128 concepts is formal and can be used to generate and run NetLogo code.

COOL,   the classroom object-oriented language [2] is a language to teach compiler construction. It is a small object-oriented language that is simple enough to be handled in a short time frame. COOL is also complex enough to have all the essential features of a best-practice modern language. The COOL MPS project[5] with 38 concepts provides an IDE for COOL and translates COOL to Java.

---

[4]https://github.com/uiano/odd2netlogo.

[5]https://github.com/uiano/COOL-MPS.

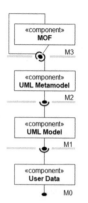

OMG Level	Examples	Java example	OCL example
3 = meta meta model	MOF	EBNF/ English	MOF
2 = meta model	UML MM	Java language	OCL language
1 = model	UML Model	a Java program	a formula
0 = instances	objects of UML classes	a run	a truth value

Fig. 1 Four-level modelling architecture according to OMG [27]

ACT ONE   is a language for algebraic specifications [11], which is used in another course at our university. As there are no existing tools for ACT ONE, students have created an IDE for ACT ONE with 23 concepts for creating and running specifications.[6] The IDE is in its early phase, and its usability can be improved.

During the years, students have created several publications in this course, or in follow-up projects after the course, for example, in bachelor projects, master projects, or PhD projects. [12–16, 21, 34, 35, 57].

3 Meta-languages

Language-oriented programming is always concerned with two different artifacts: the language description and the solution description. When we consider the OMG four-level architecture as shown in Fig. 1, then the language description is placed on level M2,[7] while the solution description is placed on level M1. There are also different roles connected to these two levels: a language designer works on level M2 and a solution designer works on level M1

The course on generative programming is mostly related to language designers and handles the tools and mindset needed to create languages and associated tools. However, a good understanding of solution design and architecture is an essential precondition to becoming a good language designer.

Language designs are essentially also solution descriptions—in a very limited domain. Here, we need language descriptions that lead to language tools. Language descriptions describe languages completely with all their aspects. Meta-modelling

---

[6]https://github.com/uiano/ACT-ONE.

[7]A meta-language description is placed on level M3.

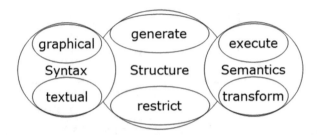

Fig. 2 Aspects of a computer language description

has often stopped at incomplete language descriptions consisting only of structure (defined using MOF [38]) and constraints (defined using OCL [56]). However, a language description has more aspects; in particular, concrete syntax and semantics have to be considered [26]. In [35], a language definition is said to consist of the following aspects: structure, syntax, and semantics (see Fig. 2).

Structure, also called abstract syntax, coincides with a narrow understanding of meta-model. It consists of two sub-aspects, namely, the definition of possible concepts with their connections and the restriction of those using constraints. Sometimes, a restriction could be expressed as a structure or the other way around.

Syntax stands for concrete syntax, and it defines how instances of the language are shown. This can be the definition of a graphical or textual concrete language syntax, or something in between, like tables, diagrams, or formulas.

Behavior explains the semantics of the language. This can be a transformation into another language (denotational or translational semantics), or it defines the execution of language instances (operational semantics).[8]

These aspects are not always as strictly separated as they seem in the illustration; constraints are shown as overlapping with structure since constraints interact closely with the structure-related technologies in building up (and restricting) the structure of the language. However, constraints can also be used for defining restrictions for presentation as well as behavior. The structure is the core of the language; it contains the concepts that should be part of the language and the relations between them. A meta-model-based approach to language design focuses on the structure. A well-defined language structure is the starting point to define one or more textual or graphical presentations for the language, as well as to define code generation into executable target languages such as Java.

MPS features a large set of meta-languages, and some of them match the aspects shown in Fig. 2. Section 4 provides more details about the MPS concepts used in the course. The definition of possible concepts in the *structure* aspect is handled by the structure meta-language. At the same time, restrictions can be expressed

---

[8]Another type of semantics is axiomatic semantics that gives meaning to phrases of a language by describing the logical axioms that apply to them. Axiomatic semantics is not relevant in this article.

using the constraints and the type system meta-languages. The editor meta-language handles the *syntax* aspect covering both text syntax and diagrammatic syntax. *Transformation semantics* is handled by the textgen meta-language for model-to-text transformations and by the generator meta-language for model-to-model transformations. MPS does not support *execution semantics*; it can be captured using parts of the action meta-language.

In addition, MPS allows influencing the user appearance of the generated IDE using the intentions, the refactorings, and the usages meta-languages. Moreover, MPS allows using low-level implementation details in the language design, for example, using the actions meta-language. Finally, MPS provides means to describe tool-related information, for example, how the described IDE is built. These parts are not essential in a language design course.

Domain-specific languages are always about the correct abstraction level. They enable to express the knowledge of the domain. A DSL can describe a complete solution on a suitable abstraction level. Of course, it is necessary to know the domain well to come up with a good domain-specific language.

As meta-languages are also domain-specific languages, the same is true for them. They have to be on the correct abstraction level. Since the domain of language descriptions is relatively new, there are only a few good patterns of language description available. Most often, the implementation is guiding the concepts provided because language designers are often solution designers knowing how to write a code.

An essential part of this course concerns finding a suitable abstraction level to facilitate code generation from models. In this respect, tools for language description are used as an example. Therefore, it is essential to have excellent high-level abstractions available and explain how these are translated into low-level code by the tools. However, it is a challenge to find tools and technologies that work on a high abstraction level for each language aspect.

If the abstraction level is too low, too many seemingly irrelevant details will create complications and complexities, making it more difficult for the students to get started with the tools. On the other hand, if the abstraction level is too high, it may not be possible to generate working tools from the language specification. For structure and textual syntax, some meta-languages provide a suitable level of abstraction, while it is more difficult to find the right abstractions for the other language aspects.

3.1 Concepts for Structure

The structure of a language specifies what the instances of the language are; it identifies the significant components of each language construct [8] and relates them to each other. Although there are proven methods for finding the concepts of a domain [25], most of these methods are not applicable for inexperienced students. Therefore, the course uses extensive feedback to make sure the concepts identified are useful. There are several ways to express structure; grammars, meta-models, database schema descriptions, RDF schemata, and XML schemata are all examples of different ways to describe structure. The following concepts are considered essential for structure for an introduction to language design:

- Concept and abstract concept
- Enumeration
- Property, child, and reference

3.2 Concepts for Constraints

Constraints on a language can put limitations on the structure of a syntactically well-formed instance of the language. This aspect of a language definition mostly concerns logical rules or constraints on the structure that are difficult to express directly in the structure itself. Neither meta-models nor grammars provide all the expressiveness that is needed to define the set of (un)wanted language instances. The constraints could be first-order logical constraints or multiplicity constraints for elements of the structure. The following concepts are considered essential for constraints for an introduction to language design:

- Name binding with definition and use, uniqueness, identifier kind, and scope
- Lexical constraints
- Multiplicity constraints
- General constraints
- Type systems: definition and comparison of types

3.3 Concepts for Syntax

The concrete syntax of a language describes the possible forms of a statement of the language. In the case of a textual language, it tells what words are allowed to use in the language, which words have special meaning and are reserved, and what words are possible to use for names. It may also describe what sequence the elements of the language may occur in: the syntactic features of the language. This is often expressed in a grammar for textual languages.

For a graphical, diagrammatic, or tabular language, the situation is similar: the appearance of each concept has to be defined and the possible placements in relation to other concepts. The following concepts are considered essential for syntax for an introduction to language design:

- The appearance of concepts including keywords
- The appearance of properties, children, and references
- Placement of elements (over, under, left, right, in) and indentation

- Notational freedom for users
- Ambiguity
- Highlighting and context assistance

3.4 Concepts for Transformation

The behavior of a language describes what the meaning of a statement of the language is. Two main types of formal ways of defining semantics are called operational and denotational semantics [49]. Denotational semantics in the strict sense is a mapping of a source expression to an input–output function working on some mathematical entities. We use a form, called translational semantics, that is related to model transformations, thereby defining an "abstract" compiler. The following concepts are considered essential for transformation for an introduction to language design:

- Model-to-model and model-to-text transformations
- Template-driven and data-driven transformation descriptions
- Navigation in the input and the output

3.5 Concepts for Execution

Operational semantics [49] describes the execution of the language as a sequence of computational steps, thus defining an "abstract" interpreter. Operational semantics is described by state transitions for an abstract machine, for example, using abstract state machines (ASM) [7]. The state transitions are based on a runtime environment, describing the possible runtime states. The following concepts are considered essential for execution for an introduction to language design.

- Runtime environment with elements independent on the program (e.g., program counter) and elements dependent on the program (e.g., variable locations)
- State changes
- Application of state changes related to sequential order and concurrency

3.6 Tool-Related Concepts

There are many more aspects of languages that could be important when designing real-life languages. MPS has dedicated meta-languages for some of those, for example, languages to design actions, refactorings, intentions, usages, connections to source code control, data flow, stand-alone versions of a tool, and many more. For a compiler course, these aspects are disturbing, and they are not taken into account in the teaching of the course. However, these meta-languages can be relevant for the concrete student projects.

4 Using MPS Meta-Languages for Teaching

MPS has many meta-languages, and not all of them are useful for novices. Here, we look at how MPS handles the essential concepts introduced in Sect. 3.

4.1 Concepts for Teaching Structure

Given the concepts for structure in the previous section, EMOF (essential MOF) is a clear candidate to fulfil all the requirements. Full MOF [38] could also be used, but it includes a lot of advanced concepts that are overkill for students.

The structure meta-language of MPS provides all the needed constructs and some more that are not needed for students and that may disturb the understanding. MPS is missing an overview of the concepts of the language with their dependencies, as it is easily provided with EMOF class diagrams. Such an overview is helpful in case students start to work on an existing project or in general need to get an overall understanding of the concepts involved.

Figure 3 shows how an MPS concept declaration covers the needed constructs in relation to an EMOF class diagram. MPS also allows defining enumerations.

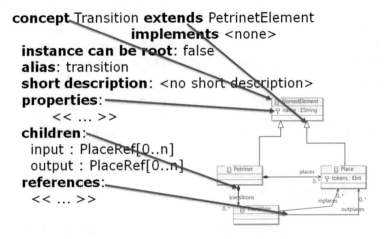

Fig. 3 Structure definition in MPS and EMOF

```
constrained string datatype: number|

    matching regexp: (0|-?[1-9][0-9]*)([.][0-9]+)?
```

Fig. 4 Lexical constraints in MPS

4.2 Concepts for Teaching Constraints

Constraints (sometimes called static semantics) are restrictions that are checked on the syntax tree *after* checking the restrictions of the syntax.

The traditional method to specify constraints is OCL [56], which allows formulating (logical) expressions over the abstract syntax. This is not very domain-specific for the language definition. A better approach exists for the handling of name resolution in [29].

The structure meta-language captures multiplicity and also allows to define lexical rules using constrained data types; see Fig. 4.

MPS has a general meta-language for constraints covering general constraints including uniqueness and scoping. In this context, also the behavior meta-language is used. The general MPS idea of the constraints language relates to a syntax check, where an input that does not match the constraints is *not* included in the model. It is possible to define correctness in the sense of static semantics using the type system checking rules. In the course, the use of checking rules is recommended for general constraints instead of using the constraints meta-language.

The type system meta-language gives a very high-level way to describe types and their connections using inference rules, subtyping rules, and checking rules as shown in Fig. 5.

The most significant abstraction gap is in the handling of name resolution. MPS handles definitions using INamedConcept, but this is very rigid and cannot be defined after the structure is in place. References are defined as reference constraints and are code-level, not high-level. The same is valid for uniqueness.

4.3 Concepts for Teaching Syntax

There are two main approaches for handling concrete syntax of a language: generation (pretty printer) and recognition (parser). Editors would typically do both sides.

The editor meta-language of MPS allows the definition of projectional editors, i.e., editors built on the idea of model-view-controller (MVC). This means that the tool always knows about the elements of the specification, and therefore ambiguity is considered unimportant. However, as [21] argues, ambiguity might not be essential for the tool, but still for the user. A check of the ambiguity of the notation could be useful.

```
checking rule ParameterNumberCheck {
  applicable for concept = OperatorReference as oR
  overrides <none>

  do {
    if (oR.parameters.size != oR.ref.parameters.size) {
      error "Wrong number of parameters! Expected: " + oR.ref.parameters.size + "
        oR;
    }
  }
}
inference rule typeof_SortReference {
  applicable for concept = SortReference as sR
  applicable always
  overrides false

  do {
    typeof(sR) :==: sR.reference;
  }
}
subtyping rule AnyRule {
  weak = false
  applicable for concept = Sort as sort

  supertypes {
    return node-ptr/ANY/.resolve(null).sorts.first;
  }
}
```

Fig. 5 Some type system rules of the ACT ONE language

As MPS does not support grammars and recognition-based text handling, this is handled in the course using separate tools (JavaCC). Still, the handling of lexical constraints can be used as an example of recognition; see Fig. 4.

MPS editors support a two-way connection between the syntax and the corresponding structure, providing feedback from the syntax analysis in the form of syntax highlighting, error messages, code completion suggestions, etc.

The projectional nature of MPS is well aligned with teaching graphical and textual projectional approaches. Even though MPS does not provide full graphical editors, the principles are clear enough as can be seen in Fig. 6.

MPS does not allow much notational freedom for the user, so this has to be explained separately as well. The inspector view of MPS can be used as an example of user freedom, which is not visible in the main notation defined; see Fig. 7.

MPS allows defining editors automatically from the structure as proposed in [22]. This gives a quick win, even though the generated editors often have to be adapted. Providing high-quality editors in MPS is very advanced and well beyond

```
<default> editor for concept Entity
   node cell layout:
   [-
   [/
        [> The entity { name } has colour % colour % and shape % shape % and it
        [> Entity { name } has the attributes <]
        (/ % userDefinedAttributes %                                                        /)
            /empty cell: [> Press enter to add attribute to    { name } <]
        <constant>
        ? Press enter to add another entity
        [> <constant> *context assistant menu placeholder* <]
   /]
   -]
```

```
   inspected cell layout:
      <choose cell model>
```

Fig. 6 An editor from the ODD language

```
Style:
hint {
   << ... >>
}
```

```
Common:
```

cell id	<default>
action map	<default>
keymap	<default>
menu	<none>
transformation menu	<none>
attracts focus	noAttraction
show if	(editorContext, node)->boolean {
	return node.next-sibling.index < 0;
	}

```
Constant cell:
```

text	Press enter to add another entity
text*	<none>

Fig. 7 The inspector view of the editor in Fig. 6

the capacities of ordinary students. Here, a much higher level of abstraction would be needed, as shown in [5, 47, 55].

In particular, the division of syntax between the inspector and the regular editor is puzzling for the students and disturbs their understanding. In the course, it is recommended to avoid using the inspector view when defining a textual representation.

4.4 Tools and Technologies for Teaching Transformation

There are many tools available to express transformations, and MPS provides a very high abstraction level for transformations. MPS allows both template-driven and data-driven definitions. The meta-language generator allows the definition of model-to-model transformations, as shown in Fig. 8. In contrast, the meta-language textgen provides means for the definition of model-to-text transformations, as shown in Fig. 9.

Model-to-model transformations are simple in MPS, while model-to-text is a bit less convenient. In particular, the description capabilities are too different between the two kinds of transformations.

4.5 Tools and Technologies for Teaching Execution

MPS does not provide dedicated meta-languages to handle execution. There are some possibilities to define debuggers. Moreover, it is possible to define simulators using the underlying base language (Java). High-level descriptions of operational semantics as proposed in [33, 40, 44–46, 48] are missing. Besides, state transitions could be defined on a higher level using ASM [7] or QVT [36]. In the course, the

```
template reduce_LetReference
input    LetReference

parameters
<< ... >>

content node:
public class xxx {
  public ITerm ccc() {
    final ITerm var = null;
    return <TF [($SWITCH$ switch_IStorable=>ITerm[Specification.Sort]) ->$[var]] TF>;
  }
}
```

Fig. 8 Model generation from ACT ONE to Java

```
text gen component for concept Entity {
  (node)->void {
    append {breed[ } ${node.name} { a-} ${node.name} { ]} \n;
    foreach e in node.userDefinedAttributes {
      append ${node.name} {-own} {[ } ${e.name} { ]} \n;
    }
  }
}
```

Fig. 9 Text generation from ODD to netlogo

concepts of executions are introduced, and possible implementations in MPS are discussed.

5   Experiences and Evaluation

Having used Eclipse and Microsoft Studio and MPS in teaching language handling, there are several remarks to be made about the suitability of MPS for teaching and the pitfalls for the teaching situation. Please note that we use MPS in the specific context of students, being novice programmers and not experienced in language design. By running the language handling course, the following experiences were gathered.

Students are no experienced developers.   MPS may work well for experienced developers, who use many keyboard shortcuts regularly. For those, MPS feels very natural. Students are novice programmers, and they most often try to write some text and copy-paste existing specifications. This is often tricky or impossible with MPS due to its projectional nature.

MPS shows best practice.   It is good to use a running example where aspects are added to complete a simple sample language. It is also beneficial to cover all language aspects within one platform. MPS has the advantage that the definitions of all MPS meta-languages are accessible in addition to several sample languages. This allows copying from best practice examples.

The theory comes before tools.   The understanding of the concepts of language design is strengthened by showing their implementation in MPS. However, students tend to drown in the tool details of MPS, which hampers their under-standing. It is often easier to start with the high-level theoretical concepts before showing the implementation.

MPS is heavy.   MPS is a heavy tool to use in teaching. The learning curve is very steep, and students take a long time to get used to the tool. There are very many details, and for a novice, it is not easy to see what is essential and what not and where to look for a place to change unwanted behavior. We try to limit the complexity of the projects by focusing on the concepts mentioned in Sect. 3.

Distinguishing languages and specifications is tricky.   In MPS, both languages (level M2) and meta-languages (level M3) and even specifications (level M1) are shown in the same way and in the same editor window; see Fig. 10. They are also represented internally in the same way. This is a challenge for students as they need to understand the difference between languages and specifications. The teaching tool LanguageLab makes it easier to see this difference [14].

Learning MPS is possible.   Despite the heavy tool and the heavy tasks, the students consistently report that they learn a lot in this course and that they can use this in their future job. This is visible in the results from the course, which are good grades and decent languages in most of the cases. After the course, the students have a good understanding of language handling and how it can be used.

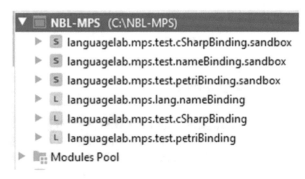

Fig. 10 Level confusion in MPS: lang.nameBinding is a meta-language (M3), test.petriBinding is a regular language (M2), and test.petriBinding.sandbox is a collection of specifications (M1)

From our experiences, there are several possible improvements for MPS which are as follows. Most of them relate to the complexity of the tool and the associated steep learning curve for new users. There are plugins for some of the points mentioned, which should be included in the standard version of MPS.

Have a simpler starting user interface. It would be a good idea to adapt the user interface to the experience of the user. A set of essential features could be a starting point for a novice user, and then the user interface could grow in line with the new experiences of the user. The concepts presented in Sect. 3 would be a good starting point for the essential features.

Restrict expressivity. Currently, most of the MPS meta-languages have a procedural core that allows expressing everything computable in the sense of Java. However, in many cases, a higher level of abstraction would restrict some functionality but would increase precision. A good example is the handling of type systems. A bad example is the behavior aspect which collects everything that does not fit somewhere else.

Have a web version of MPS. It would be excellent if students could work in a (simplified) version of MPS online, including shared documents. This would also improve the teaching process a lot. Besides, it also simplifies version handling and migration.

Provide an overview of the structure. The individual definition of concepts in MPS gives a lot of freedom, but it is easy to lose the overview. Class diagrams are an excellent way to present such an overview. These diagrams could be generated from the structure definitions. For large languages, an overview of the concepts is essential, and support for this is needed.

Improve meta-languages The current meta-languages are not always the most abstract languages to express the needed information. It would be essential to have grammar cells in the core of MPS and even improve on this idea and introduce more high-level patterns. The second area of improvement of meta-languages would be in the area of name binding, as described in [29]. It might be possible to create a version of MPS using simpler meta-languages by using bootstrapping as explored in [41, 42].

Provide a decent meta-language for execution. This requirement might not be most pressing for practical application, but it is essential for teaching in the area of language processing. As the examples of MPS show, interpreters are useful, and a good meta-language should be available.

6 Conclusions

As language technology is complex, it is crucial to keep the incidental complexity of the tool used as low as possible. MPS might not be the best tool in this regard, but it can be used in a way that lets students grasp the essential concepts. This works out if the teaching setup is aligned with the features of MPS and introduces functionality step by step.

This approach is aided very well with the stability and adequate documentation of MPS such that students get all the information they need. With this approach, students can understand the underlying concepts, and thereby they master the tool MPS.

Still, there are some serious shortcomings of MPS with regard to teaching. Fixing them might even help the general applicability of MPS. The work on appropriate meta-languages is a significant part of this improvement process.

Acknowledgments The course and the work on the teaching setup would not have been possible without my PhD students Themis Dimitra Xanthopoulou, Renée Schulz, Vimala Nunavath, Terje Gjøsæter, Trinh Hoang Nguyen, Liping Mu, and Merete Skjelten Tveit.

References

1. Aho, A.V., Sethi, R., Ullman, J.D.: Compilers: Principles, Techniques, and Tools. Addison-Wesley Longman Publishing Co., Inc., Boston, MA (1986)
2. Aiken, A.: Cool: a portable project for teaching compiler construction. SIGPLAN Not. **31**(7), 19–24 (1996). https://doi.org/10.1145/381841.381847
3. Atkinson, C., Kühne, T.: Model-driven development: a metamodeling foundation. In: Software, IEEE (2003)
4. Bennedsen, J., Caspersen, M.E.: Model-Driven Programming, pp. 116–129. Springer, Berlin, Heidelberg (2008). http://link.springer.com/book/10.1007%2F978-3-540-77934-60
5. Bettini, L.: Implementing Domain-Specific Languages with Xtext and Xtend. Packt Publishing, Birmingham (2013)
6. Bézivin, J., Gerbé, O.: Towards a precise definition of the OMG/MDA framework. In: Proceedings of ASE'01, Automated Software Engineering (2001)
7. Börger, E., Stärk, R.F.: Abstract state machines: a method for high-level system design and analysis. Springer-Verlag New York, Inc., Secaucus, NJ (2003)
8. Clark, T., Sammut, P., Willans, J.S.: Applied Metamodelling: a Foundation for Language Driven Development, 3rd edn. (2015). CoRR abs/1505.00149. http://arxiv.org/abs/1505.00149

9. Dai, N., Mandel, L., Ryman, A.: Eclipse Web Tools Platform: Developing Java Web Applications. Eclipse Series. Addison-Wesley, Boston (2007)
10. Dmitriev, S.: Language oriented programming: the next programming paradigm. JetBrains onBoard **1**(2) (2004)
11. Ehrig, H., Mahr, B.: Fundamentals of Algebraic Specification 1: Equations and Initial Semantics, 1st edn. Springer Publishing Company, Incorporated, Berlin, Heidelberg (2011)
12. Gjøsæter, T., Prinz, A.: Teaching computer language handling - from compiler theory to meta-modelling. In: Fernandes, J.M. , Lämmel, R., Visser, J., Saraiva, J. (eds.) Generative and Transformational Techniques in Software Engineering (GTTSE2009). Revised Papers. Lecture Notes in Computer Science, vol. 6491, pp. 446–460. Springer, New York (2009). https://doi.org/10.1007/978-3-642-18023-1_14
13. Gjøsæter, T., Prinz, A.: Teaching model driven language handling. ECEASST **34** (2010). https://doi.org/10.14279/tuj.eceasst.34.591
14. Gjøsæter, T., Prinz, A.: Languagelab 1.1 user manual. Tech. rep., University of Agder (2013). http://brage.bibsys.no/xmlui/handle/11250/134943
15. Gjøsæter, T., Isfeldt, I.F., Prinz, A.: Sudoku - a language description case study. In: Gasevic, D., Lämmel, R., Wyk, E.V. (eds.) Software Language Engineering (SLE2008). Revised Selected Papers. Lecture Notes in Computer Science, vol. 5452, pp. 305–321. Springer, New York (2008). https://doi.org/10.1007/978-3-642-00434-6_19
16. Gjøsæter, T., Prinz, A., Nytun, J.P.: MOF-VM: instantiation revisited. In: Proceedings of the 4th International Conference on Model-Driven Engineering and Software Development, pp. 137–144 (2016). https://doi.org/10.5220/0005606101370144
17. Glässer, U., Gotzhein, R., Prinz, A.: The formal semantics of SDL-2000: status and perspectives. Comput. Netw. **42**(3), 343–358 (2003). https://doi.org/10.1016/S1389-1286(03)00247-0
18. Gosling, J., Joy, B., Steele, G., Bracha, G.: Java Language Specification. The Java Series, 2nd edn. Addison-Wesley Longman Publishing Co., Inc., Boston, MA (2000)
19. Grimm, V., Berger, U., DeAngelis, D.L., Polhill, J.G., Giske, J., Railsback, S.F.: The ODD protocol: a review and first update. Ecol. Modell. **221**(23), 2760–2768 (2010). https://doi.org/10.1016/j.ecolmodel.2010.08.019
20. Grimm, V., Polhill, G., Touza, J.: Documenting social simulation models: The ODD protocol as a standard, pp. 117–133. Springer, Berlin, Heidelberg (2013). https://doi.org/10.1007/978-3-540-93813-2_7
21. Guttormsen, S.M., Prinz, A., Gjøsæter, T.: Consistent projectional text editors. In: Pires, L.F., Hammoudi, S., Selic, B. (eds.) Proceedings of MODELSWARD 2017, pp. 515–522. SciTePress, Setúbal (2017). https://doi.org/10.5220/0006264505150522
22. Heidenreich, F., Johannes, J., Karol, S., Seifert, M., Wende, C.: Derivation and refinement of textual syntax for models. In: Paige, R.F., Hartman, A., Rensink, A. (eds.) Model Driven Architecture - Foundations and Applications, pp. 114–129. Springer, Berlin Heidelberg (2009)
23. International Telecommunication Union: Z.100 Series, Specification and Description Language SDL. Tech. rep., International Telecommunication Union (2011)
24. JetBrains: MPS meta programming system. https://www.jetbrains.com/mps/
25. Kelly, S., Tolvanen, J.P.: Domain-Specific Modeling. Wiley & Sons, Inc., Hoboken, NJ (2007)
26. Kleppe, A.: A language description is more than a metamodel (2007). This paper is published through a website (megaplanet.org) only. No paper copy available.; 4th International Workshop on Software Language Engineering, ATEM 2007
27. Kleppe, A., Warmer, J.: MDA Explained. Addison-Wesley, Boston (2003)
28. Klint, P., van der Storm, T., Vinju, J.: Easy meta-programming with Rascal. In: Proceedings of GTTSE'09, pp. 222–289. Springer, Berlin, Heidelberg (2011)
29. Konat, G., Kats, L., Wachsmuth, G., Visser, E.: Declarative name binding and scope rules. In: Czarnecki, K., Hedin, G. (eds.) Software Language Engineering, pp. 311–331. Springer, Berlin, Heidelberg (2013)

30. Madsen, O.L., Møller-Pedersen, B.: A unified approach to modeling and programming. In: Proceedings of the 13th International Conference on Model Driven Engineering Languages and Systems: Part I, MODELS'10, pp. 1–15. Springer, Berlin, Heidelberg (2010). http://dl. acm.org/citation.cfm?id=1926458.1926460

31. Mellor, S.J., Balcer, M.: Executable UML: A Foundation for Model-Driven Architectures. Addison-Wesley Longman Publishing Co., Inc., Boston, MA (2002)

32. Microsoft: Getting started with domain-specific languages. https://docs.microsoft.com/de-de/ visualstudio/modeling/about-domain-specific-languages?view=vs-2019

33. Mosses, P.D.: Structural operational semantics modular structural operational semantics. J. Log. Algebr. Program. **60**, 195–228 (2004). http://dx.doi.org/10.1016/j.jlap.2004.03.008

34. Mu, L., Gjøsæter, T., Prinz, A., Tveit, M.S.: Specification of modelling languages in a flexible meta-model architecture. In: Software Architecture, 4th European Conference, ECSA 2010, Copenhagen, August 23–26, 2010. Companion Volume, pp. 302–308 (2010). https://doi.org/ 10.1145/1842752.1842807

35. Nytun, J.P., Prinz, A., Tveit, M.S.: Automatic generation of modelling tools. In: Rensink, A., Warmer, J. (eds.) Proceedings of ECMDA-FA 2006. Lecture Notes in Computer Science, vol. 4066, pp. 268–283. Springer, New York (2006). https://doi.org/10.1007/11787044_21

36. OMG Editor: Meta Object Facility (MOF) 2.0 Query/View/Transformation Specification, Version 1.1. Tech. rep., Object Management Group (2011). http://www.omg.org/spec/QVT/ 1.1/

37. OMG Editor: Unified Modeling Language: Infrastructure version 2.4.1 (OMG Document formal/2011-08-05). OMG Document. Published by Object Management Group, http://www. omg.org (2011)

38. OMG Editor: Meta Object Facility (MOF). Tech. rep., Object Management Group (2016). https://www.omg.org/spec/MOF

39. Pech, V., Shatalin, A., Völter, M.: JetBrains MPS as a tool for extending Java. In: Proceedings of the Conference on Principles and Practices of Programming on the Java Platform: Virtual Machines, Languages, and Tools, PPPJ '13, pp. 165–168. ACM, New York (2013). https://doi. org/10.1145/2500828.2500846

40. Plotkin, G.D.: A structural approach to operational semantics. Tech. Rep. DAIMI FN-19, Aarhus University (1981). http://opac.inria.fr/record=b1049300

41. Prinz, A., Mezei, G.: The art of bootstrapping. In: Hammoudi, S., Pires, L.F., Selic, B. (eds.) MODELSWARD 2019, Revised Selected Papers. Communications in Computer and Information Science, vol. 1161, pp. 182–200. Springer, New York (2019). https://doi.org/10. 1007/978-3-030-37873-8_8

42. Prinz, A., Shatalin, A.: How to bootstrap a language workbench. In: Hammoudi, S., Pires, L.F., Selic, B. (eds.) Proceedings of MODELSWARD 2019, pp. 345–352. SciTePress, Setúbal (2019). https://doi.org/10.5220/0007398203470354

43. Prinz, A., Scheidgen, M., Tveit, M.S.: A model-based standard for SDL. In: Gaudin, E., Najm, E., Reed, R. (eds.) Proceedings of SDL 2007: Design for Dependable Systems. Lecture Notes in Computer Science, vol. 4745, pp. 1–18. Springer, New York (2007). https://doi.org/10.1007/ 978-3-540-74984-4_1

44. Prinz, A., Møller-Pedersen, B., Fischer, J.: Object-oriented operational semantics. In: Proceedings of SAM 2016, LNCS 9959. Springer, Berlin, Heidelberg (2016)

45. Roşu, G., Şerbănuţă, T.F.: An overview of the K semantic framework. J. Log. Algebr. Program. **79**(6), 397–434 (2010). https://doi.org/10.1016/j.jlap.2010.03.012

46. Sadilek, D.A., Wachsmuth, G.: Using grammarware languages to define operational semantics of modelled languages. In: Oriol, M., Meyer, B. (eds.) Objects, Components, Models and Patterns, TOOLS EUROPE 2009. Proceedings, Lecture Notes in Business Information Processing, vol. 33, pp. 348–356. Springer, New York (2009). https://doi.org/10.1007/978-3-642-02571-6_20

47. Scheidgen, M.: Textual Editing Framework (2008). Accessed 14 April 2020. http://www2. informatik.hu-berlin.de/sam/meta-tools/tef/documentation.html

48. Scheidgen, M., Fischer, J.: Human Comprehensible and Machine Processable Specifications of Operational Semantics, pp. 157–171. Springer, Berlin, Heidelberg (2007). https://doi.org/10.1007/978-3-540-72901-3_12

49. Sethi, R.: Programming Languages: Concepts and Constructs. Addison-Wesley Longman Publishing Co., Inc., Boston (1989)

50. Steinberg, D., Budinsky, F., Paternostro, M., Merks, E.: EMF: Eclipse Modeling Framework 2.0, 2nd edn. Addison-Wesley Professional, Boston (2009)

51. Şutîi, A.M., van den Brand, M., Verhoeff, T.: Exploration of modularity and reusability of domain-specific languages: an expression DSL in metamod. Comput. Lang. Syst. Struct. **51**, 48–70 (2018). https://doi.org/10.1016/j.cl.2017.07.004. http://www.sciencedirect.com/science/article/pii/S1477842417300404

52. Szabó, T., Völter, M., Kolb, B., Ratiu, D., Schaetz, B.: mbeddr: extensible languages for embedded software development. In: Proceedings of the Conference on High Integrity Language Technology, HILT '14, pp. 13–16. ACM, New York (2014). https://doi.org/10.1145/2663171.2663186

53. Voelter, M., Benz, S., Dietrich, C., Engelmann, B., Helander, M., Kats, L.C.L., Visser, E., Wachsmuth, G.: DSL Engineering - Designing, Implementing and Using Domain-Specific Languages. dslbook.org (2013)

54. Völter, M.: From programming to modeling - and back again. IEEE Software **28**(06), 20–25 (2011). http://dx.doi.org/10.1109/MS.2011.139

55. Völter, M., Szabó, T., Lisson, S., Kolb, B., Erdweg, S., Berger, T.: Efficient development of consistent projectional editors using grammar cells. In: Proceedings of Conference on Software Language Engineering, SLE 2016, pp. 28–40. Association for Computing Machinery, New York (2016). https://doi.org/10.1145/2997364.2997365

56. Warmer, J., Kleppe, A.: The Object Constraint Language: Getting Your Models Ready for MDA, 2nd edn. Addison-Wesley Longman Publishing Co., Inc., Boston (2003)

57. Xanthopoulou, T.D., Prinz, A., Shults, F.L.: Generating executable code from high-level social or socio-ecological model descriptions. In: i Casas, P.F., Sancho, M., Sherratt, E. (eds.) System Analysis and Modeling Conference, SAM 2019, Proceedings. Lecture Notes in Computer Science, vol. 11753, pp. 150–162. Springer, New York (2019). https://doi.org/10.1007/978-3-030-30690-8_9

Printed in the United States
by Baker & Taylor Publisher Services